Design & Construction
of the
Practical Leather Holster:
Pancake Edition

George Canfield

EDC Publishing

Design & Construction of the Practical Leather Holster: Pancake Edition

Copyright © 2024
EDC Publishing

All rights reserved. This book or any portions thereof shall not be reproduced, be it—mechanically, electronically, digitally, or by any other means—without written permission from the publisher or author, except as permitted by U.S. Copyright Law. The publisher grants limited permission to photocopy only those pages listed as "Template" and noted with accompanying text. Additional resources are protected.

ISBN: 978-1-950541-20-1
First printing September 2024

Original Photography: Jacob Canfield

While he may grumble about it, George is available for select speaking engagements.
Please contact sales@EDCLeather.com

Publisher's Note:
This publication is intended for instructional purposes and is designed to provide accurate and authoritative information in regard to the subject matter covered. While the publisher and author have used their best efforts in preparing this book, they make no representations or warranties with respect to the accuracy or completeness of its contents. The advice and strategies contained herein may not be suitable for all situation. Neither the publisher nor the author shall be liable for any loss or damages, including but not limited to; special, incidental, consequential, personal, business, or other sustained by following the advice herein.

EDC Publishing
2517 E Kearney St.
Springfield, MO 65803

EDCLeather.com

Contents

Foreword	1
Introduction	3
Section 1 – Building the StitchTrace	4
Chapter 1 – Tracing the Firearm	6
Chapter 2 – Creating a Stitch Line	11
Section 2 – Concepts & Theory – Part 1	37
Chapter 3 – The Go/No-Go Zones	39
Chapter 4 – All About Cant	46
Chapter 5 – Principles of Holster Design	51
Section 3 – Securing the Holster	55
Chapter 6 – Belt Placement	56
Section 4 – Concepts & Theory – Part 2	62
Chapter 7 – Throat Reinforcements	63
Section 5 – Finalizing the Pattern	68
Chapter 8 – Pattern Design: 8 Degree Pancake Holster	70
Chapter 9 – Pattern Design: Thumb Break Holster	90
Chapter 10 – Pattern Design: SnapCake Holster	106
Section 6 – Holster Construction	125
Chapter 11 – Holster Building: 8 Degree Pancake Holster	127
Chapter 12 – Holster Building: Thumb Break Holster	170
Chapter 13 – Holster Building: SnapCake Holster	239
Templates & Tools	338

Foreword

My name is Rob Scroggins. I own Gunblinger Designs LLC out of Union, Kentucky. My main product line is gun leather, though I make a variety of other things. I'm also a registered nurse and safety director for a medical company, which affords me a fair amount of travel.

I began leatherwork as a teenager in 1977. After high school, I boxed up my leather tools and went on with my life. Eventually, I joined the Army, and later, got married and had kids.

It was during the pandemic, I decided I needed a new belt. Having the skill and knowledge, I found my old tools and made one. Shortly thereafter, a friend asked if I could build him a holster. I said why not and I did what so many others do. I watched some YouTube videos, figured it out, and went to work. I was proud of my first holster and my friend was happy with it, but looking back, I wasn't that good at it.

One of the videos I watched was by EDC Leather and this guy named George Canfield. I had never spoken to him directly but I learned a lot from his videos.

In February 2022 my work travels took me to Springfield, Missouri. On my last day there I had some downtime and decided to visit EDC Leather. I thought, What the heck. Worst thing that can happen is he says 'no'. So, I messaged George and asked if I could see his shop.

To my surprise, he messaged me back immediately. He asked where I was and then came to pick me up. We had lunch and then I got to see his shop.

I was amazed, both by his hospitality and by his shop. It was a true production shop. He had every tool one could think of for building holsters and other gun leather.

George is what I call YouTube famous. He has many videos on the subject and has helped countless people learn, grow, and build safe and functional holsters. He's mentored many leathercrafters, selflessly sharing his vast knowledge and experience.

Since meeting him, he's introduced me to so many people in the leather industry, suppliers and makers alike. I've learned about different tanneries and the various tanning processes. I've learned what makes one leather better than another for different applications and projects. And I've learned several building techniques which make it easier to accomplish what I set out to do.

George comes from a long line of leather workers and tanners. He's worked with and tanned leather nearly his entire life and has experience in so many areas of the craft. Every discussion is like being in leather school even though he doesn't realize it.

In normal conversation, unconsciously, he's always teaching you something about leathercraft or the leather business. He's an endless idea factory. But he's also as personable as can be and will help any way he can.

Since that first meeting, George and I have become great friends. I've taken the Holster Makers Bootcamp course he instructs, and worked with him on developing new products as an alpha builder. I've taught classes with him, and collaborated on several other projects, including this book.

In this book, you'll be introduced to holster making. But it's not just a set of directions. George teaches you "HOW" to build a holster and "WHY" things are done a certain way. Like all leatherwork, every piece is an individual piece of art, but holsters are Functional Art. They can be individualized in as many ways as your imagination can take you— but there are also several constants that MUST be taken into consideration for making a safe and functional holster.

We aways say, "As long as it's a safe build, it can have any look you want." This is proven by taking a look at any of our finished holsters. You will see a variety of styles, colors and embellishments (as indicated in my company name, "Gunblinger"), but all of them have the same safety features and functionality.

In this book George does a great job making it understandable for the new holster maker as well as the seasoned veteran. We're never too old to learn new tricks.

I've read this book many times between the first draft manuscript and the final published product. I've manually performed each step as it's written to ensure every detail and concept was clearly defined and understandable. I'm acutely familiar with the contents and I must say, this is the finest instructional book on holster making I've ever seen.

I was honored when George asked me to proof read and review this book. To have such a leather professional ask me to do that was incredible. He's worked on it for several months; writing, making drawings, taking photographs, writing some more. Then came the ultimate honor when he asked me to write this foreword. WOW! That's all I can say about it. I feel like I've been welcomed into the craft by a master craftsman.

I hope you will enjoy this book as much as I have enjoyed being a part of it

Rob "Gunblinger" Scroggins
Gunblinger Designs
July 2024

Introduction

Welcome to Design& Construction of the Practical Leather Holster: Pancake Edition!

There are lots of reasons people get into making leather holsters. Some people aren't satisfied with the current quality of holsters they find on the open market. Others may have specific needs for their circumstances. Whatever your reason for wanting to learn how to design and build leather holsters, you're welcome here!

We're glad to have you on board.

There are chapters on concepts, and chapters with step-by-step skills.

Take the time to read the design sections all the way through, then starting with each chapter, complete that step in your pattern or in your build.

There are a lot of correct ways to do leatherwork. I'll be showing you how we accomplish these projects, but you need to evaluate how these techniques apply to you.

There are a few rules we must follow. Safety is paramount, and your client may not understand your reasons for doing a certain job the way you do. Stay true to yourself, be safe, be responsible, and above all, enjoy the ride!

Geo

Section 1: Building the StitchTrace

Bobby Powell
Silver Wolfe Leather

I entered the world of leatherworking by complete accident. It was 1997. I'd just started a new sales job. I had fancy new business cards. So, naturally, I needed a nice leather case to keep them in.

I searched high and low for the case of my dreams, checking any and every store I thought might have what I was after. Unable to find it, my search slowed until I'd nearly abandoned it altogether.

Having nearly forgotten about it altogether, I was on my way to an appointment one day when I happened by a Tandy Leather. That shred of hope ignited once again as I reasoned, surely they'd have exactly what I was after.

I returned to the store as soon as I was able, desperate to find the case that had eluded me for so long. I must have looked lost because the lady behind the counter took pity of me. She asked what I was looking for and I was all too happy to explain. I'll never forget what she said to me afterward.

"Oh, honey, we don't sell finished goods here. I'll tell you what I do have—I have some kits that will let you make one yourself."

As they say, the rest is history.

I went on to learn how to make wallets, bags, and many other leather products. I would try anything except clothing. I read books, and once YouTube became popular, I watched and rewatched every video I could find. One of the things I came to realize, there are as many ways to make leathergoods as there are leatherworkers.

While I'd jumped headlong into the leathercrafting industry, I was hesitant to build holsters. I knew how important it was to build a safe and dependable product, especially when the user's life was on the line. I'd been asked to make them several times since I took the mantle of leatherworker for myself, and I was always a little uncomfortable with the idea of holster building.

A good friend of mine came to me, explaining he couldn't find anything he liked or wanted. He asked if I would build him a holster and after some heavy consideration, I agreed.

As I'd done so many times before I began my search for information. It didn't take long to discover there were almost no books on the subject whatsoever. I found a few about western style holsters, and some patterns for specific firearm makes and models, but I couldn't find anything, regardless of firearm type, telling me how to build a safe and secure holster from start to finish. My search eventually brough me to the internet where I learned almost the exact opposite of what I'd found previously.

There were so many holster crafting videos it would take weeks to get through all of them. I know because I did it! And I learned almost immediately, many of the people making these videos had no idea what they were talking about. I have no idea how much time and leather I wasted trying to follow their advice. And by the end of it I still didn't have what I considered to be a safe holster.

In 2018, on a Facebook page I follow, I came across a three-day class being held in Springfield, Missouri on how to make a pancake holster. I reached out to George, one of the instructors, and was able to secure a seat.

Over the course of those three days, I learned the fundamentals of safe holster design, how to identify what make a holster unsafe, recommended leather type and weight for various holster designs, and holster building techniques. I was instantly hooked and love every second of it!

I learned not only the "How's" of holster making, but the "Why's", the one major element I'd been missing. The class covered everything. I started with a blank piece of paper, a pencil, and a few simple tools. During those three days I designed a pattern and built a safe and functional pancake holster anyone could be proud of.

Since then, I've attended two other classes, and I'm always on the lookout for what they may offer next.

Chapter 1: Tracing the Firearm

Everything starts with a Pattern

Everything starts with a pattern, and in the case of holsters, every pattern starts with a tracing of the firearm. The next two chapters are the foundation to your holster design journey.

There are many right ways to do this. For example, we image a firearm, get the scale dead nuts, open it up in a CAD program, and trace it out. Then we build a stitch line with that.

We call that a StitchTrace and we sell the snot out of them.

The downside to this system is that we only have the stitch lines available for the models we build.

You'll soon discover you need models that aren't available on the market. So let's take a few minutes and learn how to make an accurate stitch line.

Safety note!!!

> Whenever you handle a firearm, always open the action immediately, visually check the chamber, and receiver and remove the magazine. Be certain that they are clear of ammunition.
> Always keep actions open when not in use. Never assume the firearm is unloaded!

A retention holster absolutely depends on an accurate stitch line and this accuracy starts with the tracing of the firearm.

So let's get started!

Chapter 1: Tracing the Firearm

Tools you'll need:
- Paper: cardstock 8.5x11
- Pencil: #2 preferred
- Ruler: metric or imperial
- Firearm, or 1:1 replica drone

Draw a line, from the top to the bottom of your paper. This will be your reference line that everything grows from.

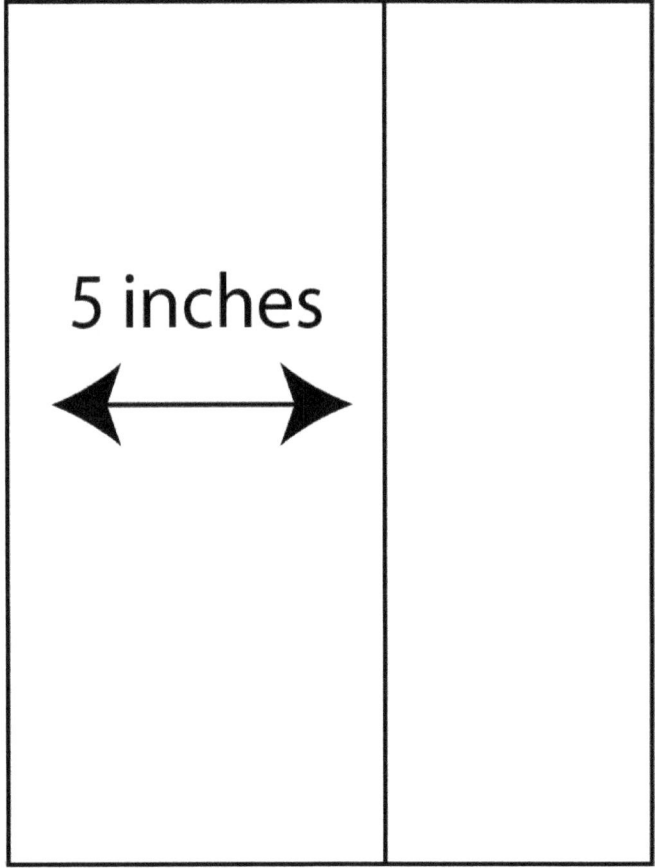

Figure 1-1

Now let's place our firearm or drone on the paper, aligning the top of the slide with the vertical line you drew.

The firearm we'll be using in this series is a Staccato P. The reasoning behind this choice is the unique challenges this firearm offers.

It has a dustcover and a large front sight. We'll be accounting for this in our design.

With a Glock, for example, you'll most likely not have a dustcover or a suppressor-height front site, and will not need to account for them in your stitch line.

Notice, the butt of the pistol goes over the edge of the paper. This part of the pistol will not be inside the holster, so we don't care!

Get the pistol aligned to the reference line you drew and let's get to tracing.

When tracing, please ensure the line you draw is as close as possible to the edge of the firearm. Remember, your pencil has dimensions, and you'll need to angle it to get your mark in-line with the object you're tracing.

Figure 1-2

Figure 1-3

Carefully trace your firearm. Remember to include the inside of the trigger guard, ejection port, and the mag release. You'll use these references when drawing the pattern.

We're looking for something kinda like this.

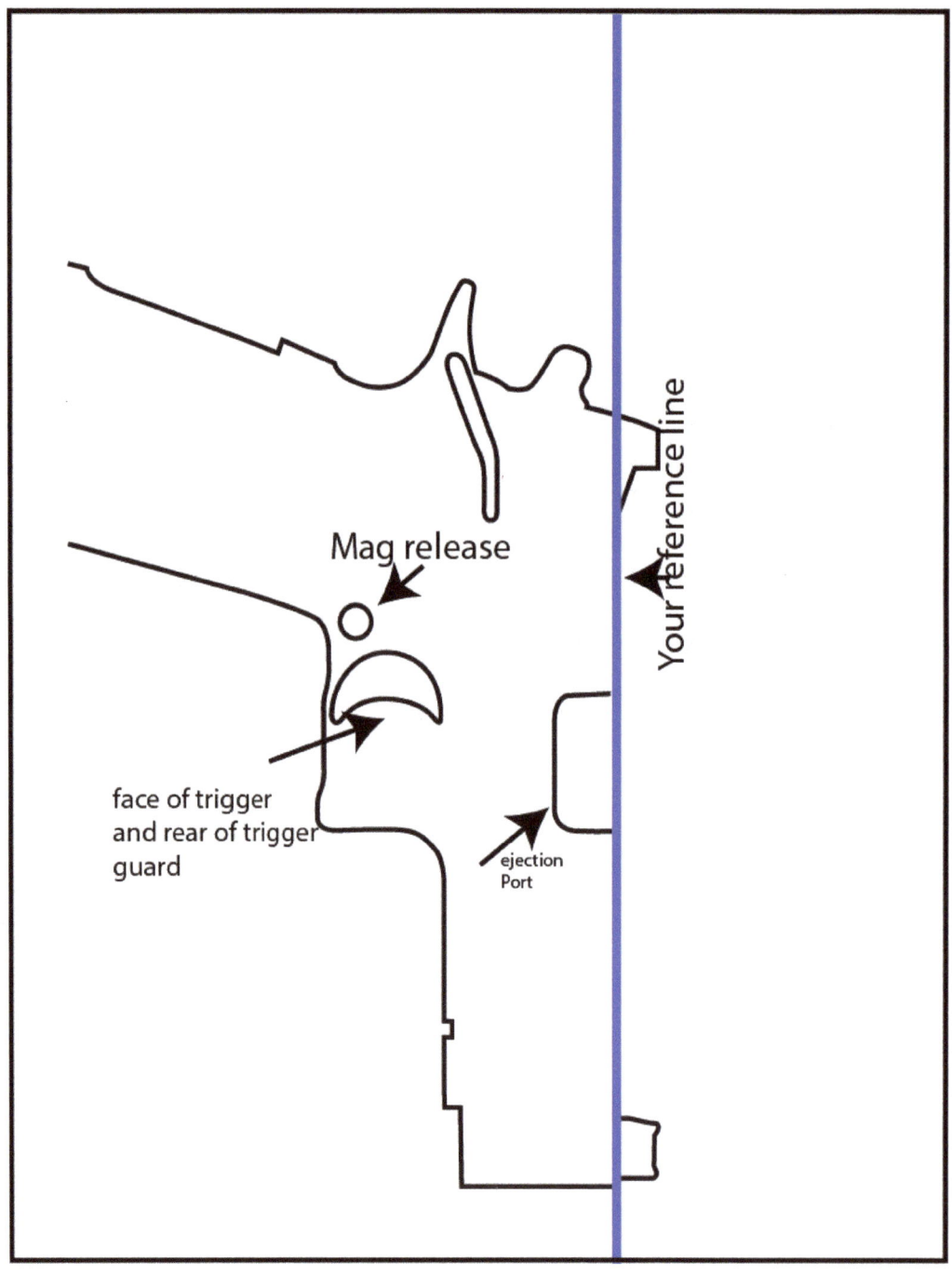

Figure 1-4

The tracing is done! Step back, pat yourself on the back. You've created the first step of your pattern! Place a five-inch horizontal line at the top, a five-inch vertical line on the side, and scan this to a file you can print many times over.

If you don't have a printer/scanner, go to the copy shop and make a dozen copies.

Please measure your reference lines to ensure the copier did not change the scale of your tracing.

Chapter 2: Creating the Stitch Line

In this chapter we're going to take your tracing and add a stitch line. Accuracy is paramount in this step of the process. Your retention and ride height will be set by this stitch line.

Tools we'll be using:
- Your tracing from Chapter 1
- Pencil: #2 preferred
- Eraser
- Ruler: metric or imperial
- Digital Caliper
- Calculator
- Firearm, or 1:1 replica drone

Figure 2-1

Safety Note!!!

> Whenever you handle a firearm, always open the action immediately, visually check the chamber, and receiver and remove the magazine. Be certain that they are clear of ammunition. Always keep actions open when not in use. Never assume the firearm is unloaded!

Let's get to work!

At the top of your pattern you're going to make a note for four measurements. You'll be writing your measurements down in this area. After we have the basic measurements, we'll be doing a little math to create our stitch line.

You can use metric or imperial measurements. For this example we'll be using imperial in a decimal format.

Let's prepare our tracing sheet to make a stitch line. At the top, note the following:
(A) **Slide**
(B) **Dust Cover**
(C) **Frame**
(D) **Trigger guard**
And the formula, **m ÷ 2 + (leather thickness)**

Center this at the top of the page. We'll be writing our measurements on the left, and do our calculations and results on the right.

Please make your sheet look like figure 2-2.

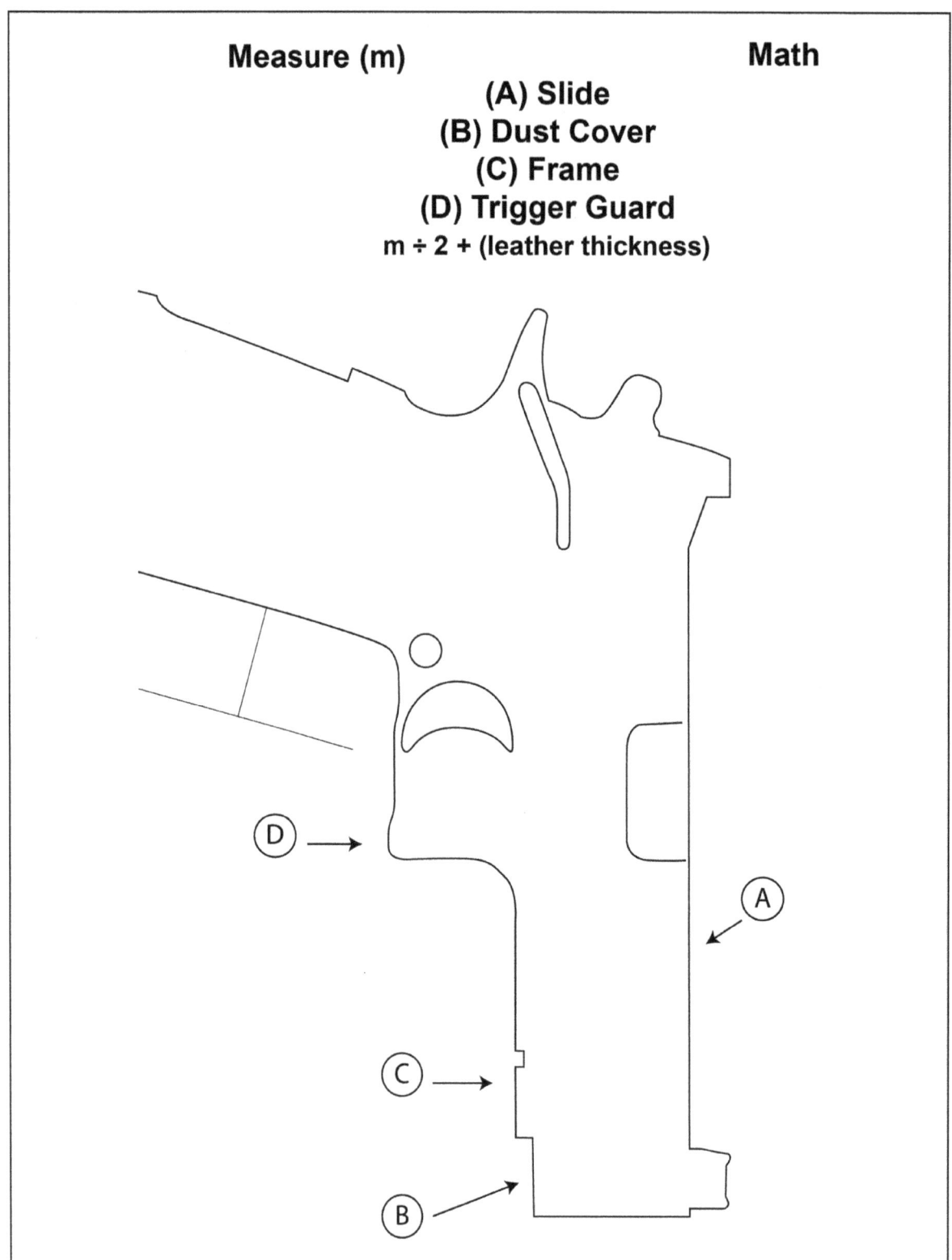

Figure 2-2

Let's grab our digital calipers and get to measuring!

You can use the metric or the imperial measuring systems. I'll be using imperial measurements in this book.

Measure the slide (A) – 0.954"

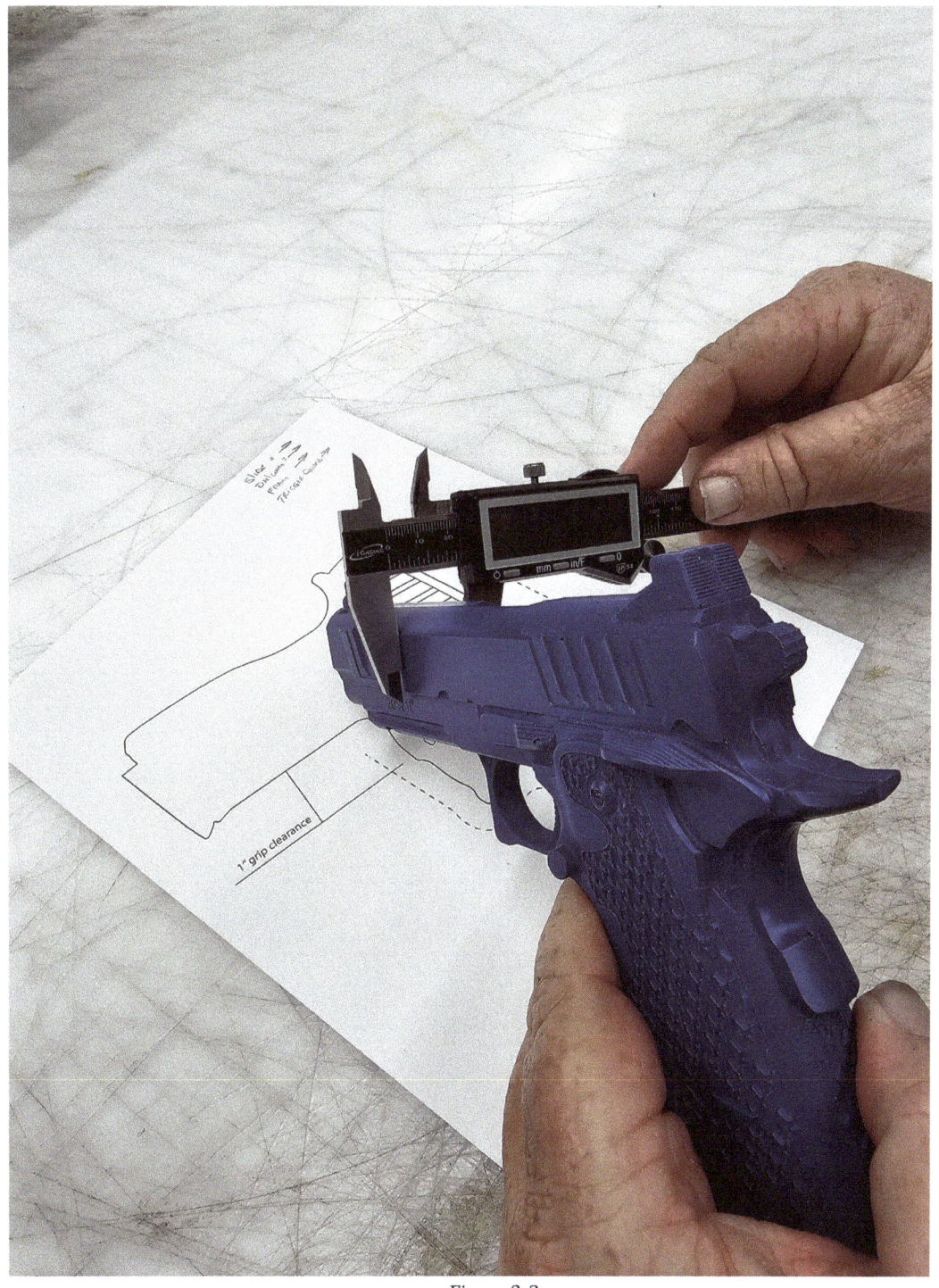

Figure 2-3

Measure the dust cover (B) (this doesn't exist on all firearm models) – 0.639"

Measure the frame (C) – 0.83"

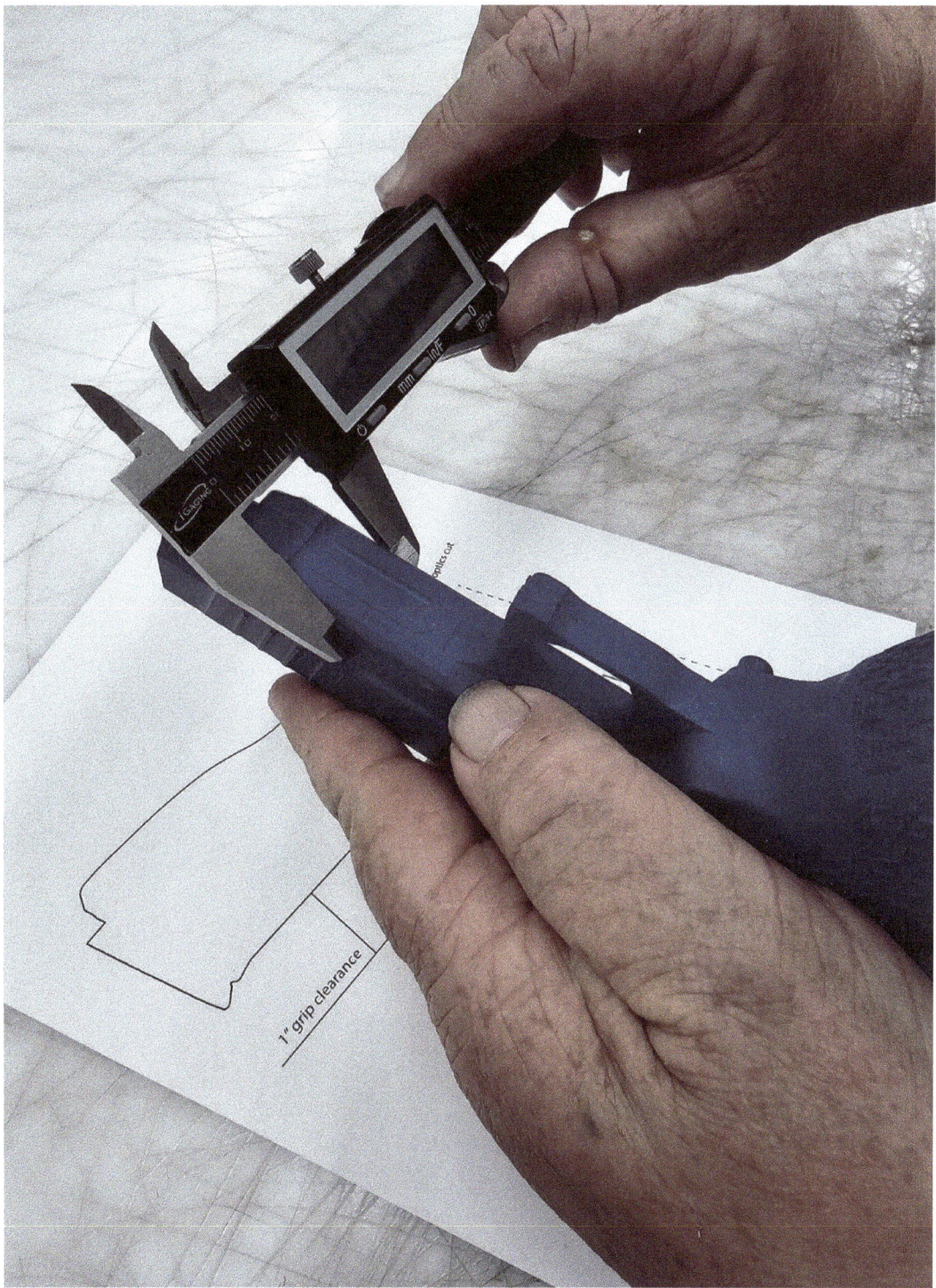

Figure 2-5

Measure the Trigger Guard (D) – 0.395"

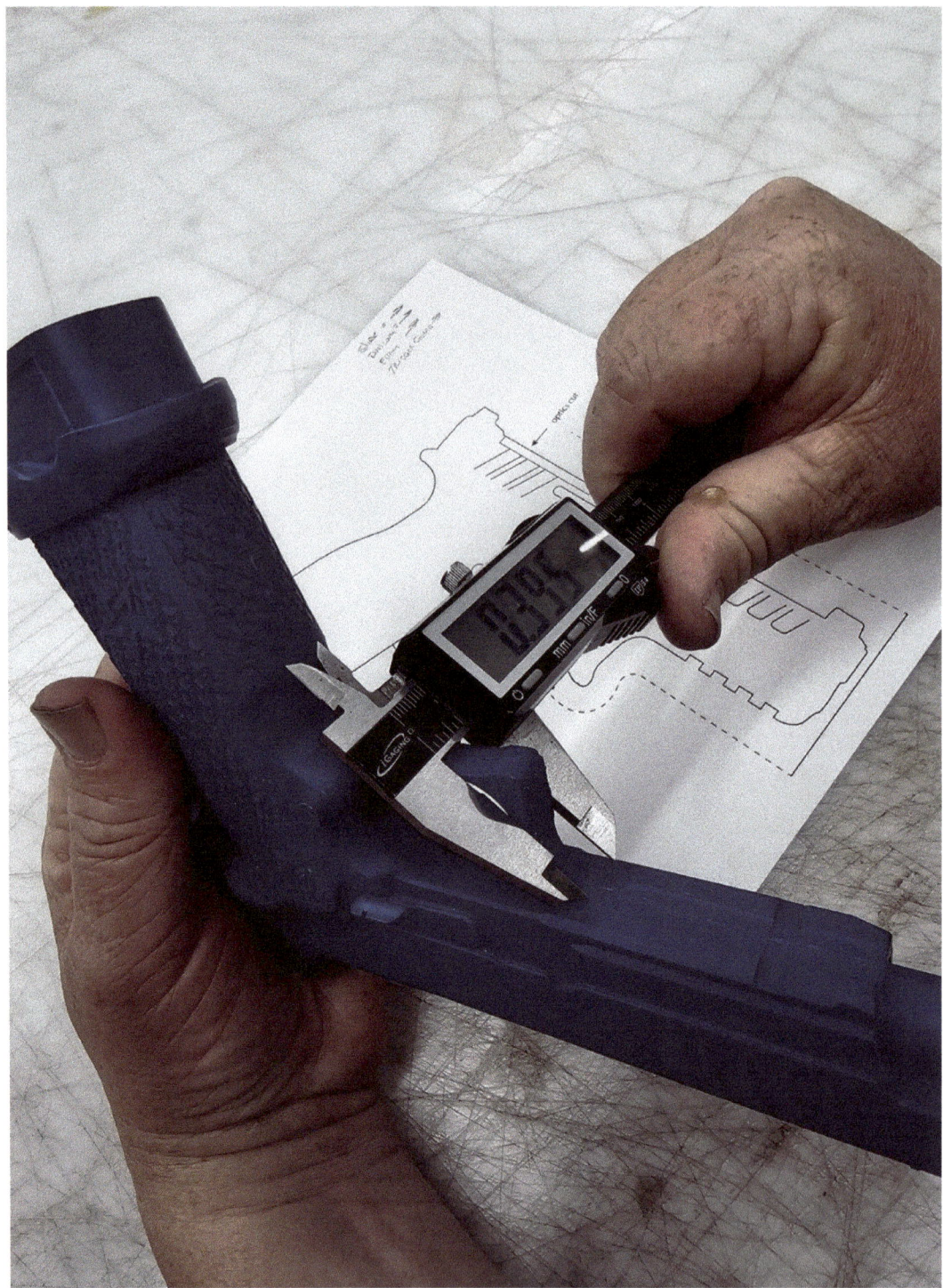

Figure 2-6

Let's put those numbers at the top of the trace sheet in the spaces you provided.

Measure (m)   **Math**

        .954   **Slide**
        .639   **Dust Cover**
        .830   **Frame**
        .395   **Trigger Guard**

$m \div 2 + \text{(leather thickness)}$

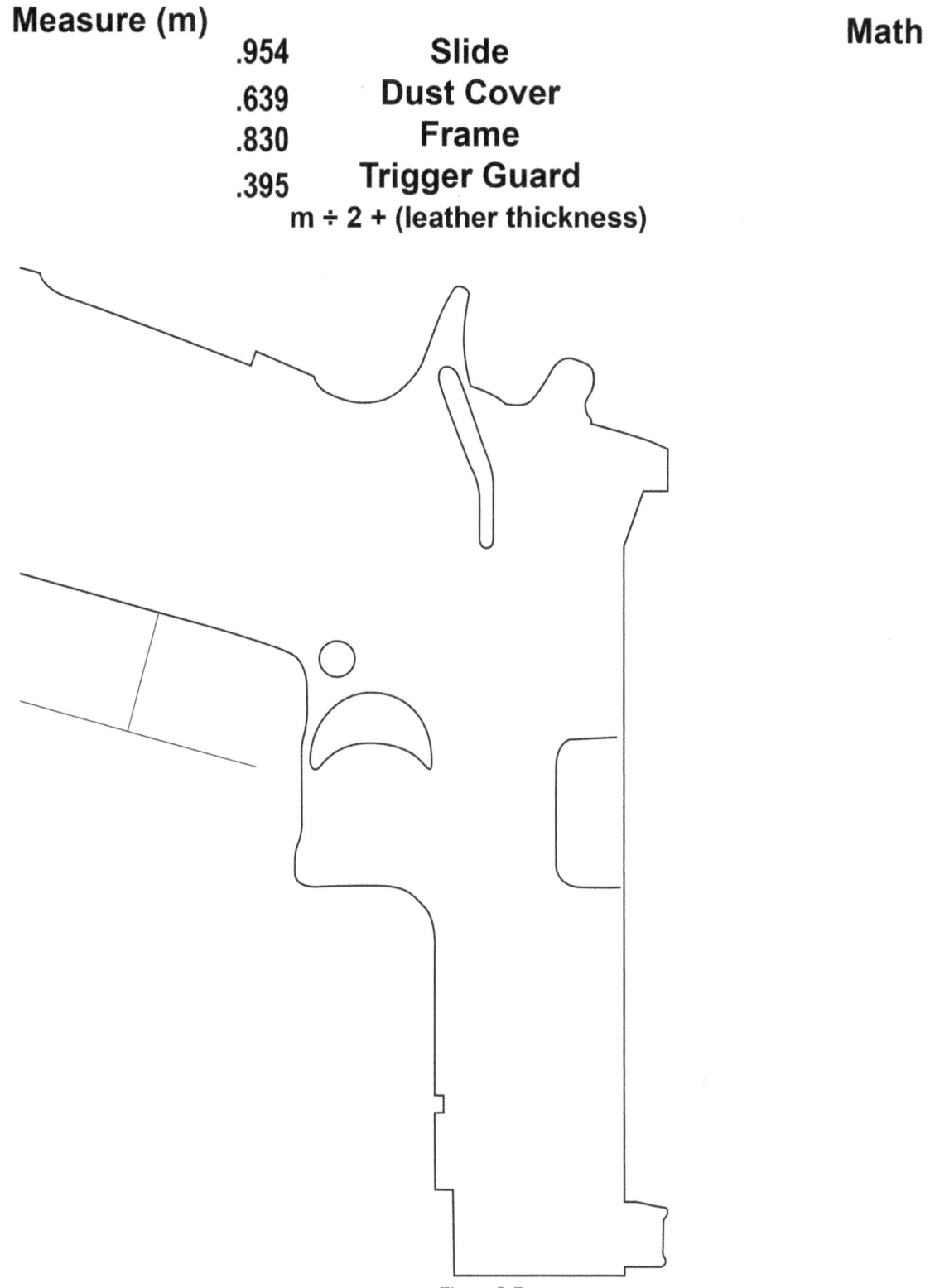

Figure 2-7

Now it's time for MATH!

Relax. This isn't rocket science, just holster science.

Each side of the holster (front & back) travels halfway around the firearm and is stitched together. So we need to divide our measurements in half.

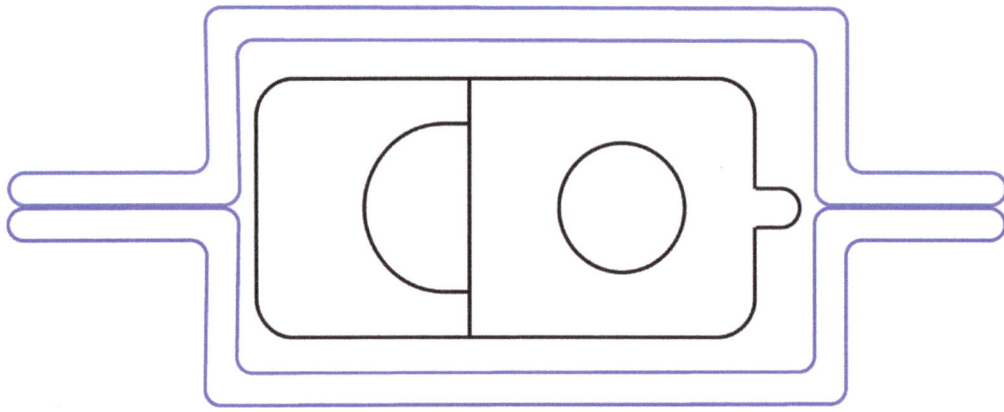

Figure 2-8

Take each of your measurements: A, B, C and D, and divide them in half. Record this to the right side of your measurements table.

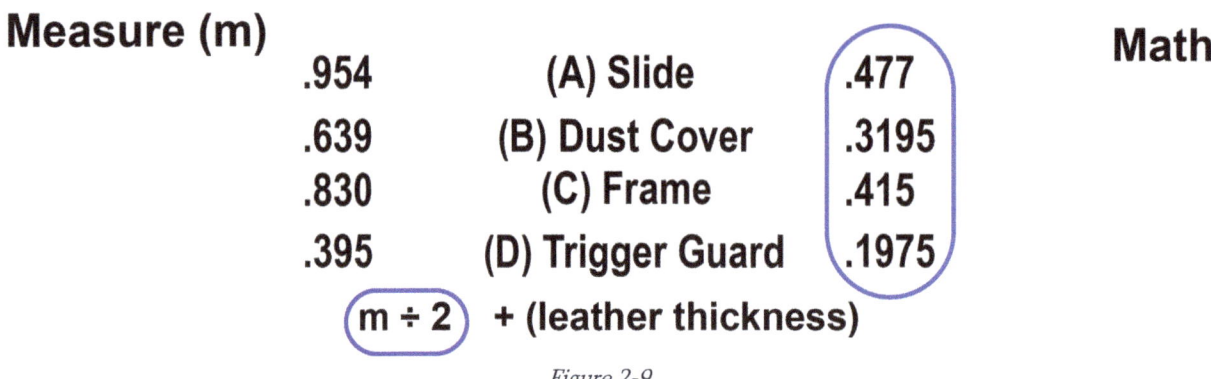

Figure 2-9

We're getting pretty close, but we must remember that leather has its own dimensions. We'll be using eight-ounce (8 oz.) leather which is one-eighth-inch thick (1/8"), or displayed in a decimal format would be written as 0.125".

When we stitch the holster together, the leather will be in-between the stitch line and the firearm, so we need to add the thickness of the leather to our calculation.

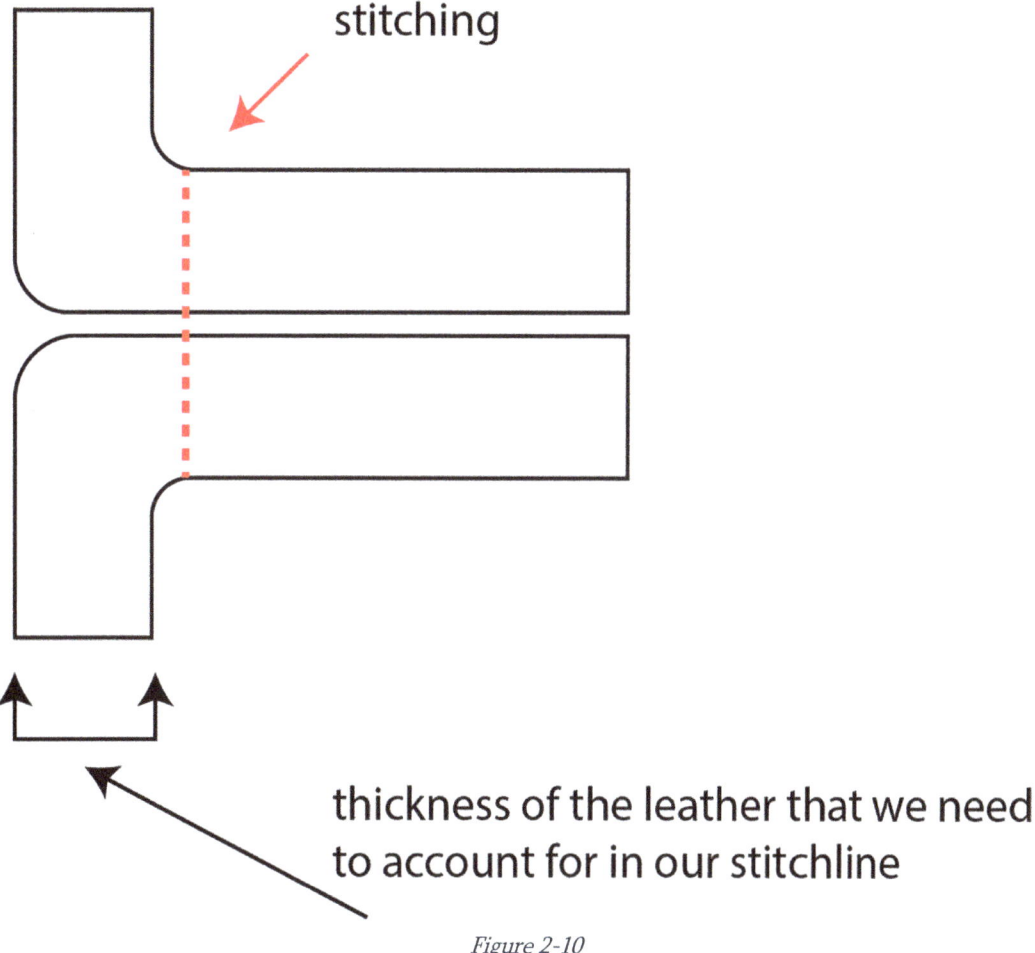

Figure 2-10

Now we'll go back to our measurements table and finish the calculation.

Figure 2-11

Chapter 2: Creating the Stitch Line

Let's round these measurements to two decimal places to keep things simple.

Measure (m)			**Math**
.954	(A) Slide	.477 + .125 =	.60
.639	(B) Dust Cover	.3195 + .125 =	.45
.830	(C) Frame	.415 + .125 =	.54
.395	(D) Trigger Guard	.1975 + .125 =	.32

m ÷ 2 + (leather thickness)

Figure 2-12

You've now got the stitch line measurements ready to add to your tracing.

We'll be using our digital calipers to mark the reference points for our stitch line. Simply find the measurement you want on the display. Tighten the lock screw. Press one of the points to the tracing. And mark the other point with your pencil.

Do this once at the beginning of your line and once at the end.

Now grab your ruler and connect the dots.

How cool is that?

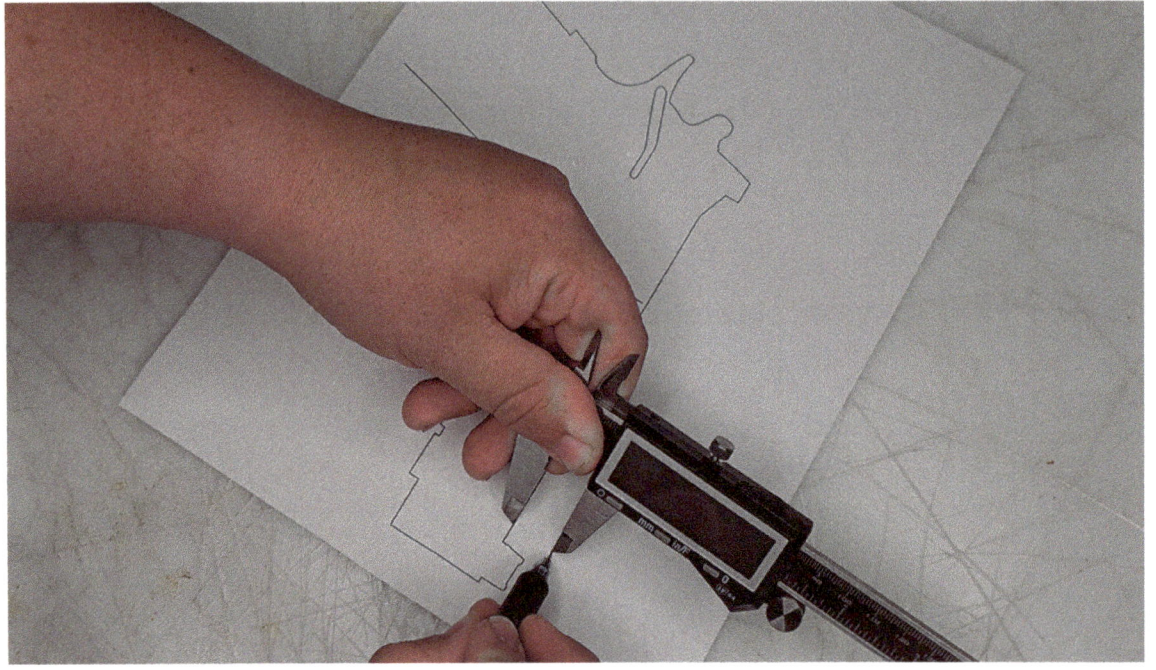

Figure 2-13

First, using your calipers, mark one end of your stitch line.

21

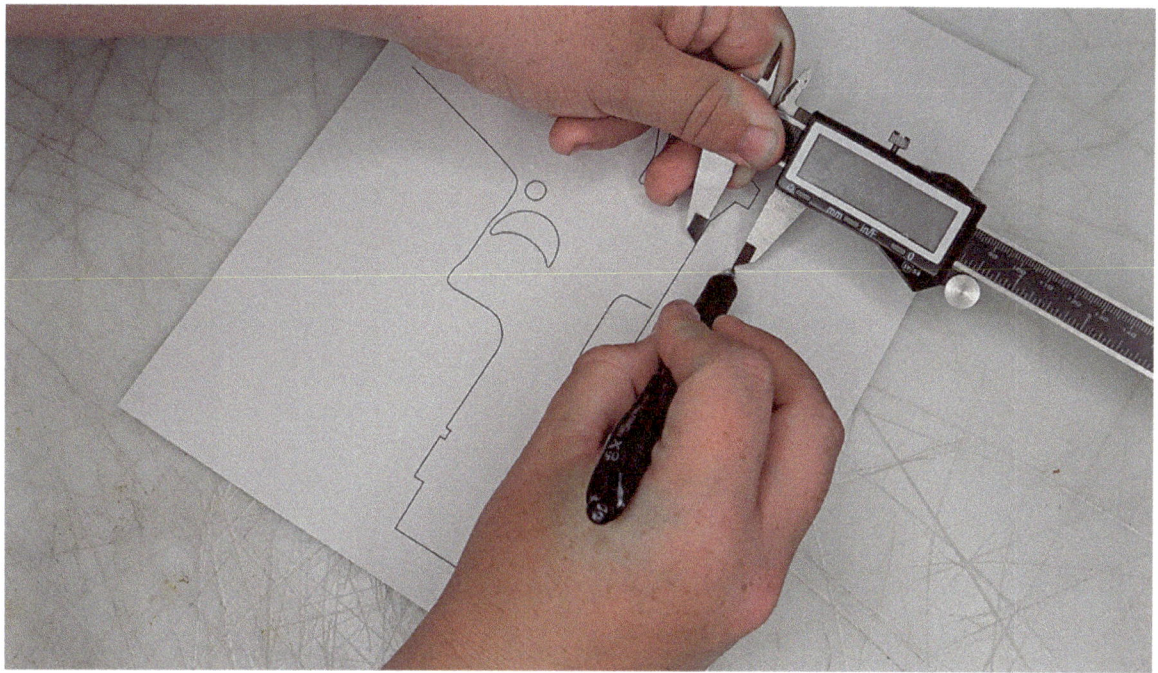

Figure 2-14

Second, using your calipers again, mark the other end of your stitch line.

Figure 2-15

Now, use your ruler to connect the marks and draw your stitch line.

Chapter 2: Creating the Stitch Line

Figure 2-16

And here is your completed slide side stitch line!

This method of marking and creating your lines will give you the accuracy we need to sew the holster.

Remember, we gain retention through friction and molding. That means we need tight stitch lines.

Now let's measure and place the rest of our stitch lines

First, we'll add the slide stitch line (A).

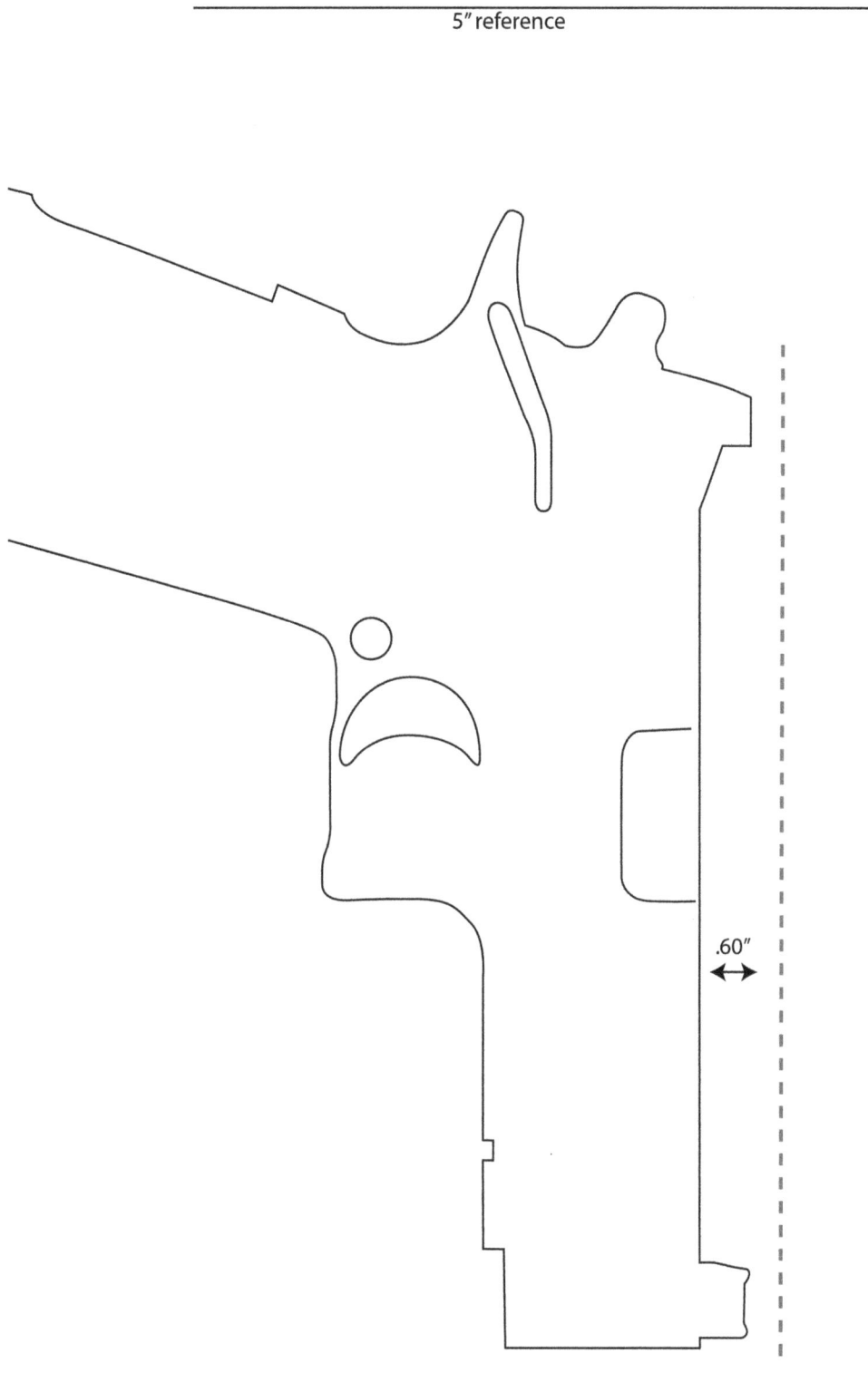

Figure 2-17

Once that's in place, we'll add the dustcover (B) and frame (C) lines. Don't worry if they extend past the transition point. We'll erase the excess after we join them.

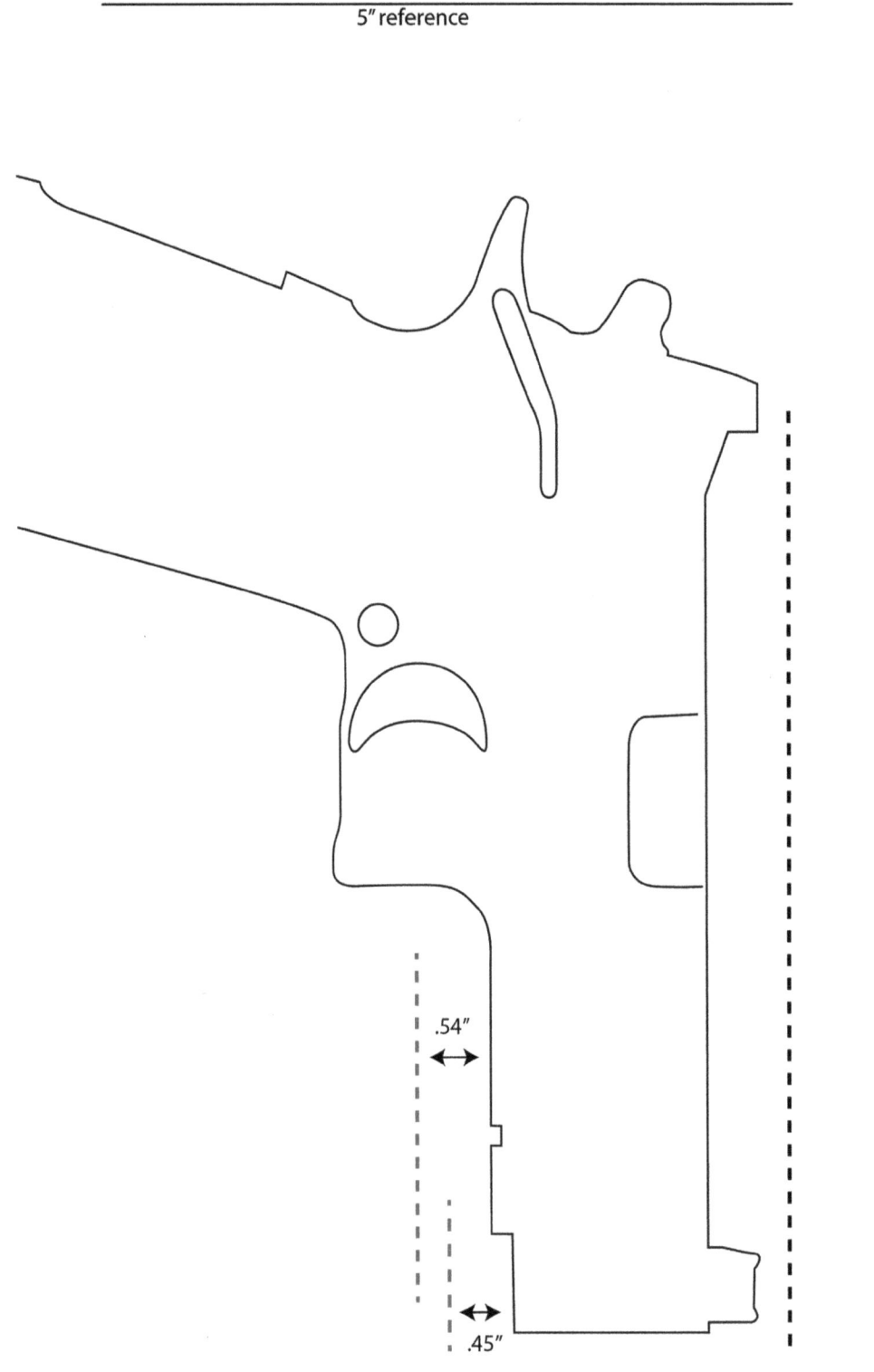

Figure 2-18

The final lines we'll drop in will be our trigger guard. This is measurement (D) on your sheet. We'll be placing both horizontal and vertical lines.

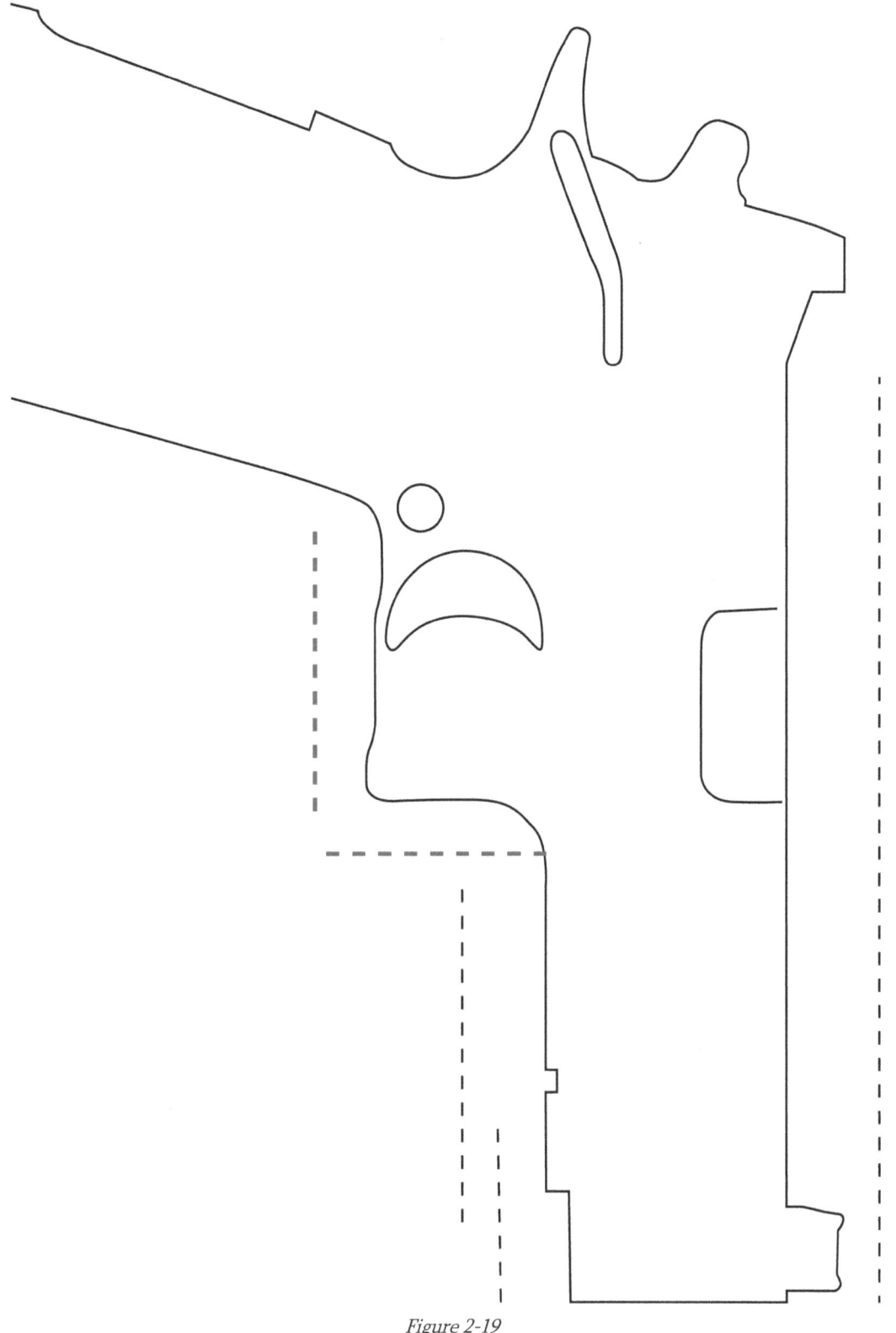

Figure 2-19

Chapter 2: Creating the Stitch Line

Now we have a bunch of straight lines along the frame side of the firearm. Let's get to connecting them.

First, we need to look at the connection point from the frame (C) to the dustcover (B).

We'll be connecting the two lines, but we will not create the connection directly adjacent to the actual transition. We're going to drop down about one-eighth-inch (1/8") or 0.125" and place our transition there.

This is because the leather will move up slightly when we mold it to the firearm.

Our transitions will look a little like this.

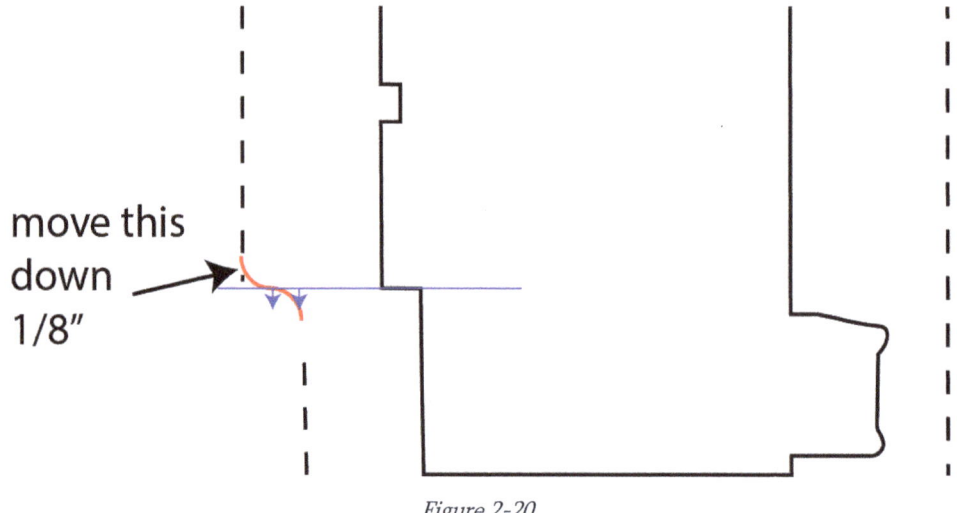

Figure 2-20

And after we move the transition down, it will look like this.

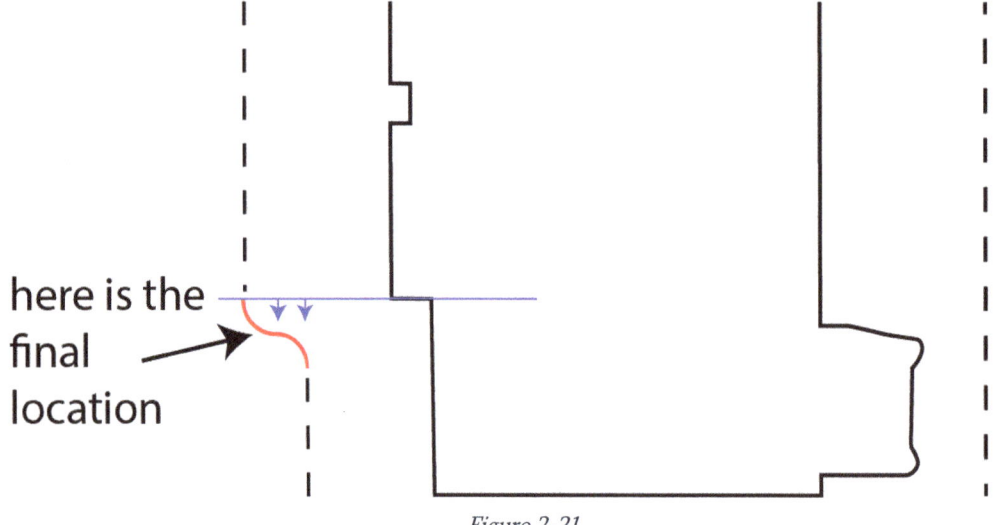

Figure 2-21

27

This small adjustment will make the transition from frame to dustcover look the way you want it.

Next, we'll be connecting the transitions around the toe of the trigger guard, and the trigger guard to the frame.

Let's use the same technique with your calipers to mark and trace the curve around the front of the trigger guard.

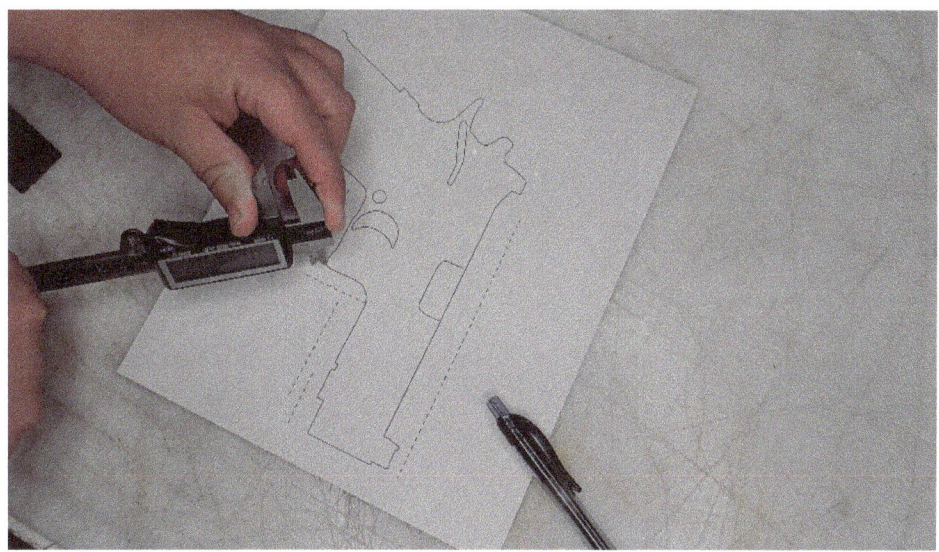

Figure 2-22

Place your calipers on your tracing and make a mark for the stitch line.

Figure 2-23

Change your location and place another mark, we'll use this technique to create three marks.

Chapter 2: Creating the Stitch Line

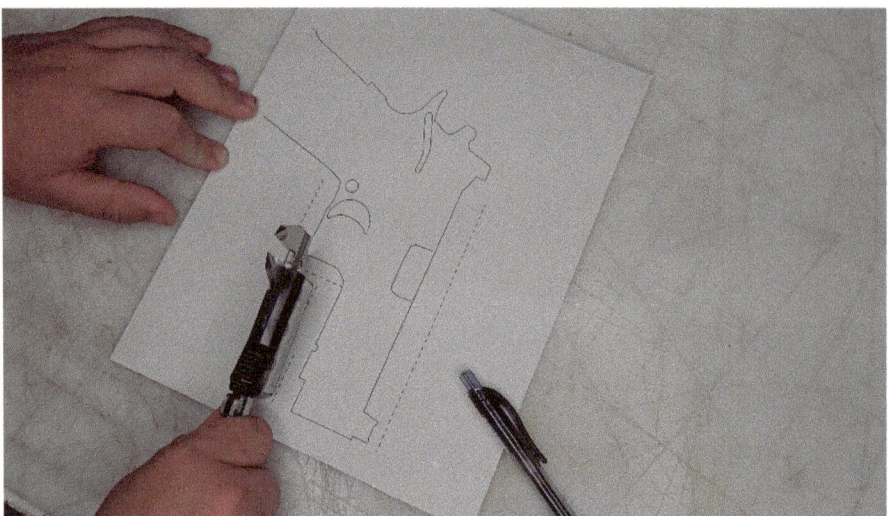

Figure 2-24

This is the last mark we'll make. Now let's play connect the dots.

Figure 2-25

When you connect your three marks you'll have an accurate curve for the bottom of the trigger guard.

Now we need connect the trigger guard to the frame. We're going to use a very high-tech tool for this!

Figure 2-26

That's right, one thin dime! This will probably be the least expensive leather template piece you'll ever buy!

Now, let's use it to connect our trigger guard to the frame. If you go much smaller, your stitches will look kind of jagged, not at all charismatic!

Figure 2-27

This is starting to look like a stitch line already.

Figure 2-28

We're getting closer!

Let's take a look at where we are on our stitch line.

Note: The transitions are in different colors.

First, we need to get our curve for the toe of the trigger guard, followed by the transition from trigger guard to frame.

And finally, the dust cover transition slid down one-eighth-inch (1/8") to allow for leather movement during the molding process.

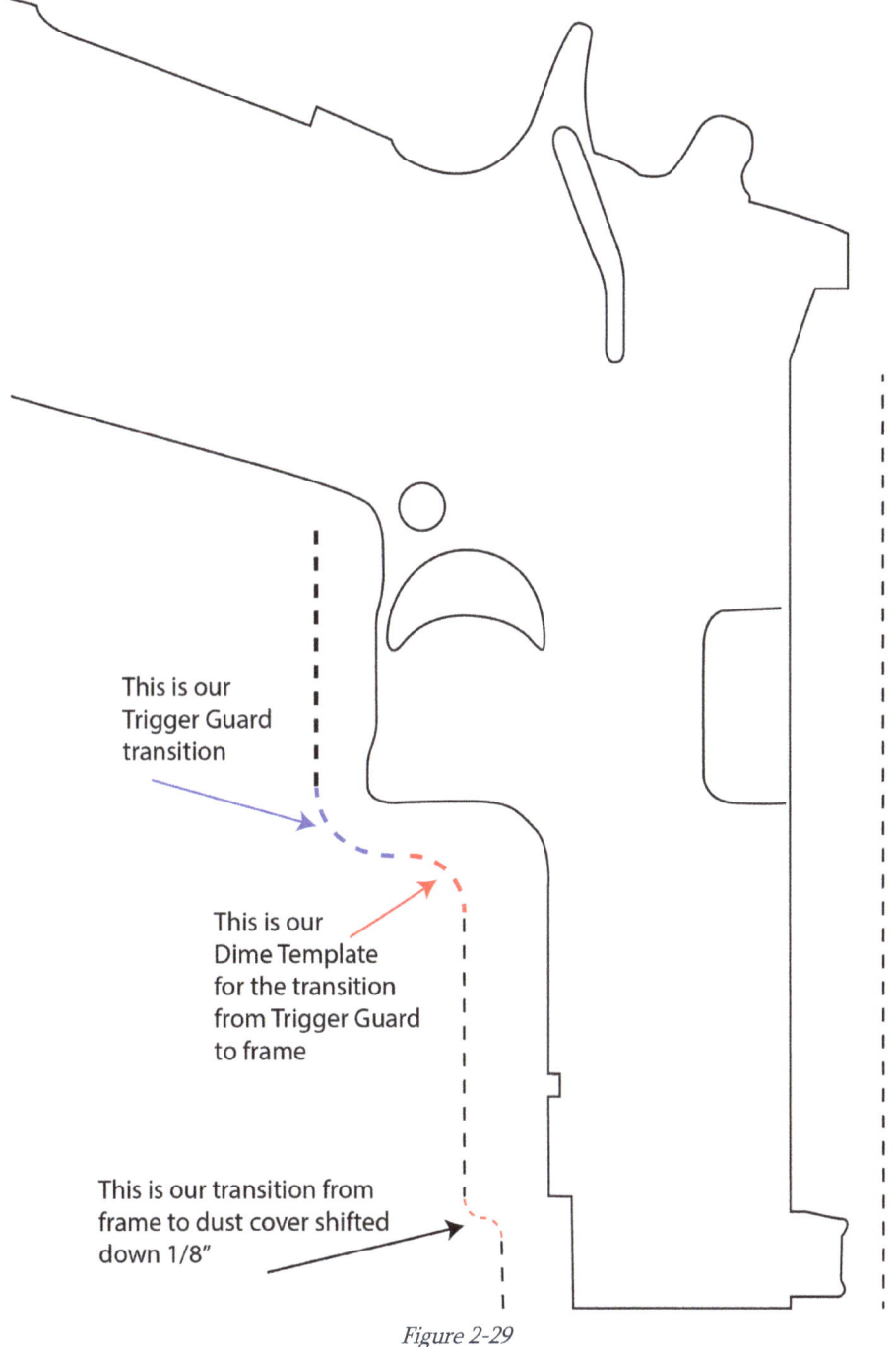

Figure 2-29

We're in the final stretch.

Let's add a horizontal line one-eighth-inch (1/8") below the bottom of the muzzle.

Our goal is to give enough leather to slightly fold in during the molding process and protect the crown of the barrel from damage.

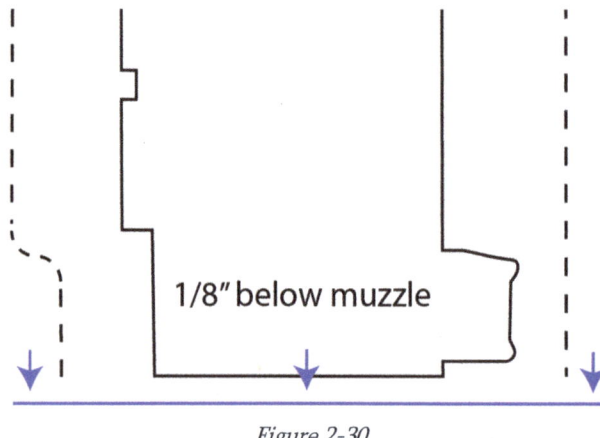

Figure 2-30

Let's place our line one-eighth-inch (1/8") below the muzzle.

Just a couple more steps and we'll have an awesome stitch line that you can use to build all your holsters for this model in the future.

There are several reasons why I chose this model of firearm for this book.

First, it offers several challenges that don't exist on all holsters. It had you design a dust cover transition. And now, we have to account for a Co-Witness front sight.

Just look at that freakin' HUUUGE sight!

If we leave the slide side stitch line as it is, this sight will drag in the leather and get occluded by leather shavings. Or, in the worst case, it can cut your stitches.

Using the muzzle line we created, we'll add one-eighth-inch (1/8") to our slide side stitch line to accommodate the sight. We don't need to add this room all the way to the top of the holster, only to the ejection port.

When the firearm is in that position of draw, it's starting to rotate and the front sight will no longer need additional space.

Starting at the muzzle end of the ejection port, we'll add a dot to our stitch line.

Now, go to your stitch line right at the bottom of the front sight and make a mark one-eighth-inch (1/8") further out.

Now connect the dots. Your stitch line should now look like this.

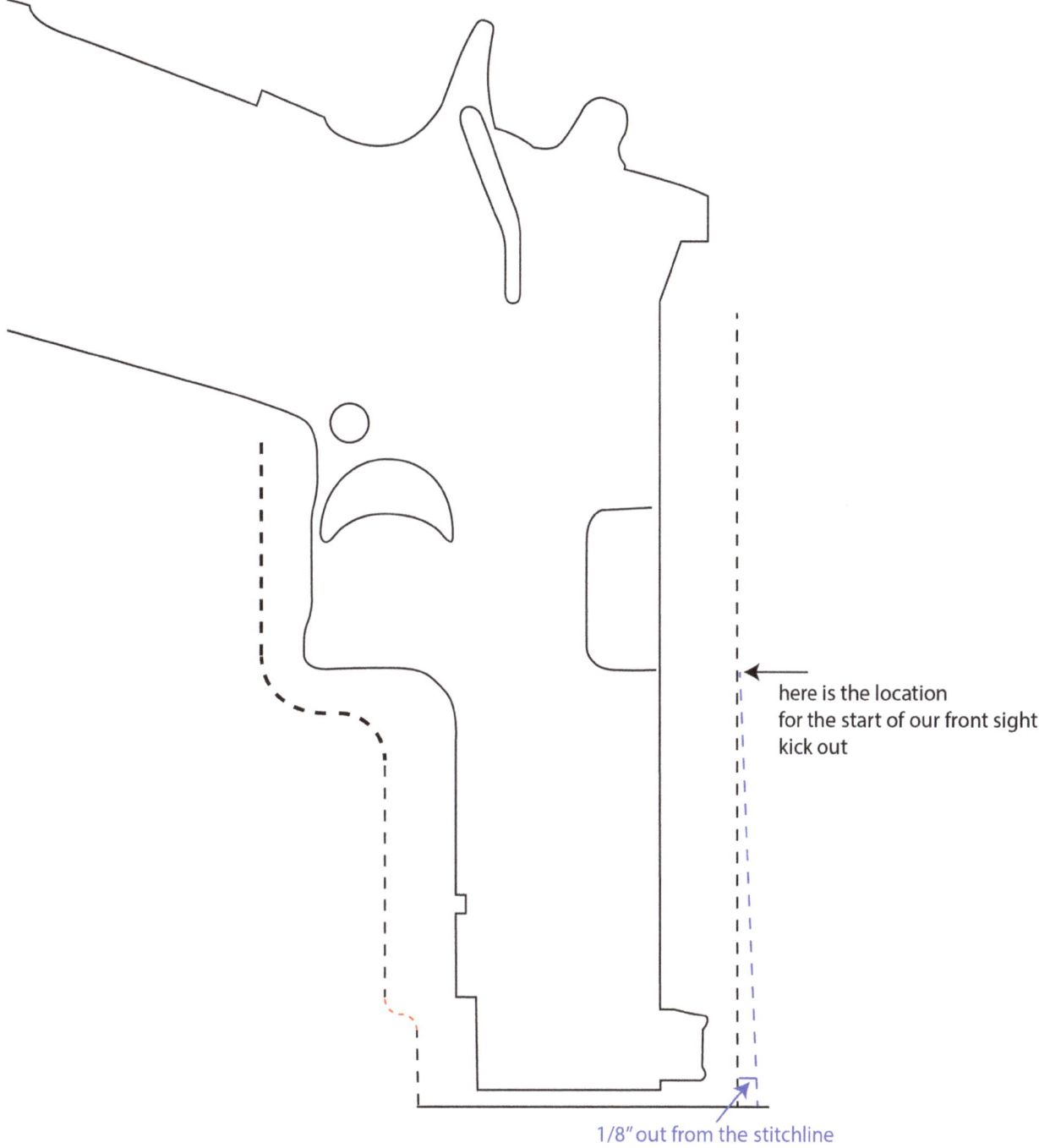

Figure 2-31

I know you're tired, but we need to add one more line to our stitch line.

When designing a holster we have to leave room for a proper combat grip while the firearm is holstered.

We'll go into more detail about that in the holster design chapter, but for now, we need to add a one-inch (1") grip clearence.

We'll do this by measuring one-inch (1") below our grip with our calipers and drawing a line.

Now, let's add a five-inch (5") horizontal and a five-inch (5") vertical line to our pattern for scale reference.

YOU WILL NOT USE YOUR ORIGINAL STITCH LINE TO DRAW PATTERNS!!!

You've bled and sweated over the creation of this puppy. You'll need to make a dozen copies on cardstock and place them in a file to use for patterns. Be sure to sign and date this puppy. Heck, frame it! This is your first step on the path of becoming a holster designer.

Design & Construction of the Practical Leather Holster: Pancake Edition

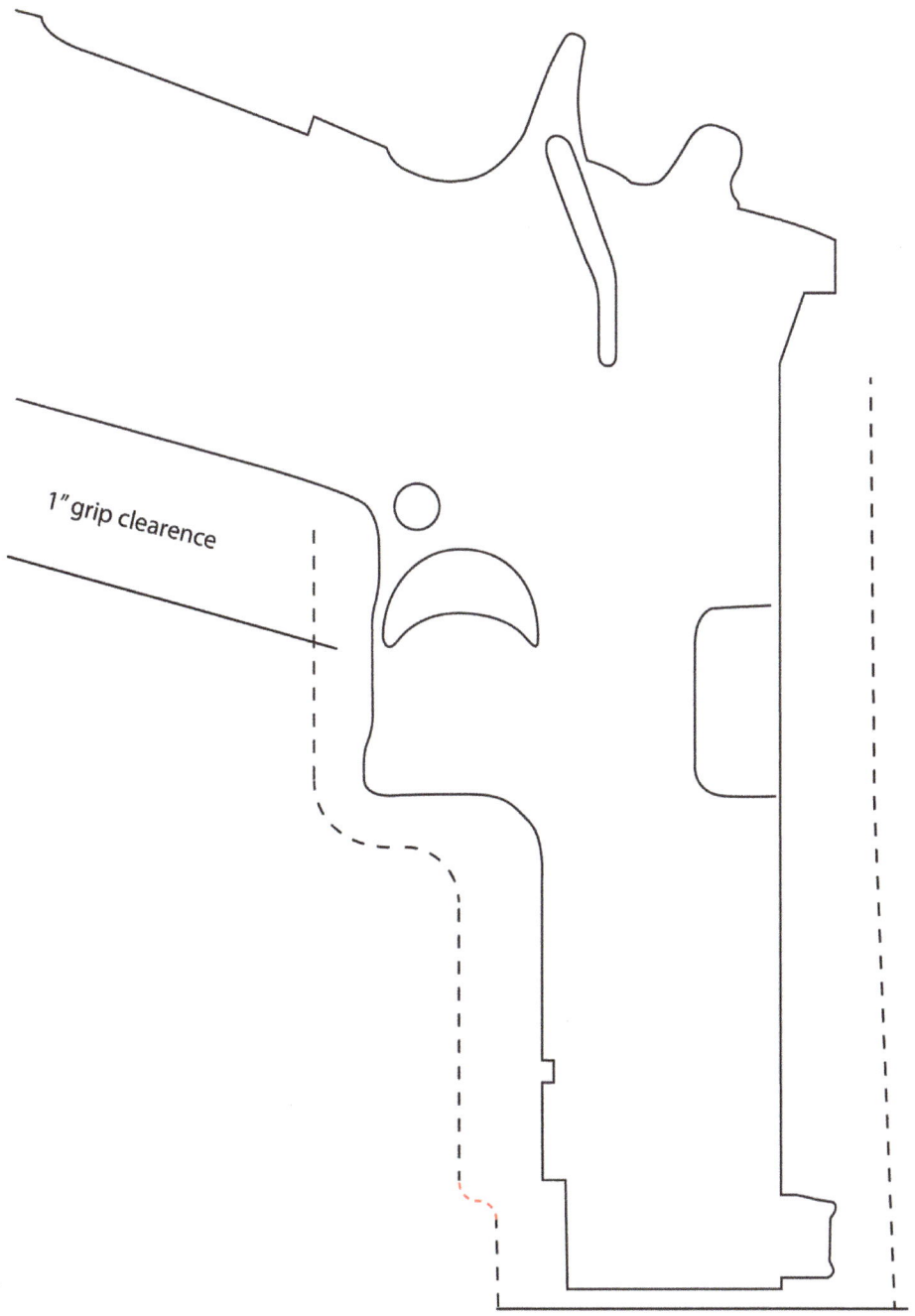

Figure 2-32

Section 2: Concepts & Theory – Part 1

Lowell Harvey on George Lawrence Co.

I've known some interesting people in my lifetime. A great deal of interesting people. Got to do a lot of holsters for a lot of people. Clint Eastwood was one of em.

That was back when I worked at George Lawrence Company. Probably the most enjoyable place I've ever worked. It really was.

I knew Bill Lawrence, the last of the family. It had been in that same family for 132 years. Started before the Civil War, in 1857, and stayed in the family att that time.

They brought their brother-in-law over from Scotland. That's where they were from. Brought the family to work in the business and take it over later on.

It was a two-story building with a water elevator. You walked into this big square lift. It had a big wooden lever you pushed and it'd transfer water from one barrel to another. The weight would pull you up, or let you down. There was no noise, it was just water raising and lowering you.

When you walked into the basement, they had like a museum. There were tools and stuff there, like buckles from the 1800's.

It was insane to work there. I found the original 60 Sumter holster sets from the civil war. We started reproducing them. I found everything down there.

I once opened up two bins, like the old flour or potato bins that tipped out. I tipped out these two bins and one was full of Confederate brass buckles; lead filled, not a hook on the back, but like an arrowhead, how they were originally made. The other was full of U.S. buckles. They were originals from the 1800's.

They had the old bullet pouches and all the patterns. They had everything.

We started making the sets for reenactors and such. You wouldn't believe what all was down there. I mean, patterns from the 1800s!

And they had every handgun that was ever made from 1857 until 1988. We had them all. Most were sand castings. We took the original and made a sand casting of it, but we had the mold. We had guns that people couldn't believe we had.

People ask why Golden Goodrich bought them. I'll tell you why—For the damn gun molds! You have no idea how much was there!

I tried to buy it. I wanted to buy it. I didn't find out it had sold until Bob Gould showed up.

I knew Bob. I'd worked as a sharpshooter. They'd hire you to come in for a few months, kind of like a travelling nurse. You'd come in and go through every station, going through like edgers, stitchers, clickers. They'd bring em through and train em to be better and more accurate.

I'd knew Bob because he was the CEO of Smith & Wesson. When Smith & Wesson sold their leather division, him and John Goodrich got together and bought it, making Gould & Goodrich. So, really, Gould & Goodrich was just Smith & Wesson. So I was real familiar with them.

Bob showed up one day. He walked through and looked into everything. I was doing a custom belt then. He looked at it and the holster, a western set, and said "I wish we could get edges like that on our holsters. We just can't get those nice edges."

That was kind of what we specialized in. We had custom burnishers that were made out of oak. And we used tallow and a little bit of turpentine in it to soften it up. That's how we got them good edges. But I didn't know he was buying the damn company then.

Chapter 3: The Go/No-Go Zones

This is a conceptual chapter. We recommend reading through the whole thing before attempting to apply the following concepts to your holster pattern design. By reading this chapter in its entirety you'll have a better understanding of the topic as a whole, and will therefore be better equipped to make the necessary adjustments when time comes to design your holster.

We're almost ready to start drawing the actual holster body, but before we do, we need to know the areas where we can place leather and the areas we cannot.

There are three No-Go Zones, and three Go Zones.

Let's get started with the No-Go Zones.

When we drew our stitch line, we marked out a one-inch (1") area below the grip to leave room for the hand to achieve a *full combat grip*. This area is a No-Go Zone.

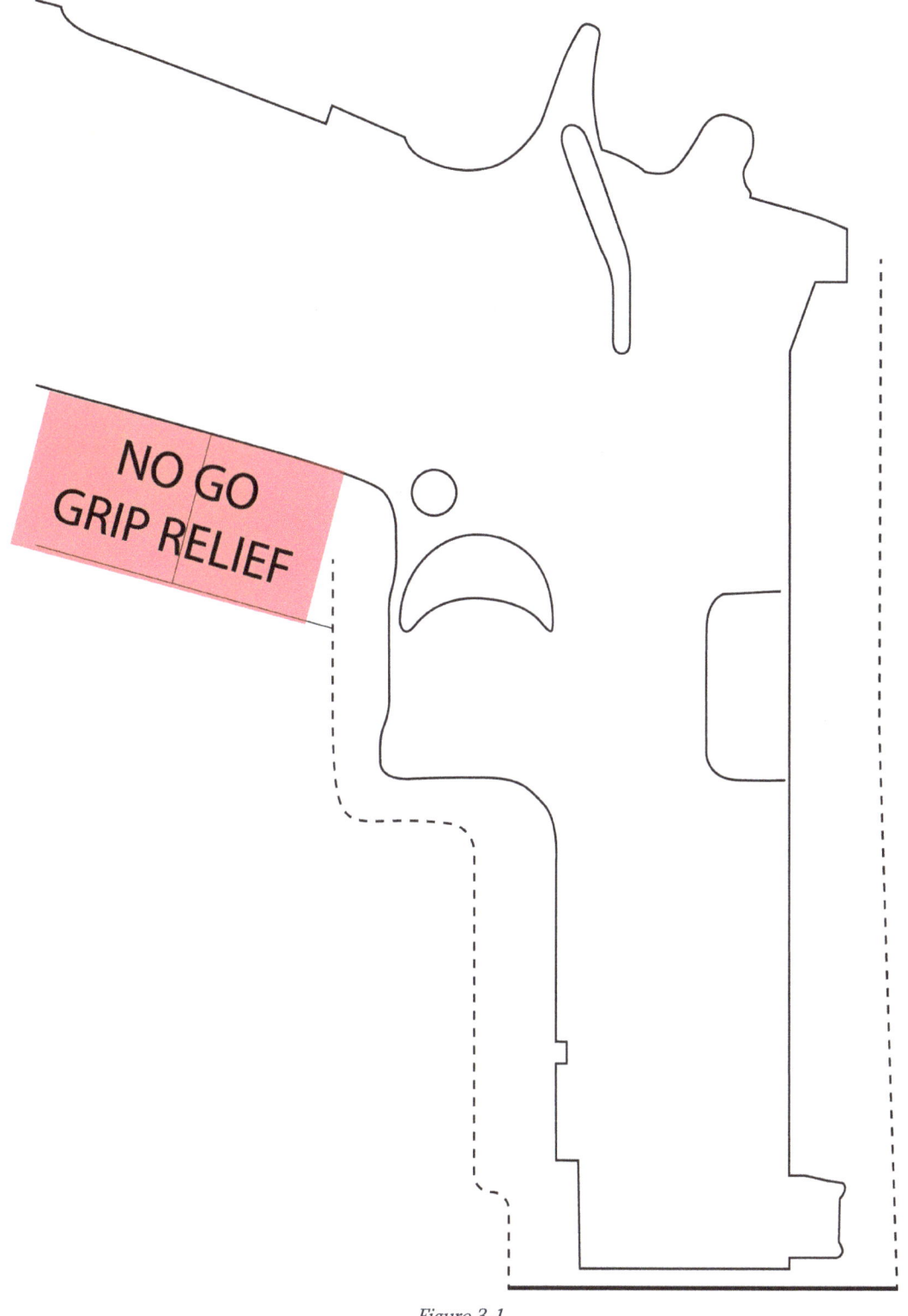

Figure 3-1

The next No-Go Zone is the rear of the grip below the slide.

When you're gripping the firearm, the web of your hand (the area between your thumb and first finger) will occupy this space.

If leather is in this area, you cannot achieve a good grip.

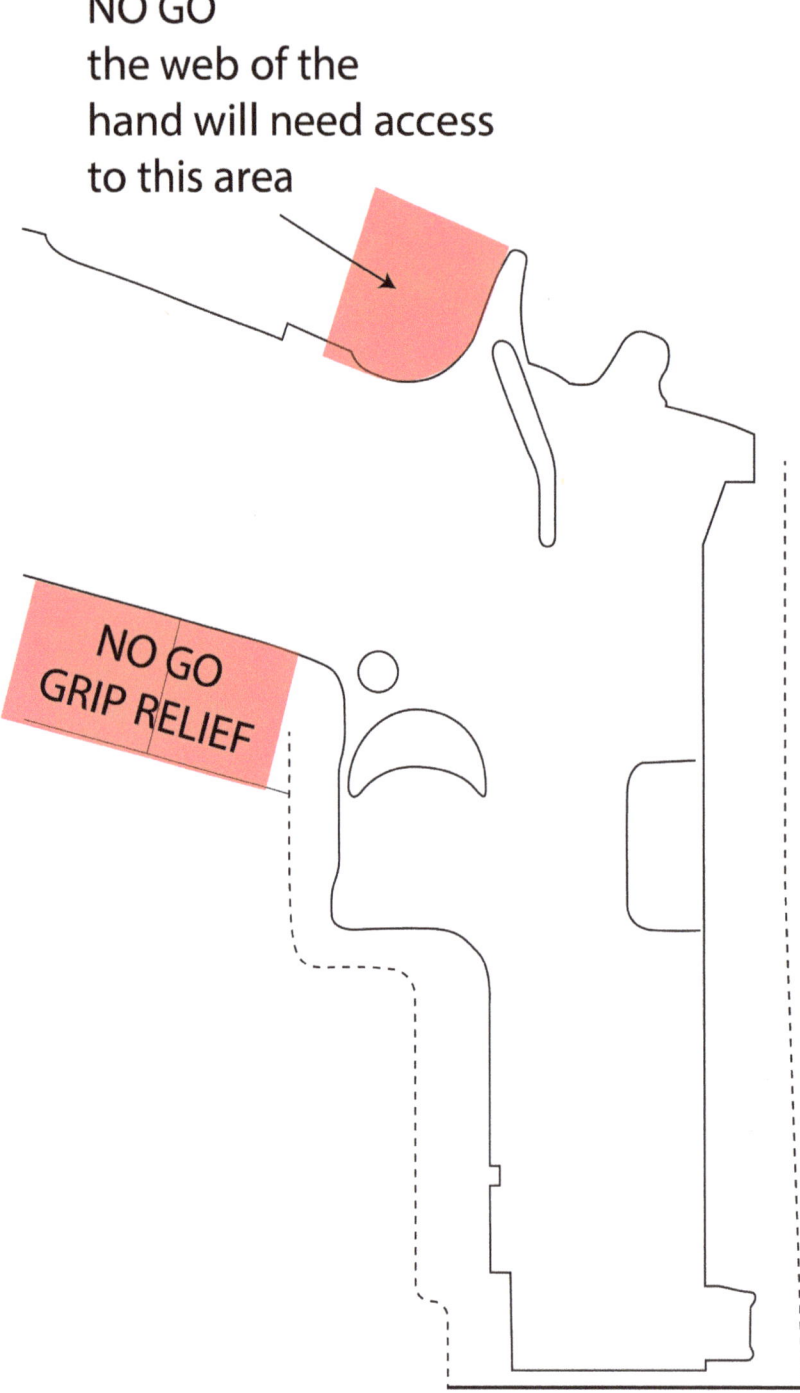

Figure 3-2

The final No-Go Zone is the mag release.

If leather is over the mag release it will impact it and eject the magazine from the pistol, leaving you with a very expensive single shot firearm.

People may try to convince you this won't happen, but it will. I'll say this again; it's not a matter of IF the mag will get ejected, but WHEN it will happen.

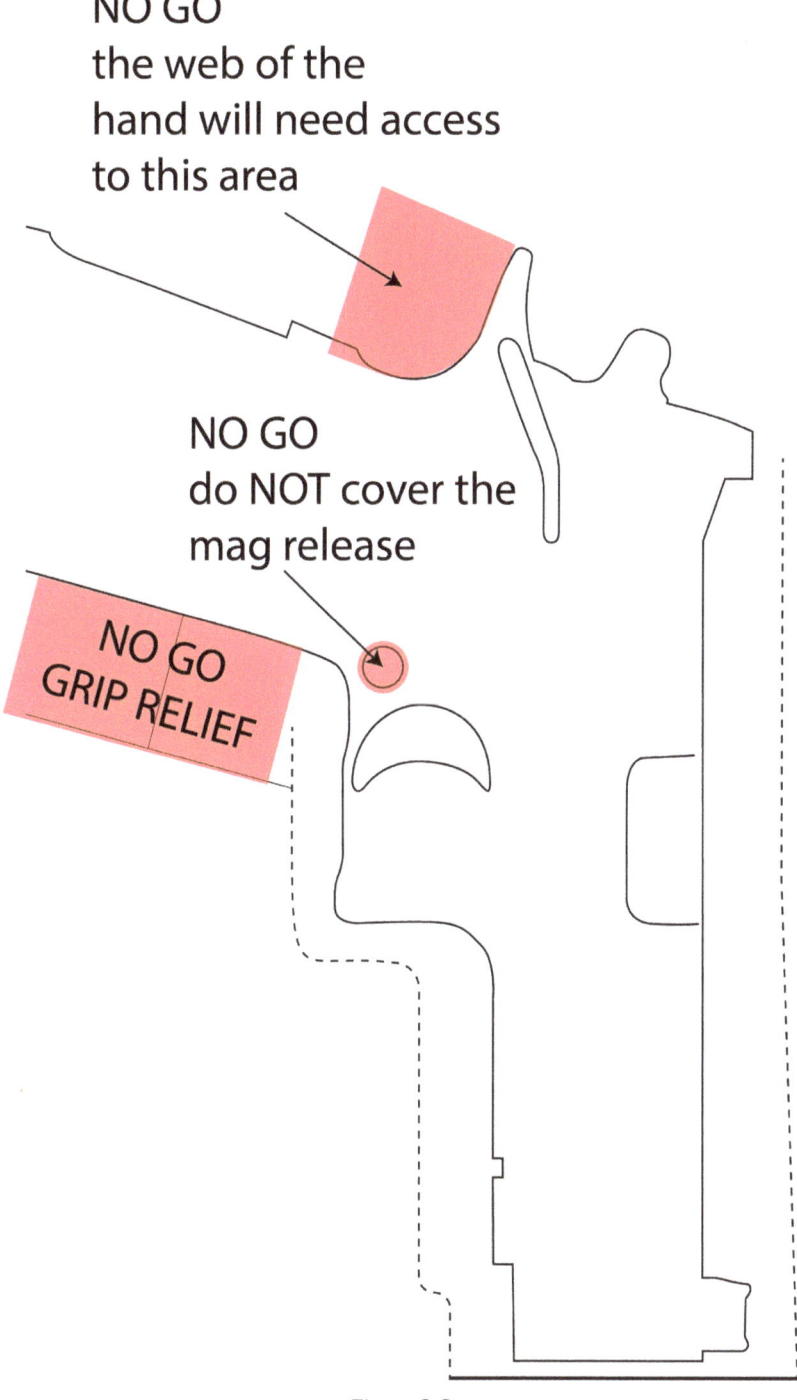

Figure 3-3

Chapter 3: The Go/No-Go Zones

Enough of the negatives, let's get to some positives. For the first Go Zone, we need to cover the muzzle.

We'll extend the leather one-eighth-inch (1/8") below the end of the muzzle.

A couple of things can happen to a pistol with an exposed muzzle. First, the crown of the muzzle can be impacted and deform, causing a loss in accuracy.

Next, when you sit down, the end of the barrel can hit a hard surface and will literally remove the firearm from the holster. WHOOPS!

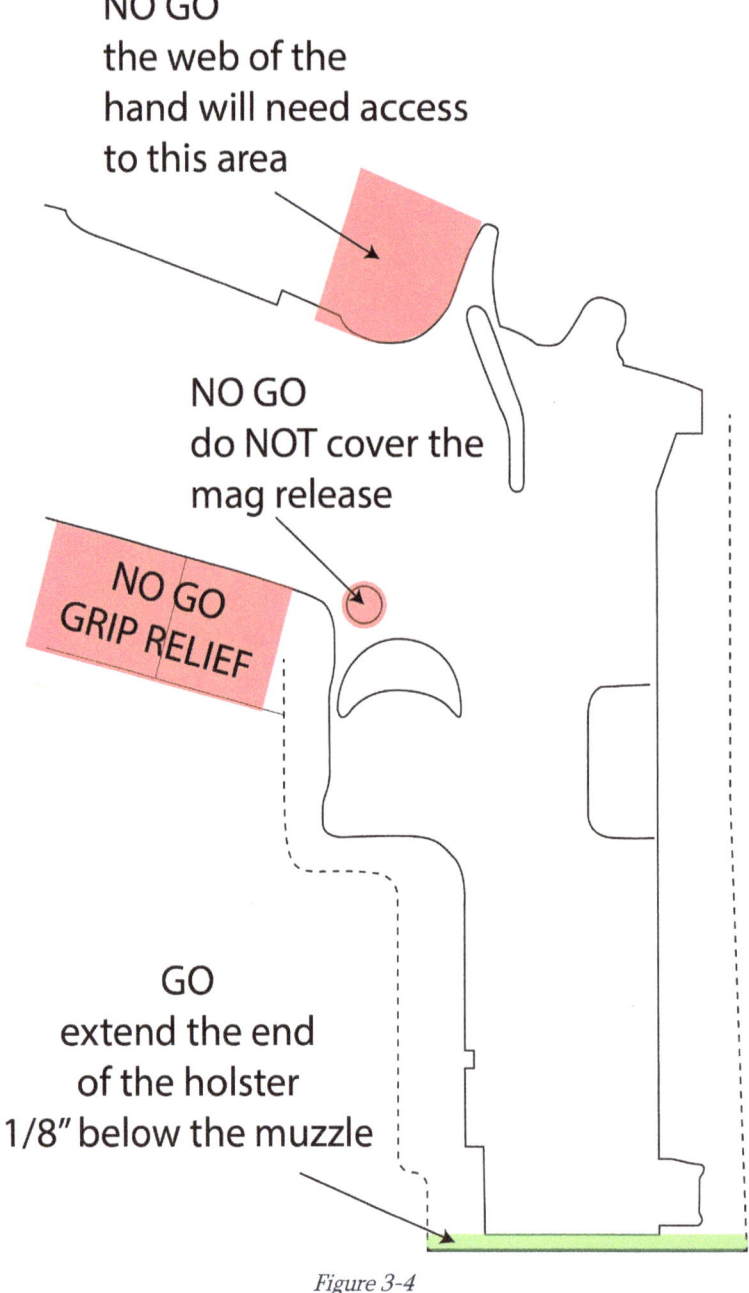

Figure 3-4

For the second Go Zone. Cover the trigger!

Many modern firearms are striker fire and do not have a manual safety. If the trigger is pulled, the firearm goes BOOM!

Fingers are not the only thing that can pull a trigger. A shirt tail can get in the trigger guard while holstering. A twig or branch can impact the trigger in the woods. A seatbelt buckle can also impact the trigger.

So let's solve this problem and cover the area with leather.

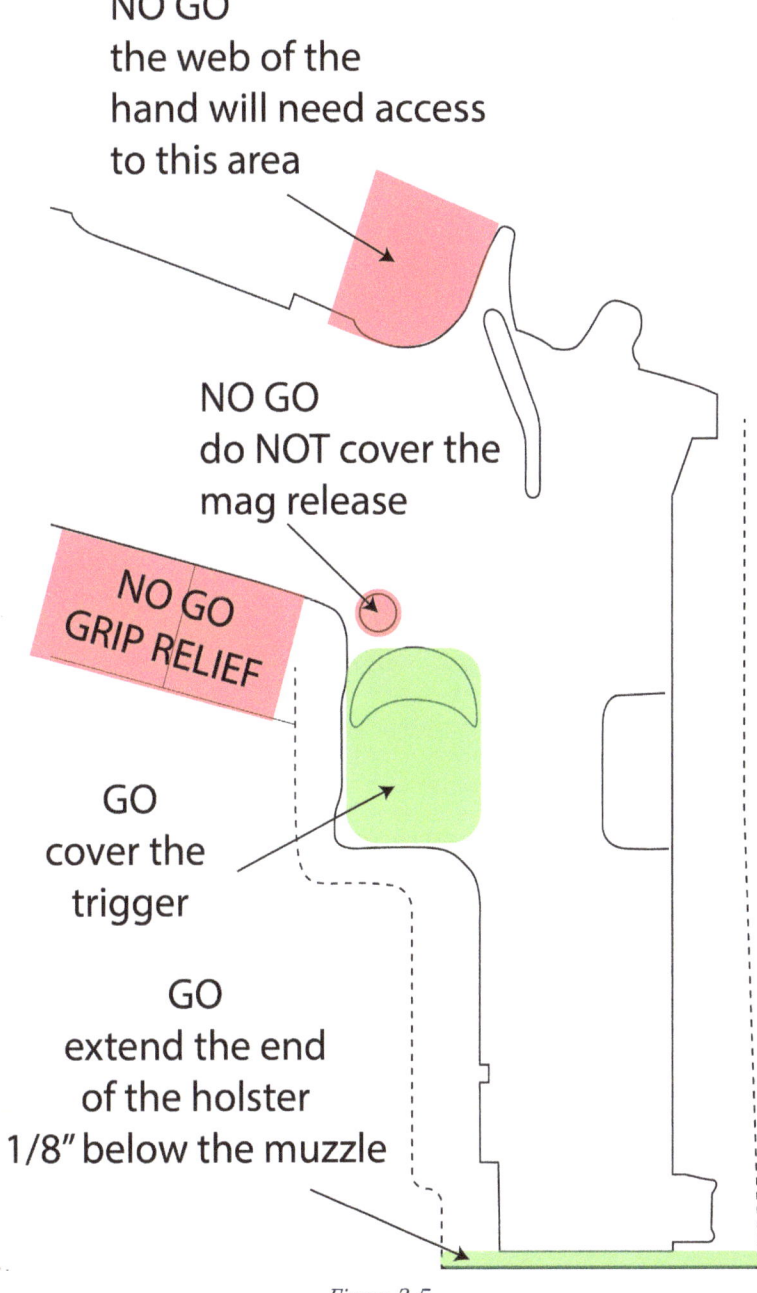

Figure 3-5

Our final Go Zone! Cover the ejection port.

When you're molding the leather on your holster, you may not always be able to use the trigger guard to achieve retention. But the ejection port will always be there and is an excellent way to achieve this.

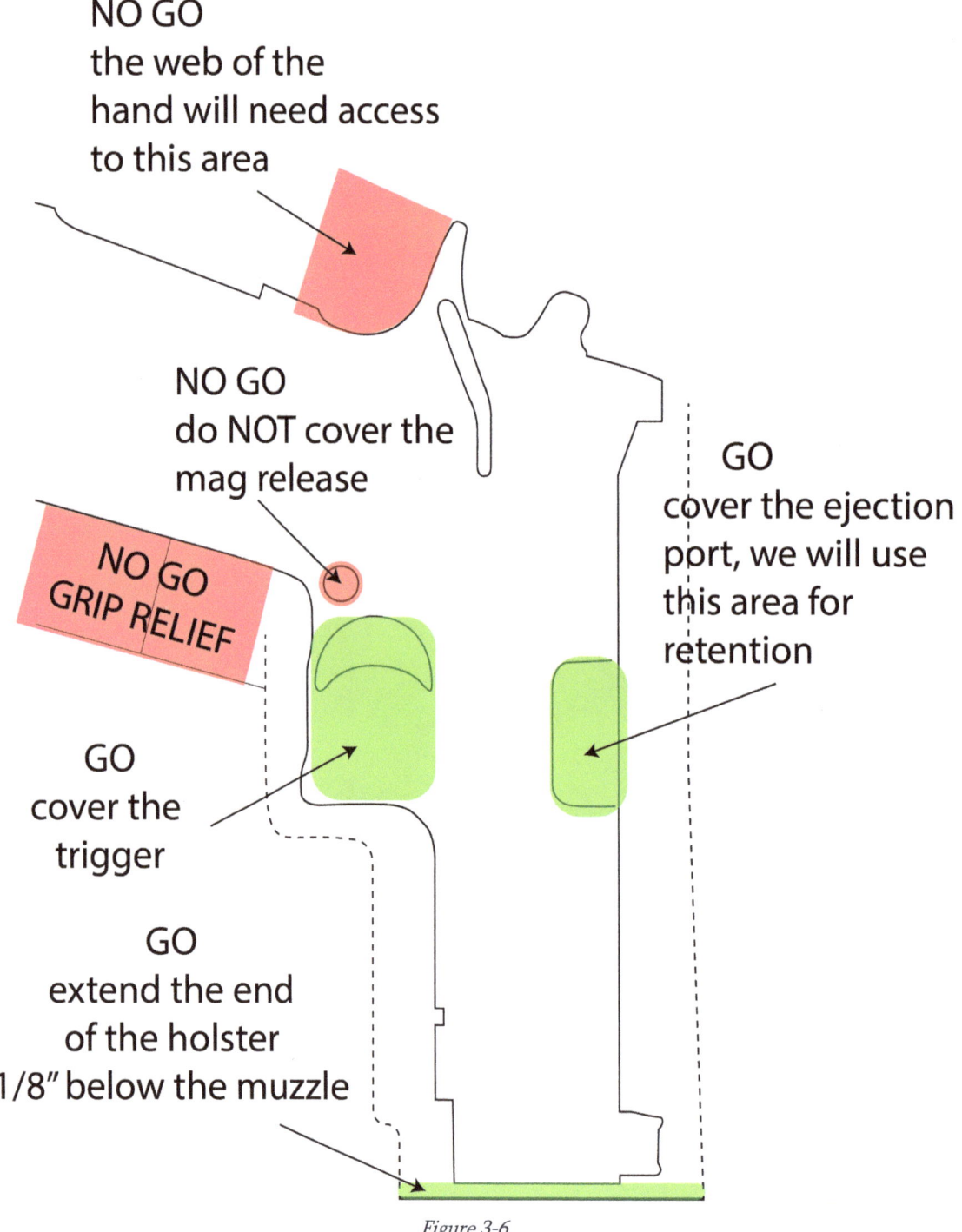

Figure 3-6

Chapter 4: All About Cant

This is a conceptual chapter. We recommend reading through the whole thing before attempting to apply the following concepts to your holster pattern design. By reading this chapter in its entirety you'll have a better understanding of the topic as a whole, and will therefore be better equipped to make the necessary adjustments when time comes to design your holster.

Before we start to draw the holster pattern, we need to know the angle (cant) the firearm will ride.

Start with an 8-degree cant, then come back and draw the same design in a neutral, (or zero) degree cant. You'll notice the 8-degree may give you a little more room to draw in some areas.

Cant is simply defined as the angle we're designing the holster to have. You can think about this as tilting the firearm either forwards or backwards while in the holster.

We simply account for this angle in our holster design when we draw our belt line and place the belt slots.

We design holsters in two primary cants, 0-degree and 8-degree.

Most firearms have been designed with a grip angle between sixteen and twenty-two-degrees.

The firearm manufacturer wants the grip angle to hold the pistol on target with a natural point of aim, (just like you're pointing with your finger).

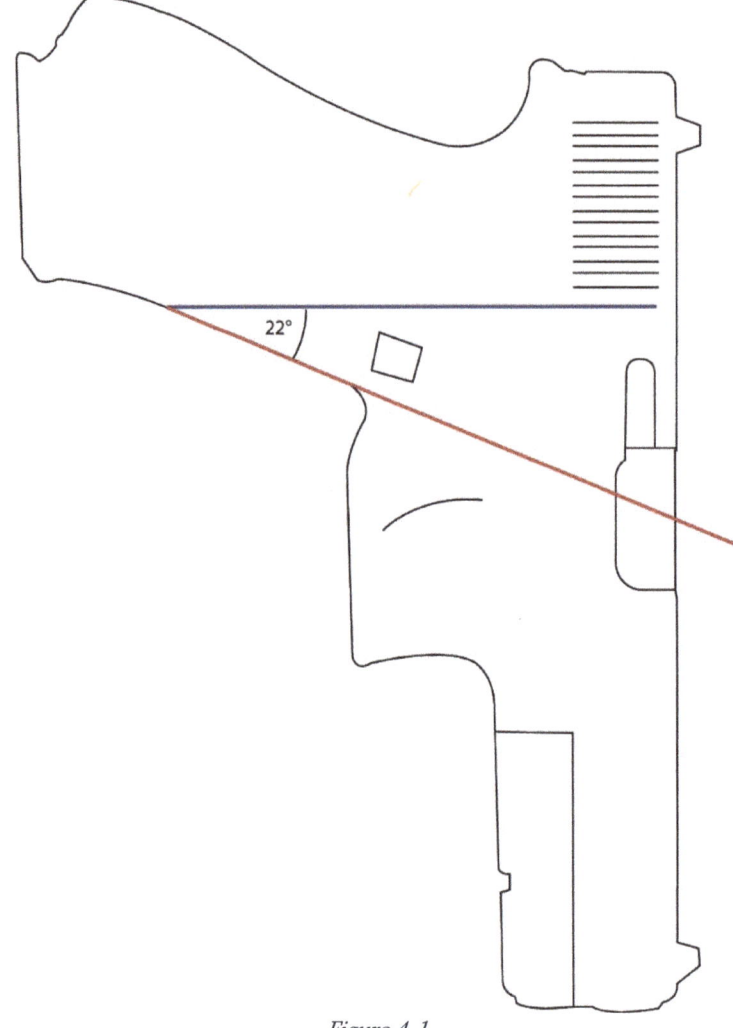

Figure 4-1

With that in mind, you'll find that your natural arm positions will work at 0-degree cant!

How cool is that?

But where the heck does 8-degree come into play?

When a client decides to carry in a position over his back pocket, (about 4:30 on the clock position) the hand will rotate as the arm reaches behind the hip and the natural grip will be about 8 degrees cant.

Figure 4-2

Let's take a look at a Glock 43 at 0-degree cant, worn at the 3-o'clock position.

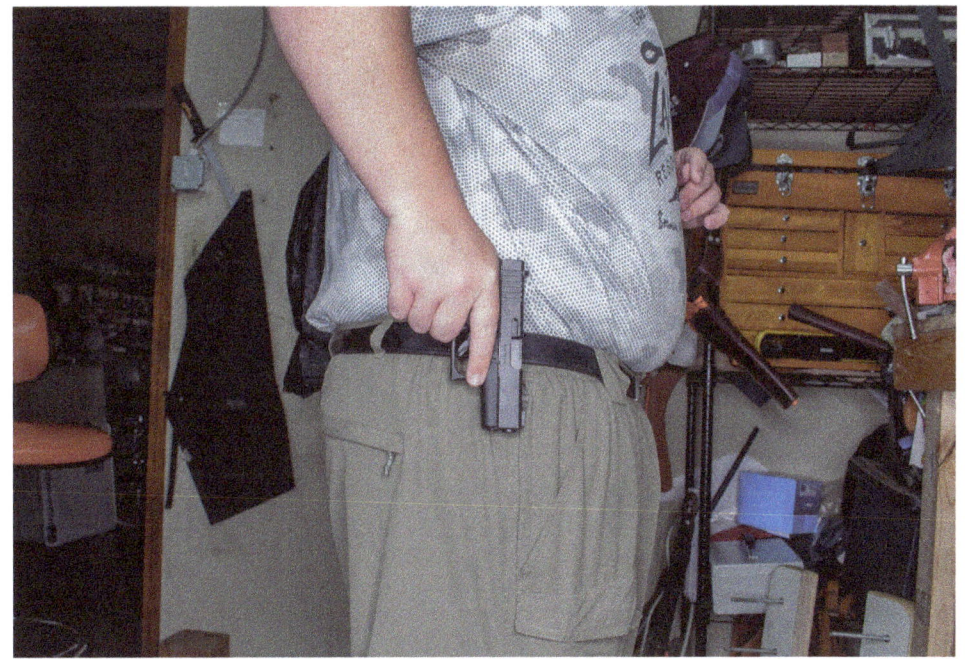

Figure 4-3

Here you can see the grip angle with a natural draw and the slide is vertical.

Let's take a look at the grip with a dowel rod taped to Jake's hand to better show the grip angle of his hand.

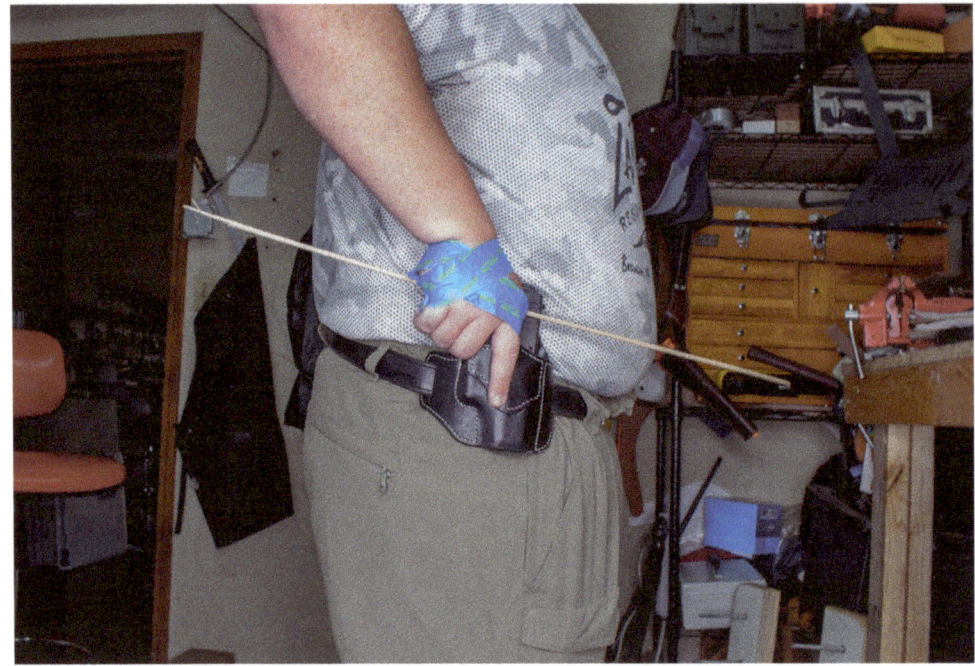

Figure 4-4

Now, let's move his hand back to the 4:30 position and see what happens there.

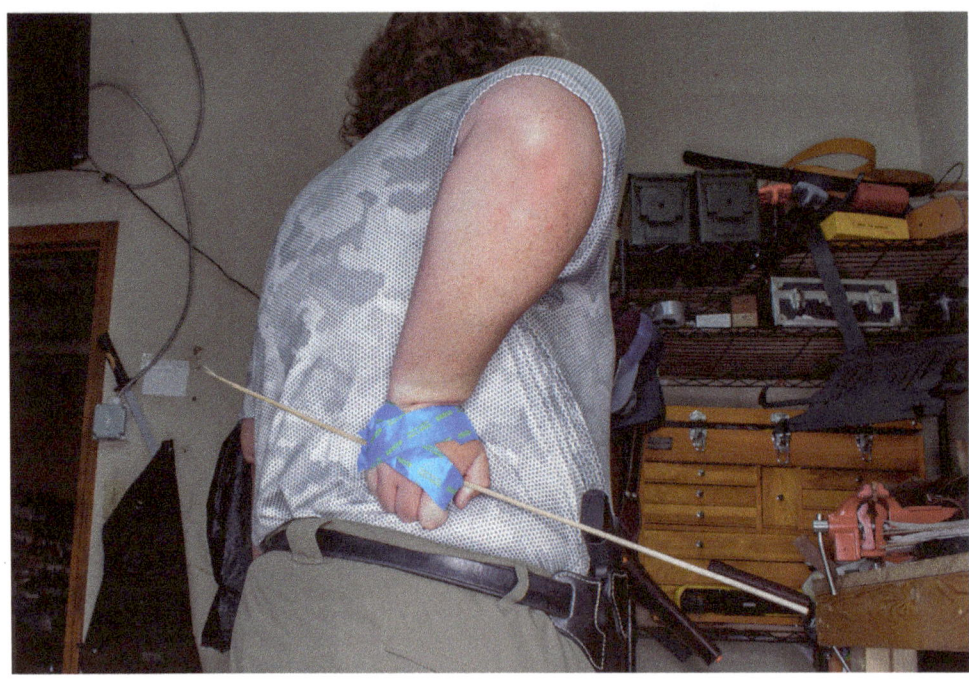

Figure 4-5

Obviously, this is a generalization, and your experience may be different. But we feel that these two cants are a good place for you to start your journey.

Things that can affect Cant

There are two primary factors that can affect cant.
The location of the holster on the belt, and barrel length.
We already discussed how moving your hand to the back of the body will change the angle of your grip, but we may have a short torso person with a five or six-inch barrel.
If this person tries to draw vertically from a 3-o'clock position they'll end up with the grip in their armpit!
In a situation like this, we may want to move the holster back to 3:45 to 4-o'clock position and give it some cant.

Chapter 5: Principles of Holster Design

The principles or elements of holster design are the source of tons of research materials. Here we're going to cover the four elements I use every time I design a holster. You may find other elements to fit your needs better than the ones I look at.

Awesome right? Remember, you're the artist!

Emphasis (gravity)

When we say emphasis, we're looking at where the viewers eyes are going to be drawn to when they first see your holster.

There are several ways we can build gravity into our design. For me, the most obvious choice is to include a throat reinforcement panel.

It resides in the center of the pattern and serves a purpose in holding the throat of the holster open when the holster is empty.

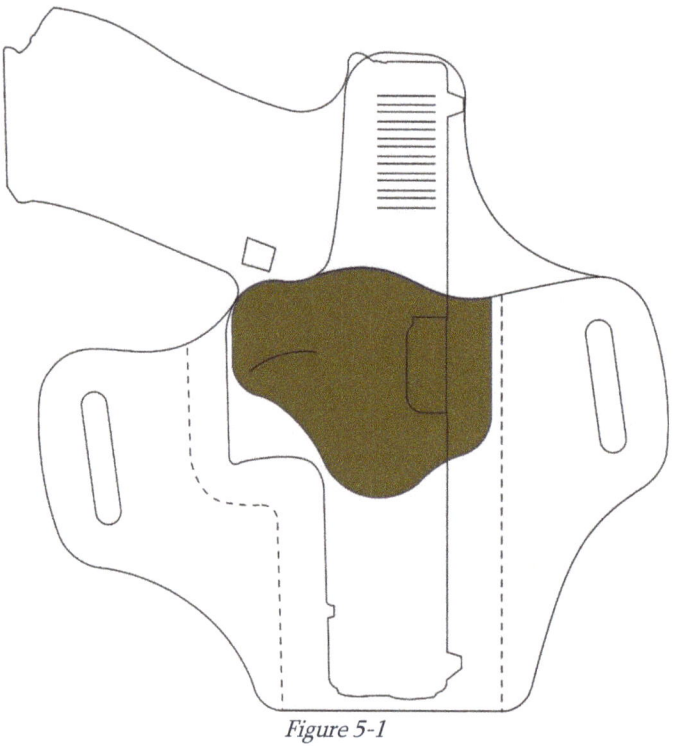
Figure 5-1

We can see the throat reinforcement panel is in the center of the pattern and draws the eye.

We can build the panel with different dye jobs or add some tooling to increase the gravity.

And don't forget, we can overlay the panel with an exotic to both increase the gravity and the retail price!

Balance (symmetry)

The primary way to achieve balance is to use the same area of your French curve on both the trigger guard and the slide side when drawing your belt slot ears.

The belt slots are also a hard line that attracts the eye. Ensuring the belt slots are perpendicular to the belt, and the distance from the stitch line are equal will help with symmetry.

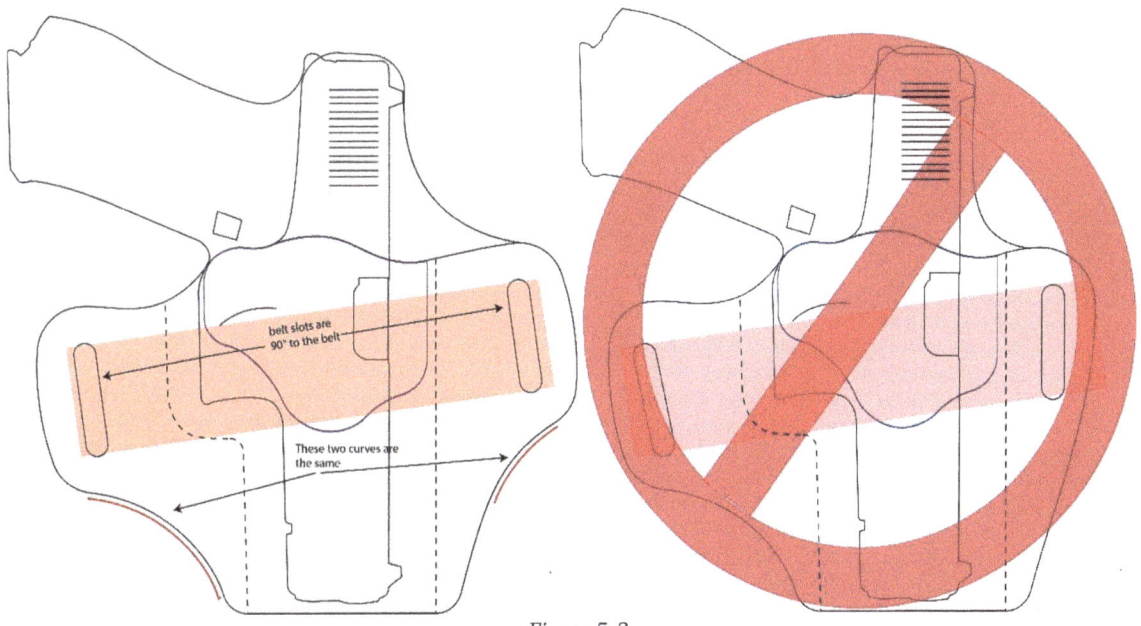

Figure 5-2

Notice the holster on the right is having problems.

You'll see new holster designers making this mistake.

The slide side belt slot matches the slide stitch line, and is too close to the firearm to give the leather room to move to the belt line.

Chapter 5: Principles of Holster Design

The belt slot on the trigger guard side is canted away from the belt line.

These designers think that this type of slot arrangement will hold the holster in place on the belt better than a perpendicular slot.

If they would cut the slots to match the belt, this would not be a problem.

What they've made is a holster that will not ride close to the body and will always create pressure points. In addition, there's no symmetry to the design, meaning that the leading edge of the holster has no design relationship to the trailing edge. **Poor Design**.

Movement

When a holster has a forward cant, (in our example the 8-degree cant) the holster appears to have forward motion.

Think of the speedy delivery service sign on the side of a van. The text leans forward creating the illusion of forward motion.

Now, let's look at a pancake holster with an 8-degree forward cant and look at the forward motion.

Pretty cool, isn't it!

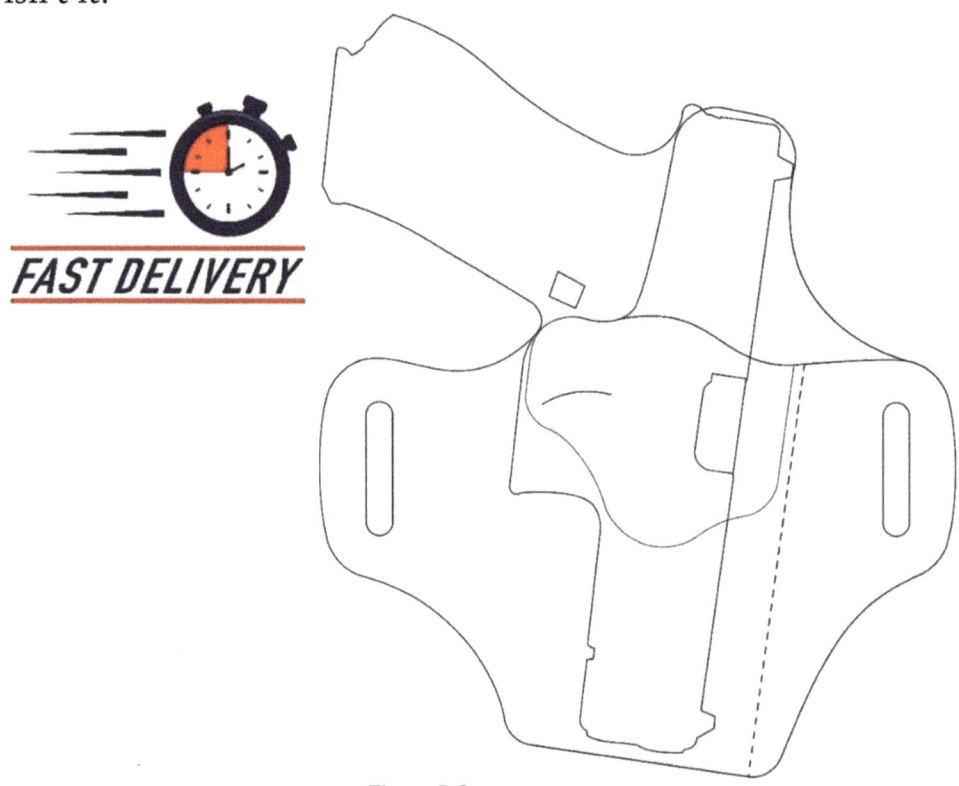

Figure 5-3

Contrast

One of my mentors once told me, "All leather goods are sold by the use of contrast in color and texture."

At the time, I kinda blew him off. But as the years have gone by, I've come to see the value in his words.

When drawing a design, think about how you can incorporate these things into your build. Things like dye choices may seem obvious. But think about airbrushing a *halo* around the edges of the holster to create a sunburst effect.

Something as simple as changing the color of the thread can have a tremendous effect on the build.

Exotic leather inlays or overlays can be awesome.

Play with all of these things. Experiment and go wild!

Section 3: Securing the Holster

George Cubic
Viktor George Leather Goods

I'm excited for the readers of this long overdue book on holster design by George of EDC Leather.

My name is George too, and I've been working leather for many decades, specializing in rugged leather goods for the serious outdoorsman and wilderness trekkers. Knife sheaths, pouches, bags, harness and saddle repair, along with reenactment gear for living historians.

Notice I didn't include holsters, even though I've built many for cowboy action shooters and some OWBs and IWB concealables.

My holster builds for everyday carry literally transformed after I found Mr. Canfield and his detailed breakdown of the mechanics of a safe, modern holster carry system.

Mr. Canfield has, in addition to his line of holster patterns and kits, taken the science of pattern design to an unprecedented level, easily explained in understandable text.

I've had the pleasure to review this book and to delve deep into every aspect of design, safety, and balance of what a holster should and should not be.

I've always felt that, as a holster maker, one should be well-trained and know the safe use of carrying a firearm for self-defense. This manual provides the Whys of the holster itself. It's broken down into exhaustive detail and I would use this book similar to a college course textbook with a highlighter to underline areas of importance for yourself.

Where has this book been all my leatherworking life?

Thank you, George, for sharing your vast knowledge in this specialized field of leather holster design. So, consider this book a great resource for learning this craft and I'd suggest you get an autographed copy because this is only the beginning of many more books to come. This is exactly the first step in becoming an expert in the field of modern holster design.

Chapter 6: Belt Placement

In our priority list of holster design, we start with an accurate tracing and a stitch line. These two steps provide us with a solid foundation for our holster design.
But now we gotta hang this thing on a belt. Meaning, we have to take things like Cant in to consideration. We covered this topic in an earlier chapter.
Now it's time to bring all these things together and blend them into our Mode of Carry.

Ride height

If we get the firearm too high above the belt we'll experience *flop.* This is when the grip of the pistol flops away from the body due to no support.
We know from the last chapter that we want the top of the belt to be as close as possible to the center of gravity limited by the need for grip clearance. This is not always possible but we can get it as close as possible.
When placing the belt on your pattern, you'll also want to place your belt slots for the holster. The slots will be perpendicular to the belt and will be large enough to allow the belt to slide through.
We can use a tool to help us both define the belt location and draw our belt slots on our pattern.
It'll look like the sample found in figure 6-1. At the end of this chapter, we'll have a full-size version of this tool you can photocopy.

Chapter 6: Belt Placement

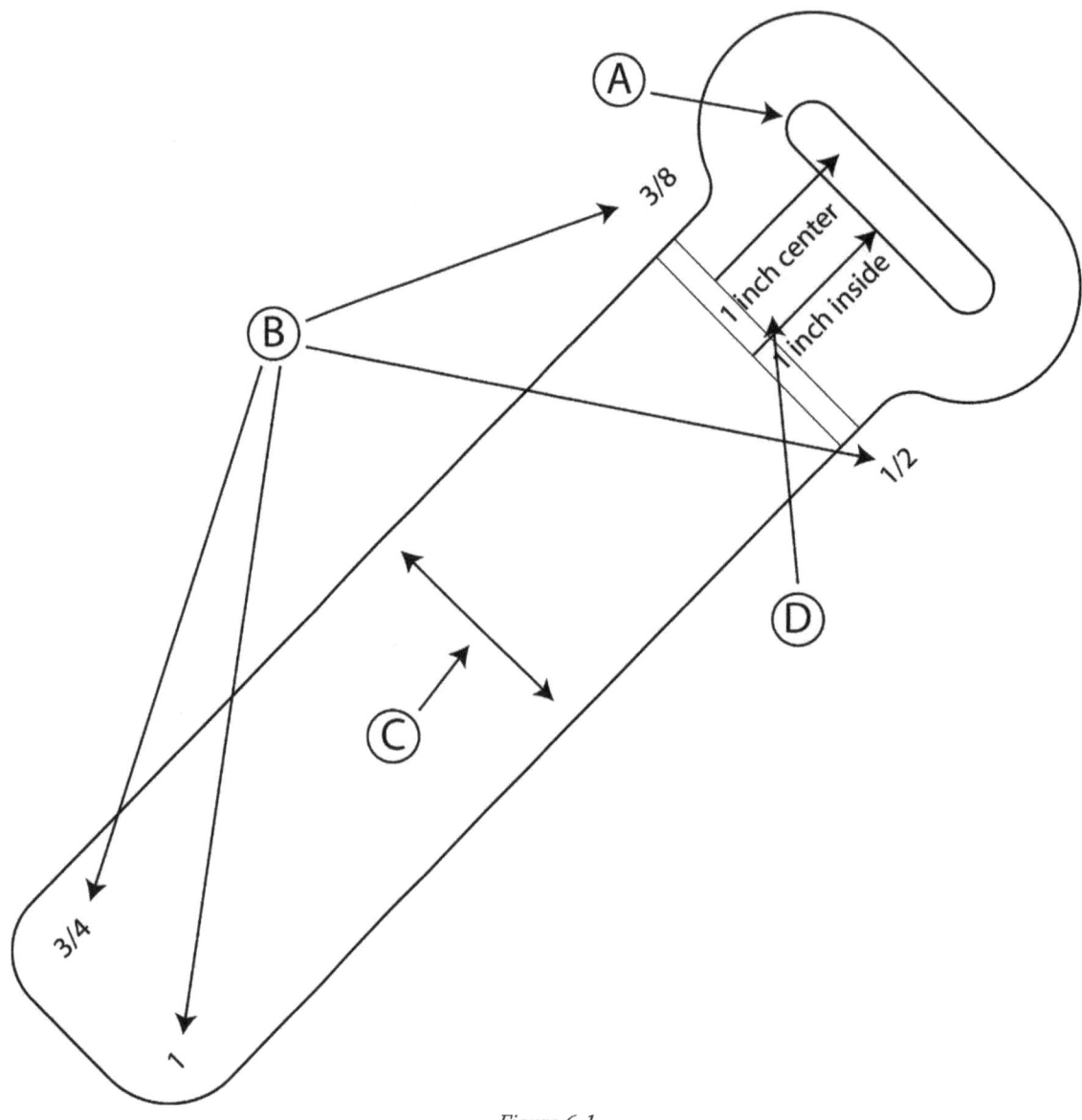

Figure 6-1

Let's take a look at this type of belt slot tool.

The slots are five-sixteenth-inch (5/16") wide and one and nine-sixteenths-inch (1-9/16") tall.

A typical gun belt is two layers of eight-ounce (8 oz.) leather with a total thickness of around one-quarter-inch (1/4").

These measurements provide one-sixteenth-inch (1/16") of slack on both dimensions. The tool also places the slot perpendicular to the belt.

57

Each of the curves on this tool are a different radius. You'll use some or all of these radii as a holster designer.

The straight edge of the tool is one and one-half-inch (1-1/2") wide, which represents the most common gun belt you'll build for.

These are two of the most common distances you'll use when standing the belt slot off from the stitch line.

Let's look at a belt placement on the stitch line you just created. We'll be designing an 8-degree holster in this example.

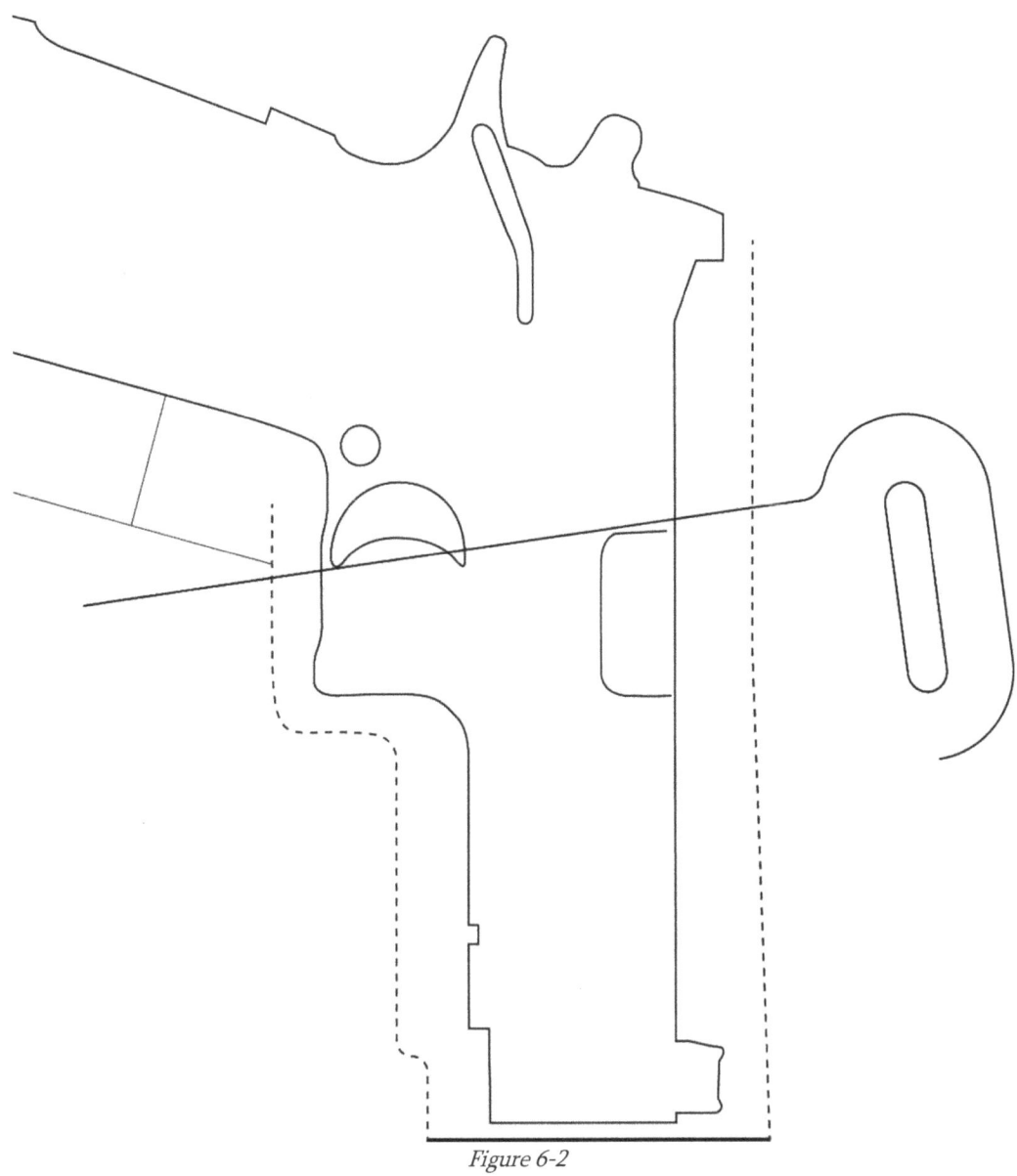

Figure 6-2

Space the belt slot away from the slide side stitch line using the one-inch (1") to inside of the belt slot mark.

Note: We'll always measure distances from the belt slot at the top edge of the belt.

Trace the top of the belt and the outside of the slot template. Also trace the actual belt slot. It should look kind of like this.

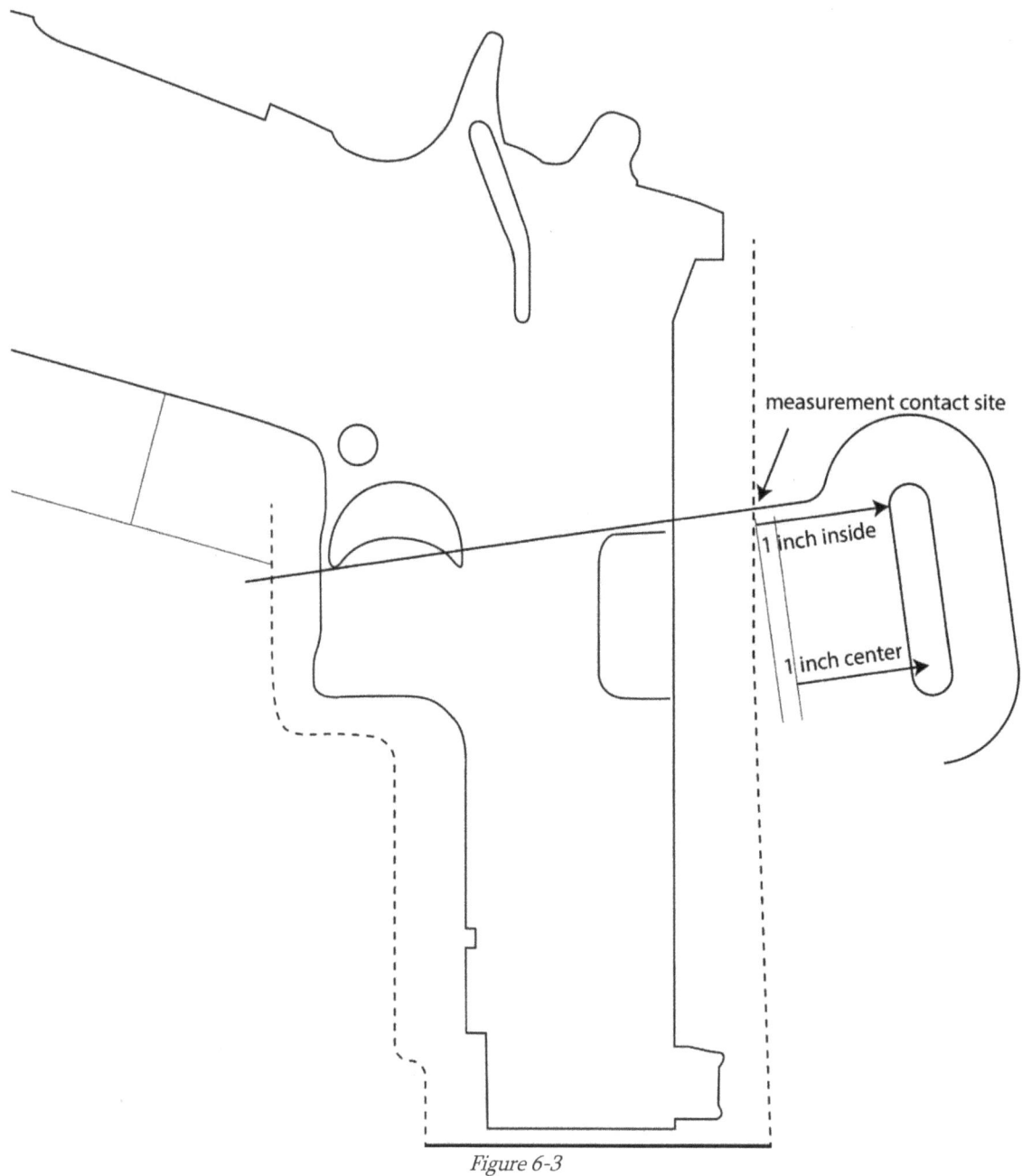

Figure 6-3

Now, let's reverse the belt slot tool and trace the trigger guard belt slot.

This time, however, we will be using the one-inch (1") to center mark of the slot line. This'll move the trigger guard belt slot a little closer to the stitch line.

The trigger guard is narrower than the slide and the slot will move in. This'll also help bring the slots closer to the center of gravity.

Place your template and trace the same areas you did for the slide side. It should look a little like this.

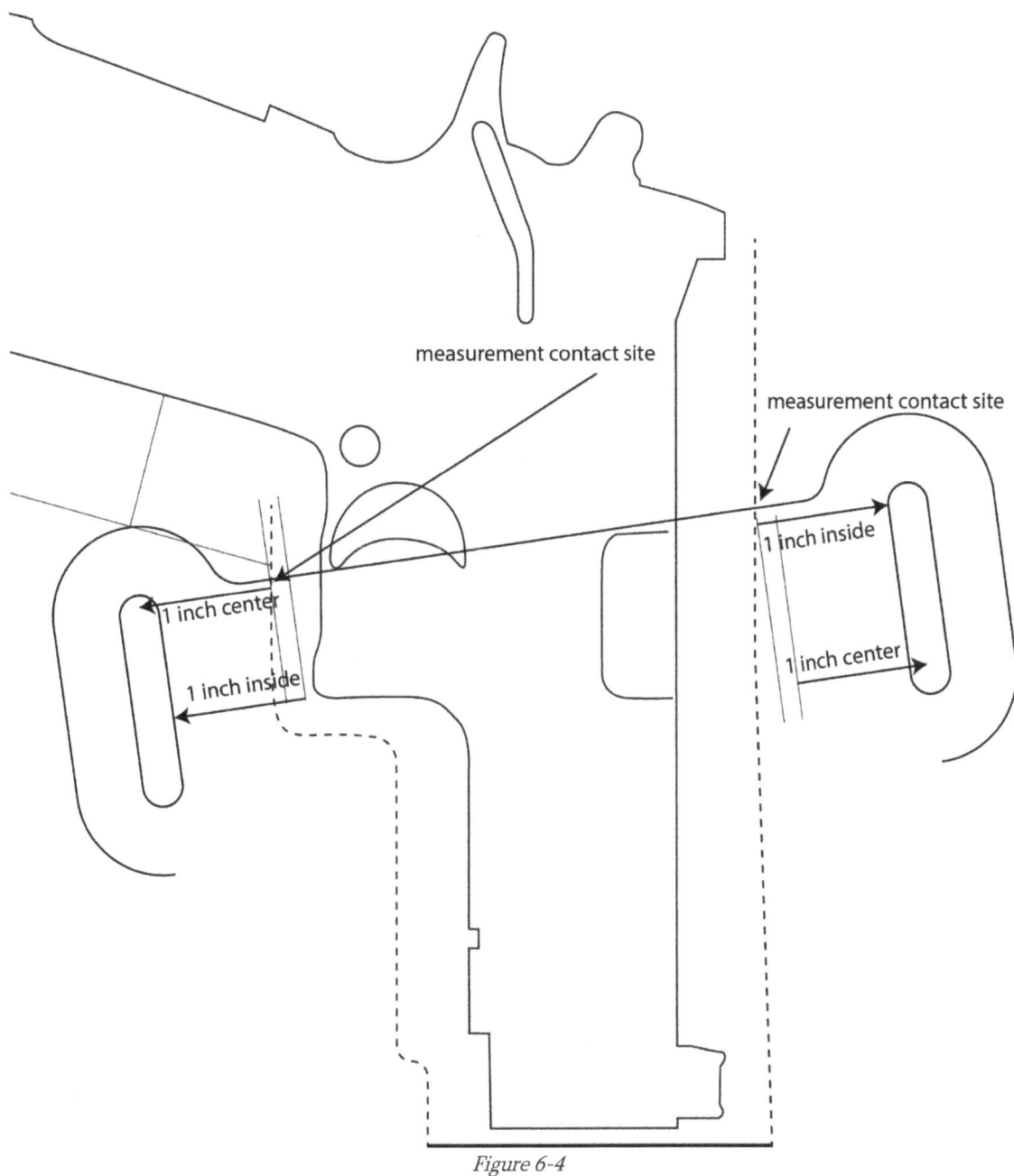

Figure 6-4

Things to note:

- Belt crosses the face of the trigger. This is as close as we can get to the center of gravity.
- Belt slots are perpendicular to the belt.
- Belt slots are spaced 1" from the stitch line to the edge of the slot on the slide side.
- Belt slots are spaced 1" from the stitch line to the center of the slot on the trigger guard side.
- There is a half-inch (1/2") leather allowance around the belt slots.
- The slots have one-sixteenth-inch (1/16") slack in both directions on belt dimensions.
- In this pattern we impinged upon the one-inch (1") grip clearance by one millimeter. This is an allowable amount. After edging and sanding you may very well see the impingement go away entirely.

Section 4: Concepts & Theory – Part 2

Eric Larsen – HBE LeatherWorks

I'd been making holsters for a few months when friend of mine, who owned the CZ forum at the time, posted a couple pictures of holsters I'd made.

One day I got a phone call. The voice on the other end said, "I'm Lou Alessi and I've got some questions for you. Are you really making holsters out of upholstery leather?"

"I don't know." I said. "I'm using the leather I get from the leather factory."

He brought up some pictures he'd seen online, pictures of my holsters, and explained they were made from upholstery leather. He then went on to ask if I mold them. And if so, how long does it take to get them to retain their shape? If they do.

I told him it took about twelve hours for the first one. I've got it down to around six hours now. "And, yes, they hold their shape just fine. Why?"

Our conversation went on for a while. I told him my holsters work quite well, and explained a few details of my process.

He laughed and said, "Well alright— I'm gonna give you one tip that's gonna change your life. It's called Veg-Tan leather." He then went on to explained how and why.

I was dumbfounded. I had no idea upholstery leather wasn't the right stuff. In my mind, leather was leather. What difference did it make? But I decided to take his advice. I went and bought some mediocre quality veg-tan. It didn't take long to discover how right he was. It did change my life.

Where my molding time had been six to eight hours, this new leather only took about an hour. Even less now. I called Lou back to thank him.

He said, "I get calls from holster makers all the time. Most I don't want to talk to. But I must respect your sheer determination. Anyone who can make soft upholstery leather work for a holster has my support. So if you want any help whatsoever, call me."

Anyway, that's how Lou became my first mentor. I worked with him for the first four or five years I made holsters.

Chapter 7: Throat Reinforcement

This is a conceptual chapter. We recommend reading through the whole thing before attempting to apply the following concepts to your holster pattern design. By reading this chapter in its entirety you'll have a better understanding of the topic as a whole, and will therefore be better equipped to make the necessary adjustments when time comes to design your holster.

At a glance, this being a conceptual chapter, it should belong in Section 2. Unfortunately, we could not place it there on account of its nature. Throat reinforcements are optional. That's what makes them conceptual.

But they're also the last patterning decision you'll make before you finalize everything.

Unfortunately, we can't place them at the end of patterning either, as the decision whether or not you're going to use one needs to be made before finalization can occur.

Placing a throat panel on a pancake holster is absolutely optional. The holster does not require one of these to function properly.

Now that I've said all of that, let's look at what this part of your design can do for you.

First, we never want the holster to collapse, as it can make it difficult to holster the firearm.

Our primary clients at EDC Leather are LEO and military organizations. The customer may end up on the ground behind cover during an incident.

The throat panel adds structure to the mouth of the holster and keeps that puppy open.

Additionally, the throat panel on the holster will create a visual focal point in the center of the rig and will add what we call *gravity*.

You can also dye this piece with a contrasting color, cover it with exotic leather, or even carve it!

We covered some of these concepts in the Principles of Design chapter.

Let's look at the minimums for our design and grow this into a piece that really lets you put your style into this rig.

Time to get started with a pattern.

Hey! Wow, you just happen to have one of those! Grab a photocopy your pattern and get started.

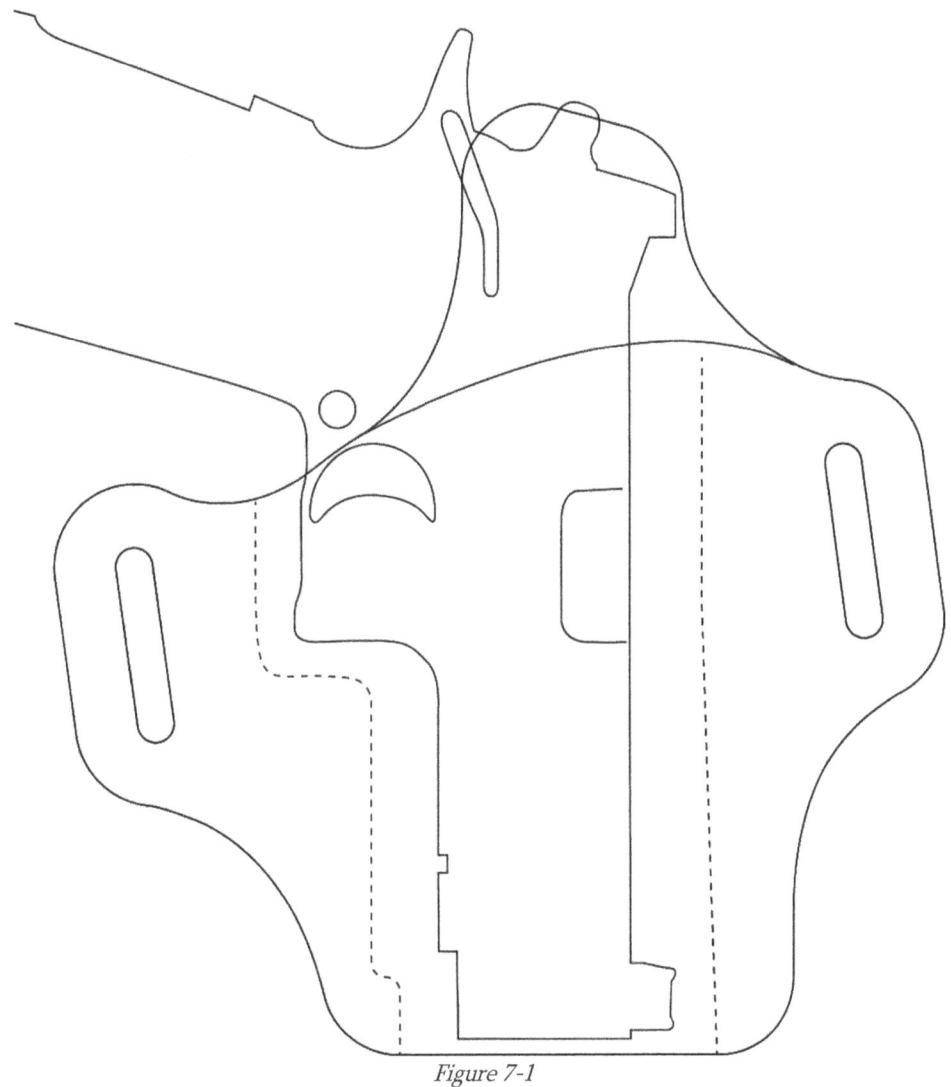

Figure 7-1

Let's consider our materials.

Since we build our holster out of eight-ounce (8 oz.) leather, let's use the same thickness for our throat reinforcement.

We want to place it one-eighth-inch (1/8") from the slide side stitch line, and be at least one-inch (1") tall. It should also match the throat of the holster.

Also, we don't want to see it cross over the trigger guard.

Let's look at that.

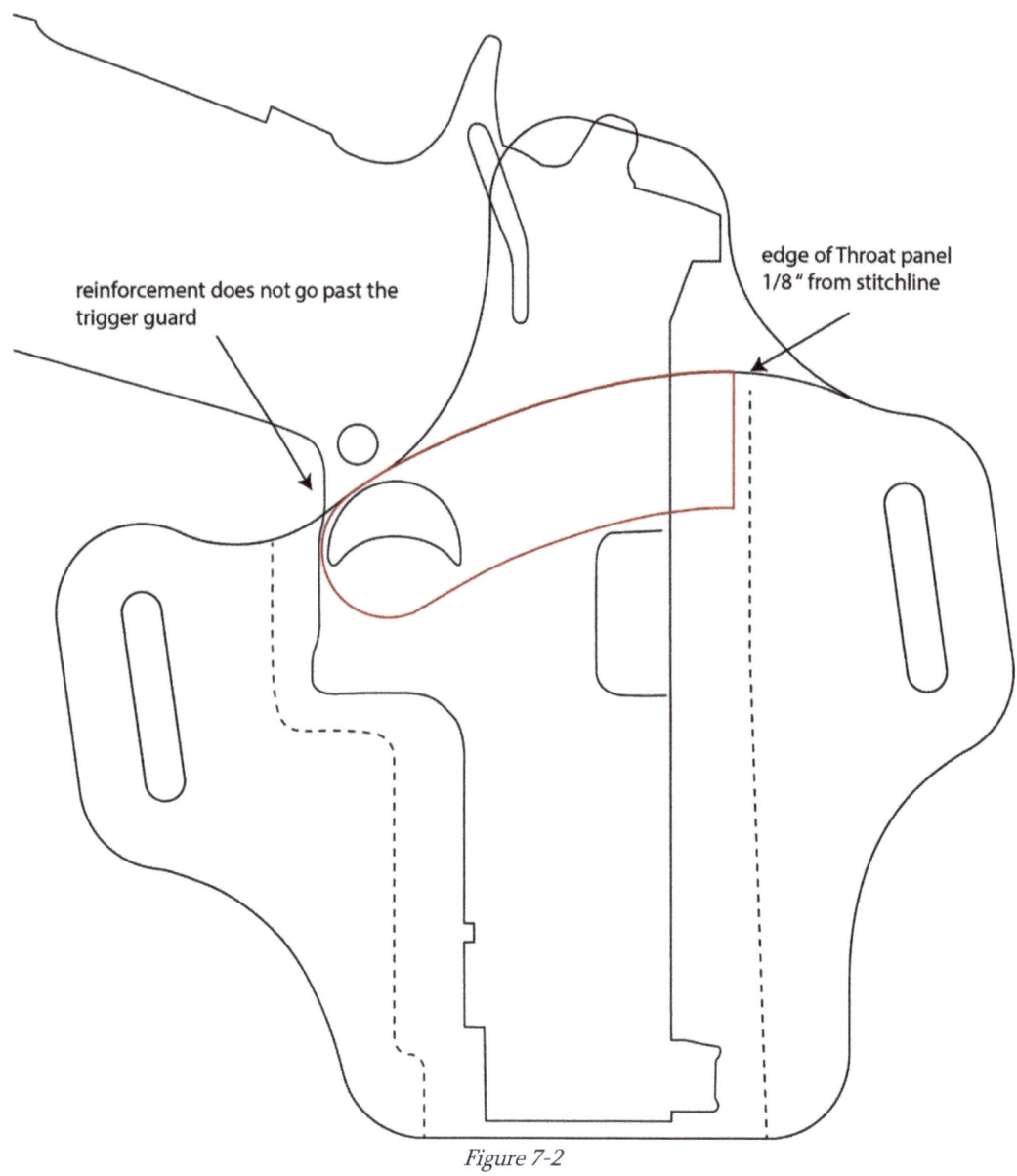

Figure 7-2

Okay, it's on there and it'll achieve the purpose of reinforcing the throat. But it really doesn't follow our guidelines of good design.

Time to get Frenchie the Curve out and play a little.

This image shows a reinforcement created of circles connected in interesting ways.

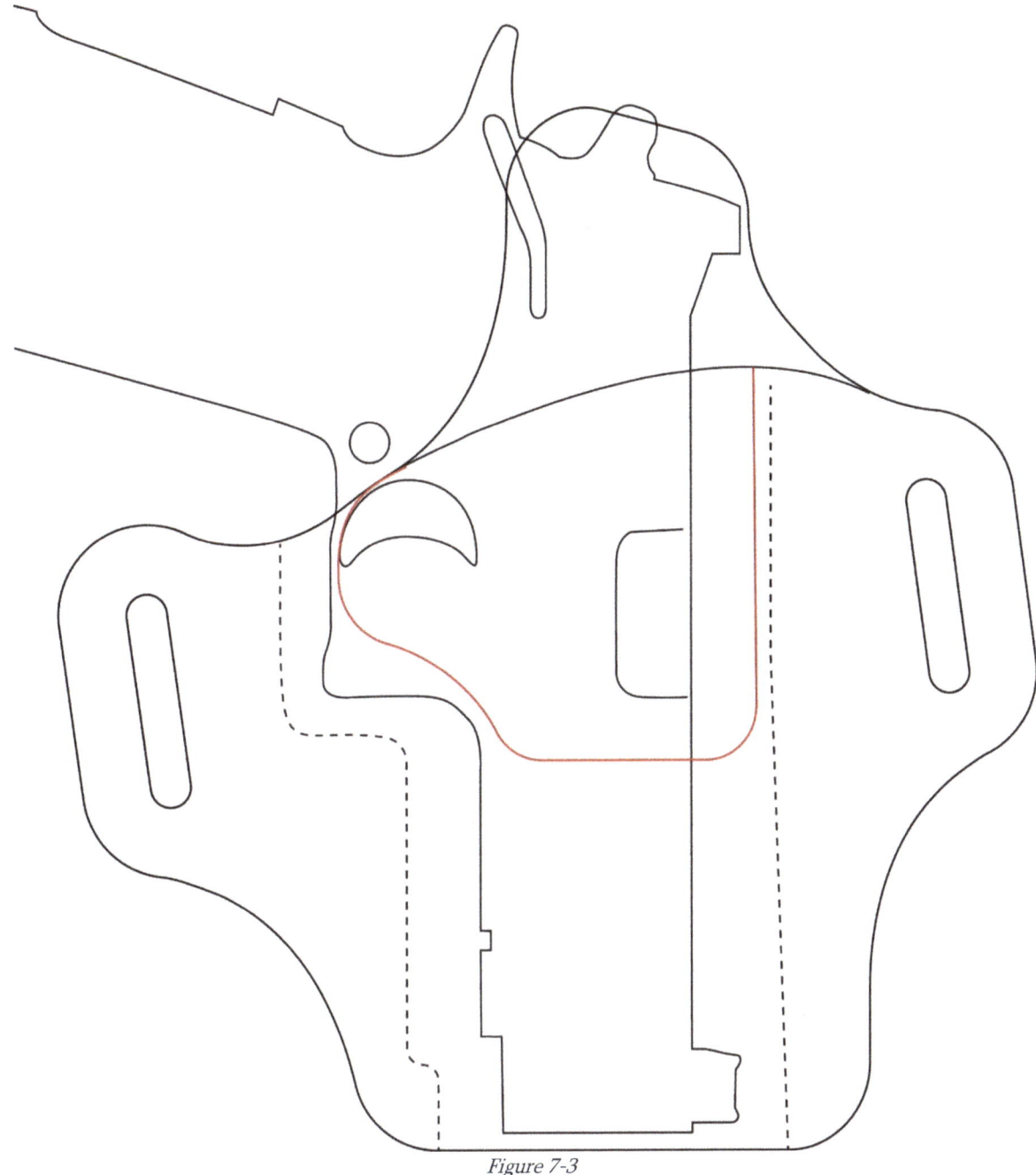

Figure 7-3

Designing your throat reinforcement is a way you can really show some personality in your holster design. Play with different shapes and dimensions.

Here are the only rules you'll need to consider:

- Build the panel out of Veg-Tan. It must provide support.
- Use at least six-ounce (6 oz.) leather, preferably 8 oz..
- Keep the slide side edge within one-eighth-inch (1/8") of the slide stitch line.
- Don't allow your reinforcement panel to *fall off* the trigger guard on the firearm tracing. It will hinder your molding of the holster later.

Section 5: Finalizing the Pattern

Lowell Harvey on Arvo Ojala – Fastest Gun Alive

On the Columbia River in Washington, the confluence of the big white salmon river flowed into the Columbia River there. Which was some of the best steelhead and salmon fishing in the country.

My folks bought a little truck stop restaurant back then it was Ridgefield. Arvo liked to fish and he liked to salmon so that was his favorite place. We had the restaurant, and the little truck stop, and we had cabins there.

He would come down on weekends and spend the night at the restaurant to go fishing.

I was fourteen when I met him. I think they'd just finished the Oregon Trail movie but at the time I didn't know who he was.

He invited me to go fishing with him one day. So I started fishing with him and still didn't know who in the hell he was. He was just Arvo. Never really knew who he was.

Then I found out.

When I first met him he drove an old Ford pick-up. But when he brought Fess Parker and a lot of the movie stars and western actors to come fishing with him, he would drive his Cadillac. They'd come down and go fishing with him, him and his big white boat that was given to him by MGM. On the side of it, it said "Fastest Gun Alive."

That's how I found out who he was.

People don't realize how little Arvo was. His reputation was pretty big, but the man himself—I was bigger than him when I was fourteen. He's tiny.

Audie Murphy was one of his great friends. People know how small Audie Murphy was. He was a giant compared to Arvo. A lot of people didn't know that about him.

Richard Boone was another. I didn't know who in the hell he was.

He was bald headed. I didn't know it. When you see them in real life they don't look like the same person.

I was just a kid. I watched them all on television, but I didn't know who any of them were at the time. I was just getting invited to go fishing.

So we fished together for quite a few years and I got to know Arvo. When I started making holsters, he got me interested in fast draw.

Arvo was a good guy and I liked him. We were good friends, me and his daughter Val. We still stay in touch.

I did loose contact with him for a long time because I went into the military. We just kind of lost track. Then years later when I was running the George Lawrence Company, I looked up one day and he came walking through the door.

He was living just out of Gresham, Oregon which was a suburb of Portland. He'd designed the rifle sling I use with the thumb hole. He came in wanting Lawrence to make his slings for him, but Lawrence was in the middle of a transition, selling to Gould & Goodrich.

They didn't want to do the sling, so I went ahead and said I'd do them.

I had a key for the shop, so I went over on the weekends and did his slings for him.

Never told anybody, that's the first time anybody will know that. All of his slings were built in Lawrence by me. He was a good friend. I enjoyed him, just a great guy.

Chapter 8: Pattern Design – 8 Degree Pancake Holster

I always prefer to start the pattern at the bottom and work up to the belt slots. In this evolution we'll use a radii card, with 4 radii from one and a quarter-inch (1-1/4") up to two-inch (2").

It looks like this.

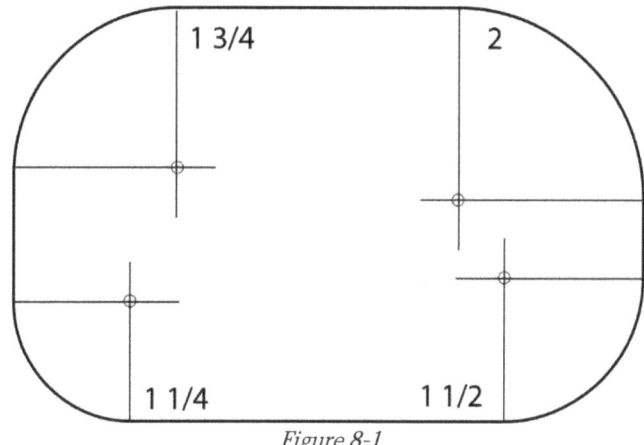

Figure 8-1

The lines on the card give a reference to the center of the circle and ninety-degrees of the radius.

There will be a full-size version of this image at the end of this book for you to photocopy and use.

We'll be using the one and a quarter-inch (1-1/4") radius at the bottom of each of our stitch lines. This'll give us a nice curve to the bottom of the holster and provide a stable platform to draw up to the belt slots.

Let's get Started!

Here, we see the radii card and the stitch line.
Let's get it moved over and traced!

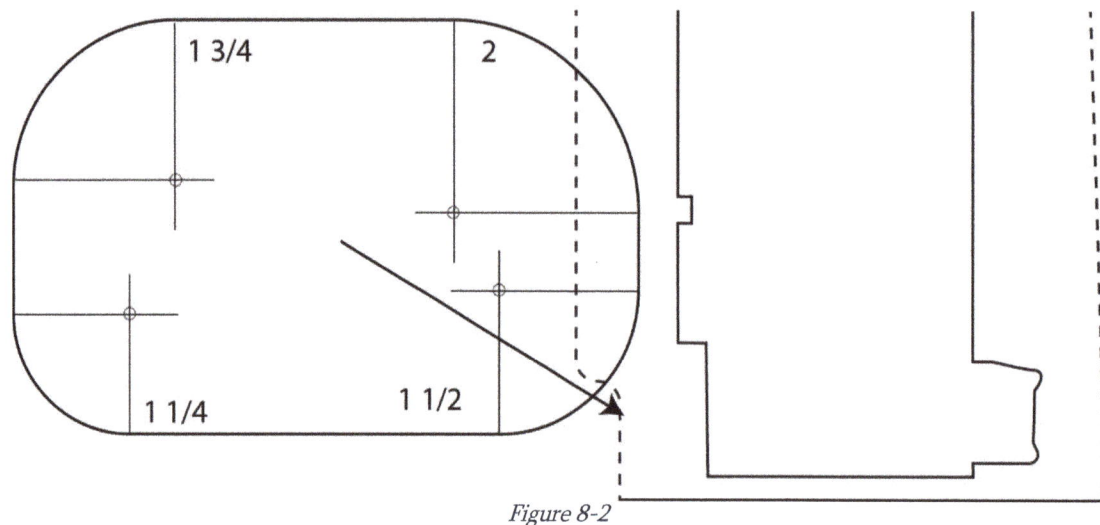

Figure 8-2

We'll be using the one and a quarter-inch (1 1/4") radius for this pattern, so all other sizes have been erased.

We'll center the radius on the trigger guard side stitch line.

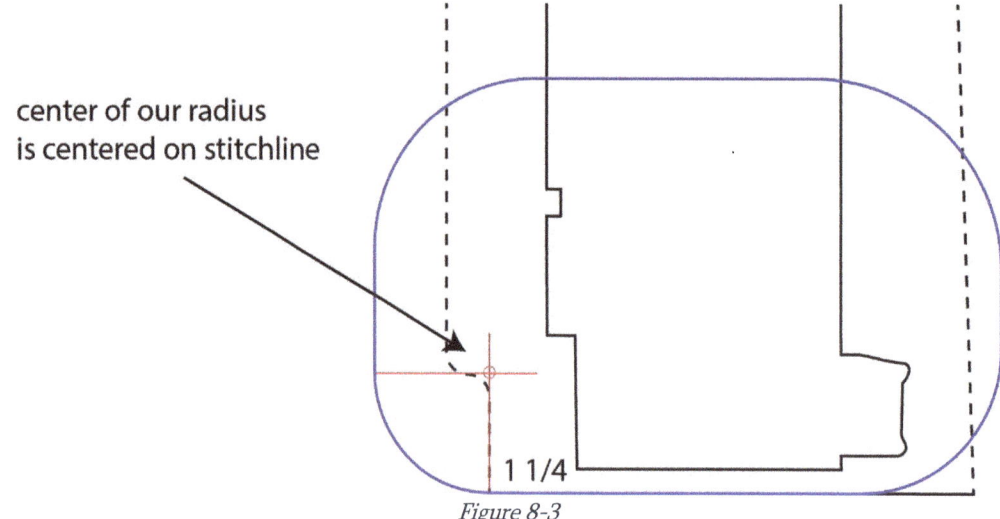

Figure 8-3

Once centered, we'll trace the radius.

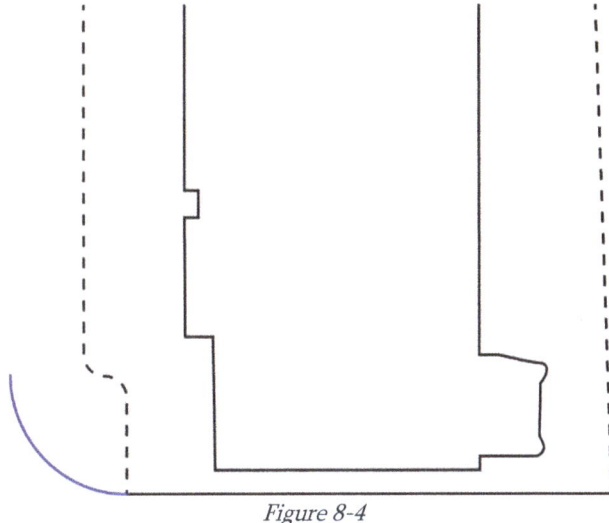

Figure 8-4

Let's move our radius card to the slide side and get that curve.

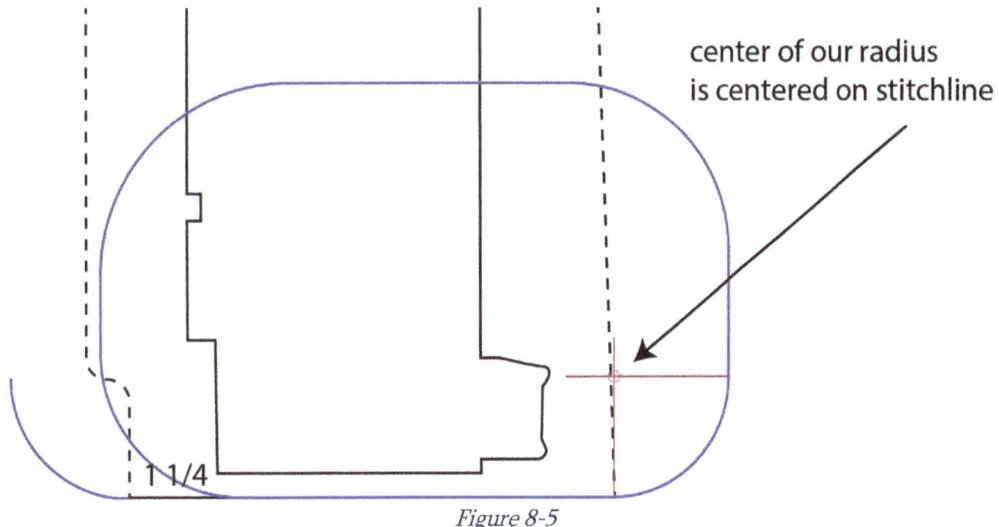

Figure 8-5

Trace the curve and remove the card from the StitchTrace.

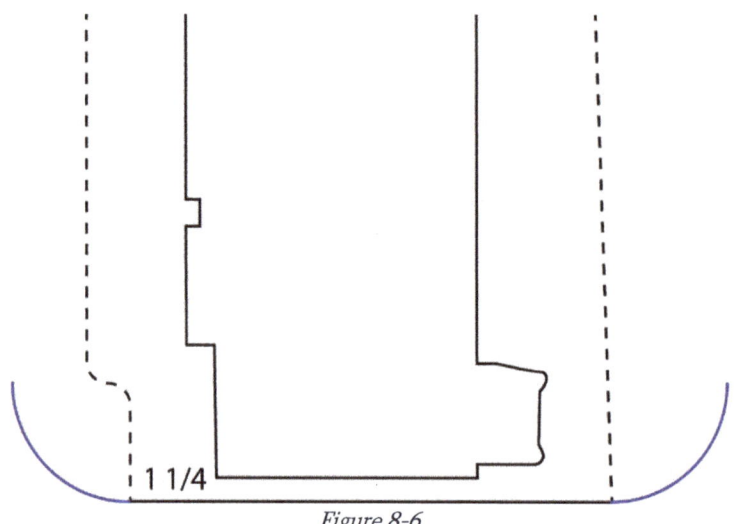

Figure 8-6

Looking pretty good gang!

Let's look at the StitchTrace with our new lines and get ready to connect to the belt slot ears.

Here is where you should be

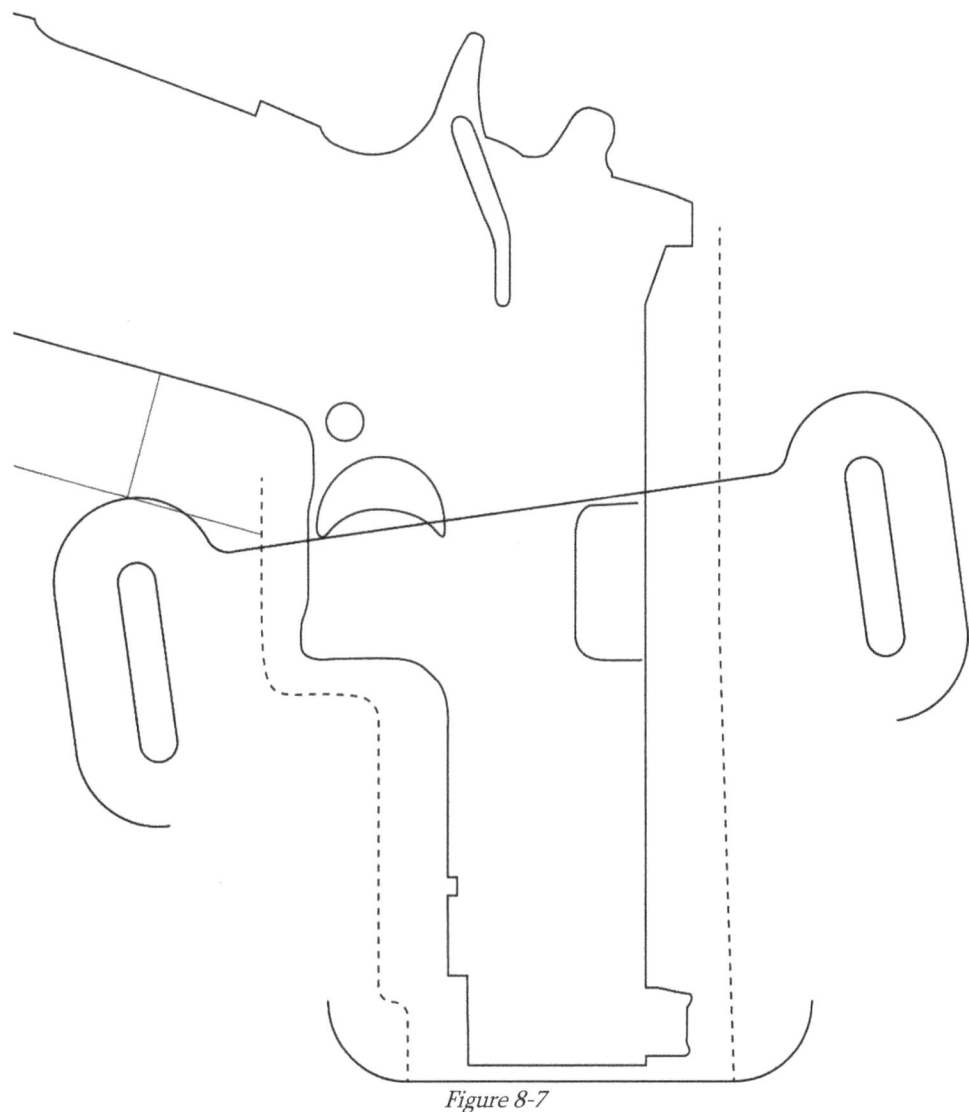

Figure 8-7

Time to raid your kids (or your) elementary art supplies. That's right, its French curve time.

We have all had these and no one ever had a use for them…

UNTIL NOW!

You're finally gonna get the chance to use this puppy for real.

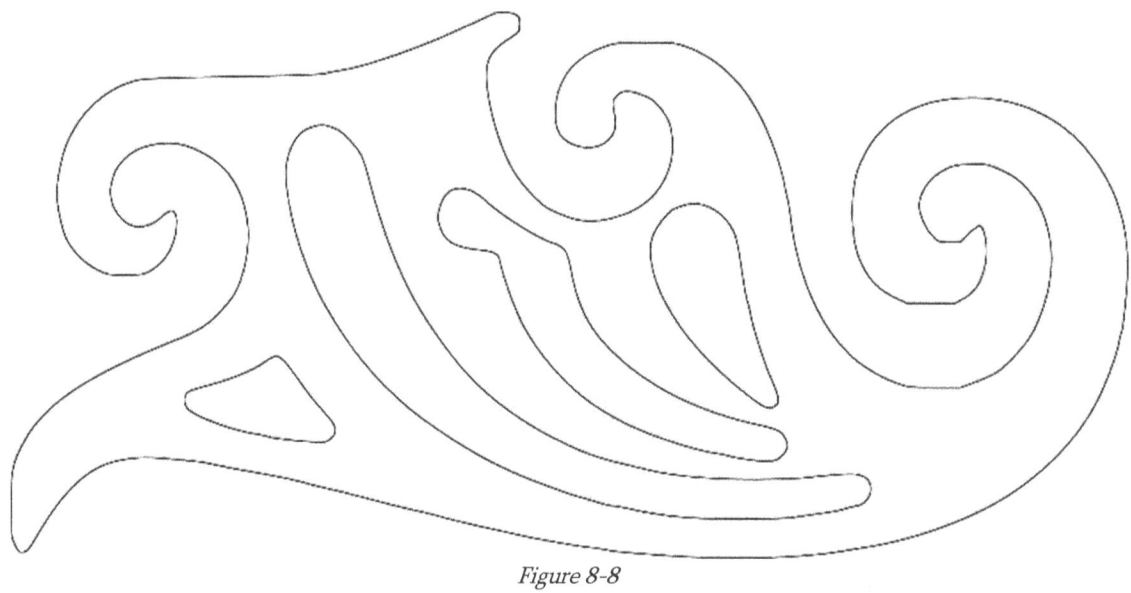
Figure 8-8

Everyone, meet Frenchie the Curve. Now Frenchie is not just a guide for curves. He can also aid you in keeping your pattern symmetrical.

We'll be marking our curve with a pencil in the areas we're tracing, ensuring we use the same areas on the other side of the pattern.

Let's place our curve on the trigger guard side of the pattern.

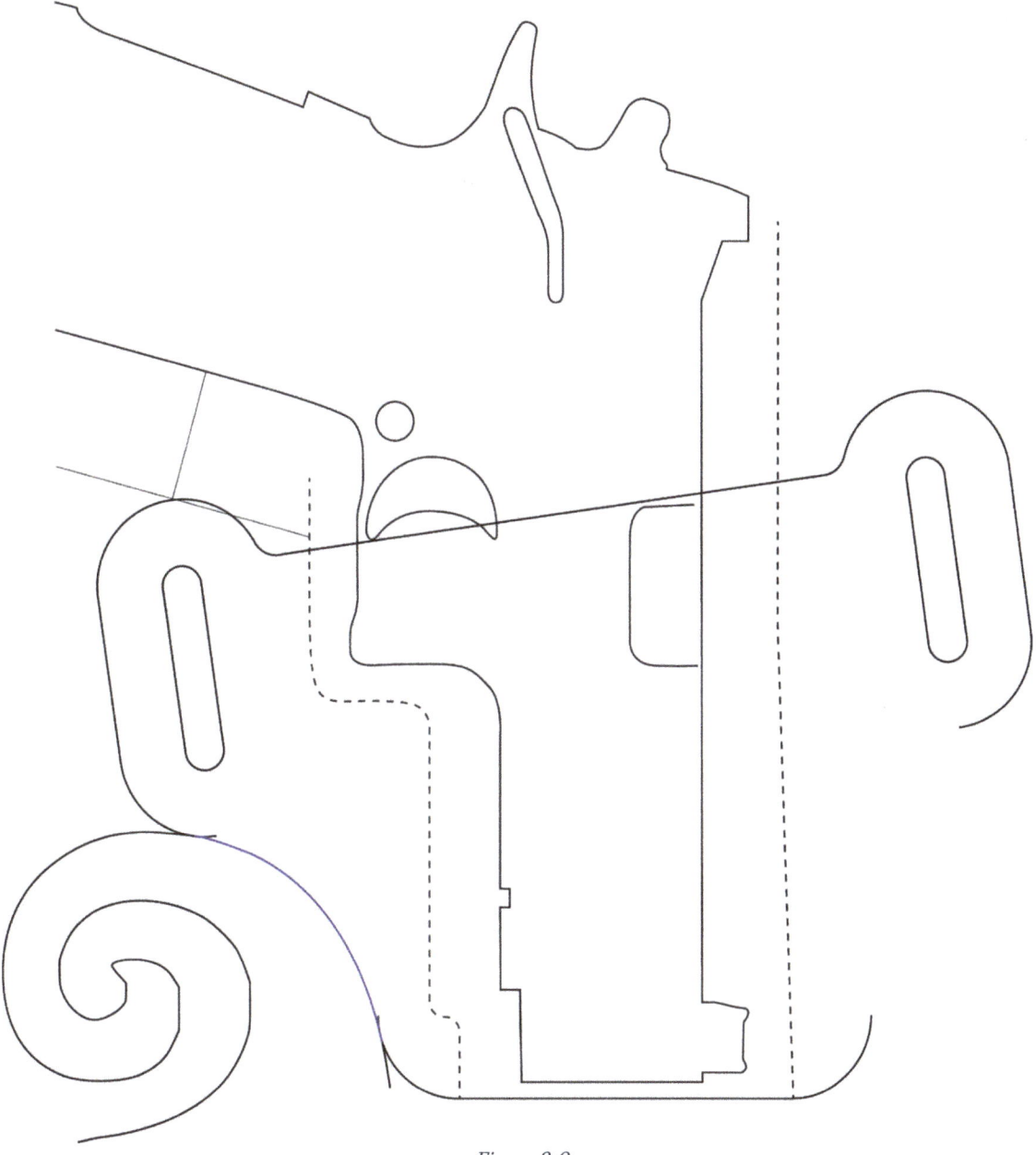

Figure 8-9

Now, we're going to flip our curve and place it on the slide side of the pattern. We'll be using the same part of the curve to provide symmetry to the pattern.

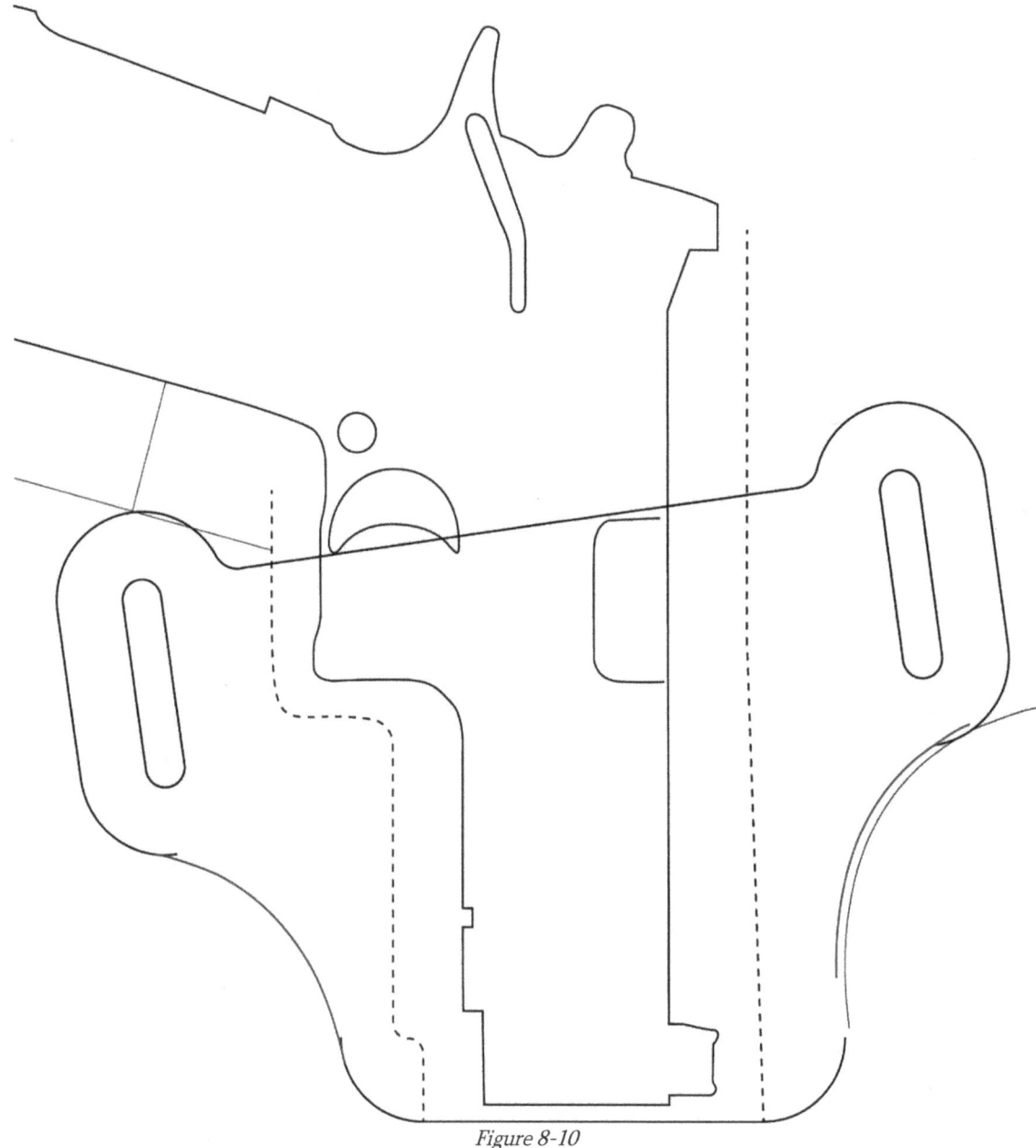

Figure 8-10

The blue lines are the same portion of the French curve.

You can see we marked our curve and kept the degrading radius.

Now let's put it all together and finish connecting the bottom of the slide side to our curve.

The blue area will be the same parts of the French curve and the red will be the connecting line. We had to rotate our curve counterclockwise a little to match the cant of the holster.

Check this out! You're doing awesome. The entire bottom of the holster is complete. The blue lines are the same area of the French curve, and the red line is a new line connecting the curve to the bottom of the holster.

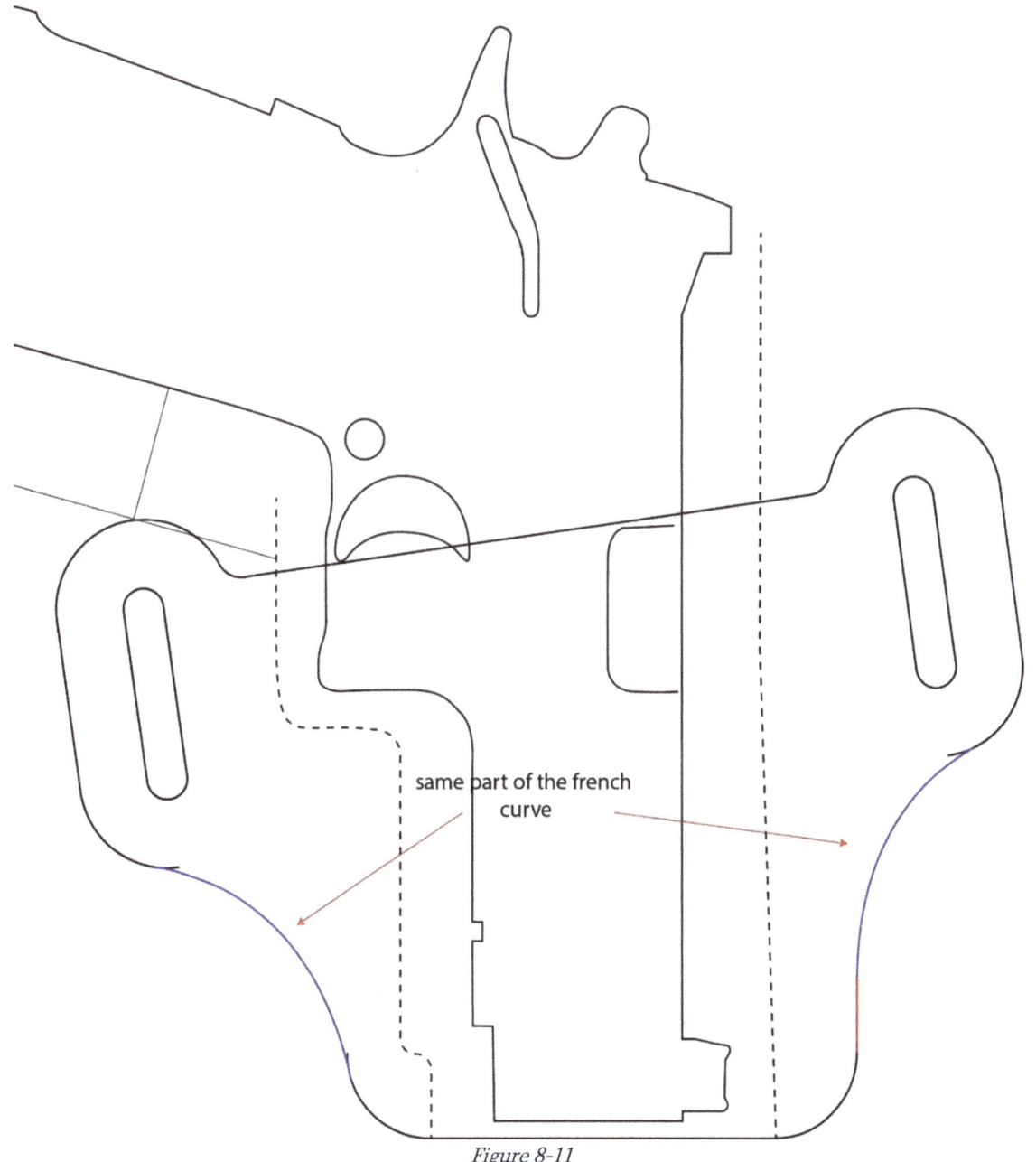

Figure 8-11

Let's work our way up.

This is where we really start to pay attention to our Go/No-Go Zones, specifically the trigger guard (Go) and all three of the No-Go Zones (Grip Relief, Mag Release, and Beavertail).

Remember, Green is Go. Red is No!

Notice we've placed a dashed line from the top of the beavertail down to the trigger guard area. This will help us draw the curve and keep us out of the beavertail No-Go Zone.

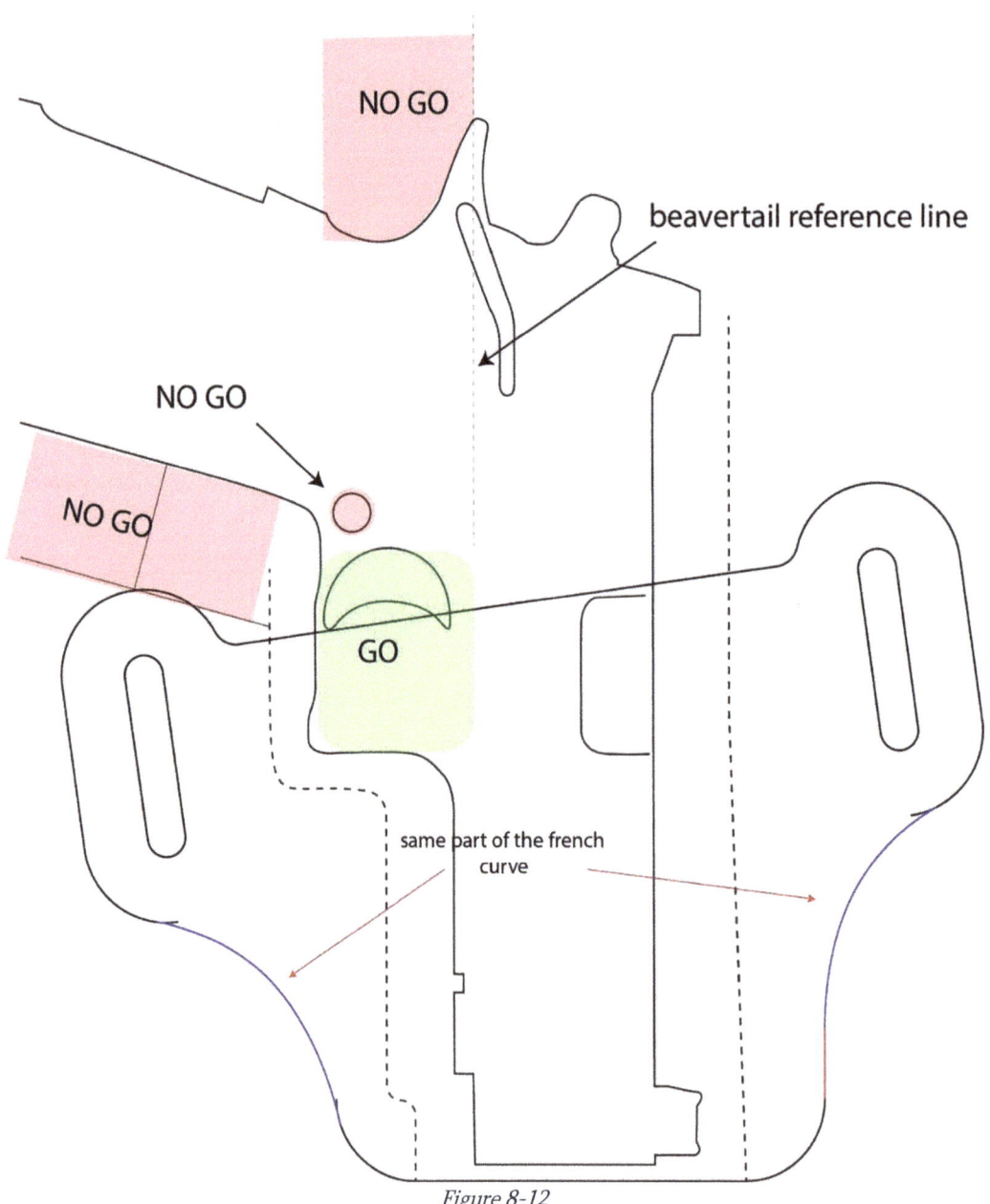

Figure 8-12

Time to grab the French curve again!

We'll start by threading the space between the mag release and the trigger guard.

Our goal is to end up with the line meeting our beavertail reference line. It should look like this.

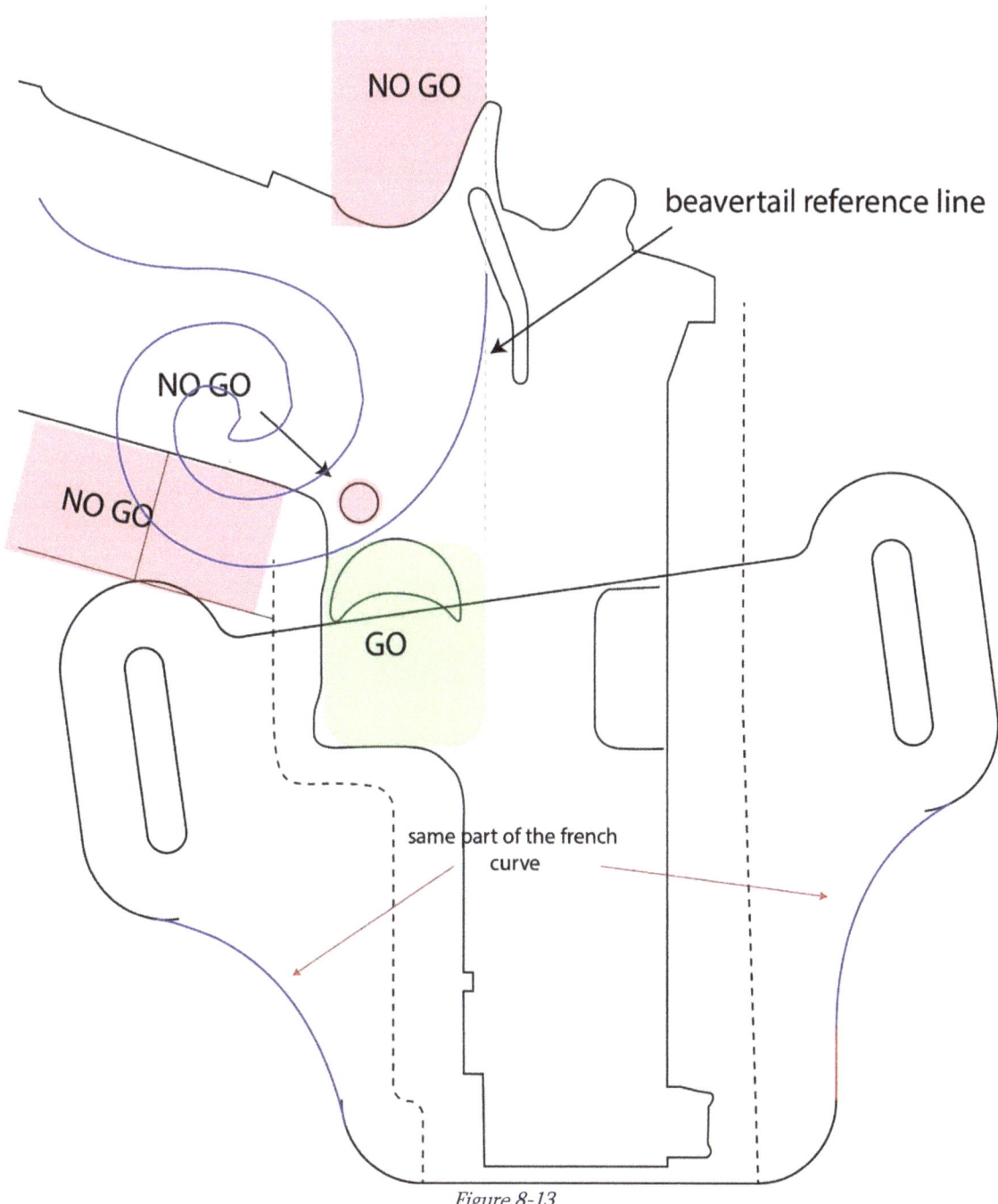

Figure 8-13

Now we need to connect the curve to the trigger guard side belt loop.

We have to impinge a tiny bit into the grip relief area, but after edging and sanding most of the leather will clear our No-Go Zone.

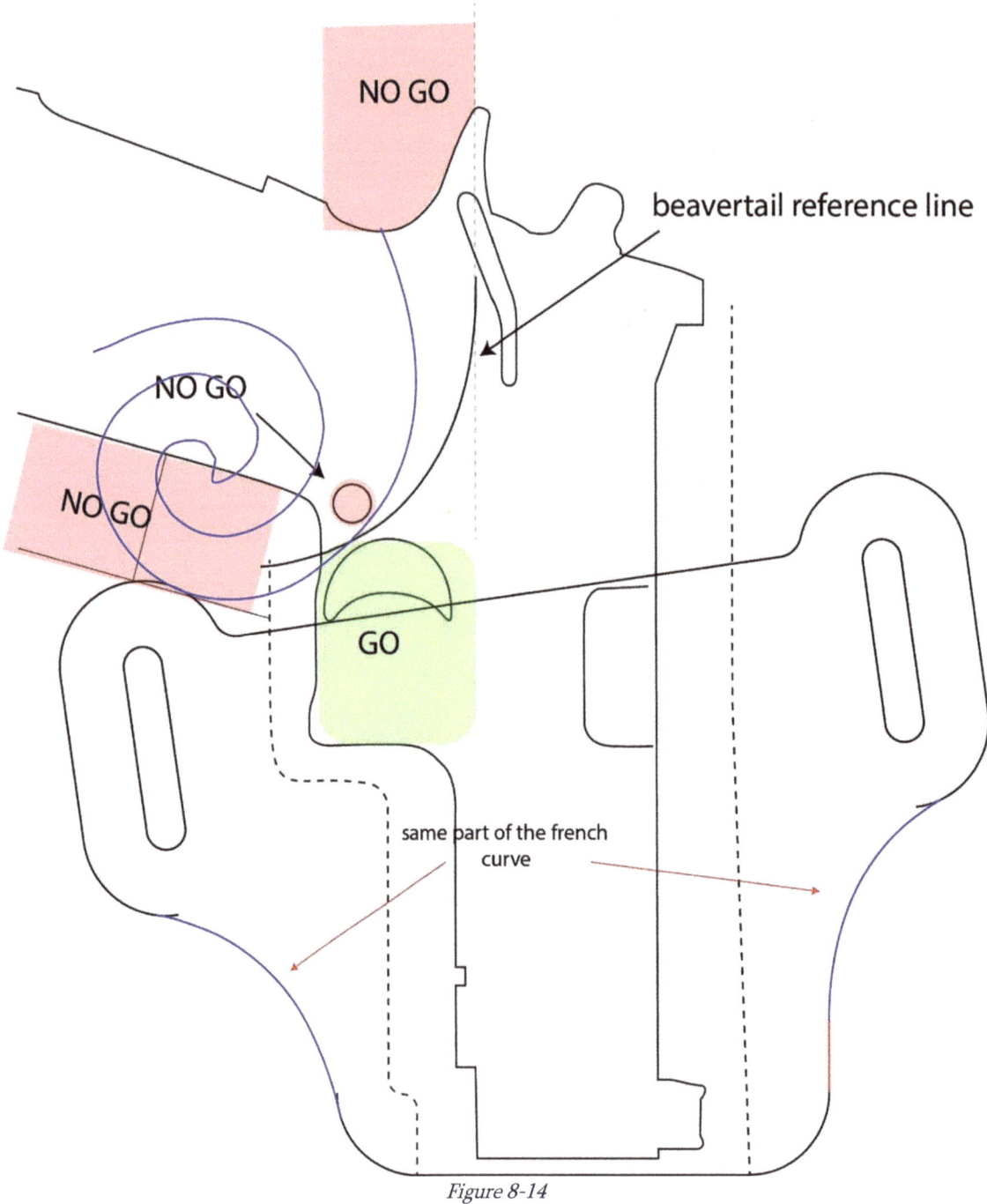

Figure 8-14

Now that we have our two curves laid into the pattern, you can see the area in the red circle where they meet.

We need to smooth this out.

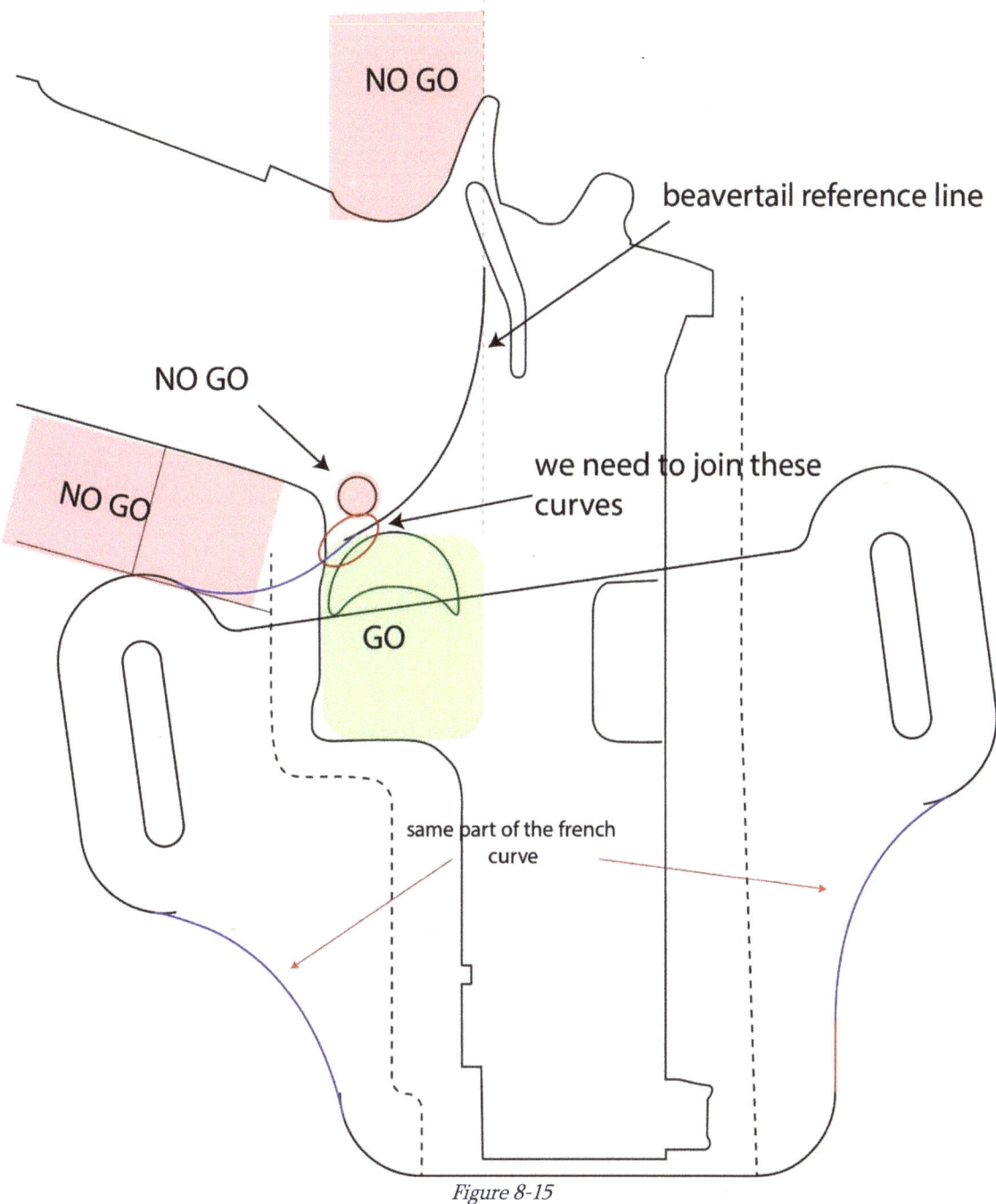

Figure 8-15

We accomplish this by turning our French curve over and drawing another reverse curve between the two areas.

Now our trigger guard curve set is done.

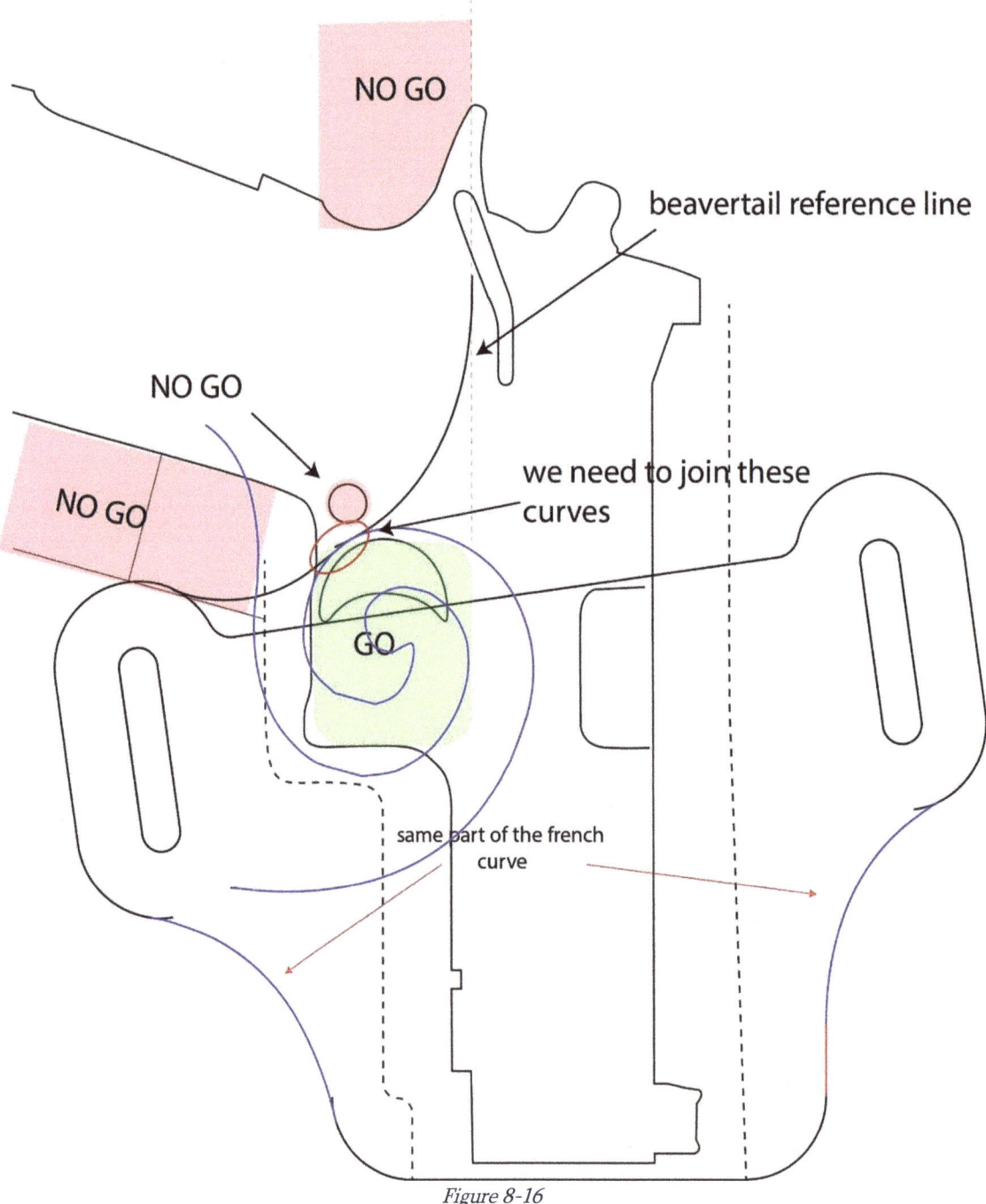

Figure 8-16

Take a moment to congratulate yourself. This is the most challenging line holster designers have to draw.

Time for a body shield. In this example we're going to bring leather all the way up to the rear of the slide.

This particular firearm has lots of sharp edges and poky corners that would be uncomfortable to the wearer.

We don't want leather to extend too far above the slide because it will fold over the rear and get in the way of holstering the firearm.

Notice we've matched the angle on the rear of the slide to draw our line. This keeps one side from being too tall and folding over.

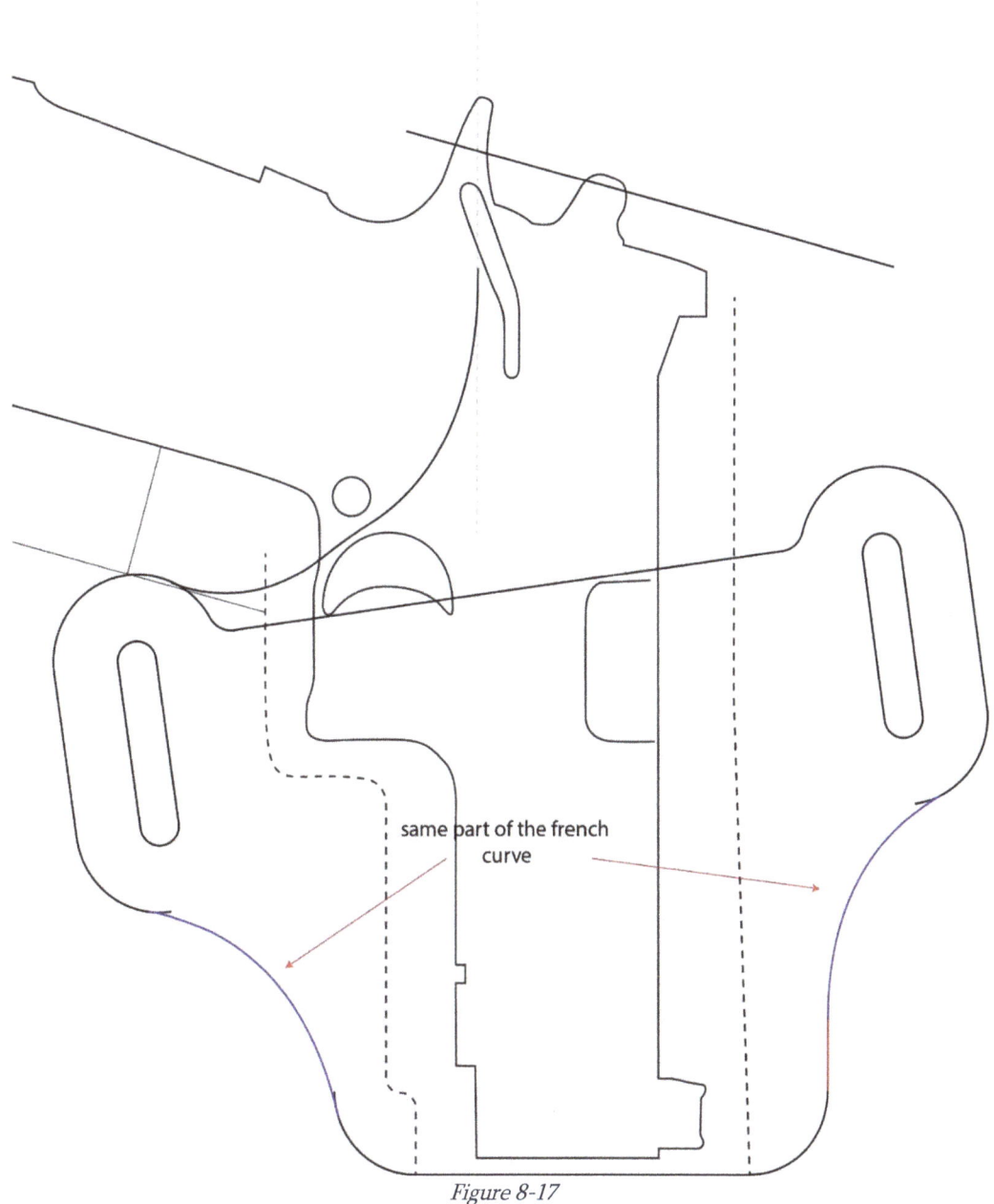

Figure 8-17

Now we're going to draw the curve from the slide side belt slot up to the body shield. Don't worry about placing the corner radius yet. Let's just get it into place for now.

Time to grab the French Curve again!

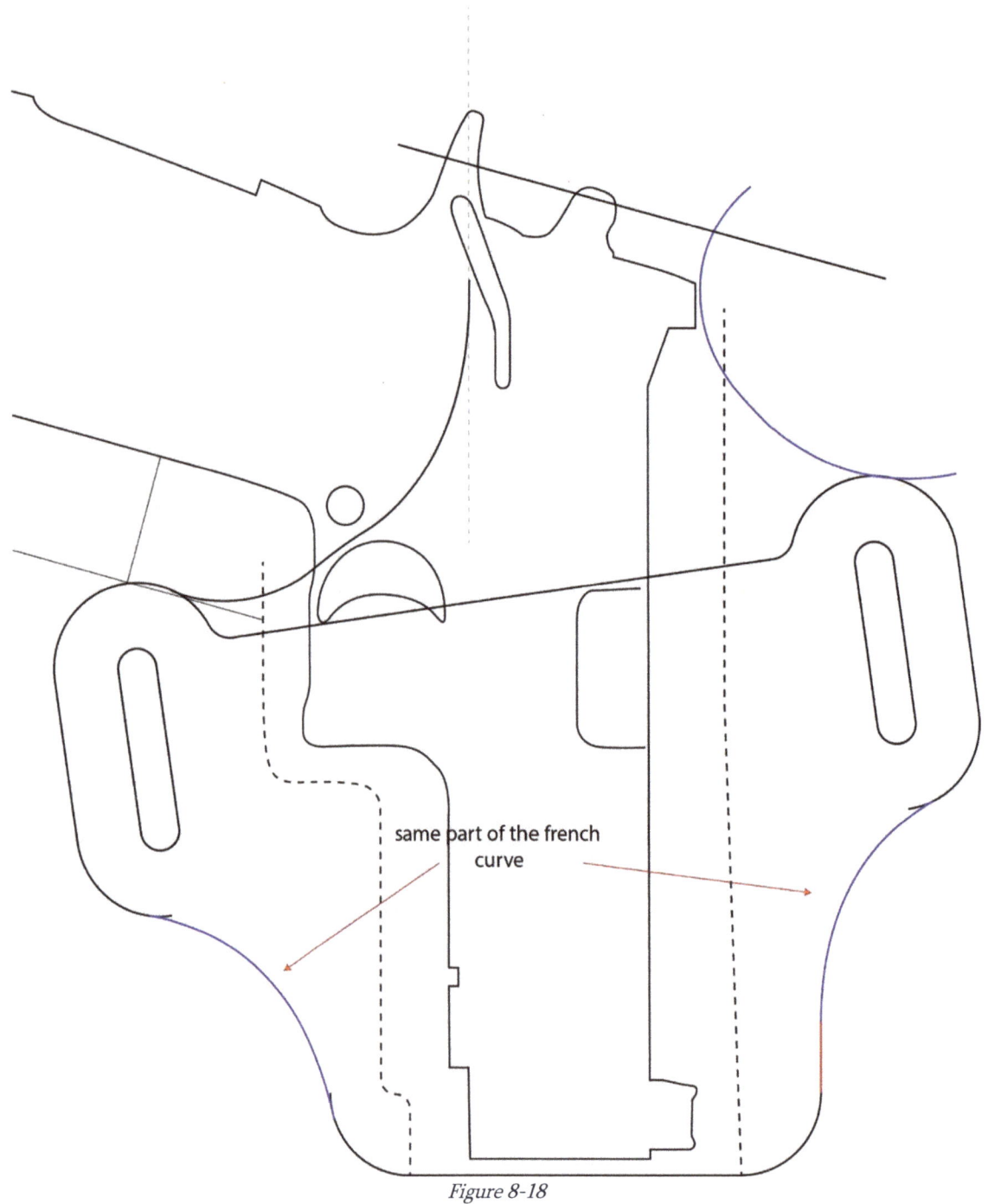

Figure 8-18

Now let's grab our radii card and connect everything!

Here's the trigger guard side of the body shield.

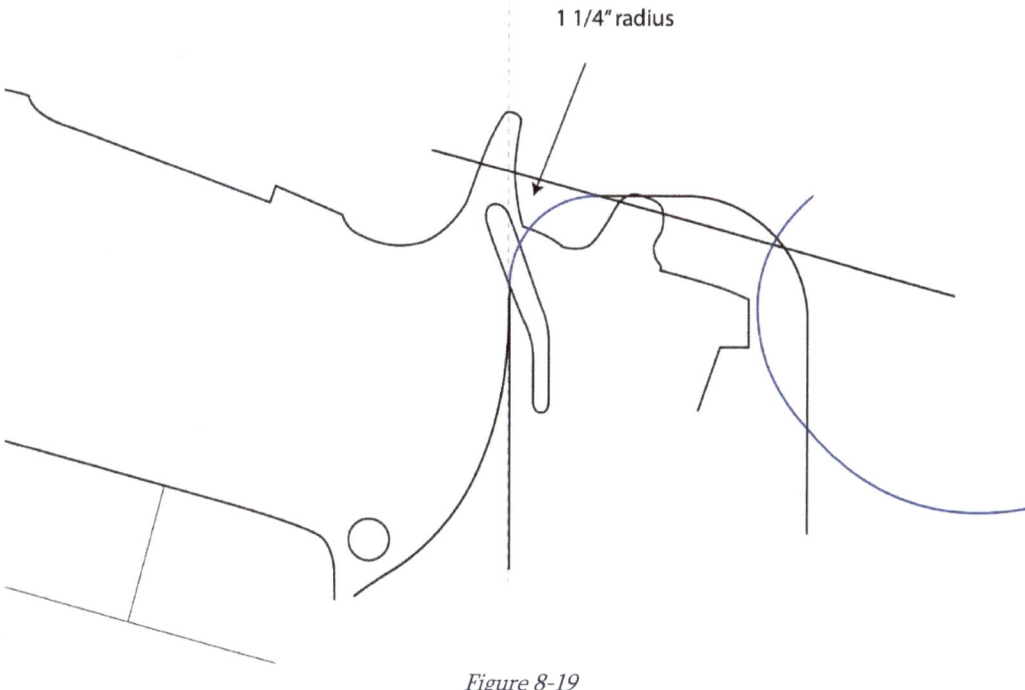

Figure 8-19

We're using the one and a quarter-inch (1-1/4") radius. We'll do the same for the slide side.

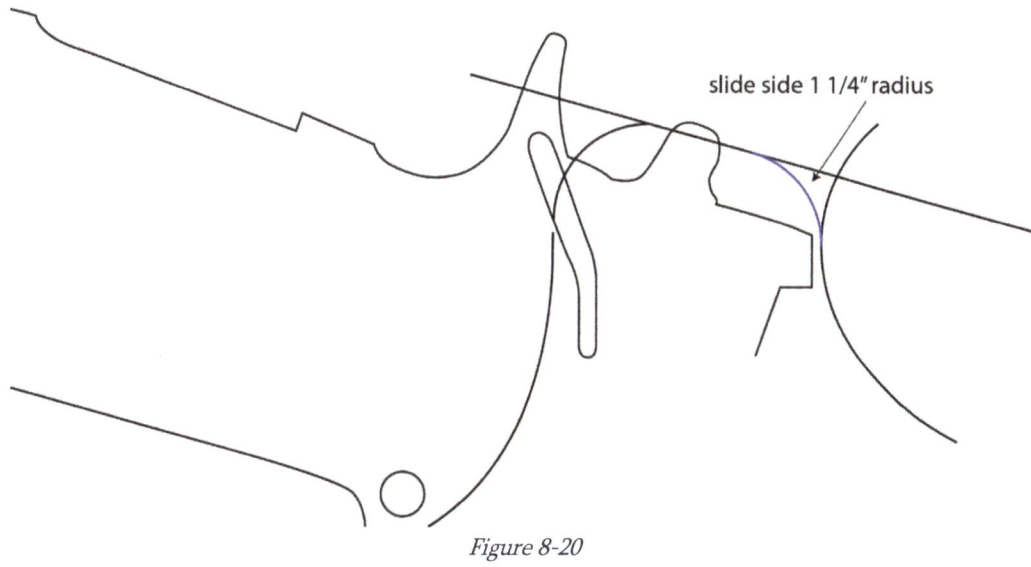

Figure 8-20

Now let's erase the belt lines, smooth all of our connection points, and erase any lines that extend past their connections points.

Your holster should look something like this.

The back of the holster is done!!!

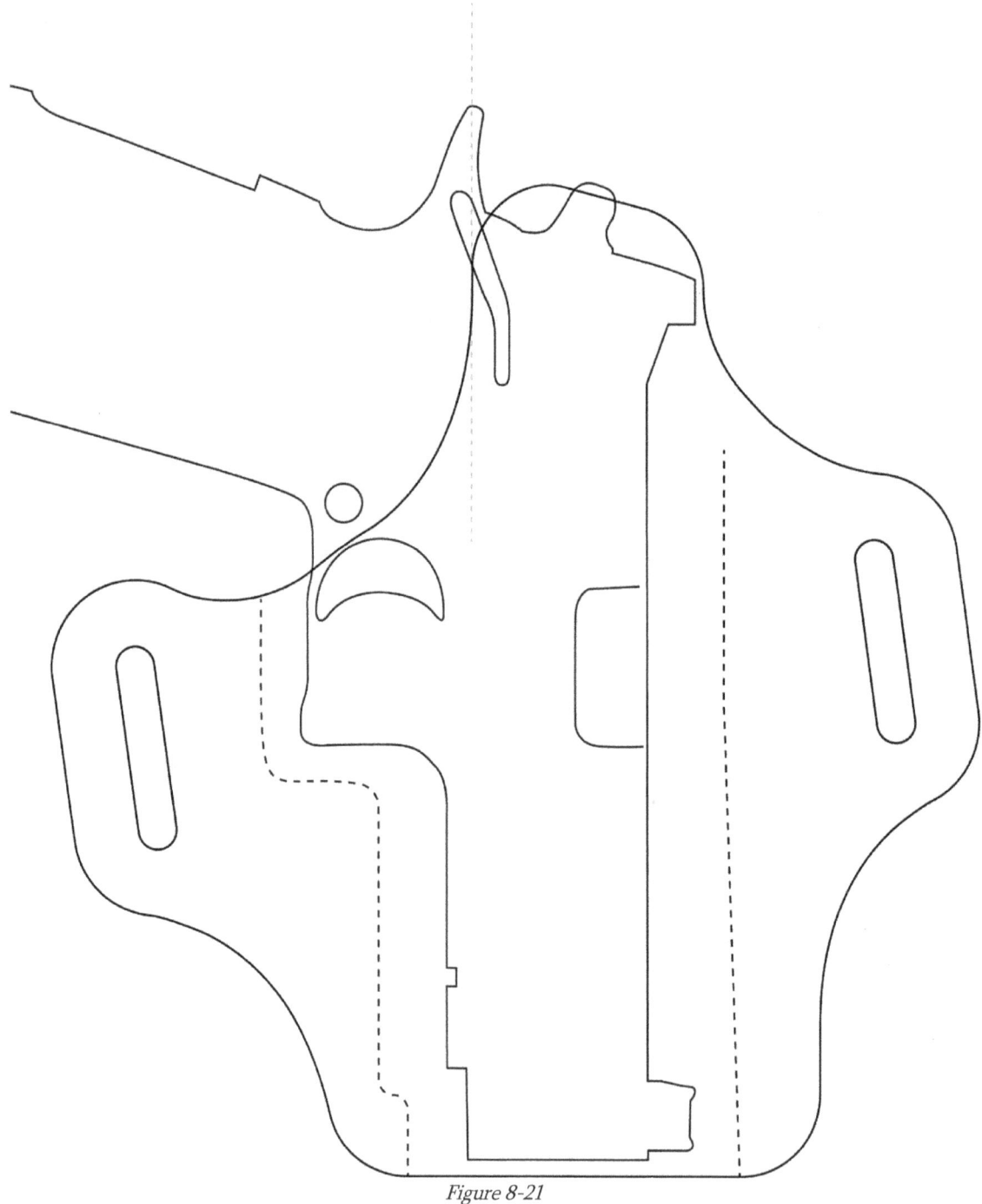

Figure 8-21

Hang in there for just a few more minutes.
Let's draw the throat (front side) of the holster now.

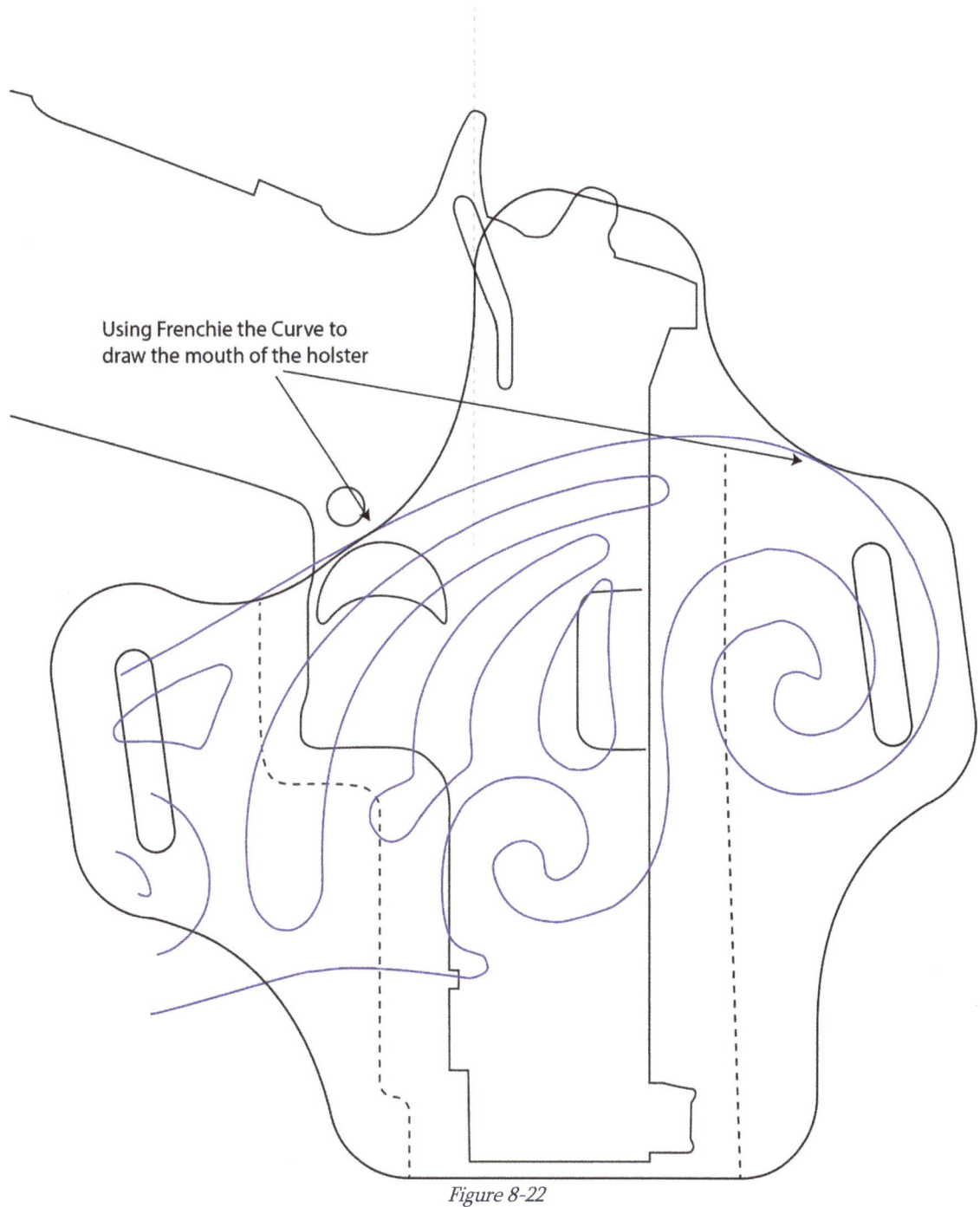

Figure 8-22

Let's draw our line and get the French Curve out of the way.
We now have a holster!

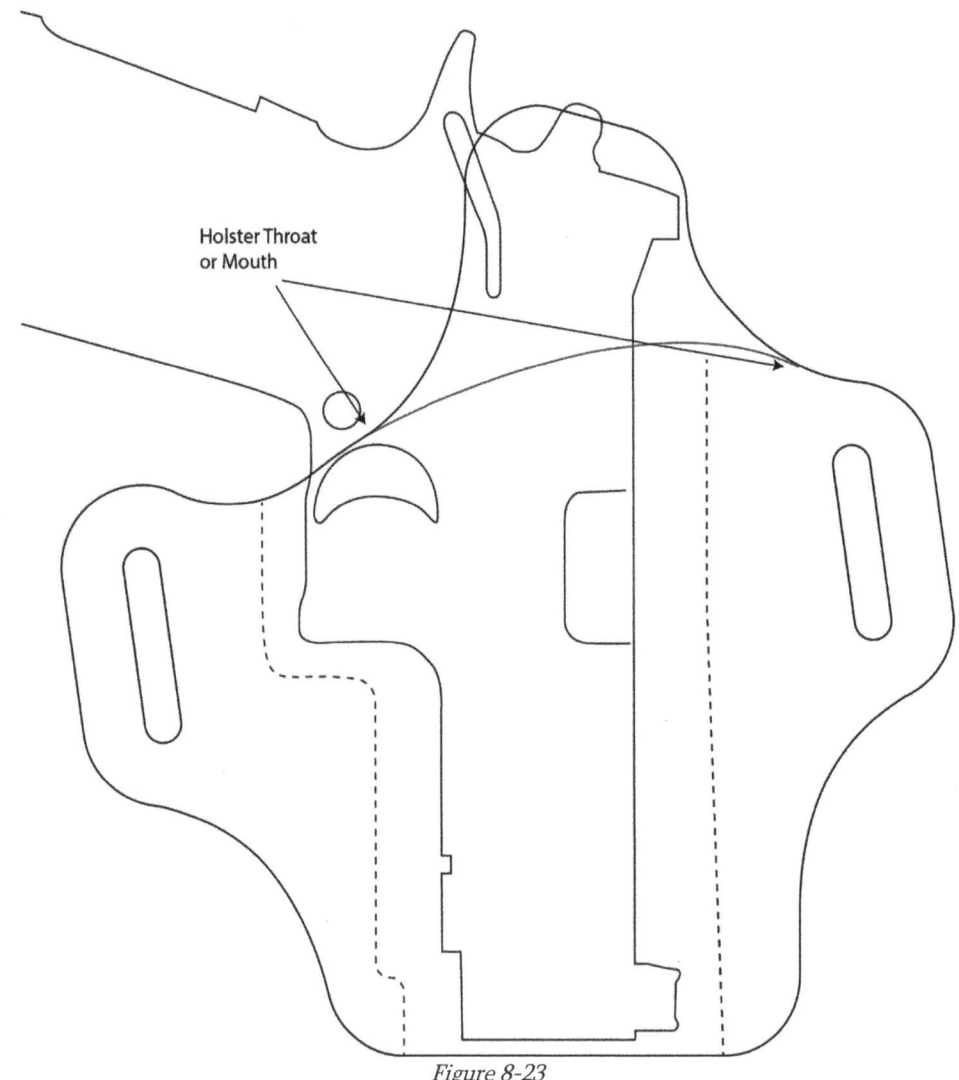

Figure 8-23

HOLY SMOKES! You did it!!!!!!!!!!!!
If you've made it to this point, you've now drawn your first holster pattern!
Do a little dance! Maybe even indulge in an adult beverage!

You've created a pattern from the ground up. Be sure to sign and date your pattern. Add in a five-inch (5") reference line, one horizontal and one vertical.

Make 3 copies, and keep your master pattern. You can always copy a new one for each build.

In the next chapter, we'll look at altering this pattern to create a thumb break.

Chapter 9: Pattern Design: Thumb Break Holster

A thumb break holster incorporates a mechanical means of retention with a strap and a snap.

This design is not dependent on friction and molding as the sole means of retention. You can absolutely detail mold this style of holster, but a properly designed thumb break will provide all necessary retention.

When the hand grips the firearm, the thumb will enter the space between the back panel of the holster and the strap opening, effectively *breaking* the connection. Thus, the term *Thumb Break*!

The thumb break holster has been kind of ostracized by many makers over the years, primarily because this design can be a bit difficult.

When you can't draw it, you tell customers it can't be any good. That's lazy thinking!

We're going to design a quick and solid break. It's up to you to decide if you want to include it in your repertoire of patterns or not.

You've completed your first holster design with the 8-degree pancake. We're going to take the exact same pattern, erase everything above the belt loops, and draw a thumb break!

So, grab your pattern, make a copy, white-out the top lines and copy again. Now you'll have something that looks like figure 9-1.

Chapter 9: Pattern Design: Thumb Break Holster

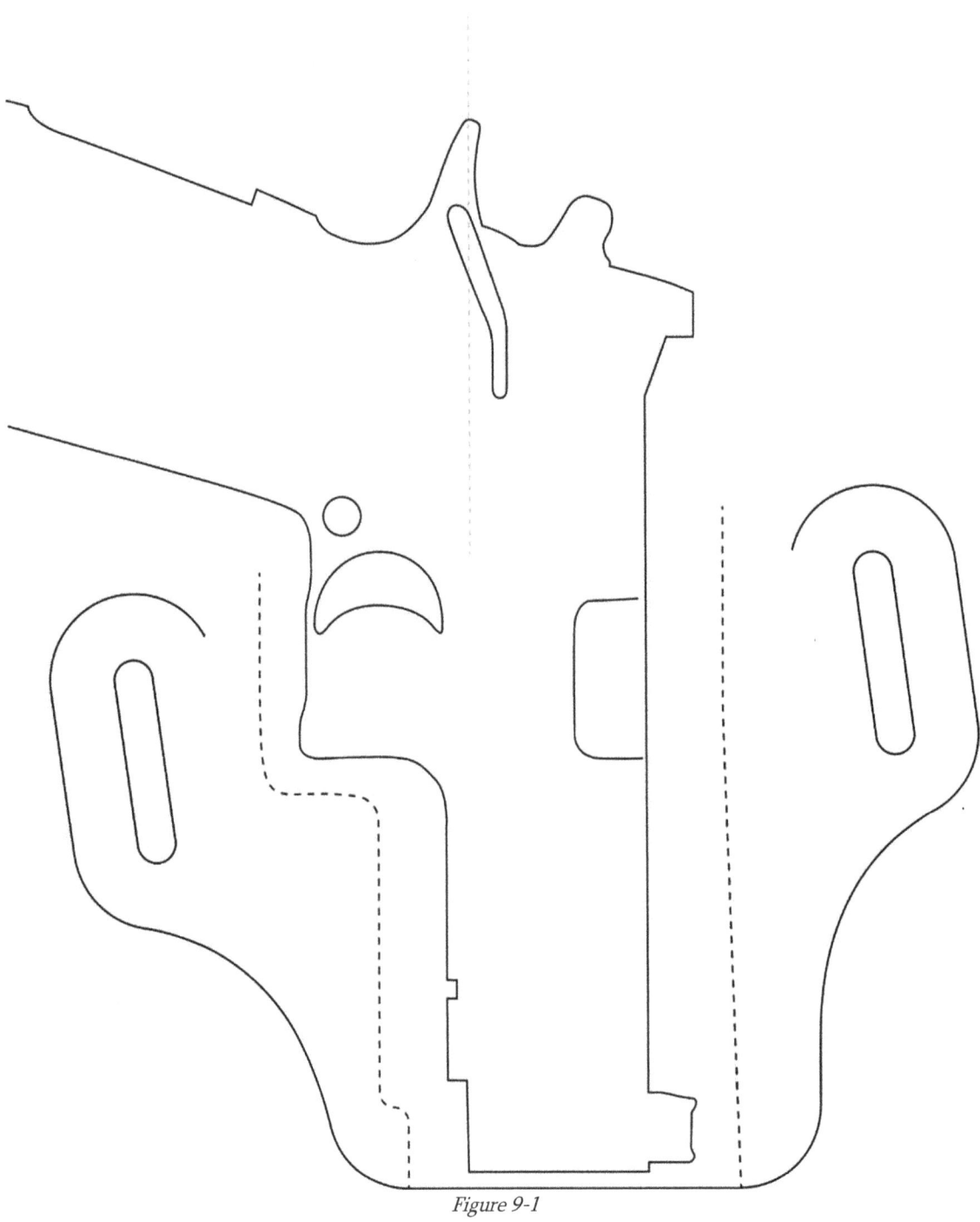

Figure 9-1

Let's get to designing!

Let's add another template to your toolbox.

This tool lays out the thumb break and the strap. You'll find a full-size image of this tool at the end of this book. Copy that puppy on cardstock, cut it out, and let's get after this design.

The larger end will be one and one-eighth-inch (1-1/8") and will have a half-inch (1/2") hole for the socket of a Line-24 Hard Action Snap.

The narrower section will be one-inch (1"), and will wrap over the rear of the slide and snap into the back of the holster.

When the hand grips the firearm, the thumb will naturally open (break) the snap. Hence the name.

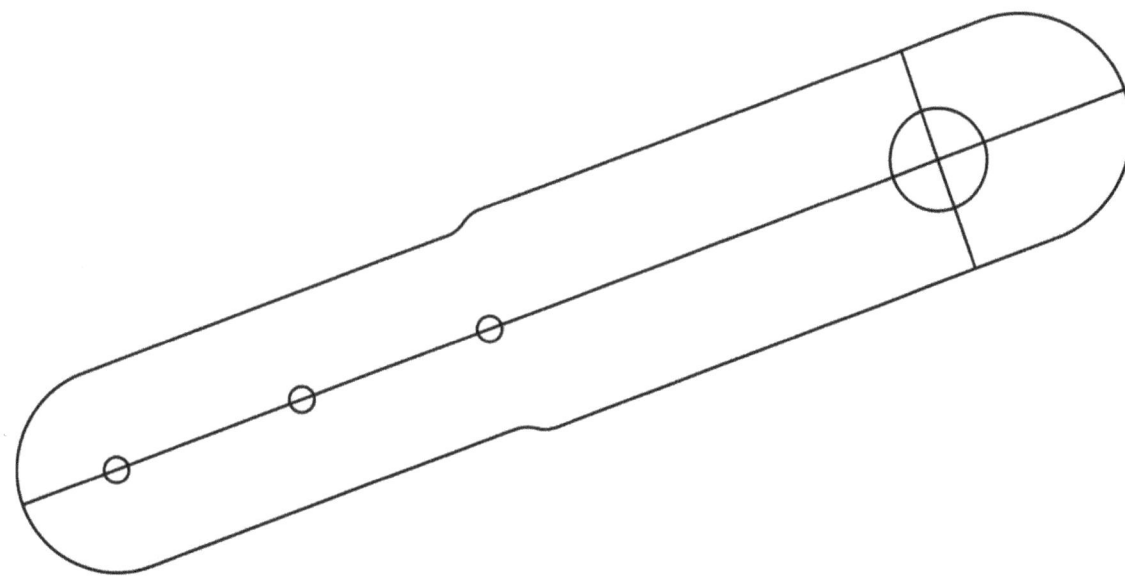

Figure 9-2

In a classic retention holster we depend on friction, created by the stitch line and the molding of leather, to create retention.

In a thumb break holster, we'll be adding a mechanical form of retention with a strap and snap.

You may want to relax the slide side stitch line by one-thirty-second-inch (1/32"). To do this you just move the slide side stitch line over to the right.

Easy Peasy!

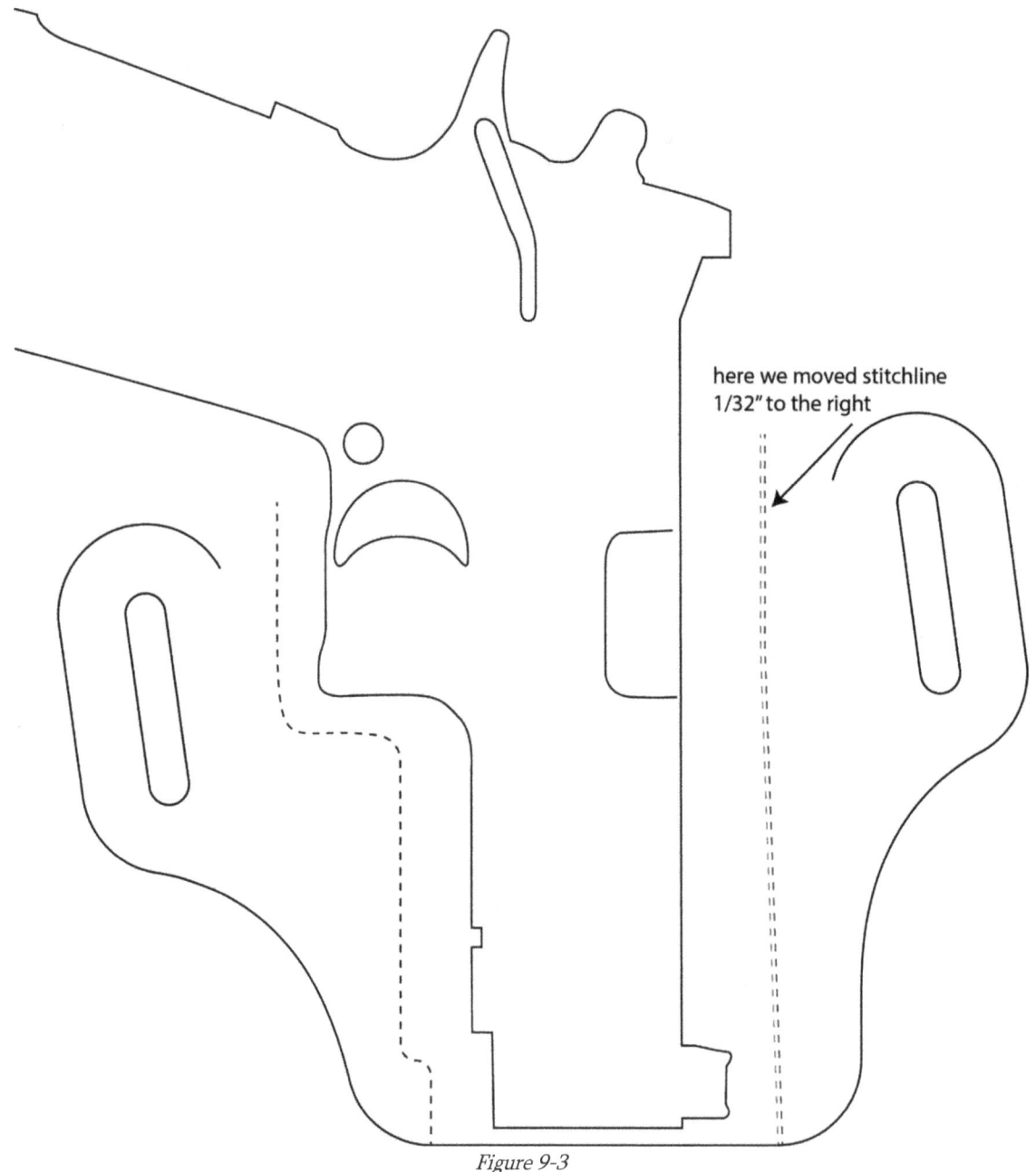

Figure 9-3

Now let's look at the location of the break.

We'll be designing this pattern with the hammer down, and we'll want the break along the back of the slide. This will allow you to set the snap by squeezing the holster between the thumb and forefinger.

We'll also be putting an angle on the break to match the back of the slide.

We'll allow the half-inch (1/2") hole for the snap socket to peak over the rear of the frame approximately one-eighth-inch (1/8").

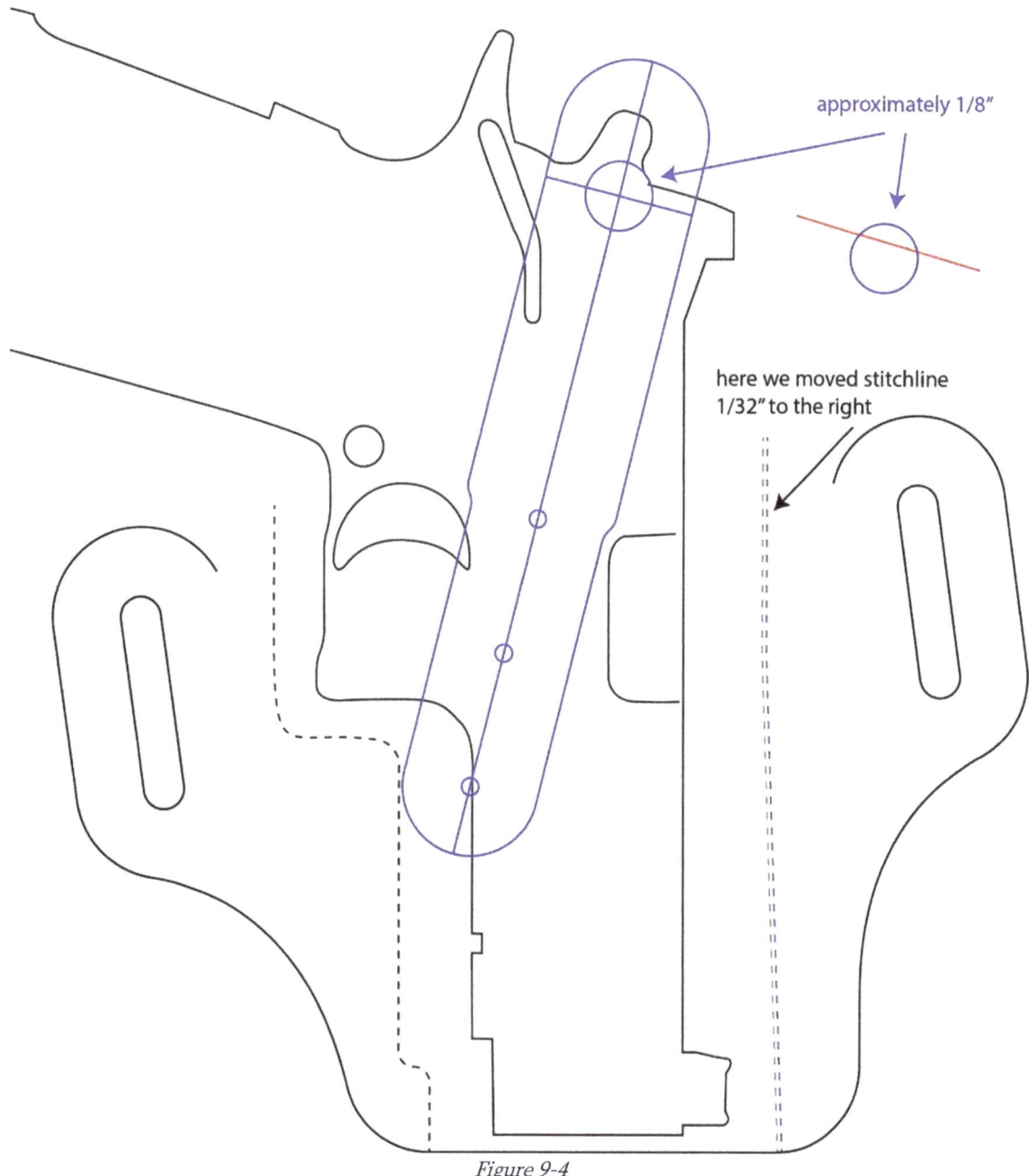

Figure 9-4

Now we'll trace the top of the template and mark the hole placement. Remove the template. Your pattern should look like this.

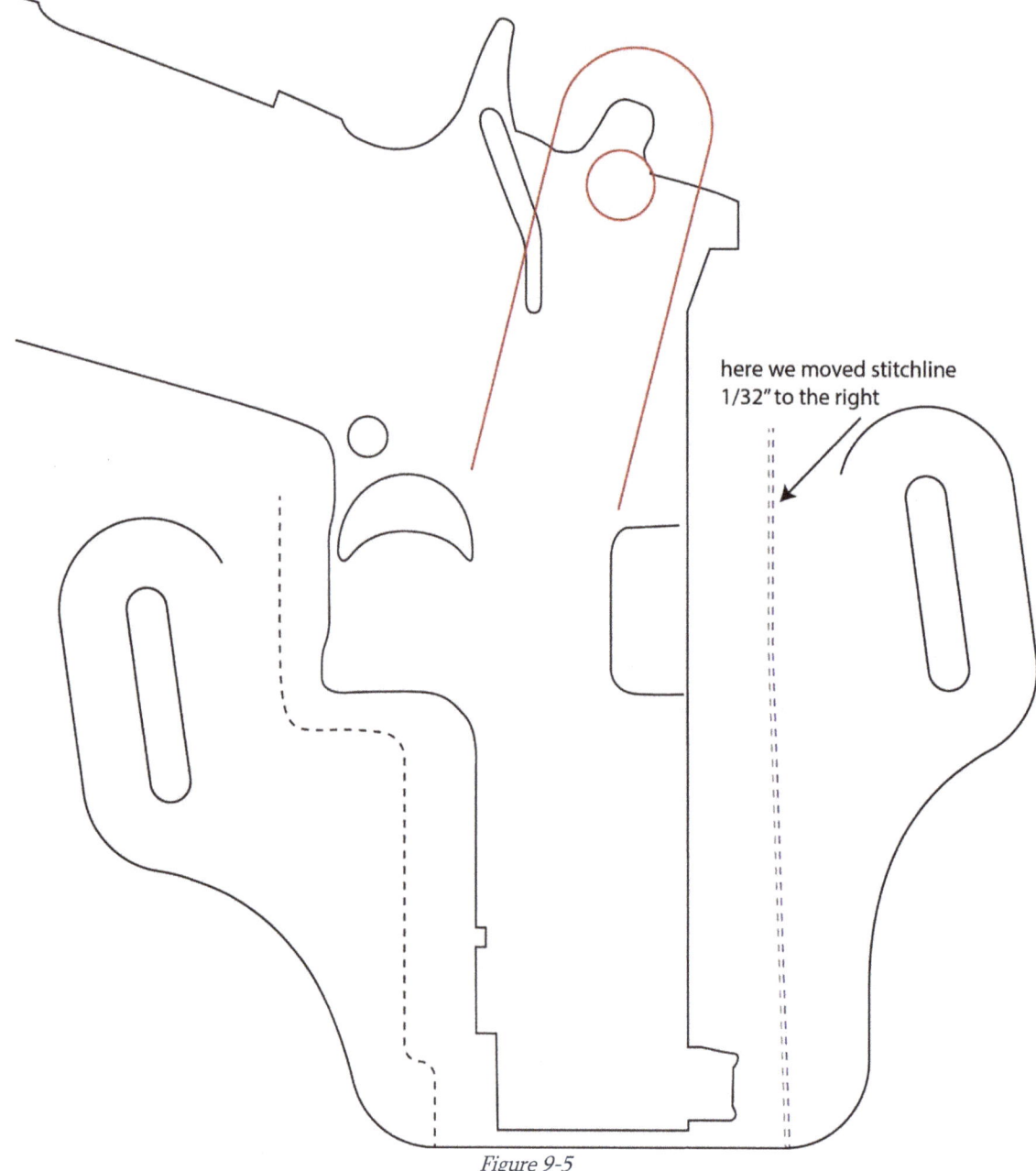

Figure 9-5

Time to get your French curve back out.

We'll connect the top of the belt slot ears to the thumb break.

We'll get fairly high up on the holster to provide structure to the rear of the pattern.

I'll place both trigger guard side and slide side in this step.

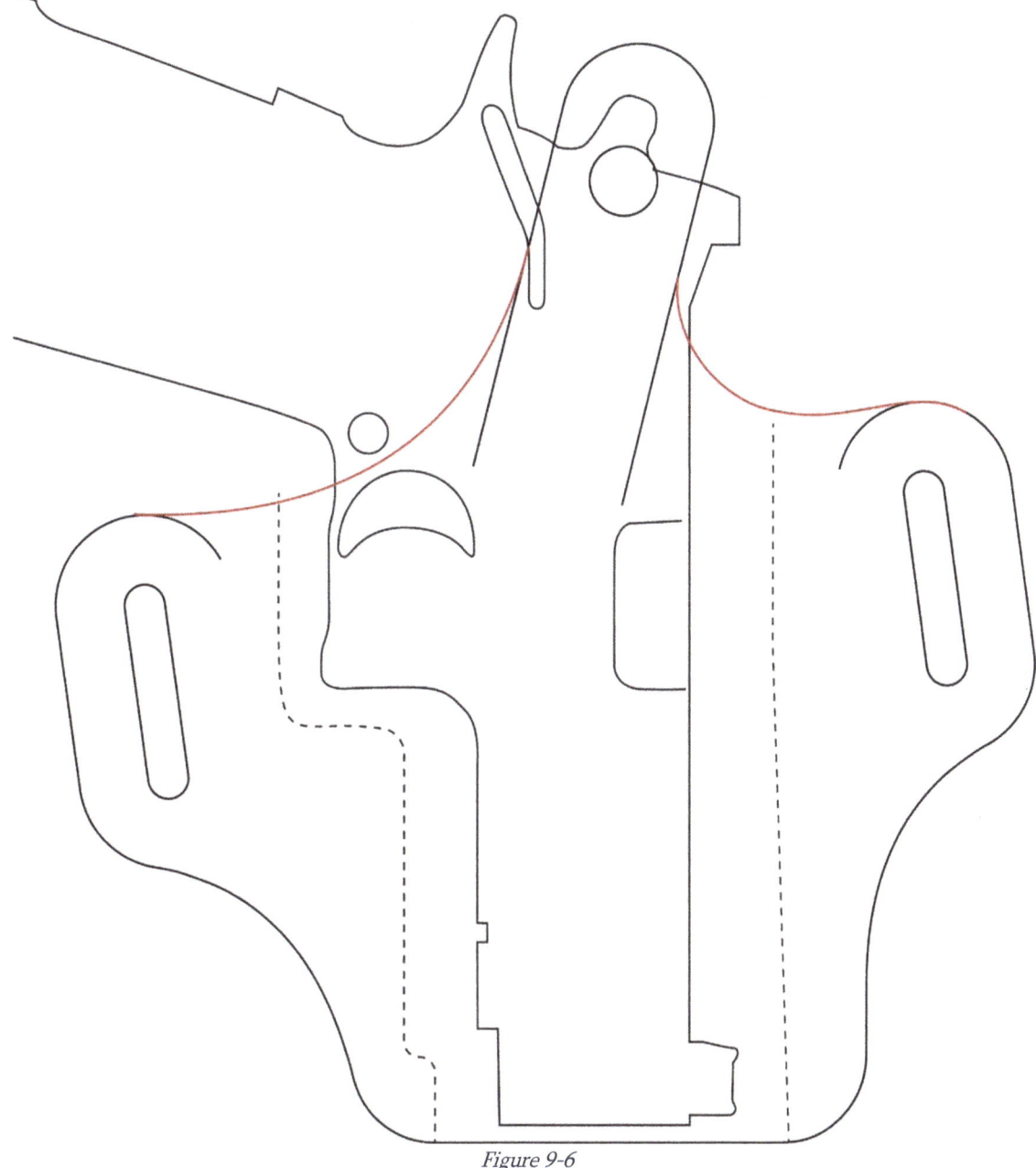

Figure 9-6

Now, let's clean up our lines and look at the back of the holster!

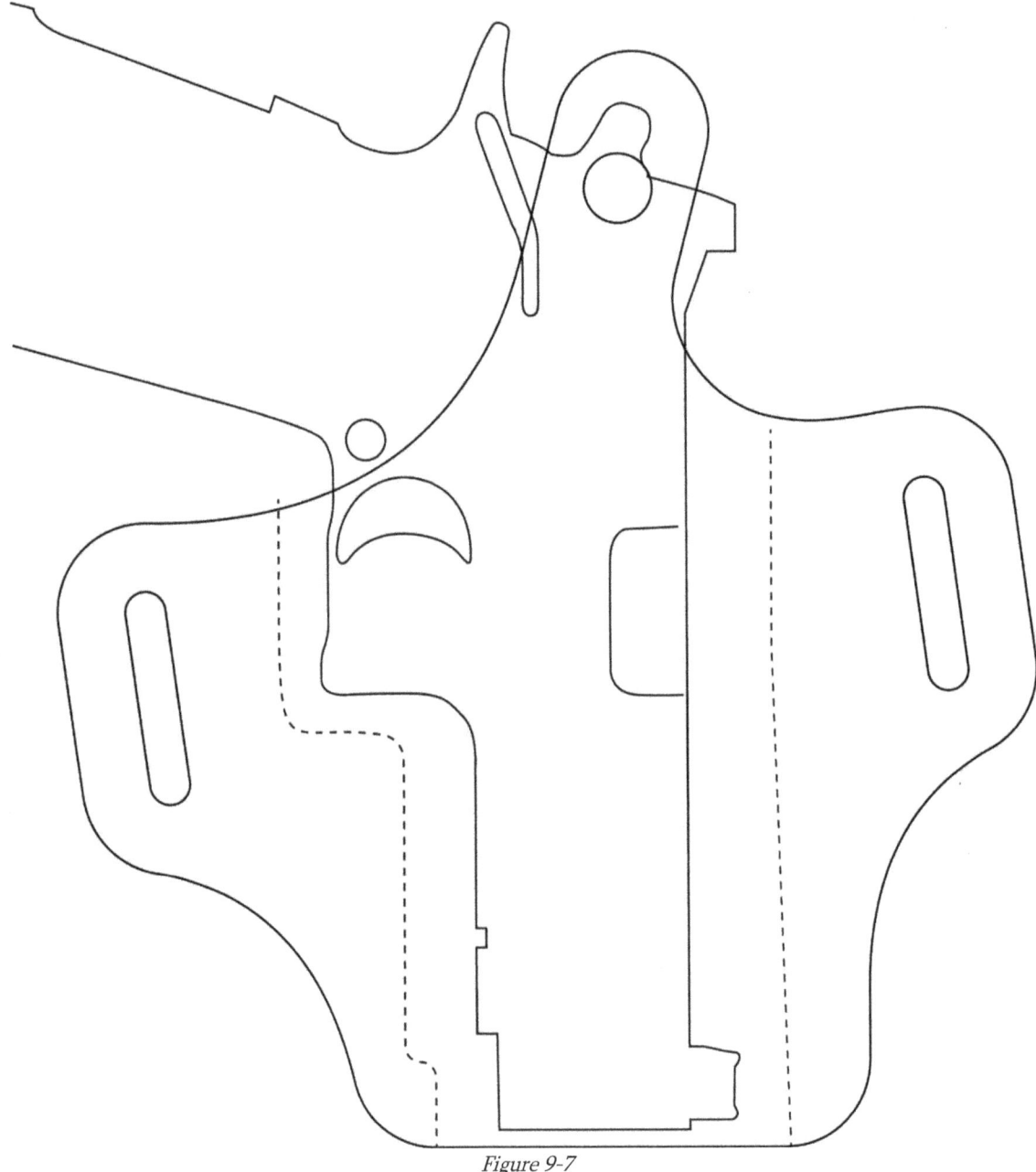

Figure 9-7

You've done it again!

The back of the holster is complete.

Now we have to draw the throat and strap that will wrap over the rear of the slide to the break.

We'll use the narrow end (1" wide) of our thumb break template tool to do this.

Once again, I'll show the placement of the tool in blue, then we will trace it out.

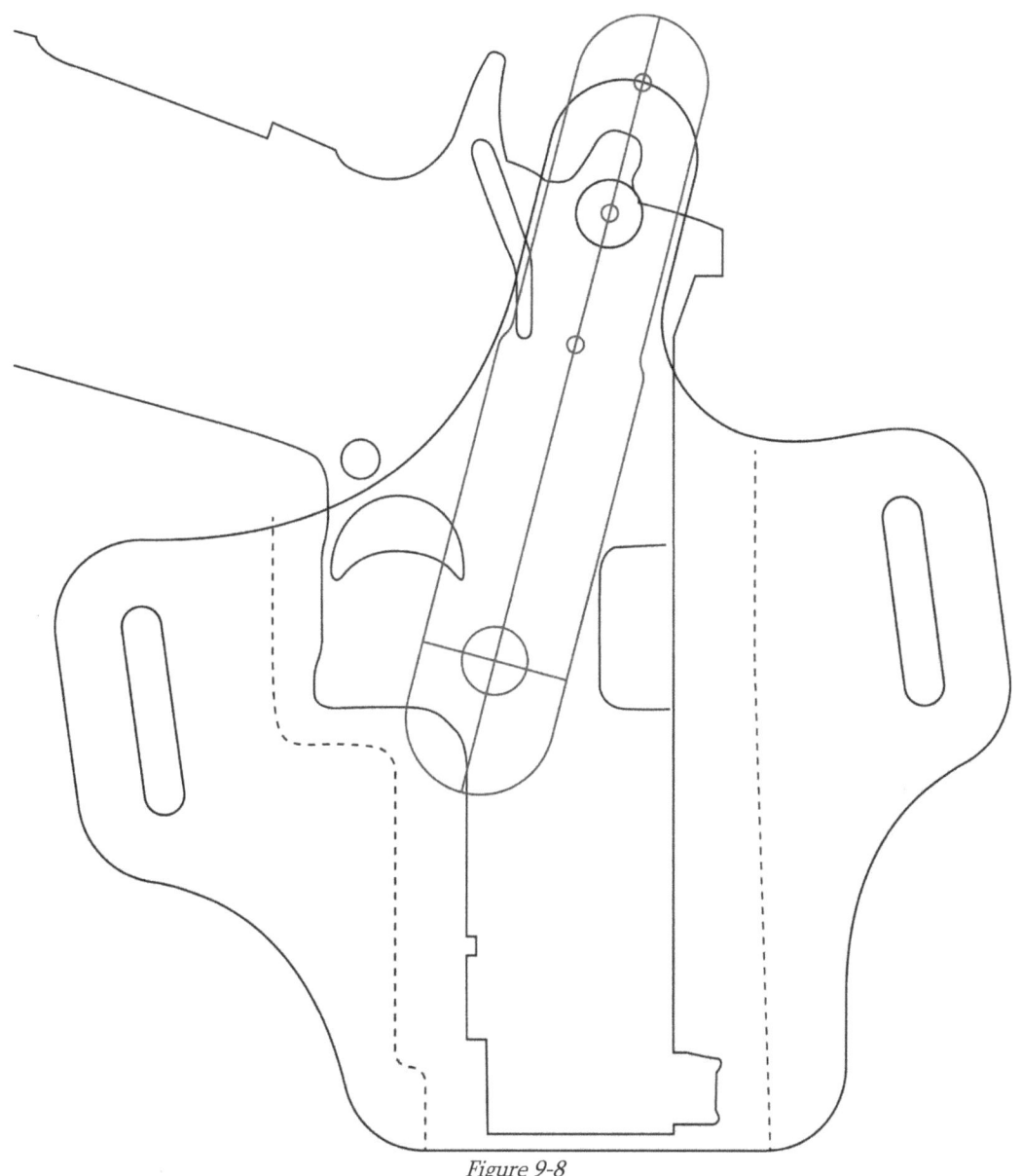

Figure 9-8

This example shows the thumb break front strap extended.

I'd like to see you extend the strap about five-inches past the end of the slide. You'll trim it back to the proper length after molding.

Each piece of leather may shrink by varying amounts depending on the attitude of the cow that day, or the method of drying used.

Here is the image of the extended strap. In the following images we'll cut it off so we can concentrate on other areas of the design.

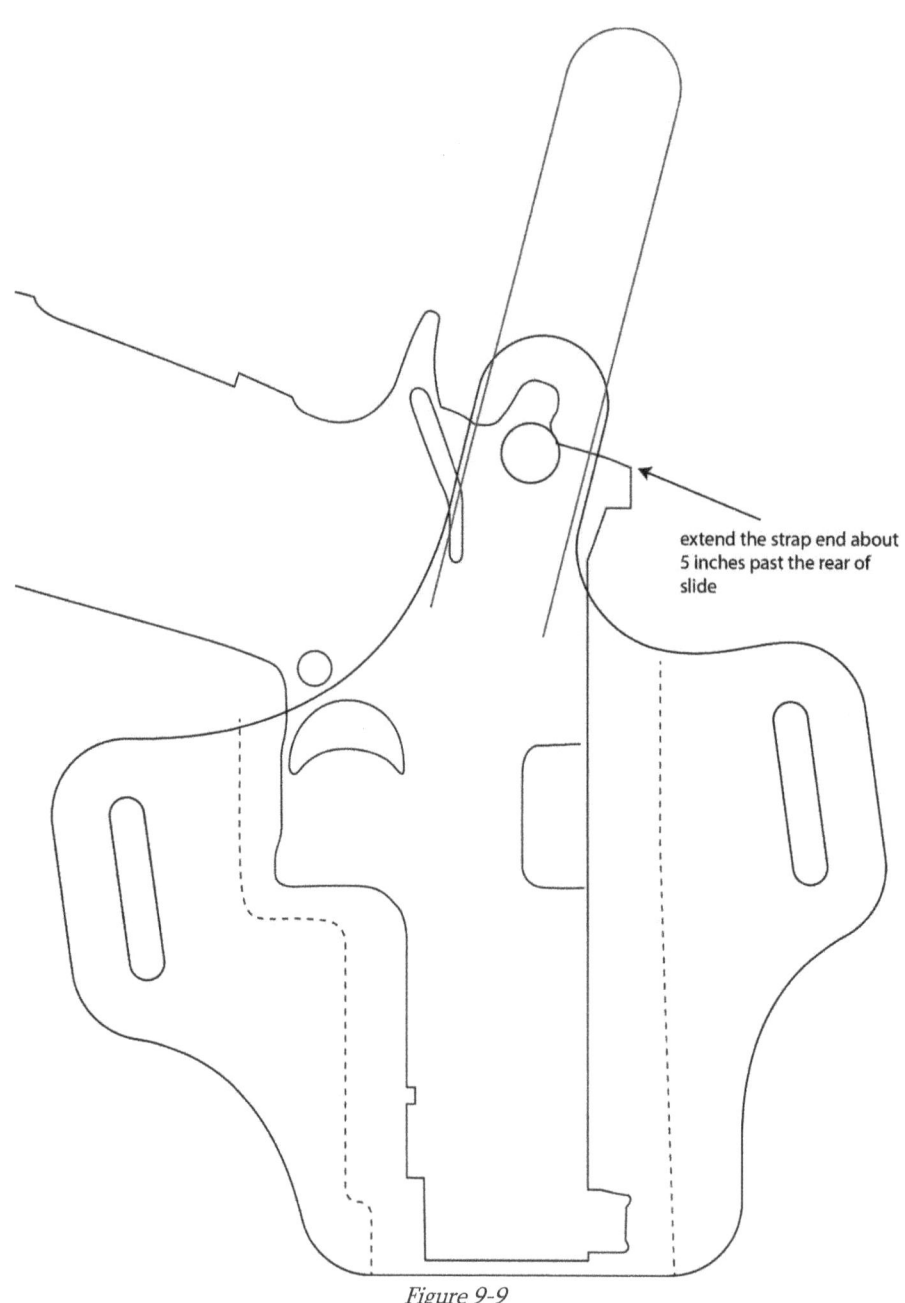

Figure 9-9

We have to connect the break strap to the front of the holster.

Our primary design concern is the edges of leather need to match-up outboard of the stitch lines.

Let's grab our French curve and give that a shot.

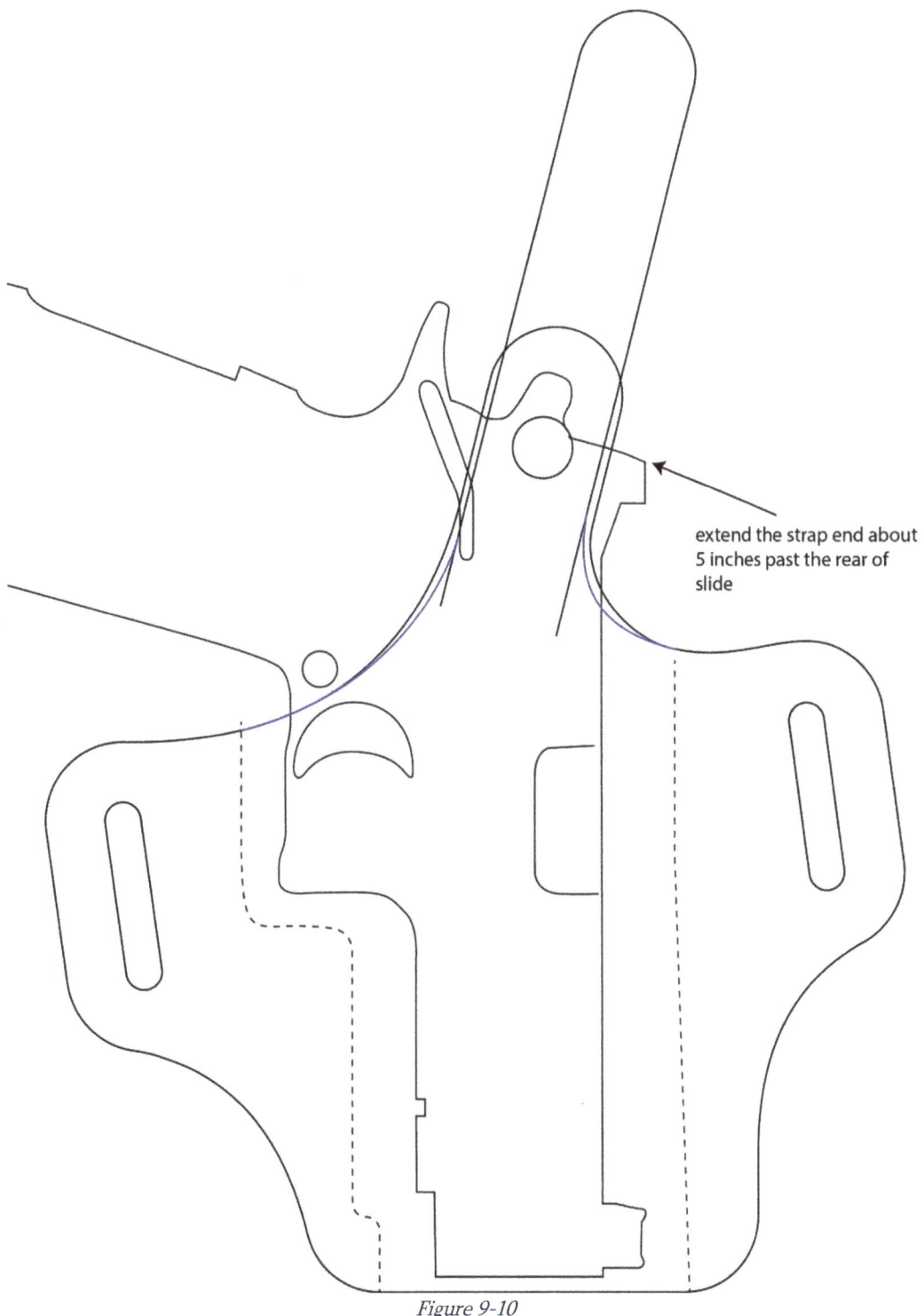

extend the strap end about 5 inches past the rear of slide

Figure 9-10

Note the line starts at the stitch line and have a smooth transition to the thumb break strap.

We'll clean this up and see what we have.

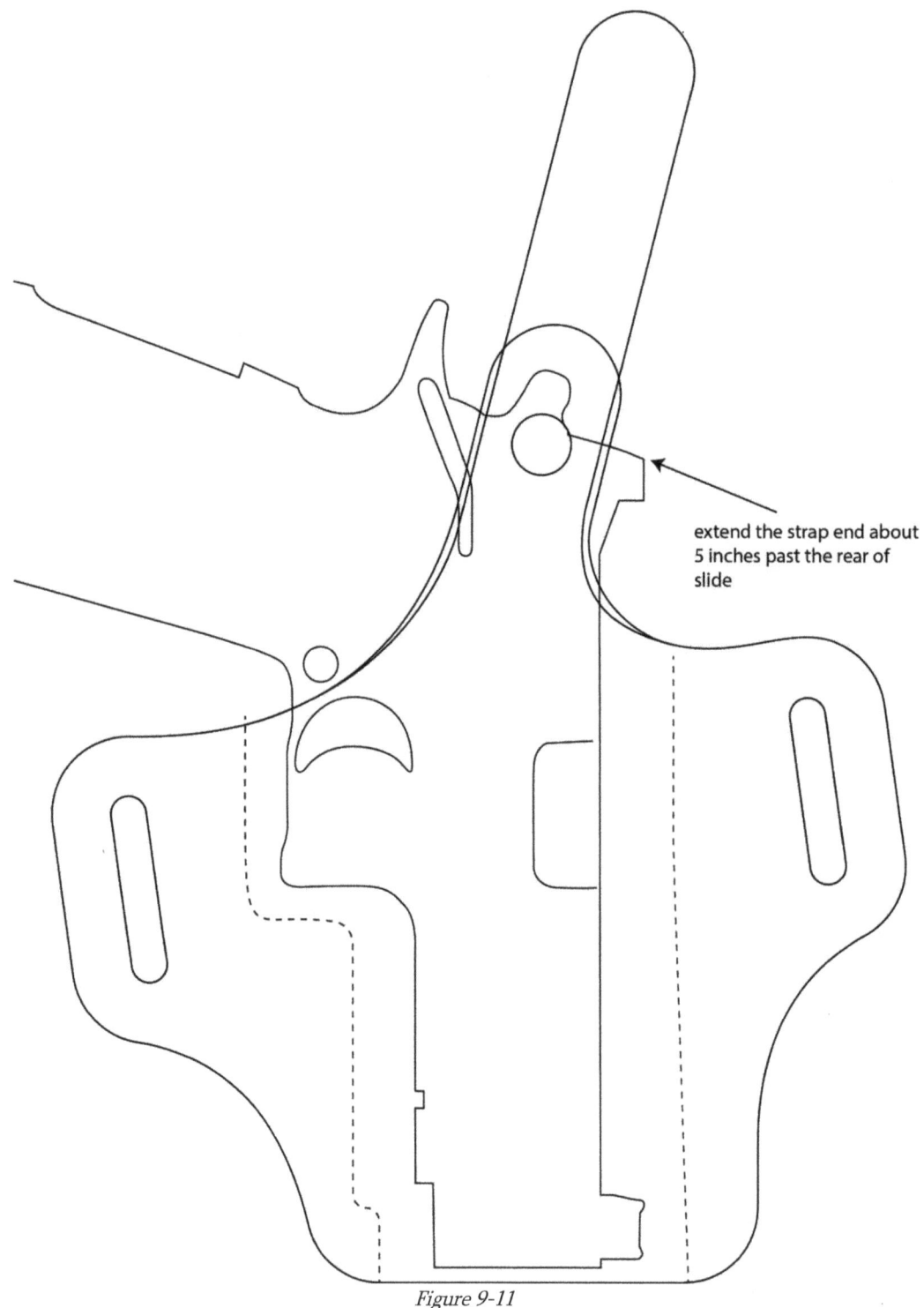

extend the strap end about 5 inches past the rear of slide

Figure 9-11

Pretty stinkin cool isn't it?

We have one more element to design and this puppy will be ready to build.

The back panel will have to be reinforced to support the thumb break. If we don't do that, the back panel of the thumb break will collapse over the throat and not allow you to holster the firearm.

We can achieve this by riveting a thumb break steel directly to the back of the body shield, but this can be a problem when sweat starts to corrode the high carbon steel thumb break.

We'll solve this problem by layering another piece of leather and *burying* the thumb break mechanism.

Let's take the back of the pattern and draw this element.

You'll see that I took a one and three-quarter-inch (1-3/4") circle and offset it from the thumb break strap.

The purpose of the offset is just to look cool. Don't read too much into it. You'll develop your own style as you move forward into your design career.

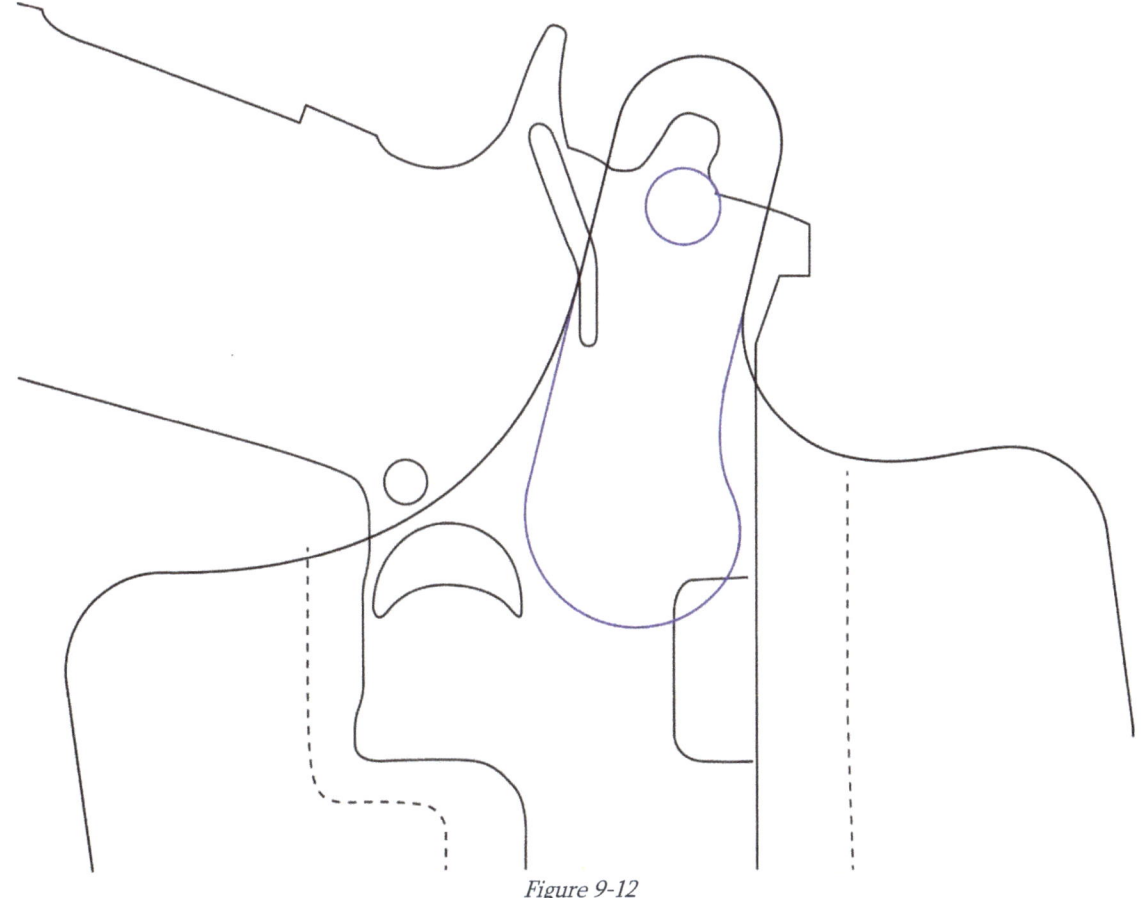

Figure 9-12

You did it!

You have now completed your second pattern.

Have an adult beverage. Are you seeing a trend here?

Let's take a look at the pattern without the firearm tracing, both as a single page, and as a breakdown of parts.

First the single page.

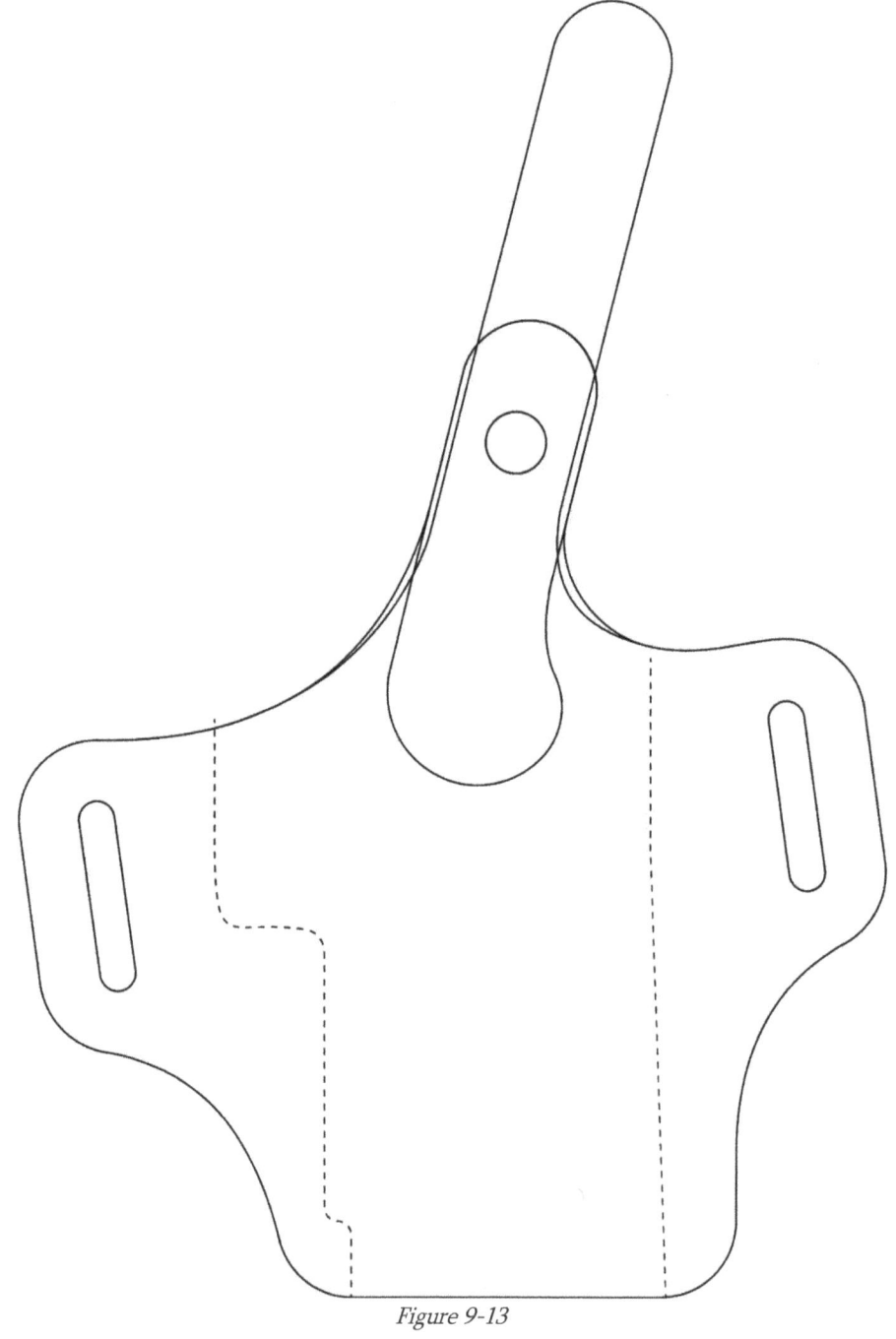

Figure 9-13

And here's the front panel and the thumb break reinforcement panel.

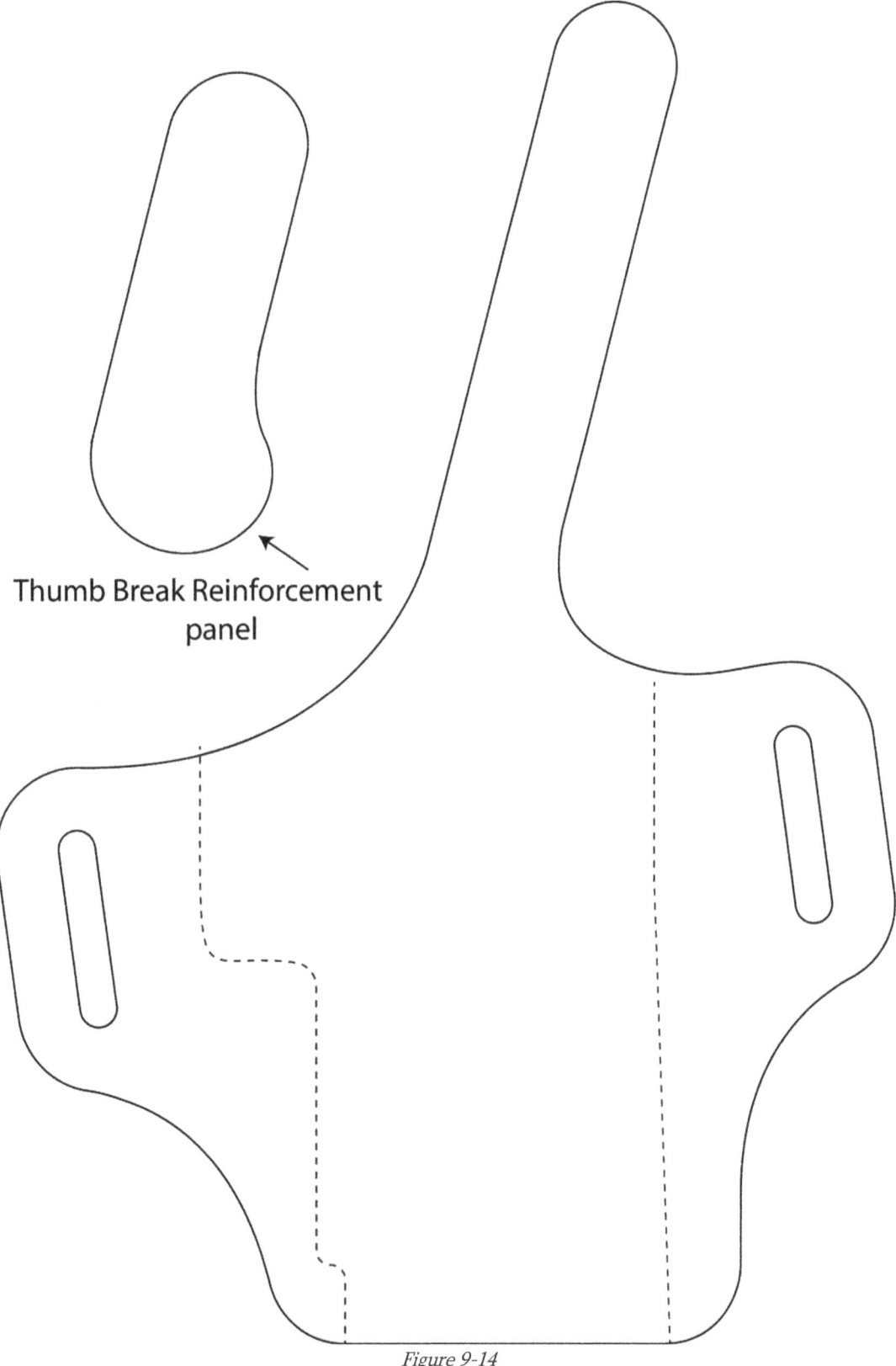

Figure 9-14

And lastly, the back panel.

Pretty sweet, right?

Your pattern won't look exactly like this one, but will be an expression of your art.

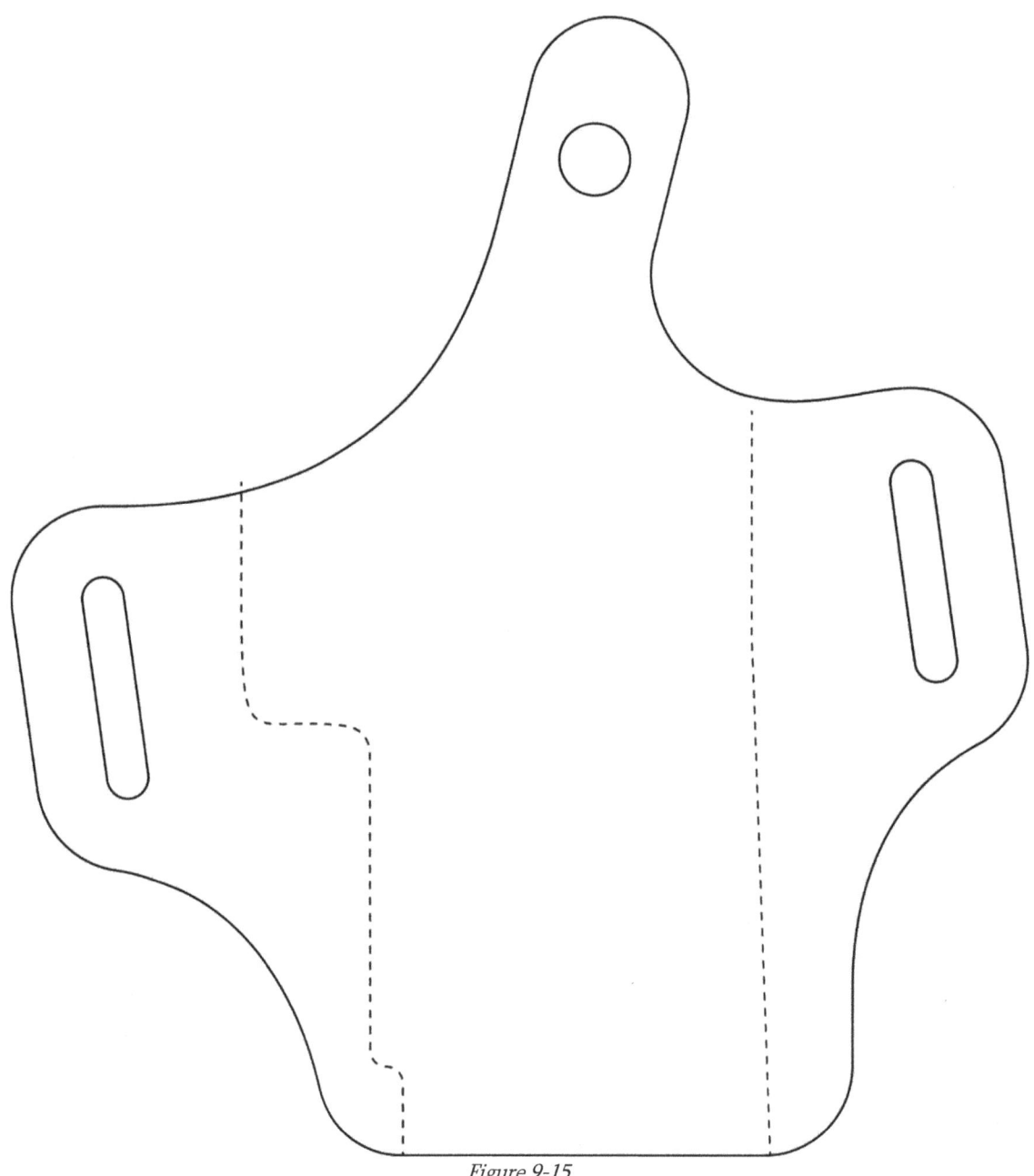

Figure 9-15

Chapter 10: Pattern Design – SnapCake Holster

Now for something completely different! SnapCakes!
This holster design is an awesome addition to your design library.

Let's take a look at some of the issues people have with wearing a holster daily.

Issues	Solutions
1. I have to unbuckle my belt to don/remove the holster.	a. The SnapCake can be placed and removed without unbuckling the belt.
2. Left-handed shooters have to just about remove their belt to place or remove the holster.	b. Same as above!

The SnapCake is another pancake design with the added feature of not having to remove the belt!

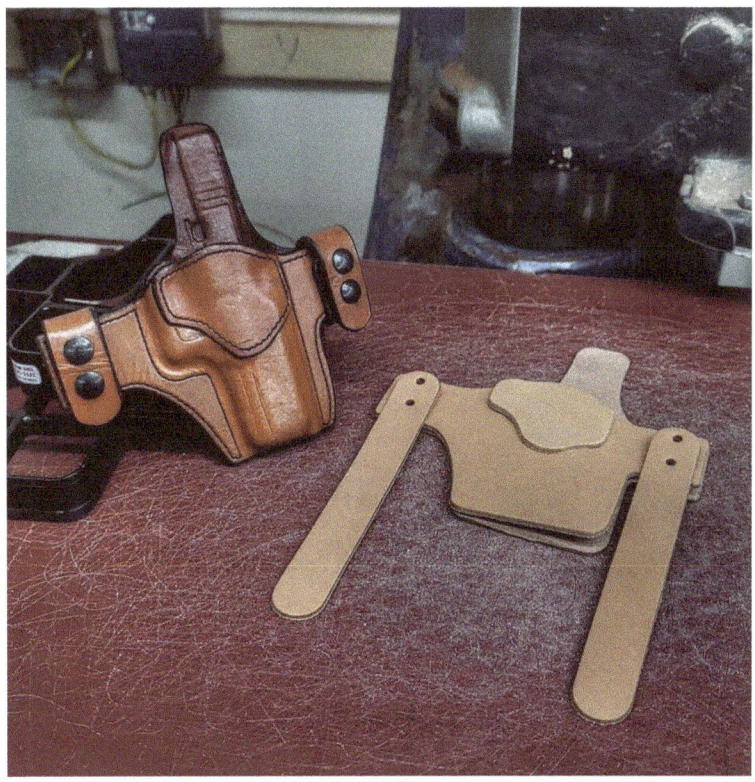

Figure 10-1

Let's get started designing this holster.

This time we're going to start from the ground up and design for a Glock 19.

We'll do this by the numbers, step-by-step. Refer to earlier chapters if you need to.

Grab your paper and draw your vertical line. Then place your firearm on the line and trace it out.

Remember: All parts of your pattern refer back to this tracing, so be as accurate as possible.

Figure 10-2

Let's place our G19 and get an accurate trace.
Remember to mark the ejection port, face of trigger, and mag release.

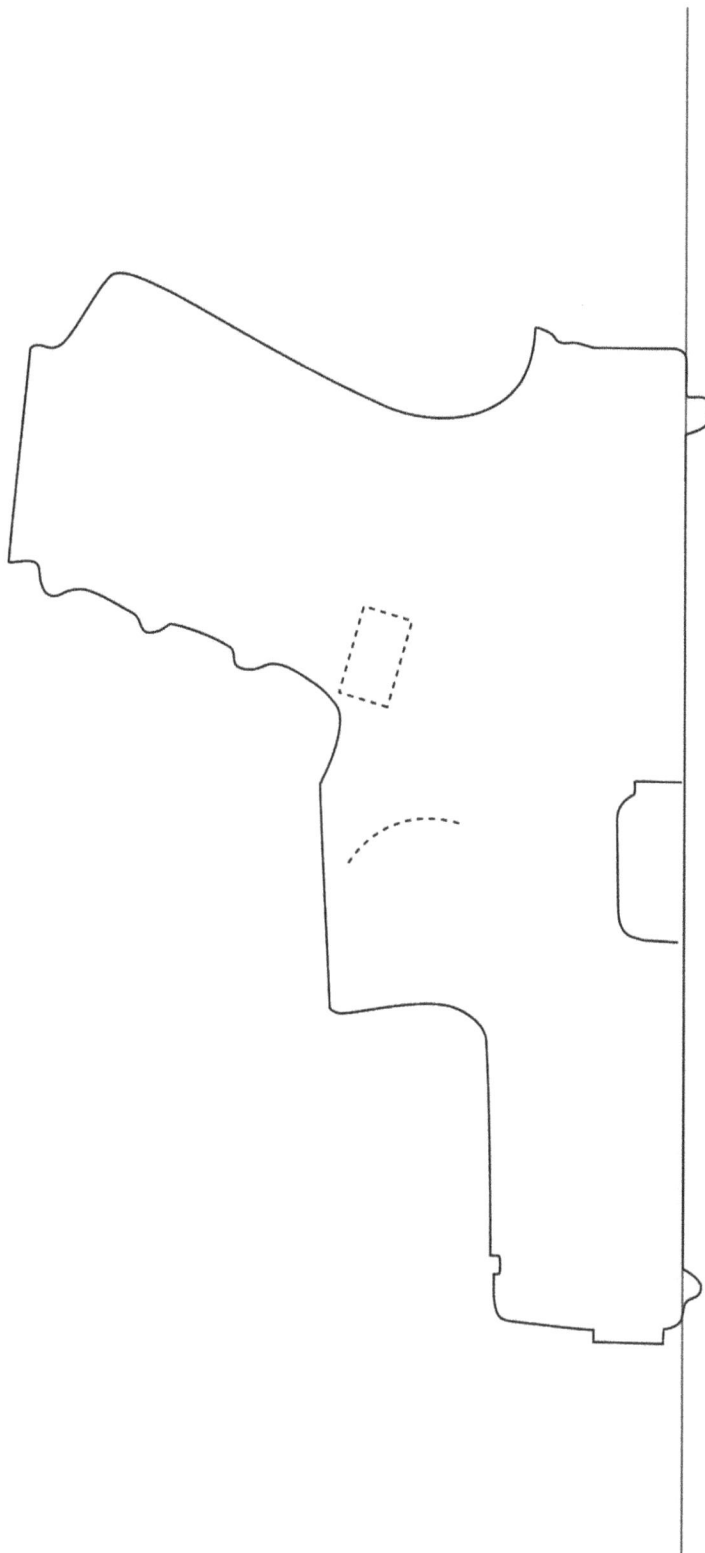

Figure 10-3

Now, let's give ourselves a grip relief of one-inch (1").

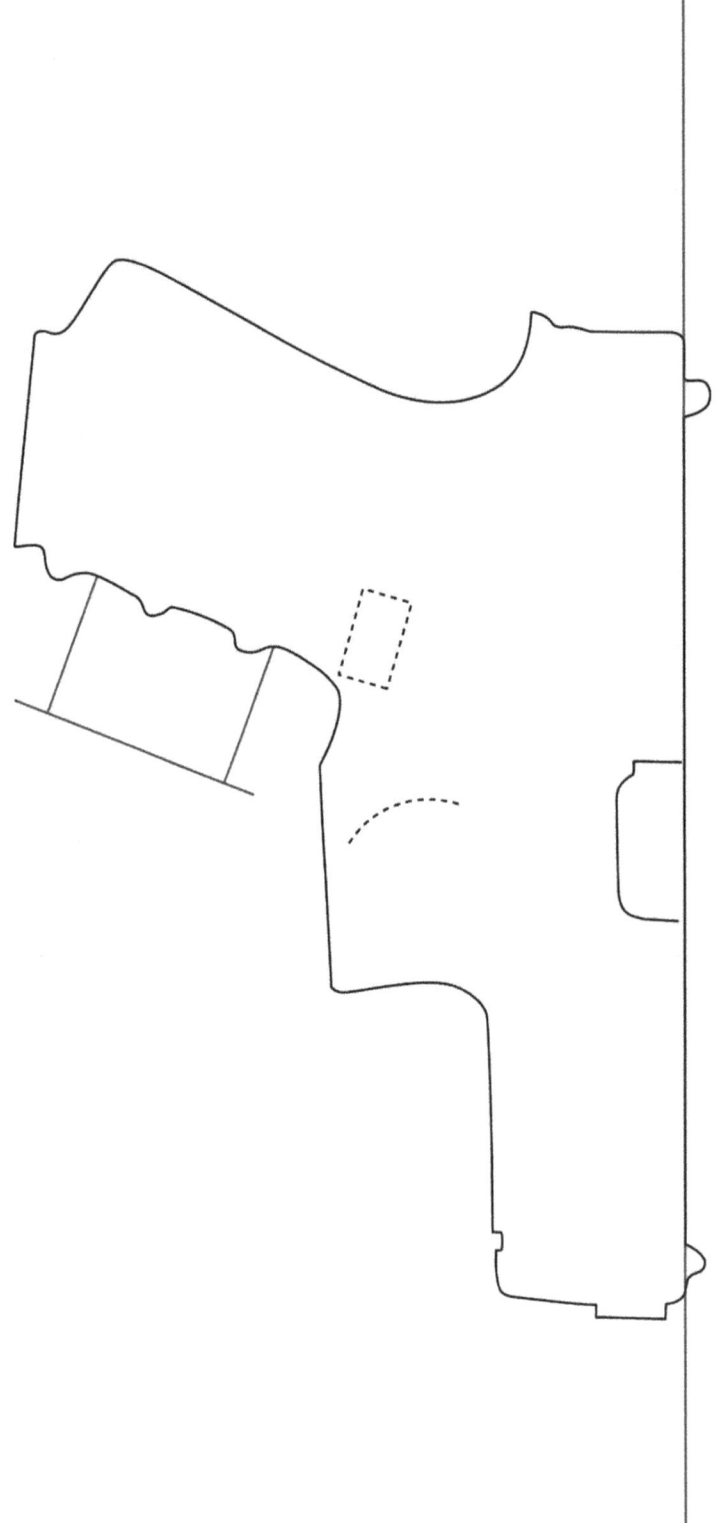

Figure 10-4

Time to measure the firearm and do some math.
Don't forget to refer to Chapter 2 if this gets a little confusing.

Measure (m)   **Math**

Measure		Math
1"	**Slide**	.625
n/a	**Dust Cover**	n/a
.83"	**Frame**	.54
.6"	**Trigger Guard**	.425

$m \div 2 + \text{(leather thickness)}$

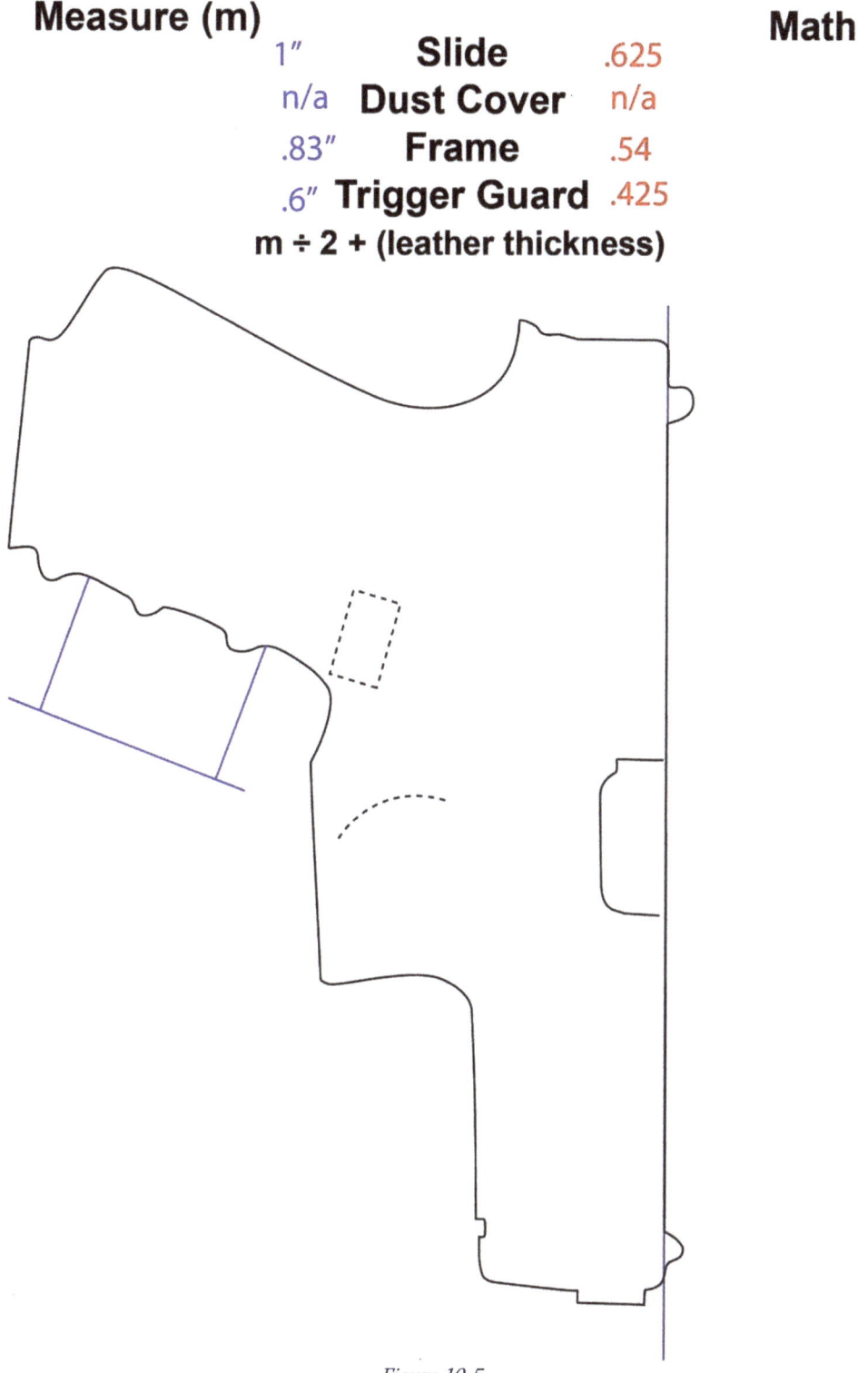

Figure 10-5

We're going to draw all of the vertical stitch lines at this point. We'll add our horizontal lines and connections in the next step.

Note: In our first pattern build, we used a Staccato P firearm and had to kick the lower slide stitch line out to accommodate the oversized front site. In this example, the G19 has a relatively normal sight height and we made no extra allowances.

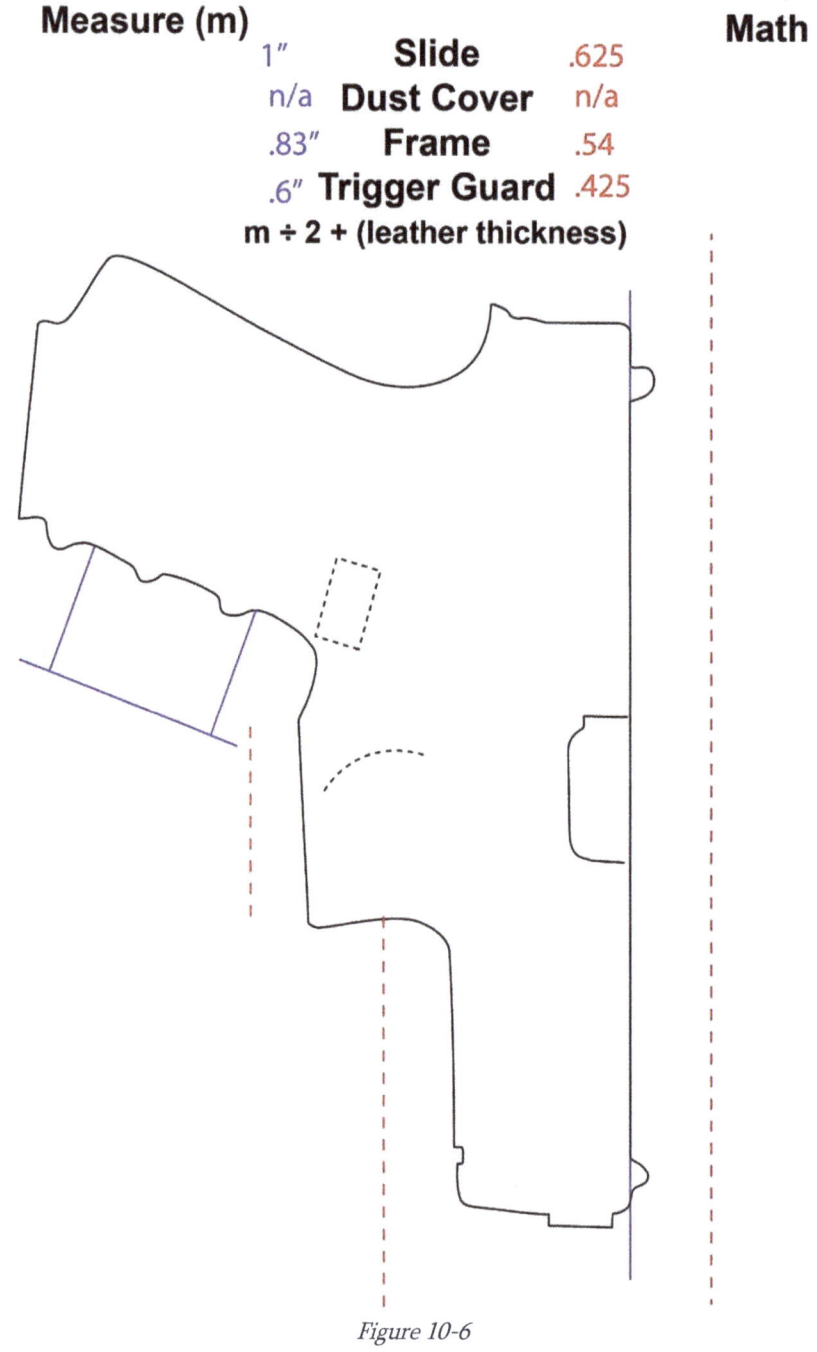

Figure 10-6

Now let's add our two horizontal lines. The first will be one-eighth-inch (1/8") below the muzzle.

And according to the math, the second will fall 0.425" below our trigger guard.

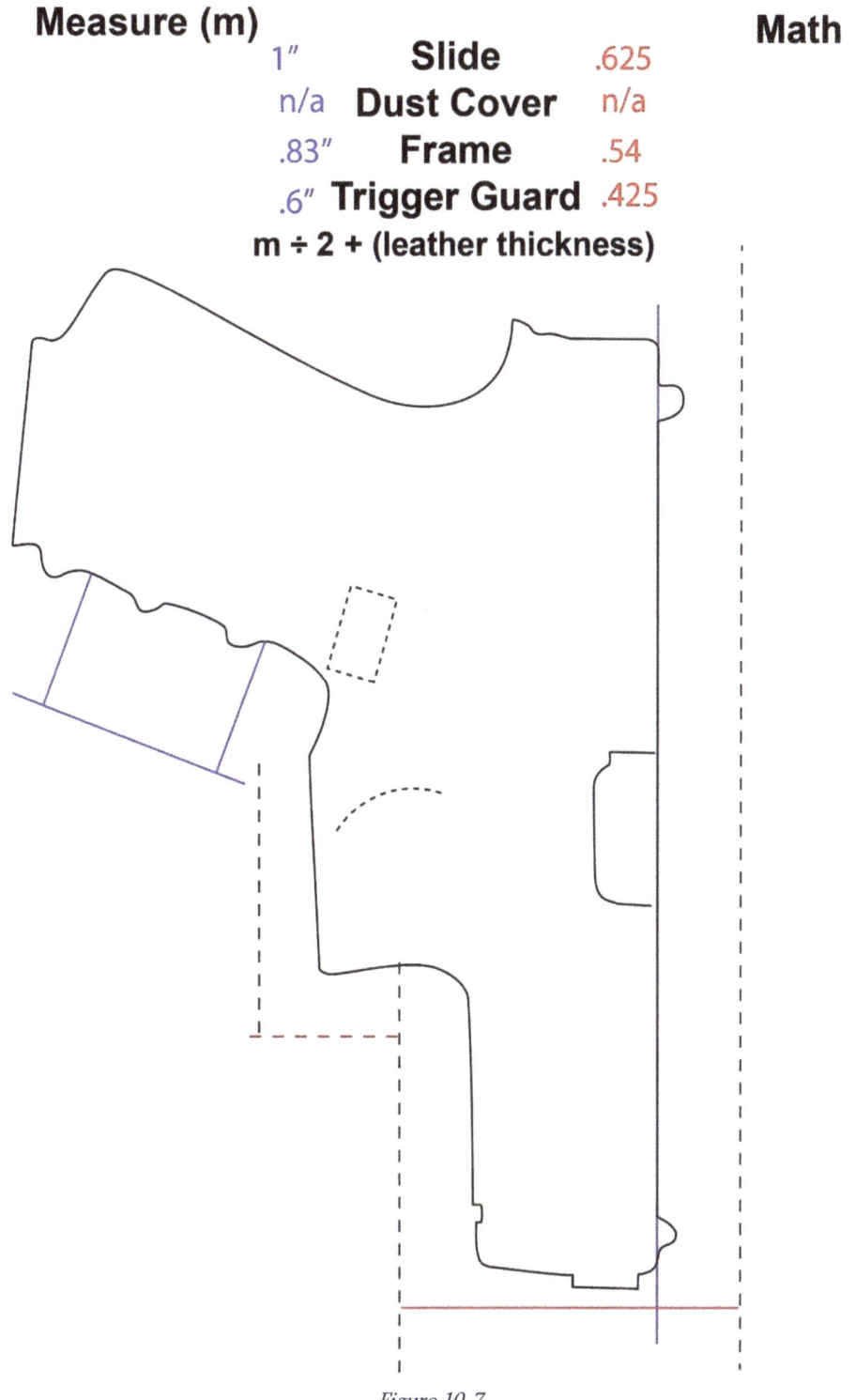

Figure 10-7

Grab your dime and let's radius our connections around that trigger guard.

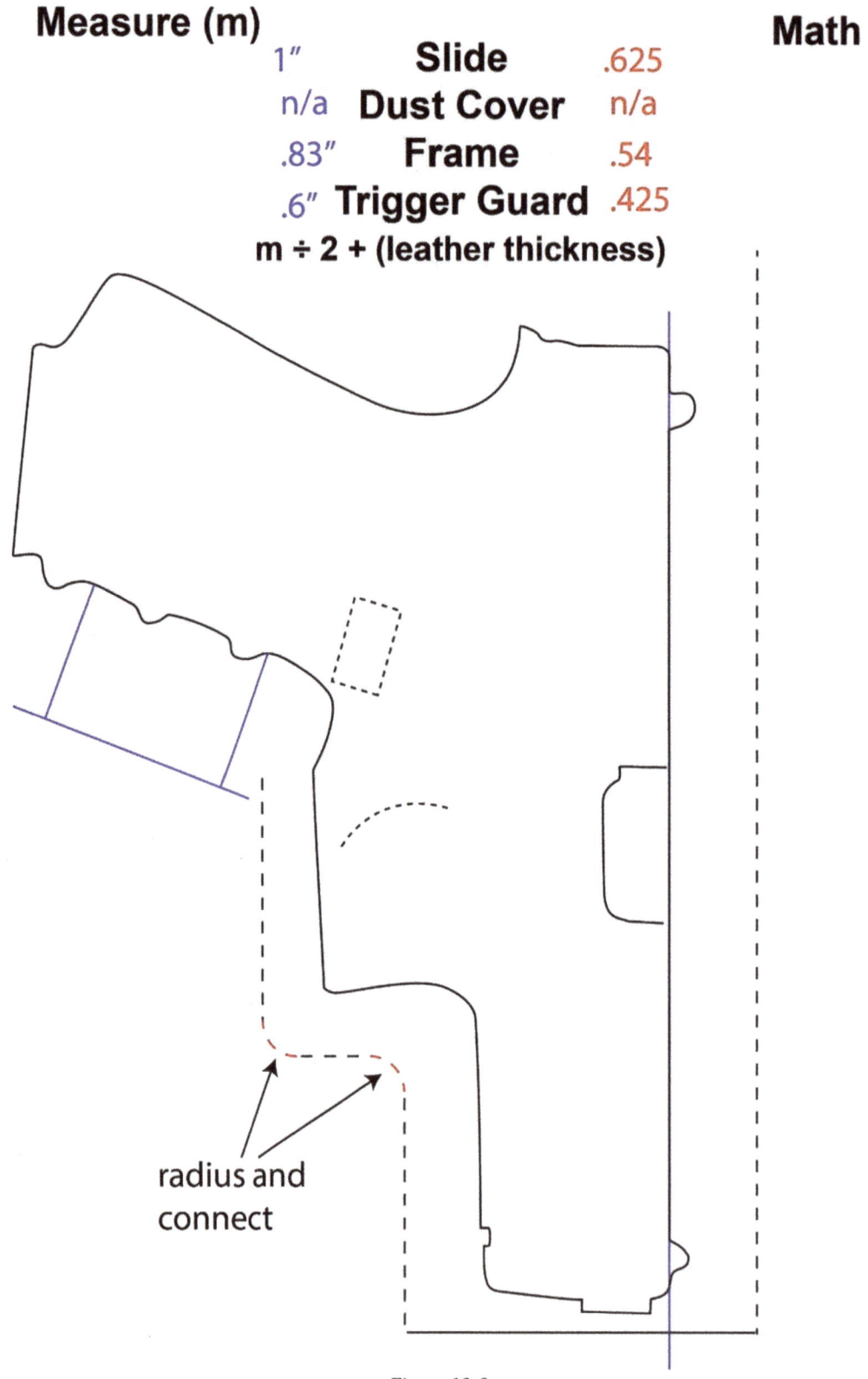

Figure 10-8

Stitch line complete! Awesome!

Now we need to lay in the attachment points for our straps.

We'll use the belt strap template.

The smaller circle represents a three-sixteenth-inch (3/16") hole you'll punch for the post of the T-Nut to ride in.

The larger circle represents the base of the T-Nut and will ensure you leave room to sew the holster together without breaking a needle.

The T-nut will be placed between the front and the back panels of the holster, with the post and spikes pointing towards the front.

We'll go into more detail on using and setting a T-Nut in the Construction portion of this book.

The reason we're using a T-Nut here is because when the snap eventually wears out, or the strap itself is somehow damaged, we're able to easily unscrew the strap from the holster and replace it with a brand new strap.

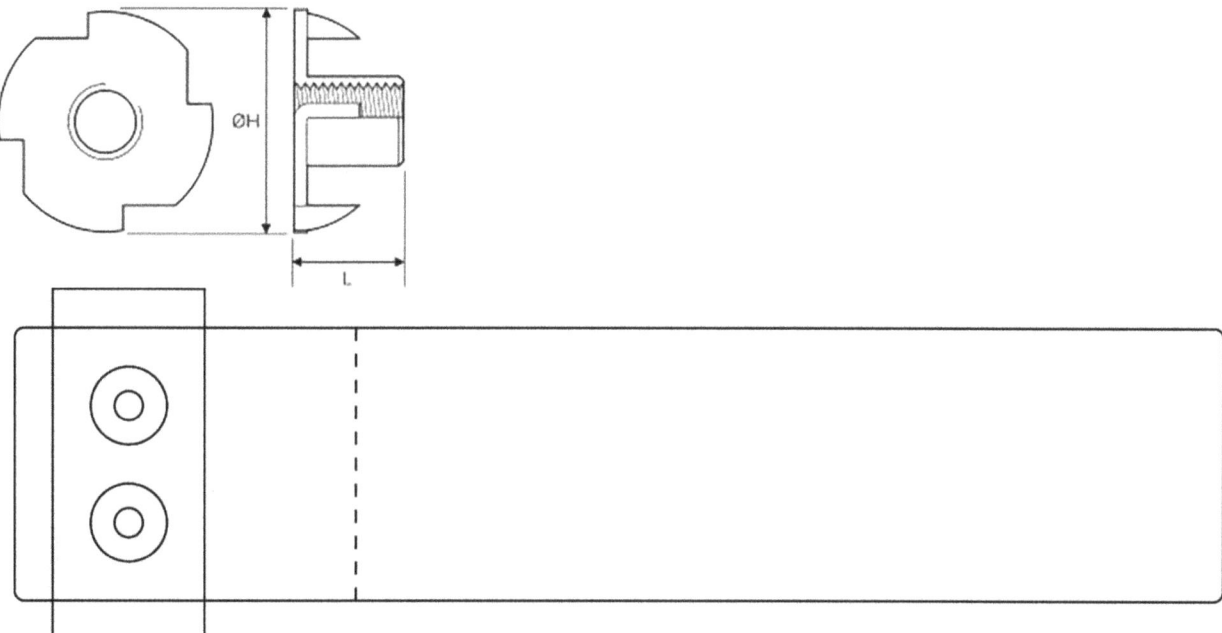

Figure 10-9

Let's add the trigger guard strap placement to the stitchline.

Please note, we've given the strap room to fold over the wing and remain outside the grip relief.

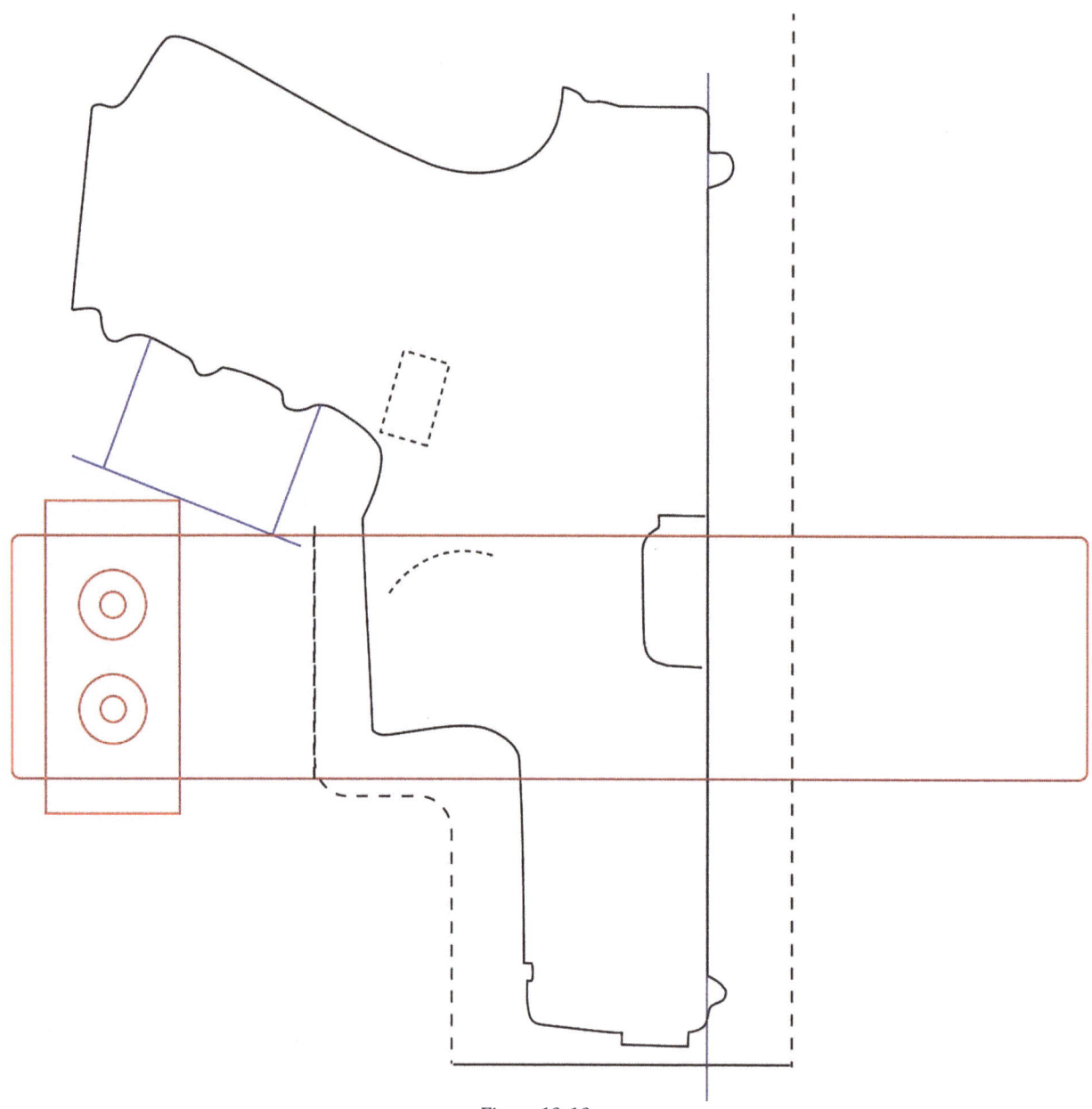

Figure 10-10

Let's place the slide side strap template and get it traced.

Notice the wings extend one-eighth-inch (1/8") past the edge of the strap. This will keep the strap from rolling over the side of the wing.

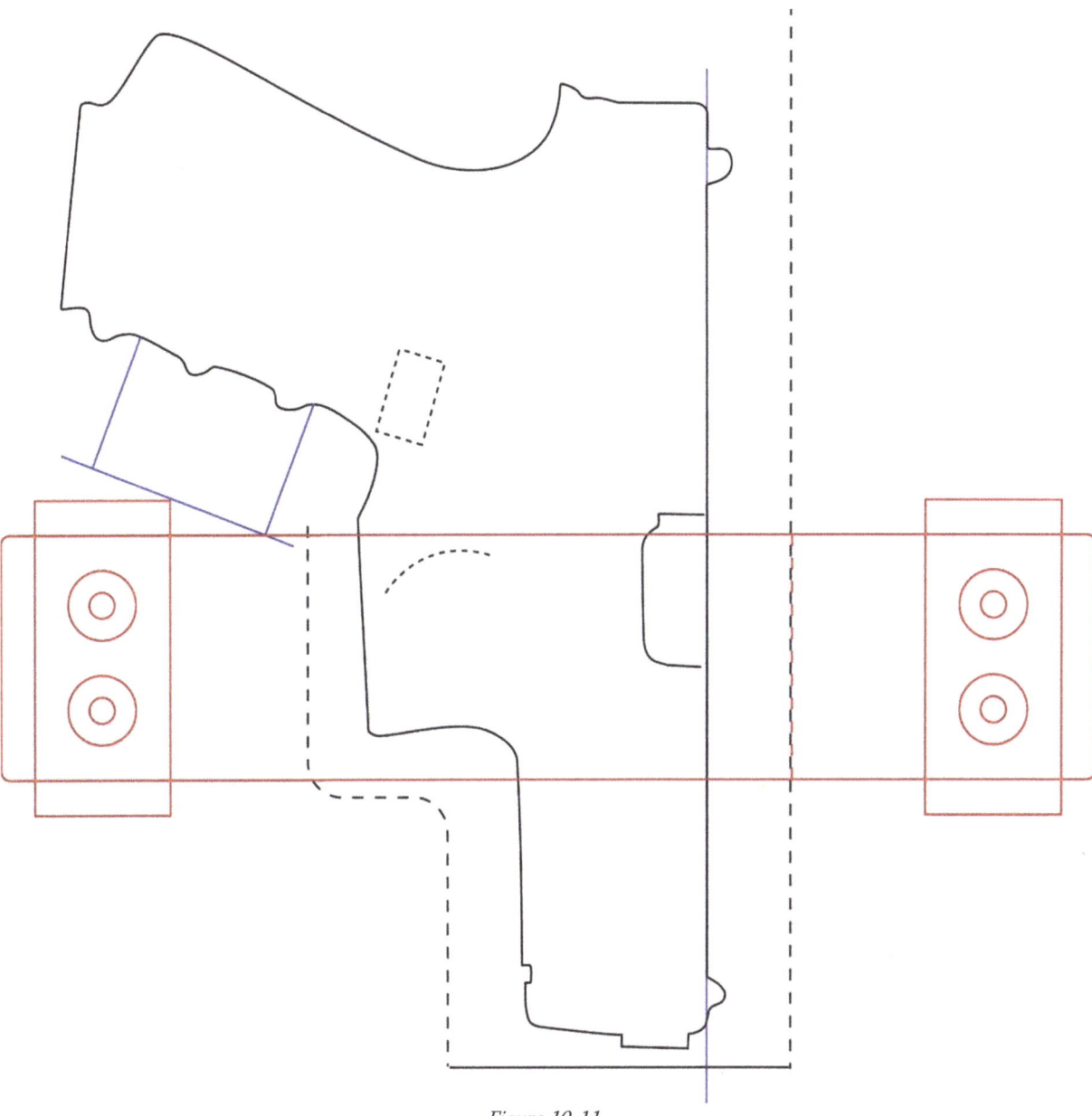

Figure 10-11

Chapter 10: Pattern Design – SnapCake Holster

Time to get the French Curve out again.

We're going to draw the bottom of the holster. This time we'll be using the one-inch (1") radius from the muzzle end, then bring the shape up with the French curve.

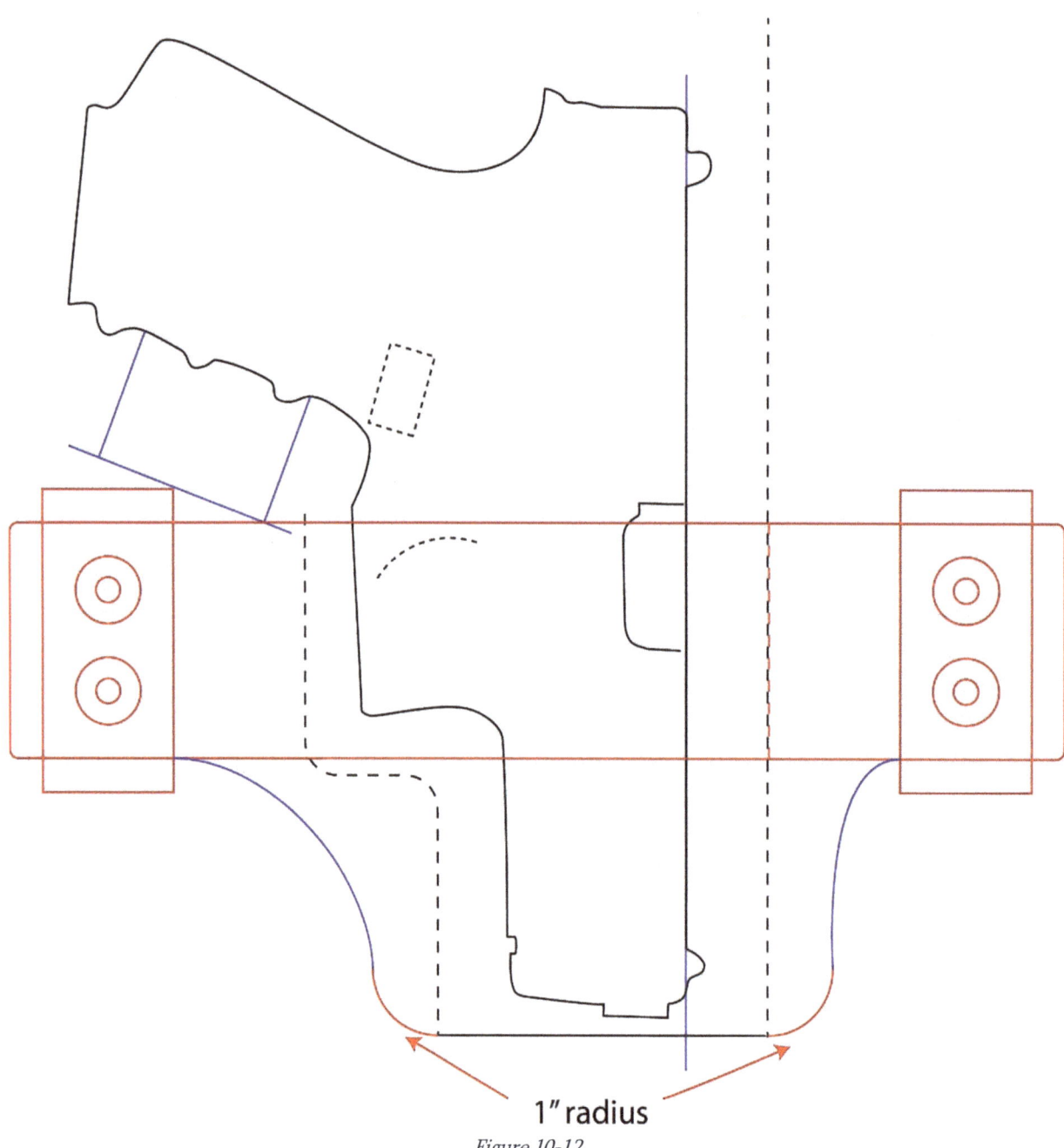

1" radius

Figure 10-12

Just as we did on our 8-degree pancake holster pattern, we'll be drawing the body shield next.

Remember our Go/No-Go Zones!

First, we'll lay in a reference mark for the grip side of the body shield. Then mark a reference for the max height of the body shield.

If we have too much leather above the rear of the slide, it'll fold over the back of the firearm and create interesting problems when you try to holster the firearm.

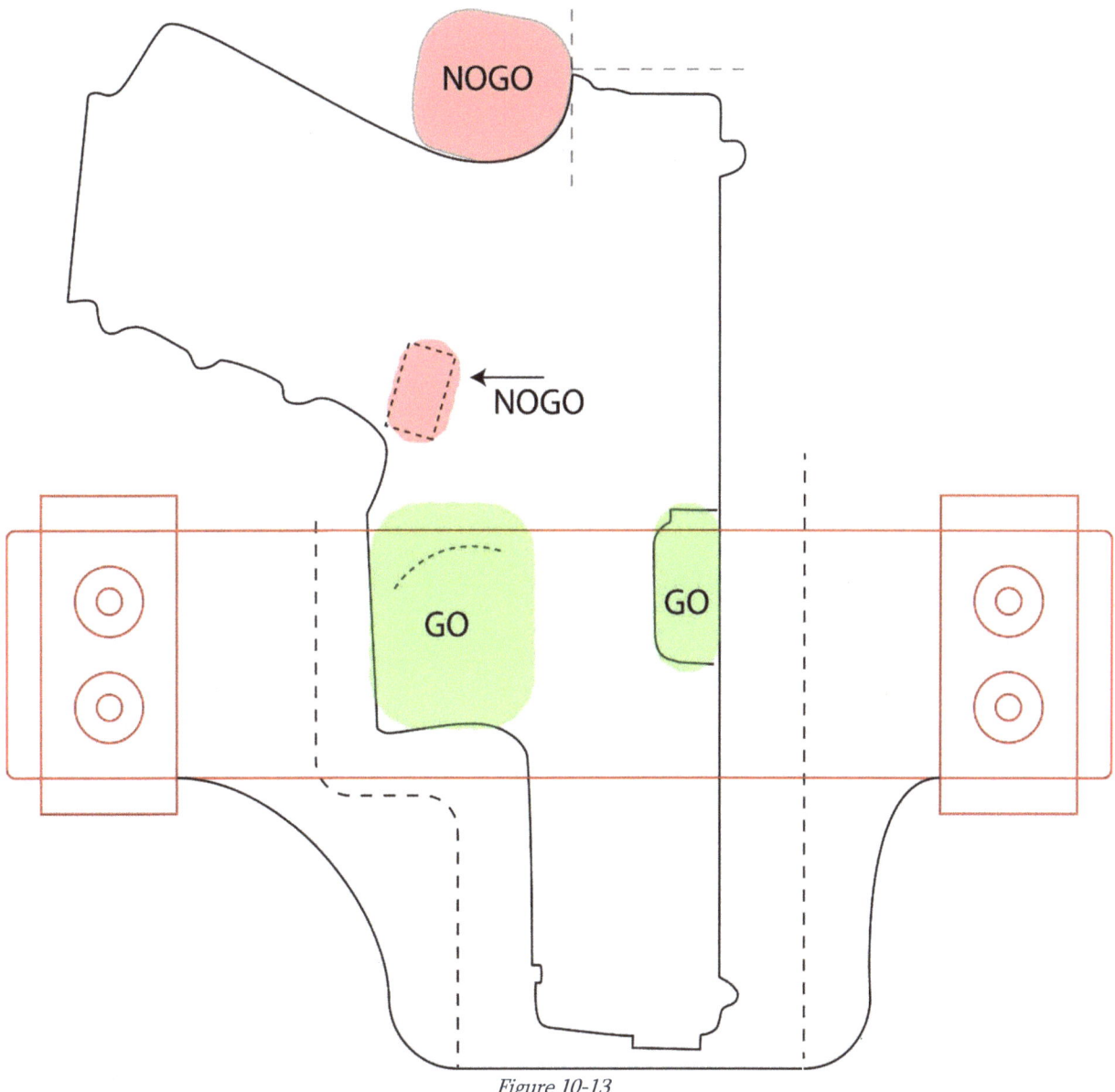

Figure 10-13

Time for Frenchy the Curve!
Let's find a radius that threads the needle of…

- Grip Clearance
- Trigger Coverage
- Mag Release Clearance
- Beaver Tail

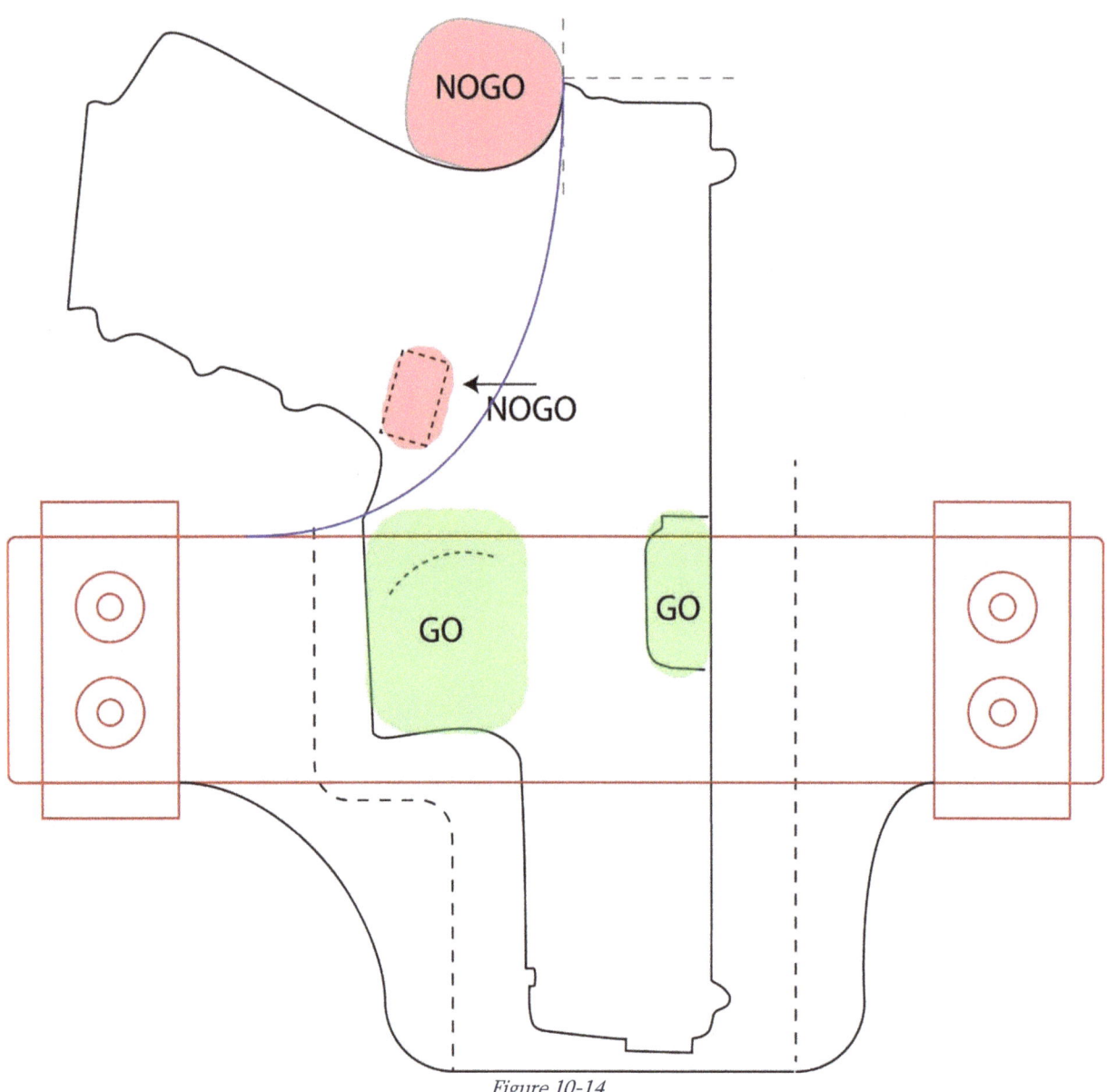

Figure 10-14

Let's use our radius card and place a three-quarter-inch (3/4") radius on both sides of the slide, and connect them across the top.

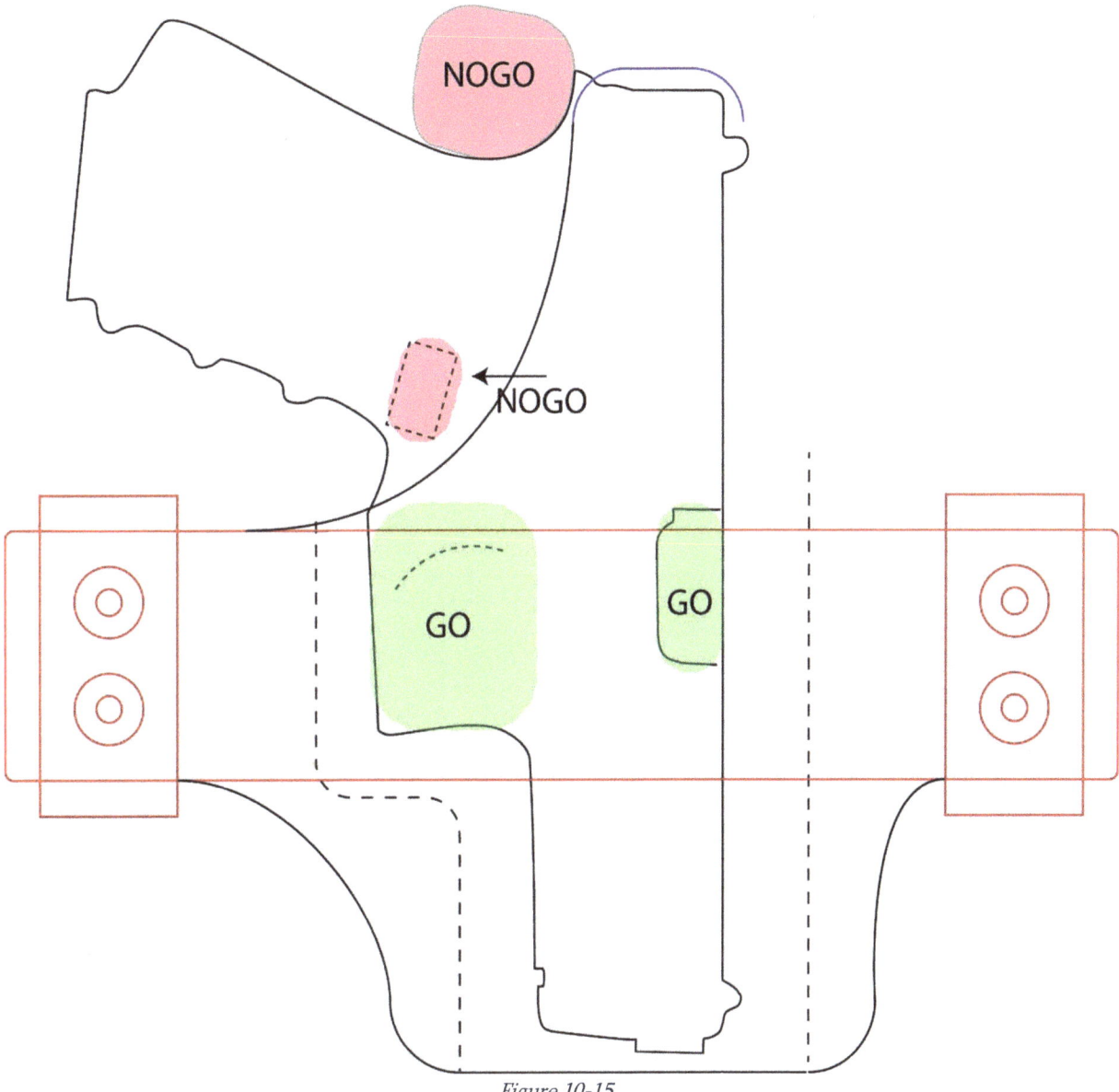

Figure 10-15

Now, let's use the French curve to lay in the slide side curve of the body shield.

Notice the radius of the curve is slightly different from the trigger guard side.

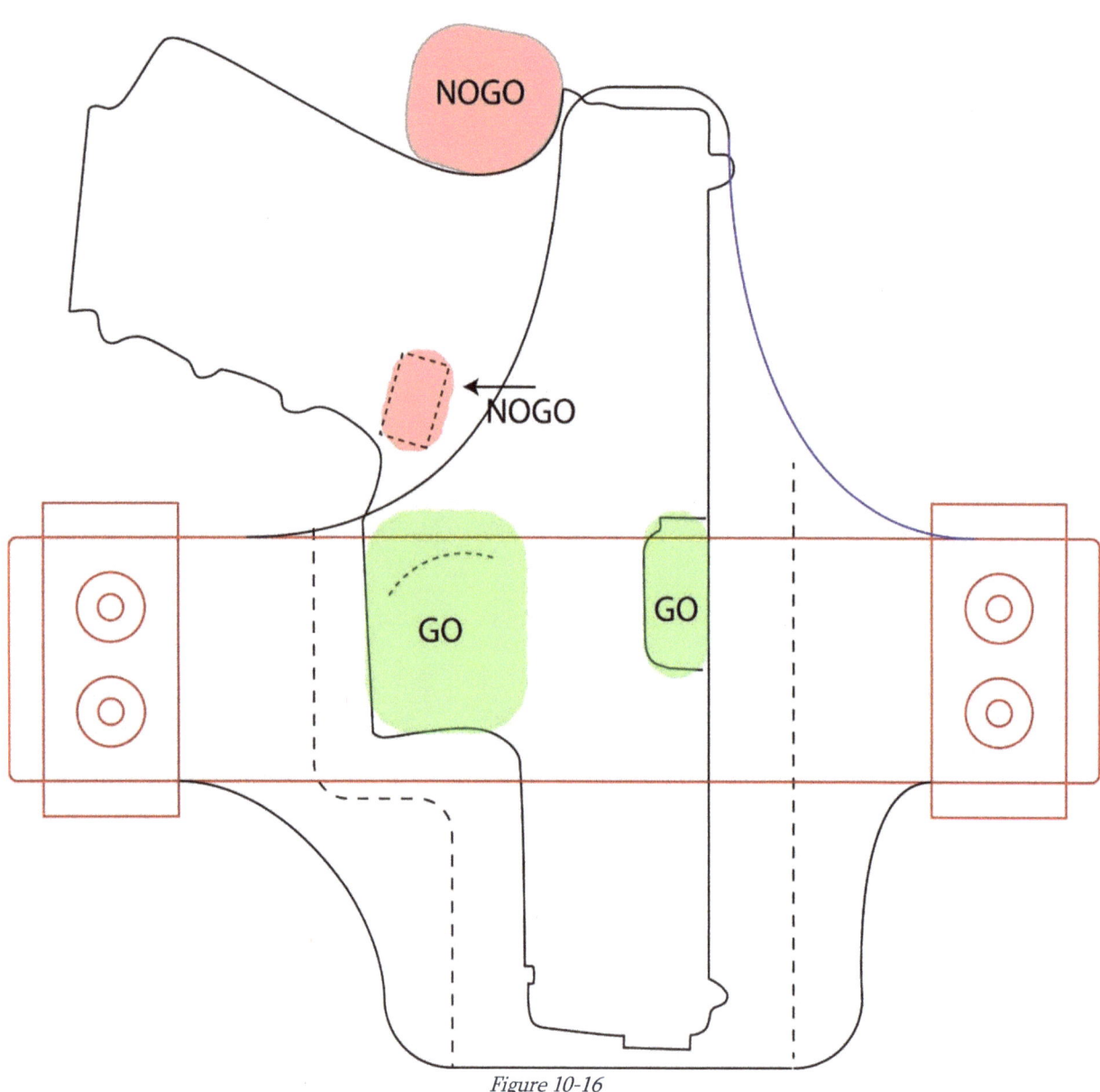

Figure 10-16

Once w clean up the pattern, you can see the back panel.
Please note the T-Nut holes will only be punched in the front panel.

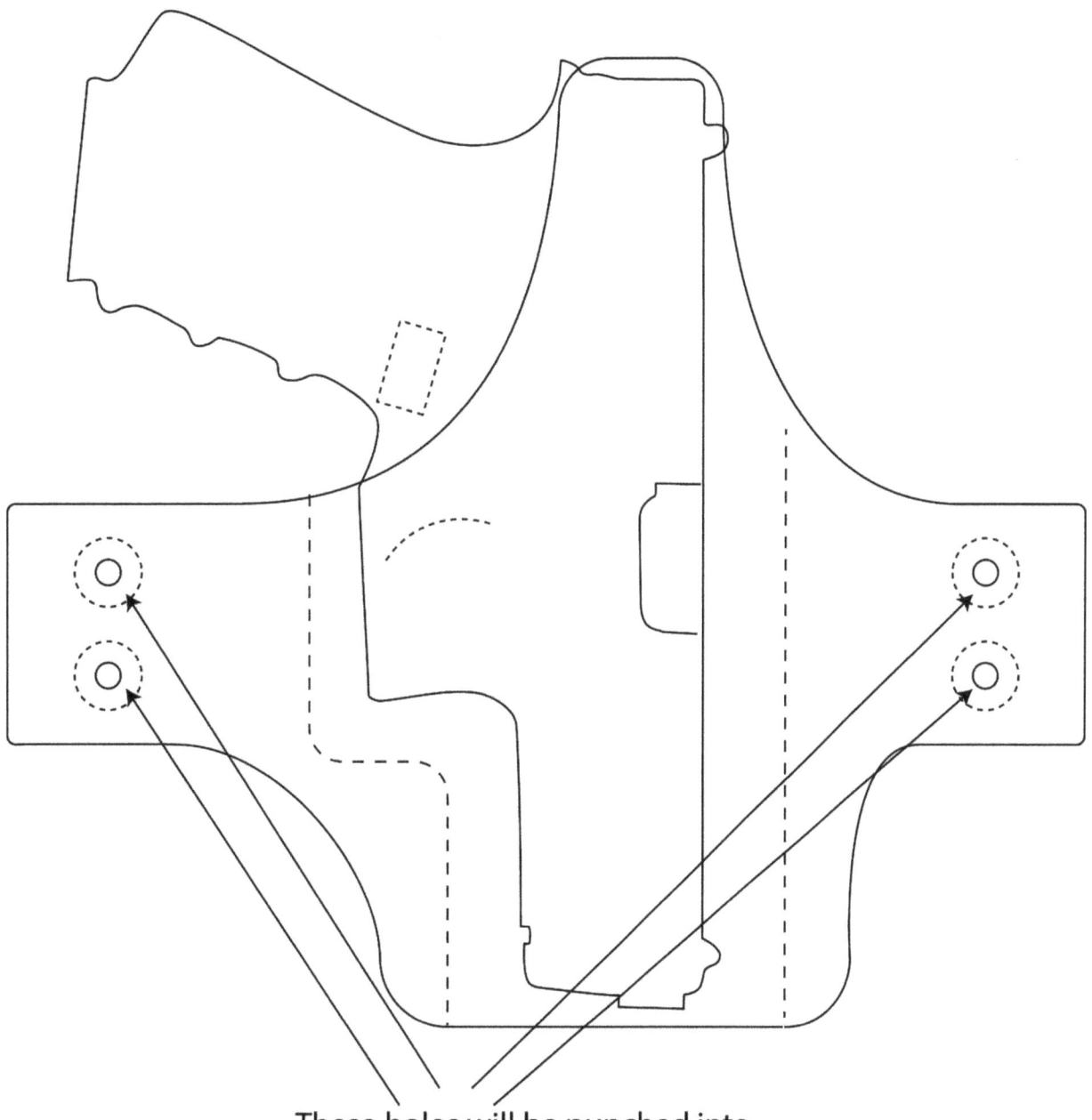

These holes will be punched into the front panel only, you will bury a T-nut between the layers

Figure 10-17

Let's grab our French curve and lay in a pleasing throat shape on the pattern. This'll be the front panel of the pattern.

We have kept the throat less than three-eighth-inch (3/8") from the rear of the ejection port. This will leave room for an optic.

Now let's add our straps and this pattern is ready to go!

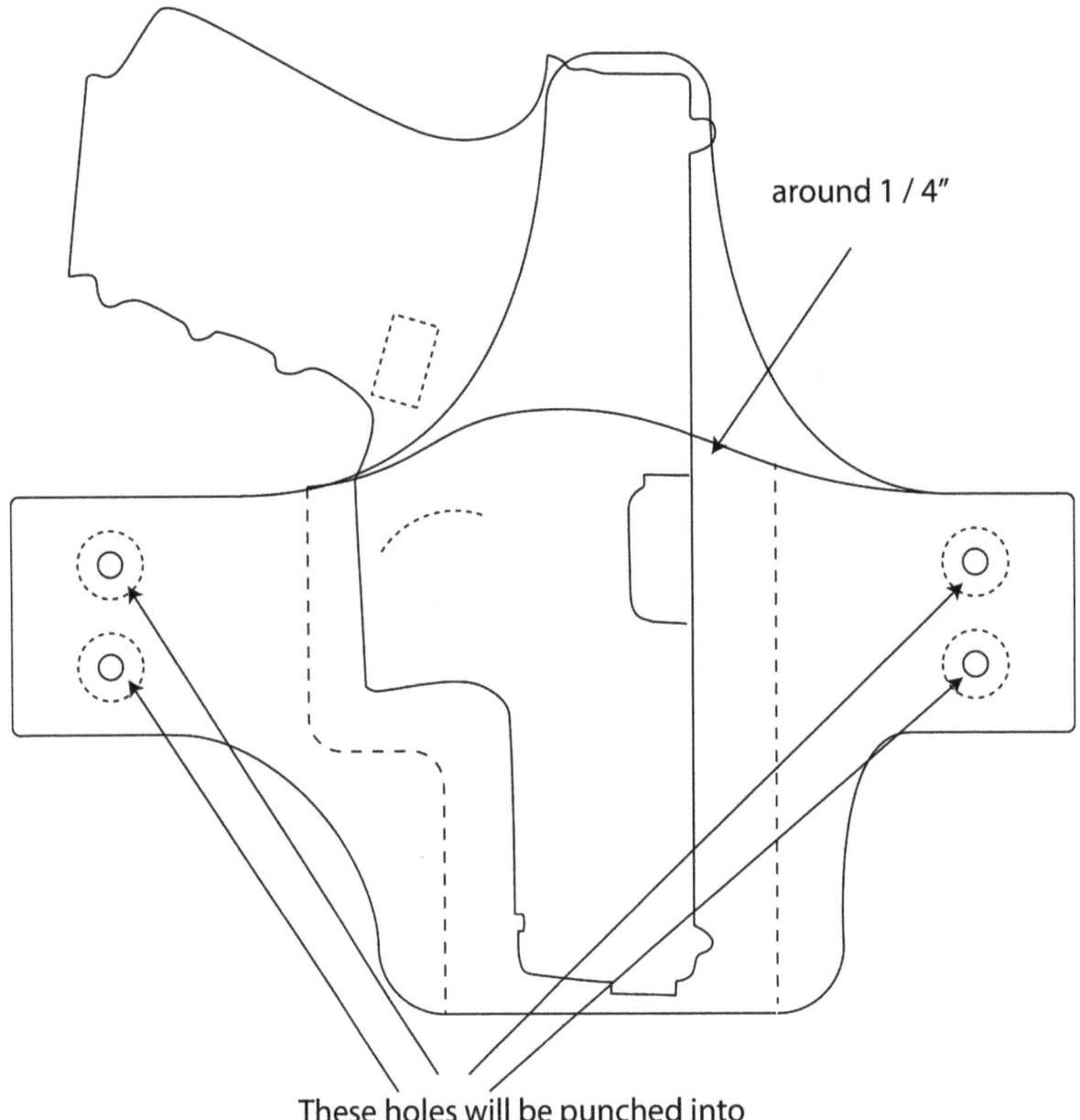

around 1/4"

These holes will be punched into the front panel only, you will bury a T-nut between the layers

Figure 10-18

Now we need a couple of straps.
I suggest cutting them long and trimming to size at the end of the build.
Let's go one and one-eighth-inch (1-1/8") wide and about eight-inches long.

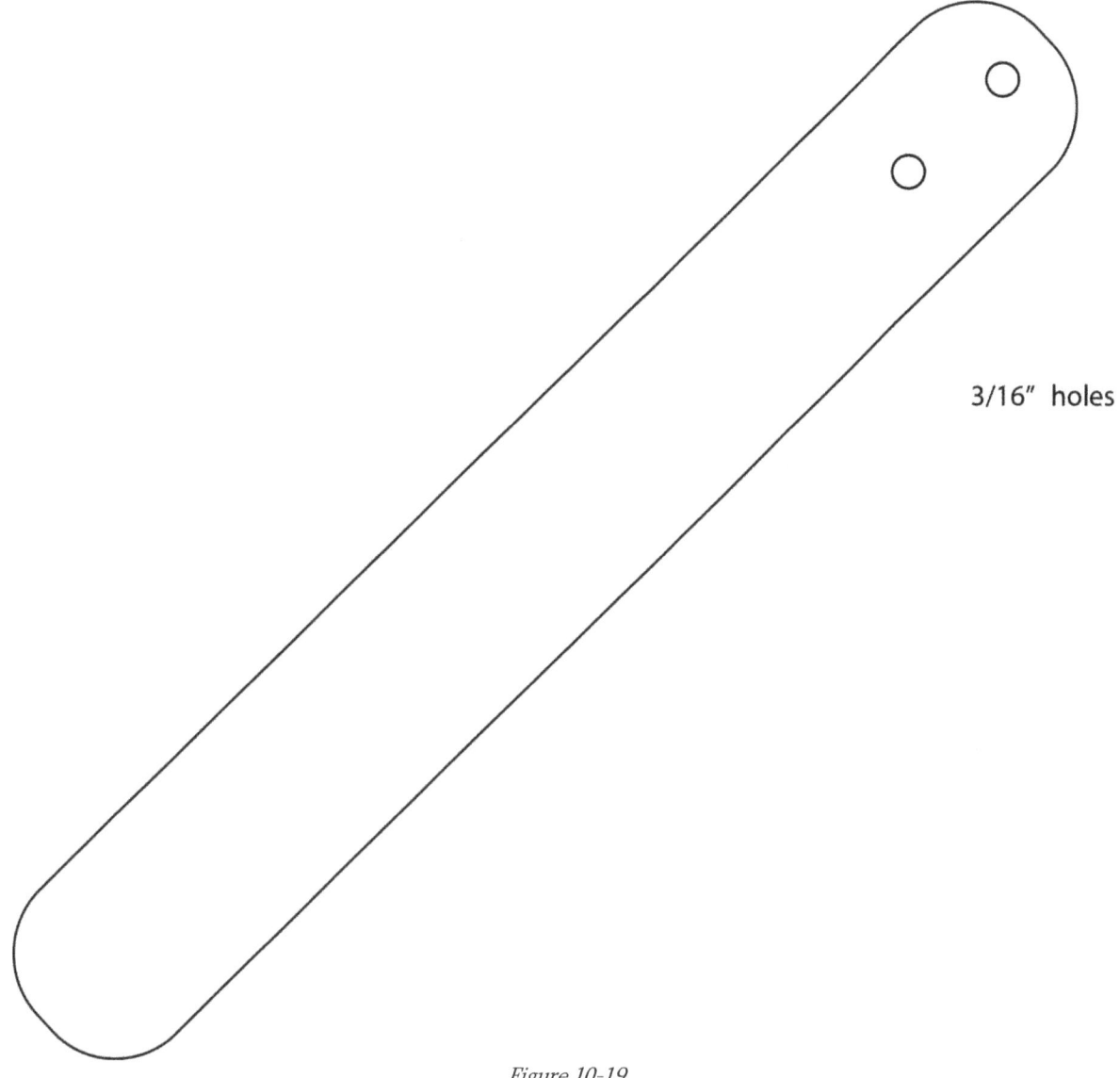

3/16" holes

Figure 10-19

WOW! You did it! This pattern is ready for build.
As before, please place both a horizontal and a vertical line with a known measurement on the page for scale. Sign and date your pattern.
This will be super helpful in the future, and will guide you in the revision process.
Also, it's kinda neat to go through your patterns after a few years and see your progress.

Section 6: Holster Construction

Lowell Harvey on Tom Threepersons

People. I'm old, everybody goes "Well, you knew Tom Threepersons."

Well, I didn't know Tom Threepersons. He was older. I got the chance to visit with him, and I got close enough but we weren't friends.

He was in a nursing home, a rest home, but I met him because he was in Safford, Arizona.

But we were in Buckhorn, New Mexico and he was from Silver City, New Mexico. He's buried in Silver City. They had his funeral there.

It's not the Shriners, but one of the Shriner types of deals. They have a cemetery there in Silver City and that's where he's buried.

I got a chance to visit, and I knew Ray Freeman. Him and Ray were good friends. That's how I met him.

Ray was also border patrol and would go over to visit. So I got a chance to visit with him and talk guns and holsters.

I'd just got out of the army in '69, and I think he died in '69, so he was in pretty bad shape.

I got the chance because I knew Arlo, the fastest gun alive. We got to talking. I didn't know till then that there's two Tom Threepersons. He said there's two of them!

He's from Oklahoma, Cherokee. The other one was an athlete. I think he may have gone to the Olympics or something.

So he said "Sometimes things get overlapped because of the names! I didn't run decathlons"

Interesting man, and I got the chance to visit with him a bit and talk holster design. And since I'd worked with Arvo, it was all fast draw western. When I talked to Tom it was more 1911's.

I'm still hooked on 1911's to this day, probably because of that.

I've seen pictures of the 1911 that he carried, the one that had the trigger guard cut off. The barrel was it, set on the bend of the barrel. It had no trigger guard.

I was like damn! But he was serious business. If you ever get a chance to read the history on him, it's crazy.

He tracked the people who killed his dad from Oklahoma to Canada. That's where he started. They killed his dad in Oklahoma. I think he was opening a gate to a pasture and two people killed him over some dispute or something. And so he tracked them all the way from Oklahoma to Canada and got even with them. He then came back, joined border patrol, and was a deputy sheriff. His whole life dedicated to law enforcement.

But he had some strange ideas for pistols. He believed in being ready and being now. He didn't' believe in playing around. He carried 1911's when most people carried the old specials.

Some people go how in the hell did you know Tom Threepersons. I'm old! But like I said, I got to meet him and got to visit with him four or five times right out of the army with Ray because I was interested in holsters. But I didn't really know him.

Chapter 11: Holster Building – 8 Degree Pancake Holster

Design time is done! Now we have to build this puppy.

Grab your pattern and make a couple of photocopies.

You'll always work from photocopies. Your original is holy and should stay in a folder so you can use it again and again.

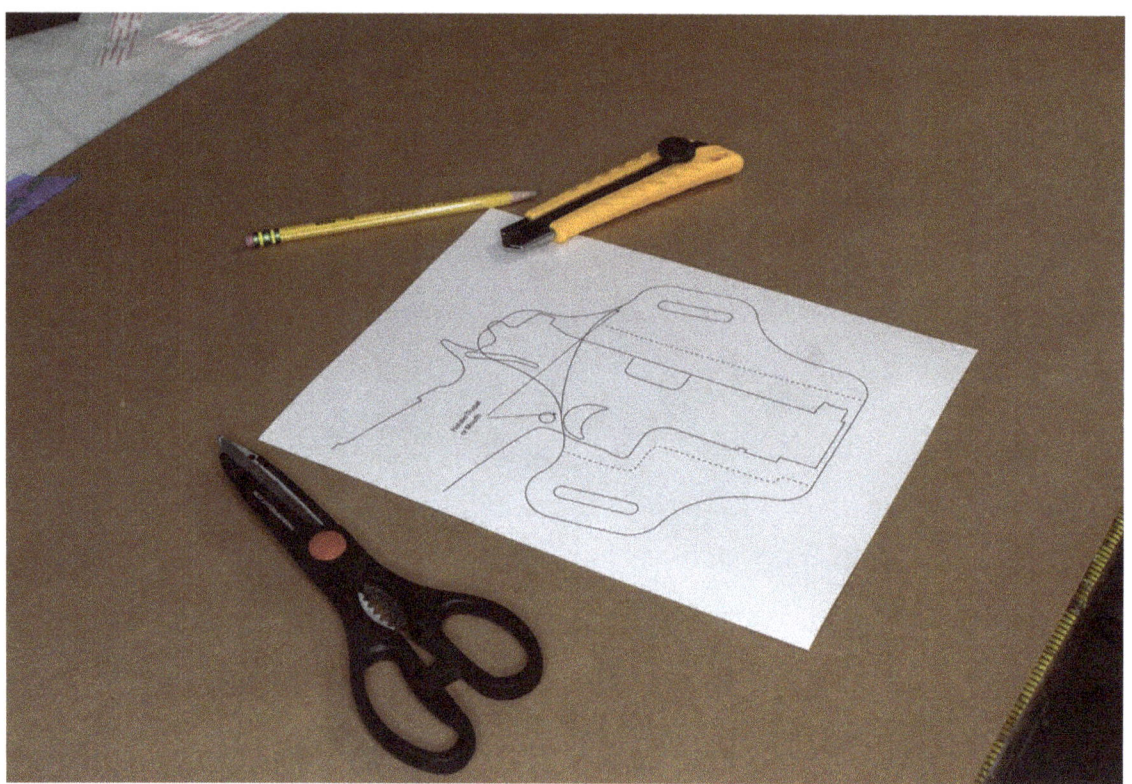
Figure 11-1

Let's take a look at your pattern. Hold it up against your belt and ensure that it's the correct hand, in this case the right-hand. Trigger guard and grip facing to the rear.

You may find that all left-handed holsters in your shop started out as right-handed for a while!

Let's cut the whole thing out and get ready to mark leather.

Figure 11-2

Now, let's write on our pattern.
RHS (Right-Hand Side) and flesh side or grain (hair) side.

Figure 11-3

Chapter 11: Holster Building – 8 Degree Pancake Holster

Mark the pattern on leather. You can use pencil or scratch awl. No ink pens!

Figure 11-4

Next, we'll cut the sweat shield off of the pattern.
What you have left will be the front panel of your rig.

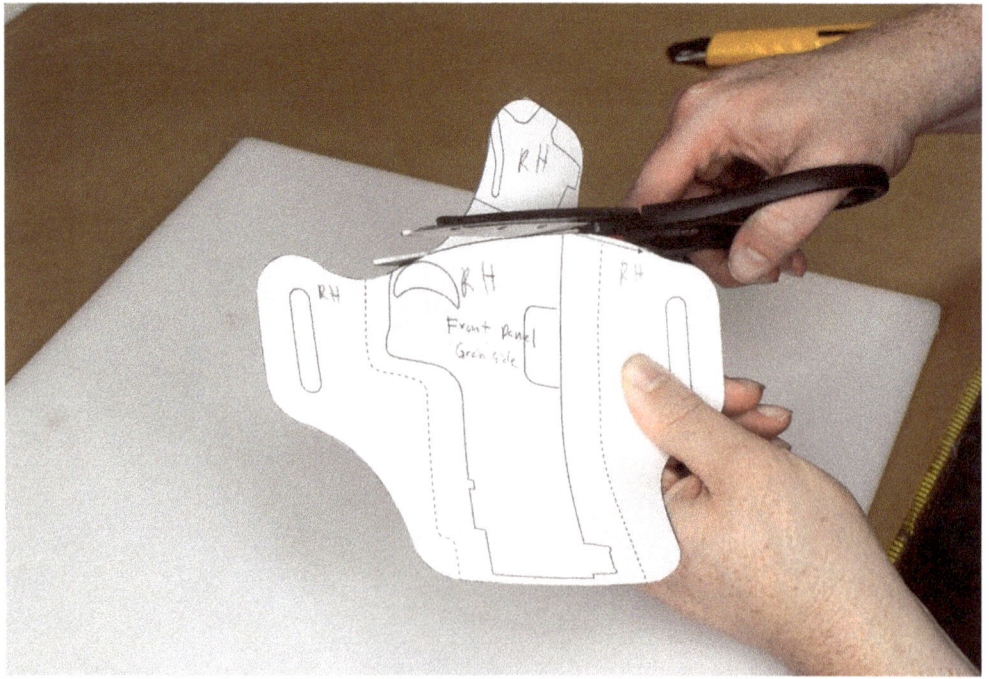

Figure 11-5

Mark the front panel onto the leather.

Figure 11-6

Now grab your favorite cutting implement and let's cut out some leather.

Figure 11-7

Now we need to chop up our pattern a little more and separate the stitch lines from the front panel.

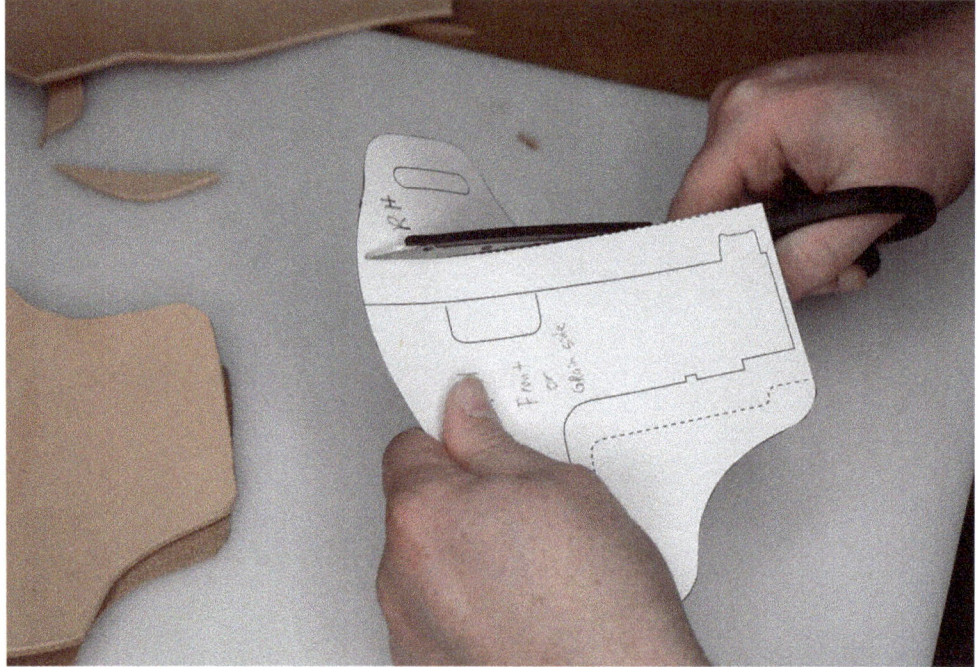

Figure 11-8

Cut both the slide side and the trigger guard side from the pattern. You'll end up with something like this.

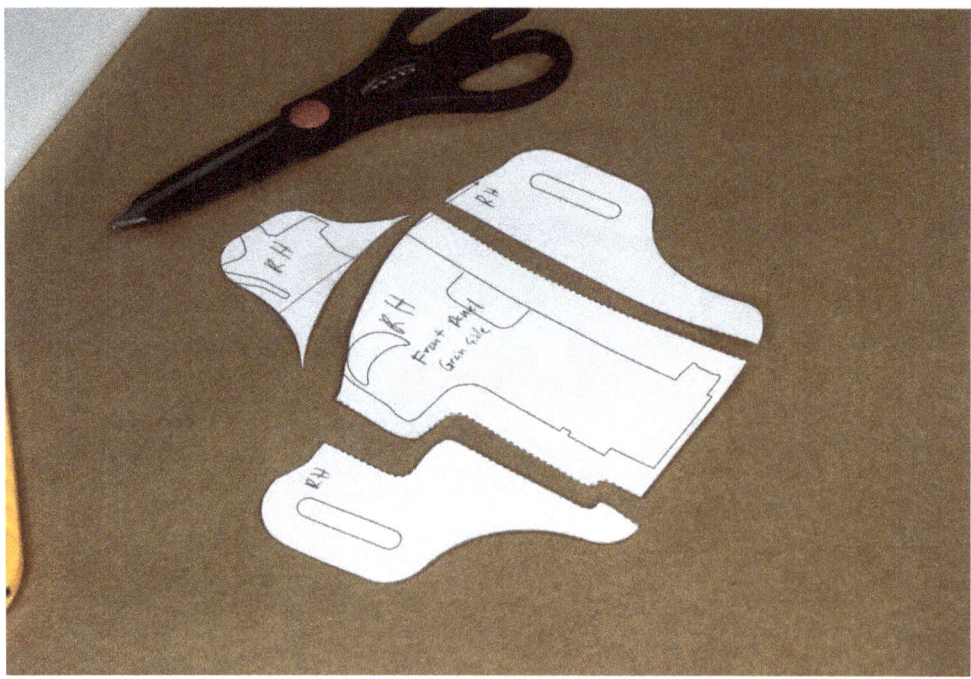

Figure 11-9

Place your stitch line stencil on the grain (hair) side of the leather and mark the top and bottom lightly with a pencil.

We'll start with the trigger guard side.

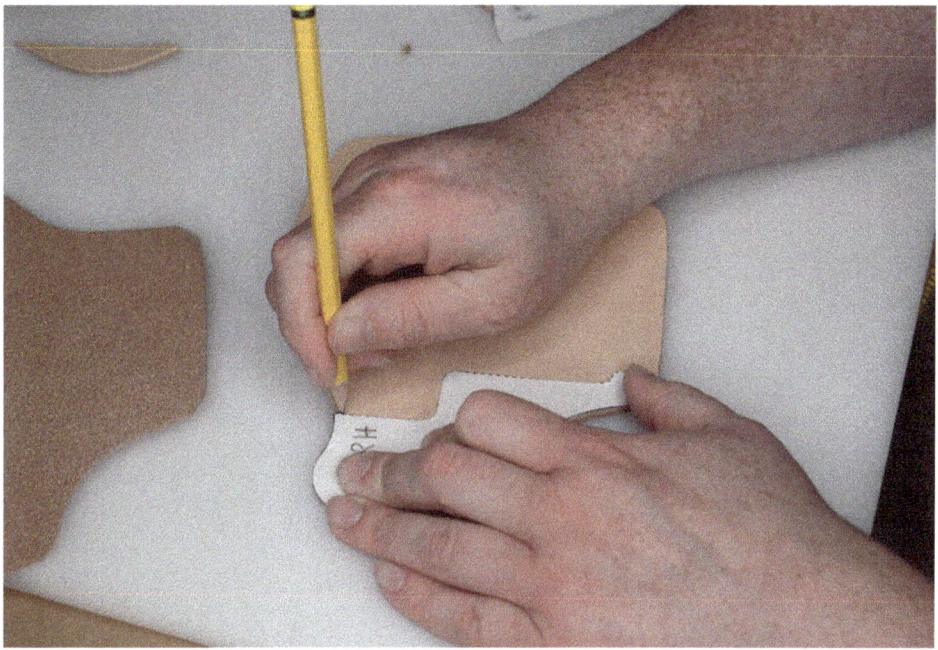

Figure 11-10

And now we mark the slide side.

Mark top and bottom. We're making tic marks, not tracing the stitch line.

Figure 11-11

These marks will serve as guides for you to do some edge beveling in places you won't be able to reach after stitching.

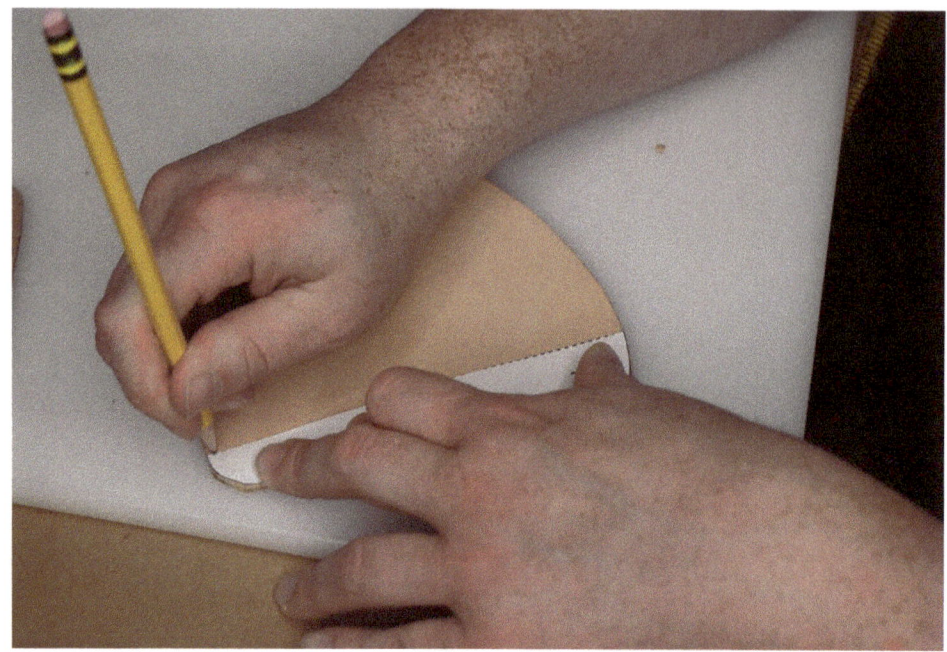

Figure 11-12

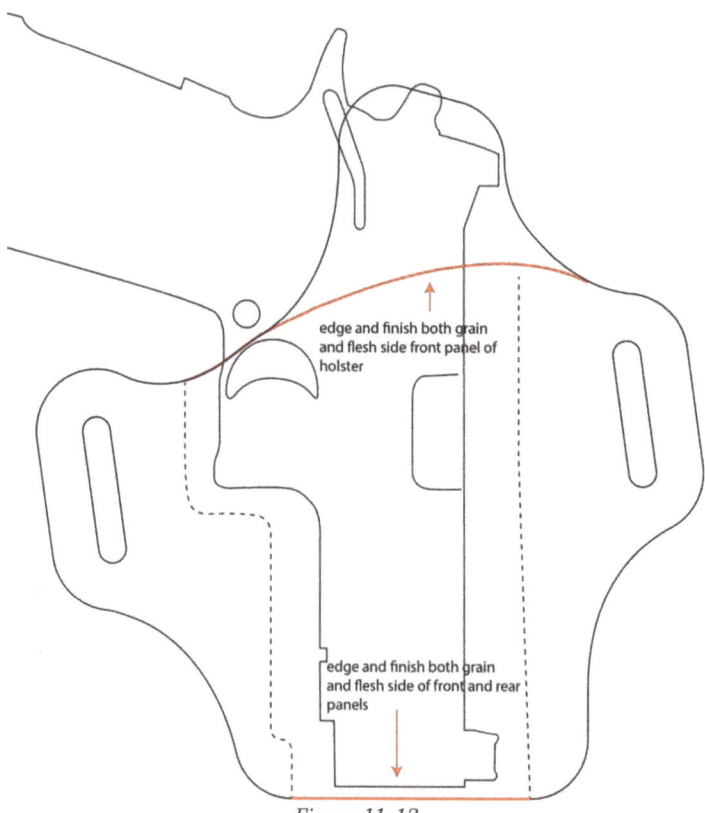

Figure 11-13

Let's edge both the grain (hair side) and the flesh side of the throat (top) of the holster. We'll be using a number 3 edger for this.

Figure 11-14

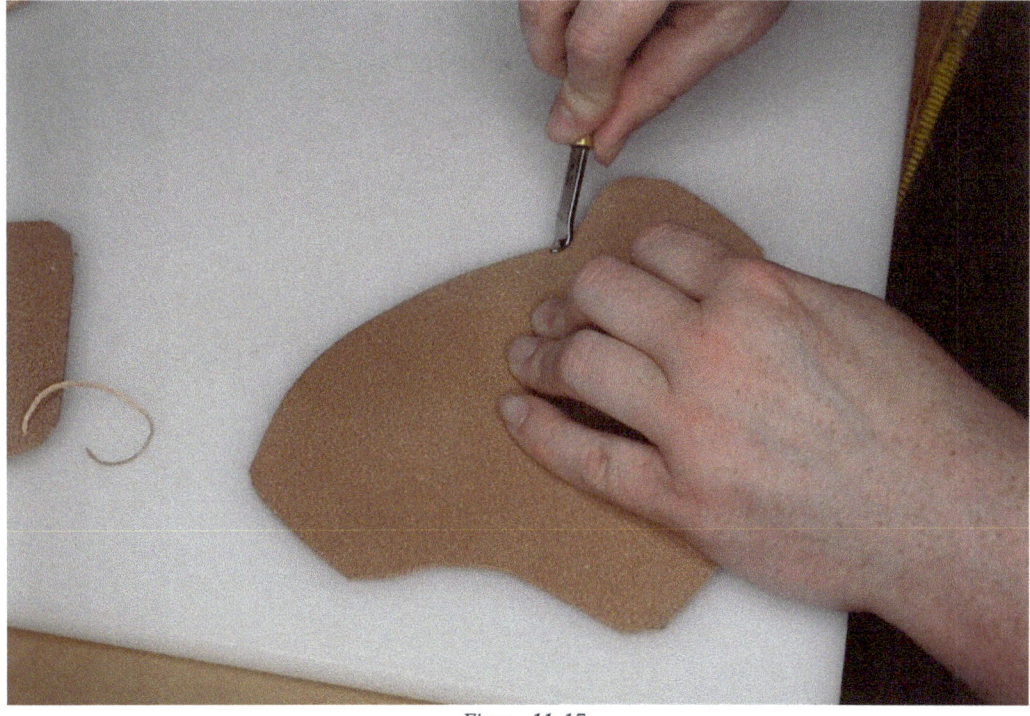
Figure 11-15

Now let's look at the bottom (foot) of the holster.

After stitching you won't be able to get to this area either.

Let's go ahead and edge bevel this as well. Be sure to do both grain (hair) side and flesh side. You'll use your pencil marks as a guide.

Figure 11-16

Figure 11-17

After edging, go ahead and burnish these areas with your hand slicker.

I don't suggest using any edging solutions at this point in the build. They may serve as a dye blocker and ruin your awesome holster.

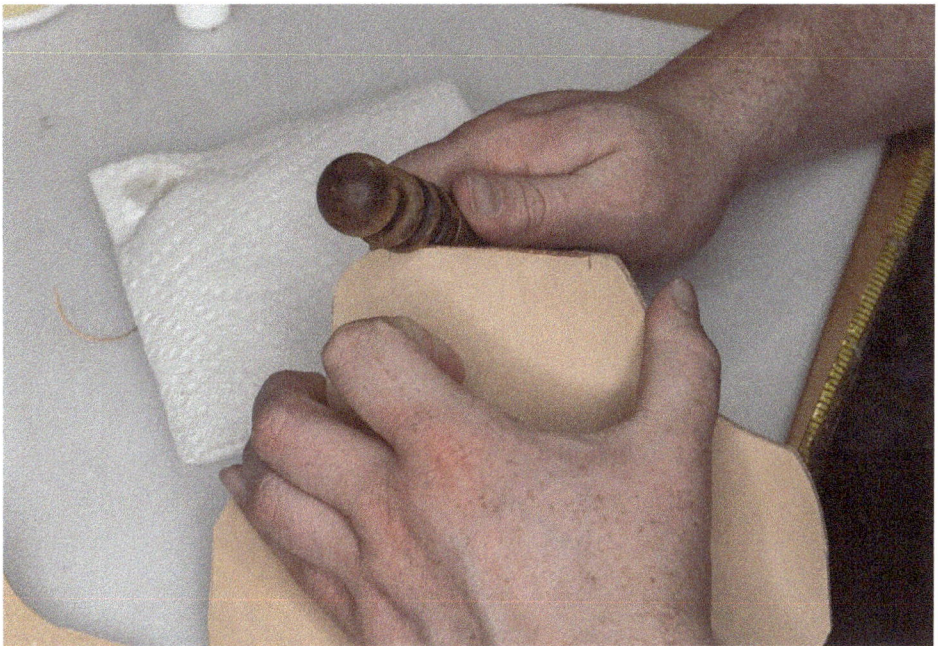
Figure 11-18

Don't forget the throat.

You'll only edge the front panel in the throat area.

Figure 11-19

There are many dyeing techniques out there. We'll be showing a couple of them in this book.

On this build we'll be pre-dyeing our panels using a dauber (large) on both grain and flesh sides.

Figure 11-20

Figure 11-21

Time for a break! Order a pizza and treat yourself to some well-deserved carbs!
We're gonna to let this dye dry for twenty-four hours.
Come back to this project tomorrow.

Welcome Back! Let's get to buffing.

There are a lot of ways to buff leather. In this example we're gonna to use a soft cotton cloth (one of Garretts old T-shirts).

Continue buffing till your cloth stays clean.

Figure 11-22

Figure 11-23

Now it's time to transfer stitch lines to the holster.

Grab the front panel cutout of your pattern and let's cut it into three pieces along the stitch lines.

Figure 11-24

Figure 11-25

Using a scratch awl, we'll trace the stitch line onto the front panel of the holster.

Please start and finish your lines one-eighth-inch (1/8") from the edge of your leather. This way you won't have unnecessary scratches in your leather above the stitch line.

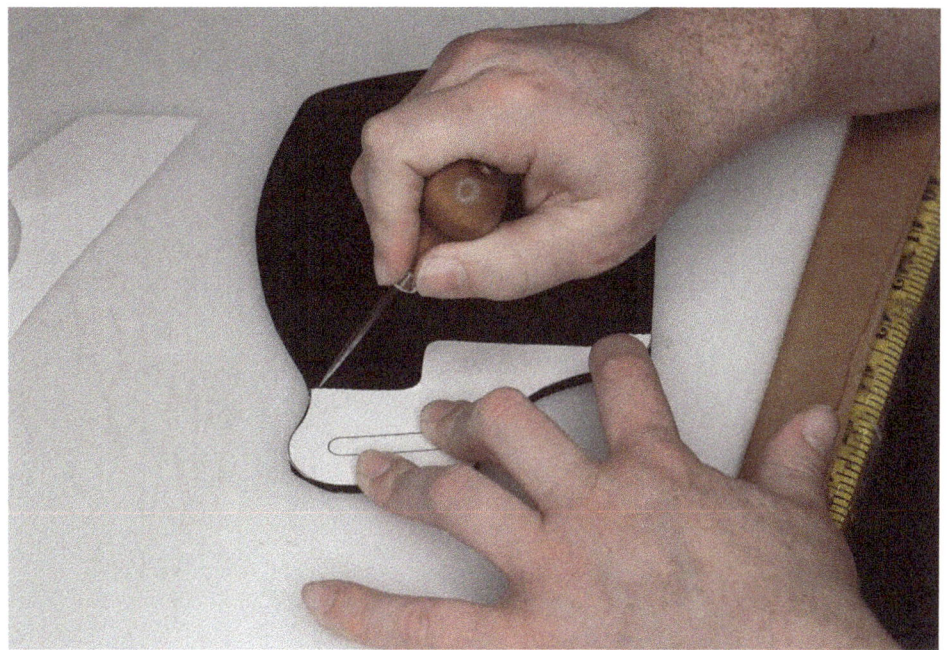

Figure 11-26

Figure 11-27

Now that the stitch lines are marked, let's get some belt slots on this holster.

Grab your pattern once again and line up the ear of the holster.

Lightly tap a punch at the top and bottom of the belt slots marked on your pattern. You're not punching through the leather at this point, just marking the leather through your pattern.

You'll only do this on the front panel of the holster.

Do this for both the trigger guard side and slide side.

Figure 11-28

Figure 11-29

Now, let's flip both panels of the holster so the flesh side is up.

We'll take both our trigger guard and slide wing pattern pieces and mark the stitch lines on the flesh side of the leather.

This will tell us where to put contact cement on the holster.

Figure 11-30

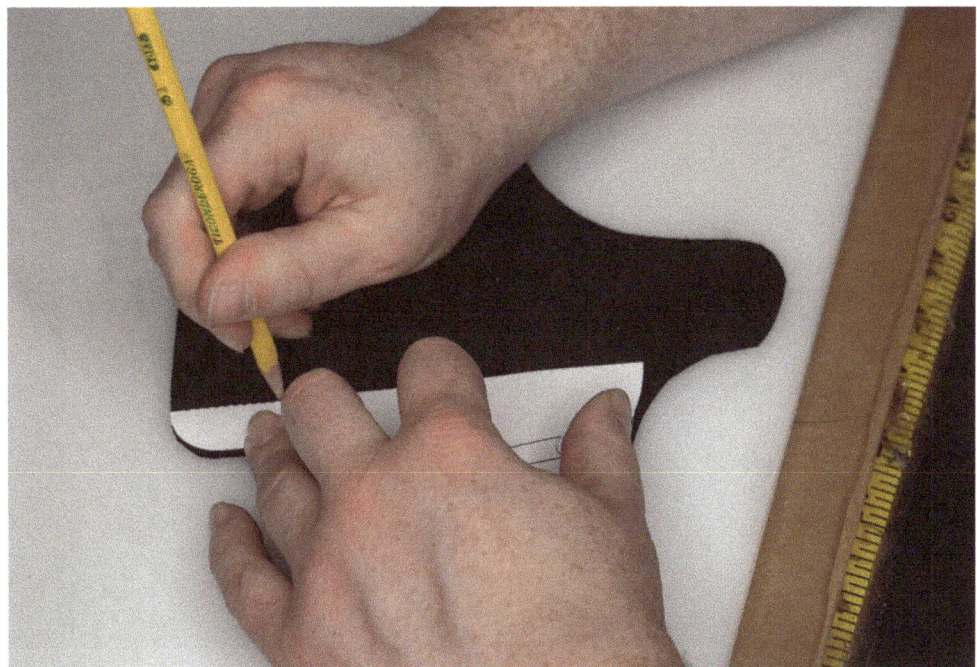
Figure 11-31

Here we can see the lines marking glue areas.

Figure 11-32

Let's grab the contact cement!

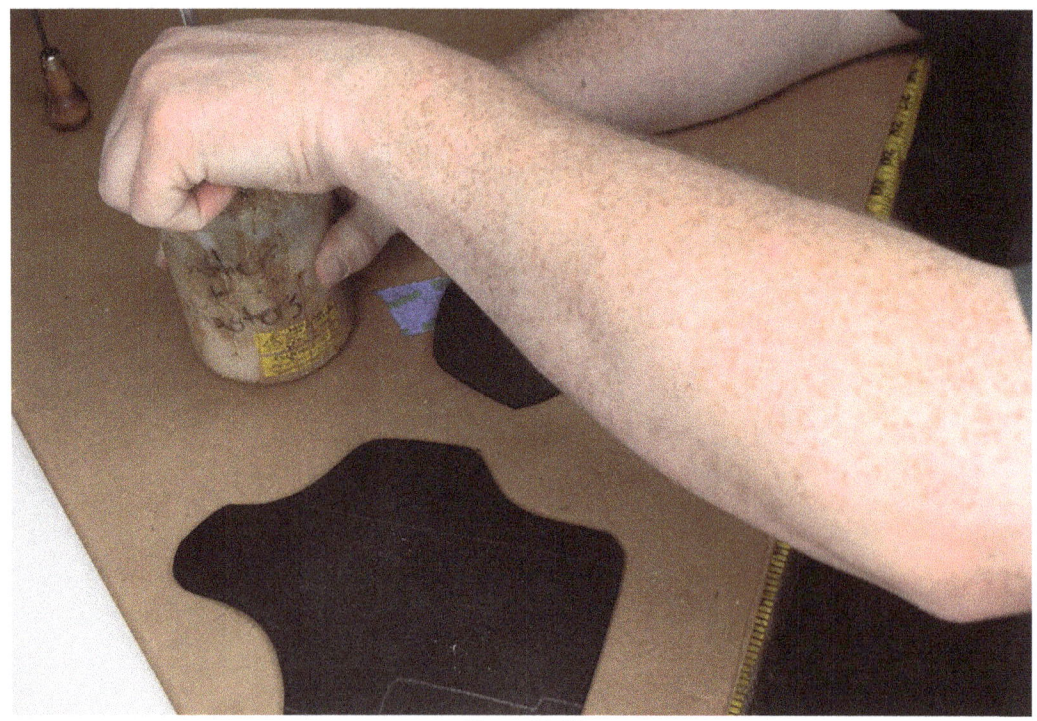

Figure 11-33

Always brush from the center of your project to the edge.
DO NOT drag your glue brush over the edge.

You'll discover new vocabulary if you're trying to sand the edges of your holster and a bunch of contact cement is in the way.

Remember, contact cement sticks to itself. You'll need to apply it to both front and back panels of the holster.

Figure 11-34

Figure 11-35

Let your contact cement sit for ten minutes or so.

Grab an iced tea. No adult beverages at this time. We're getting ready to put the front and back panels together and you need to be sober to get them to match up.

We line up the bottom of the holster and work our way up.

You may have a solution that works better for you!

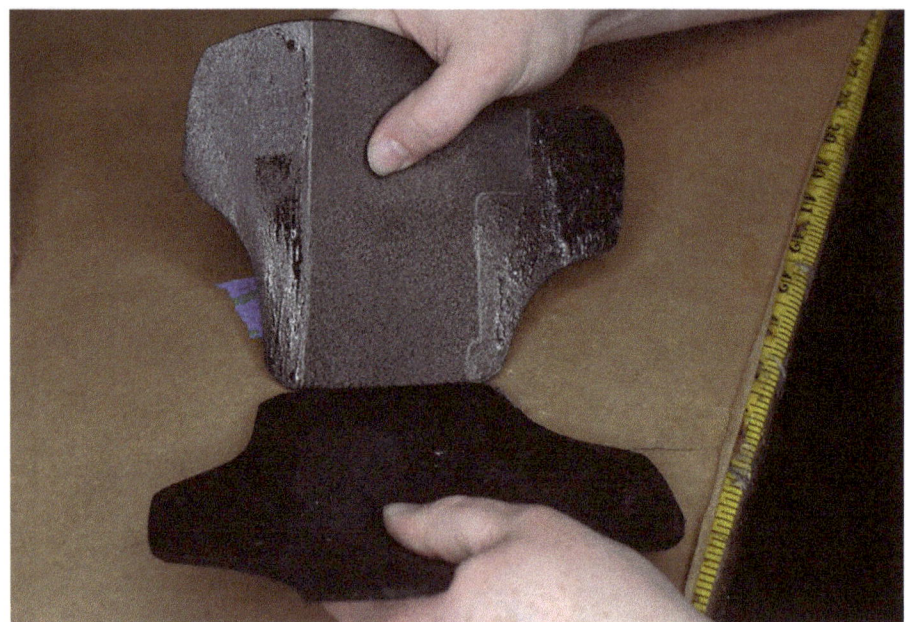

Figure 11-36

Figure 11-37

Grab your Cobbler's hammer and beat the tar out of the glued-up areas!

If you do not have a Cobbler's hammer, put a six-ounce piece of veg-tan over your project and beat the snot out of it with a regular hammer through that.

This will prevent hammer marks from appearing on the front of your holster.

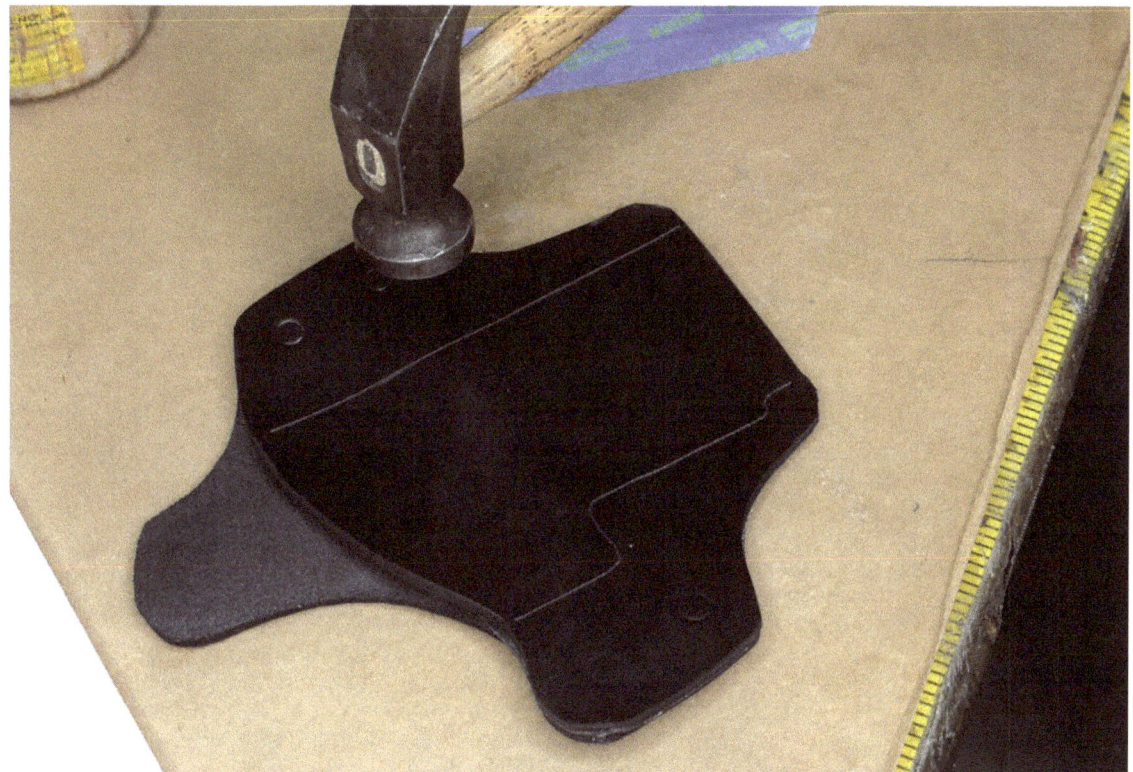
Figure 11-38

Now you can enjoy that adult beverage!

You should be seeing your design coming to life! This is the cool part.

We've let the glue set-up. Now it's time to sand the holster shapes together. You want your edges smooth and matched as close as possible.
You're going to edge finish this puppy, so let's use an inexpensive belt sander.

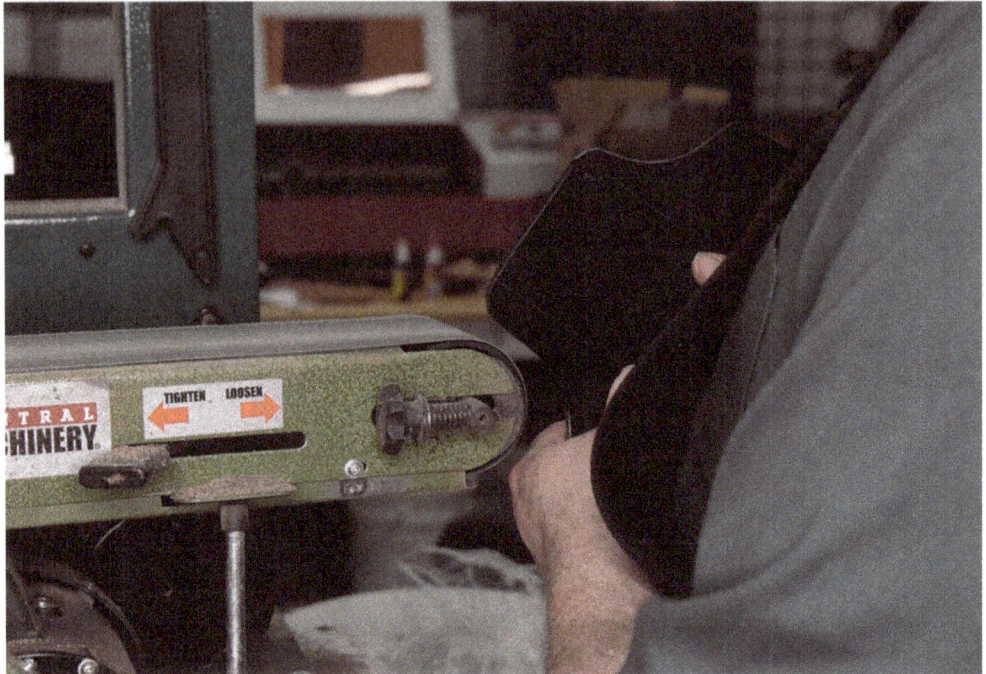

Figure 11-39

Figure 11-40

Sanding is done!
Time to edge bevel the whole rig.

Figure 11-41

The edge beveler will expose undyed leather. This isn't a problem. Just go back and carefully dye those areas.

Figure 11-42

Chapter 11: Holster Building – 8 Degree Pancake Holster

Now we dye the exposed natural leather

Figure 11-43

And now we have nice black edges!

Figure 11-44

It's time to sew this thing together.

This book is not the platform to teach you how to sew. You can either use a stitcher or hand sew.

The only thing I would like to see is you keep your stitch length to six-stitches-per-inch.

Start and stop your stitching on the outside edge of the wing so the belt covers your overstitch. This doesn't achieve any structural advantage, it just looks nice.

Figure 11-45

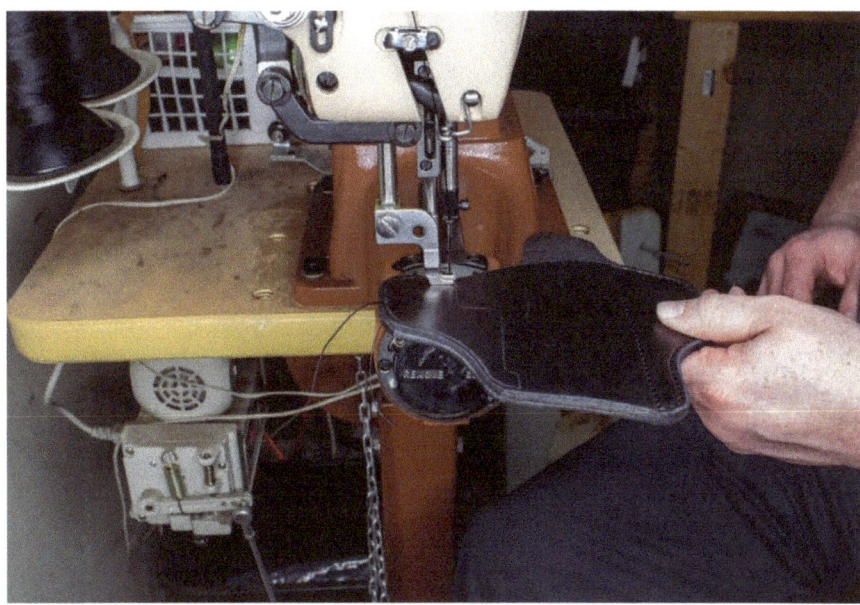

Figure 11-46

Remember when we had you mark the top and bottom of your belt slots? If you missed that step you're still okay! Go ahead and do that now.

Now, place your punch on the marked area in your leather and knock the dog slobber outa it!

You're punching through sixteen-ounces of leather. It's going to take some hard hits.

Figure 11-47

Figure 11-48

Once the top and bottom holes are punched, we'll connect them by using a chisel and your favorite hammer.

Cut each side of your punched holes.

Figure 11-49

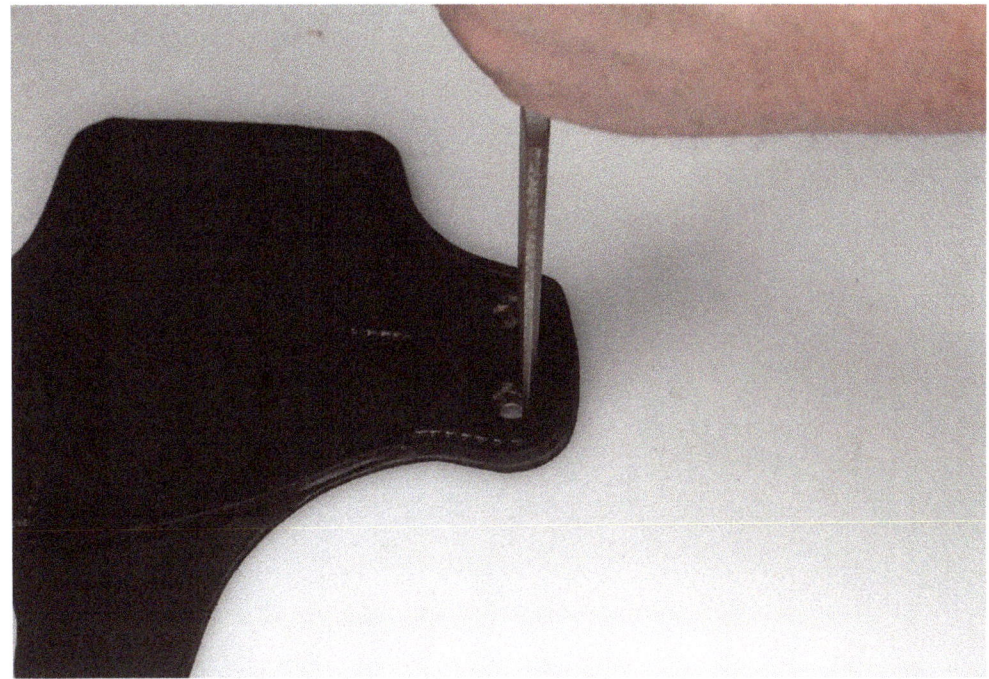

Figure 11-50

Remove that piece of leather and let's get ready to edge the slot.

We prefer the Sharp Radius Edger from Barry King Tools. There aren't a bunch of specialized tools in holster making, but this one will sure change your life.

Go ahead and edge both sides, then grab some sandpaper and wrap it around a dowel rod. Now, carefully sand the ends of the slot.

Figure 11-51

Figure 11-52

Remember when we edged the outside of the holster and we exposed some undyed leather? Well, guess what, we did it again!

Carefully dye the inside of the belt slot.

Figure 11-53

Figure 11-54

Time to get wet!

Dunk this puppy into some warm water. Treat it like an ex and hold it under till it quits bubbling!

Figure 11-55

Figure 11-56

Let's take a wooden dowel rod and cut it to length. We want it to start at the rear of the front sight and terminate at the muzzle end of the ejection port.

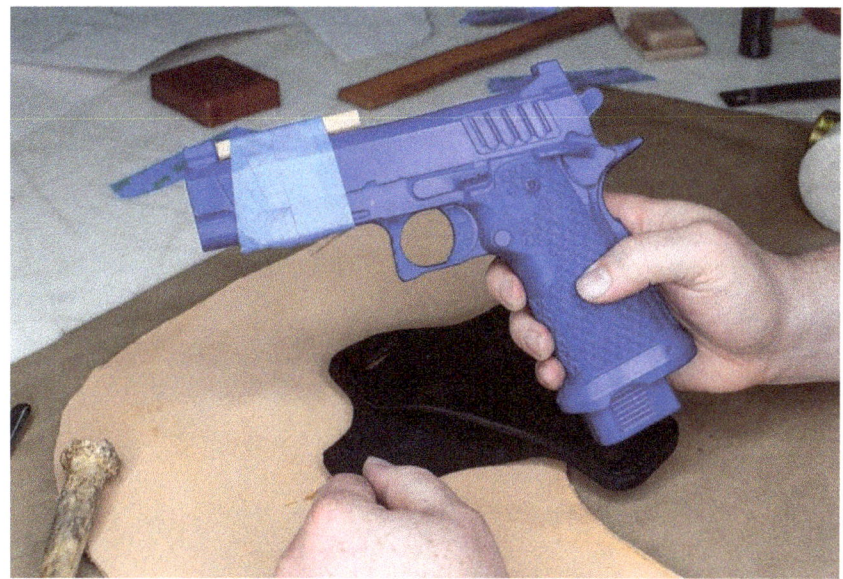

Figure 11-57

Now, let's get the gun into the wet holster.

If using a live firearm, please ensure it's clear. **BE SAFE!!!** Also, place the firearm in a freezer bag to keep it dry.

If using a BlueGun mold, just get-er-in there! Another advantage to a gun mold is, if your stitch line is really tight, you can assist this process with a poly hammer.

Figure 11-58

Mold inserted into holster!!!

Figure 11-59

Take a quick look and ensure the gun is centered in the holster.

Figure 11-60

Let's get to molding.

There are many molding techniques out there. In each of the three builds in this book we'll be showing you different techniques and tools.

This holster uses the most basic tools that most shops should have already.

Grab your wood edge slicker and start to block in the outlines of the gun.

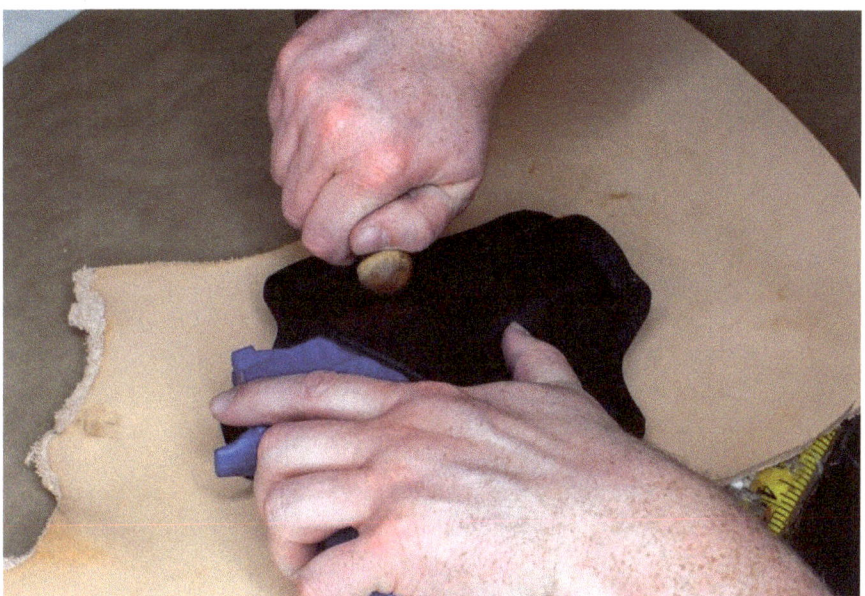
Figure 11-61

You may notice some wrinkles between the stitch line and the frame. Just rub those out.

Figure 11-62

We've completed initial blocking with the wood slicker. Now we need to grab our tooling maul and use the brass acorn nut to get a little more definition.

Figure 11-63

Now let's press the acorn nut into the trigger guard area and create a pinch point.

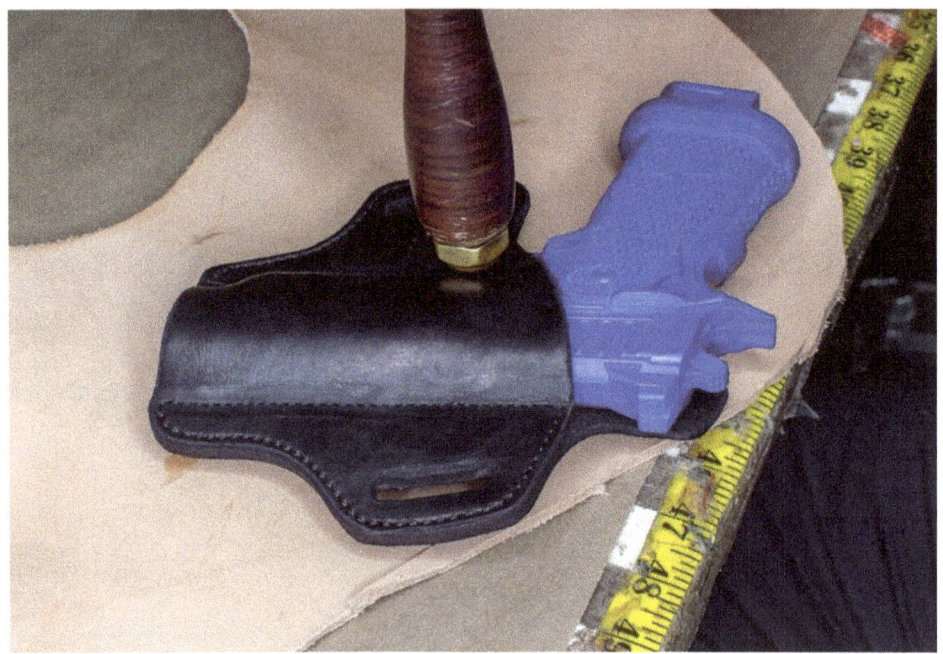
Figure 11-64

Here we're using a deer antler to work the leather into the ejection port.

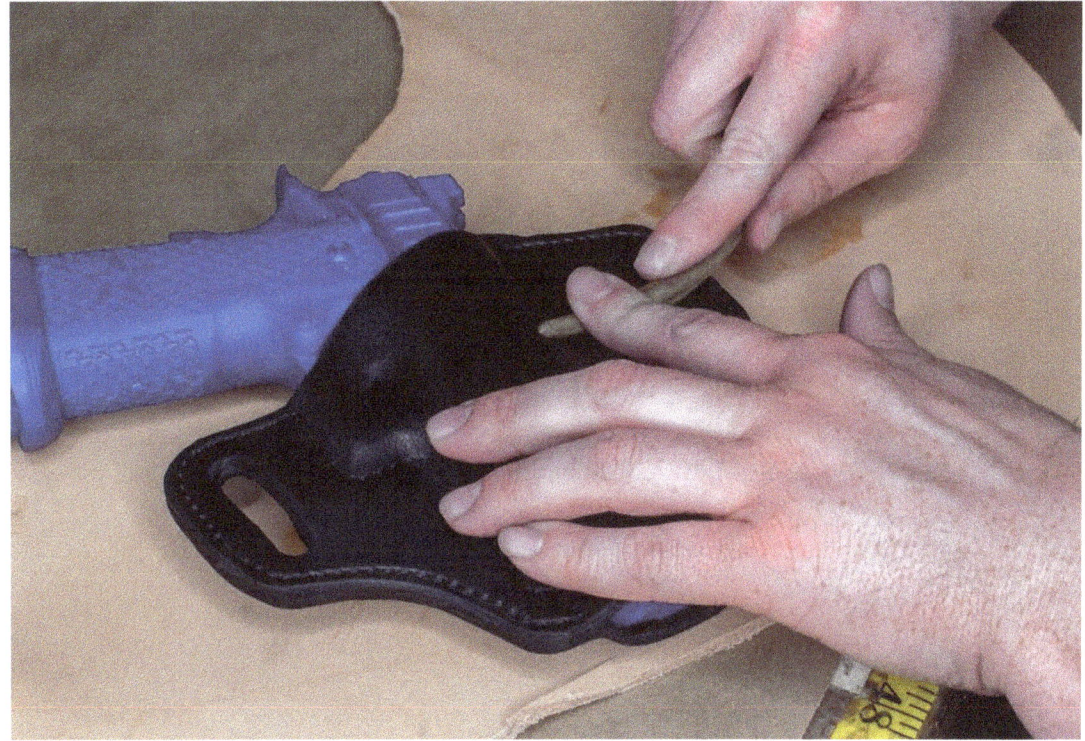
Figure 11-65

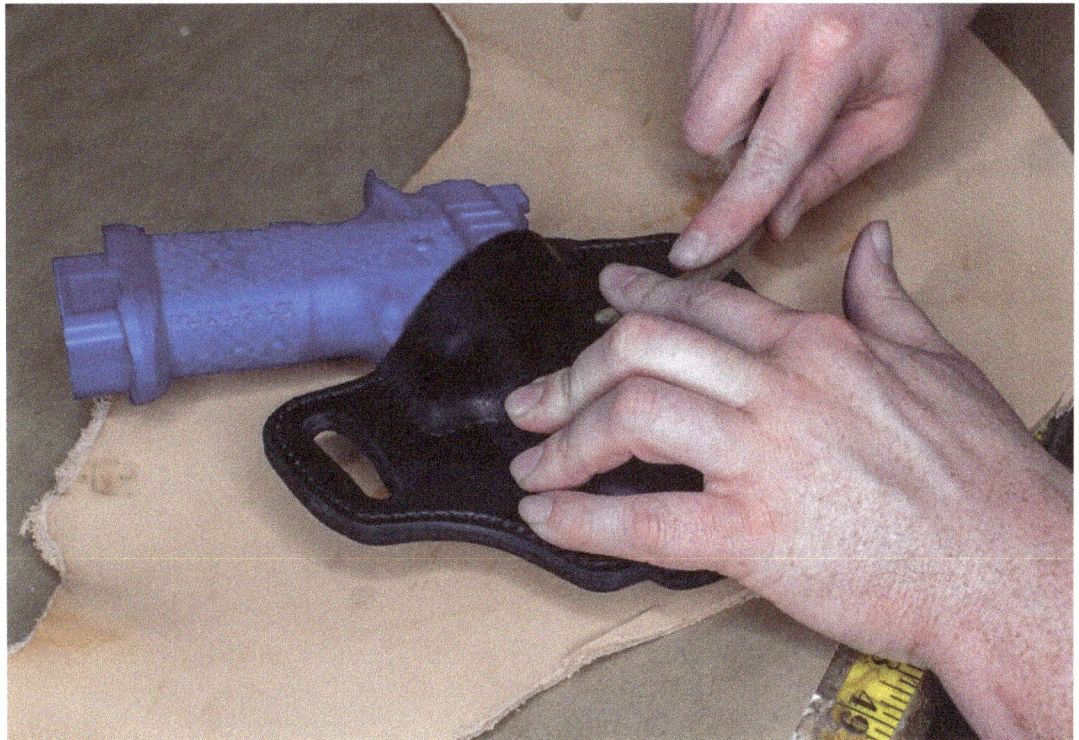
Figure 11-66

Chapter 11: Holster Building – 8 Degree Pancake Holster

Now we are using a stainless-steel boning tool from Tandy Leather

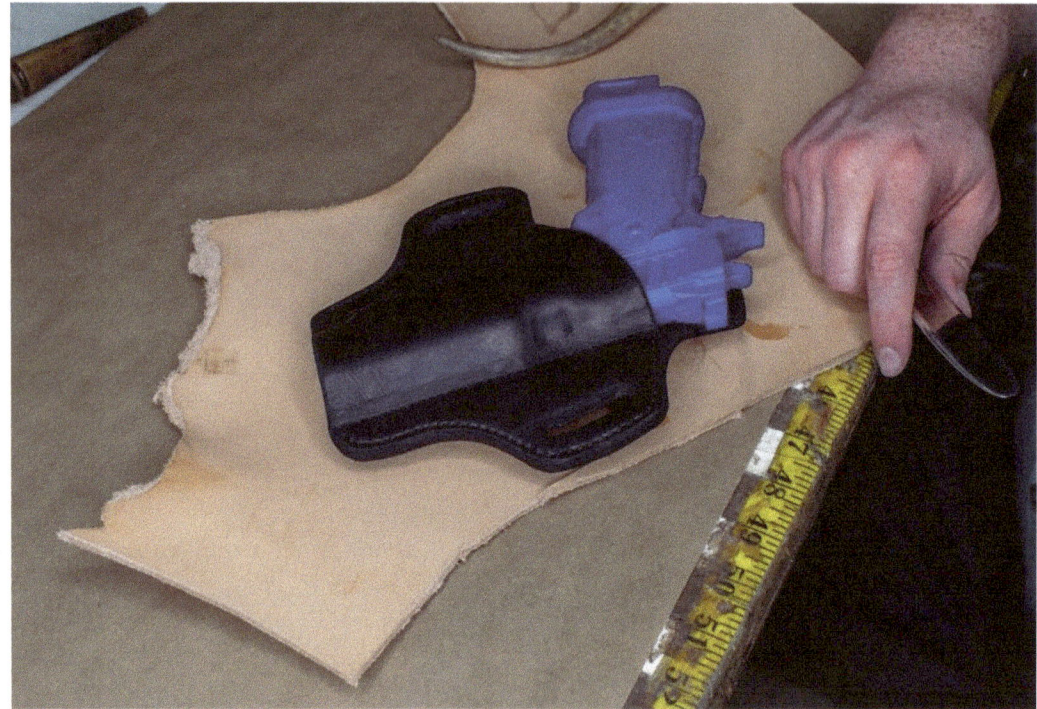

Figure 11-67

Let's mark in a couple of lines

Figure 11-68

We'll use the bone folder in the trigger guard as well.

Figure 11-69

Figure 11-70

Chapter 11: Holster Building – 8 Degree Pancake Holster

Don't be afraid to go back to your frame, slide, or detailed areas and mold or smooth them out again.

Figure 11-71

Figure 11-72

Not bad for a hand mold job!
We've gained retention at the stitch lines, ejection port, and trigger guard.

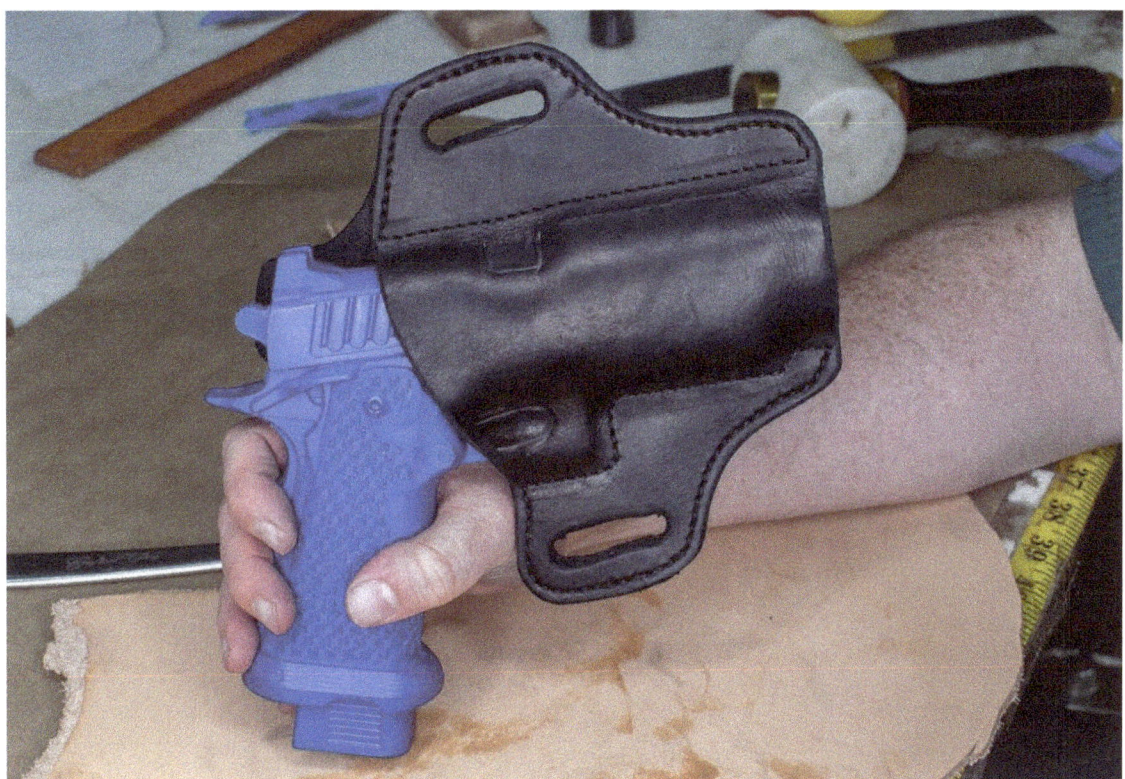

Figure 11-73

Let's get this holster hung up and let it dry.
We'll pick up from here tomorrow.

Now that your new rig is dry, we need to apply acrylic finish to it. This will provide protection from moisture and add structure to your holster.

The holster needs rigidity to provide a long service life and maintain retention. Applying acrylic will ensure the holster maintains structure for years to come.

Let's glove up!

Figure 11-74

We'll be using a foam brush in this example.

First thoroughly soak your foam brush in the acrylic. You don't want any bubbles to transfer to your holster.

Figure 11-75

Place your fingers in the throat of the holster and start applying acrylic from the bottom to the top.

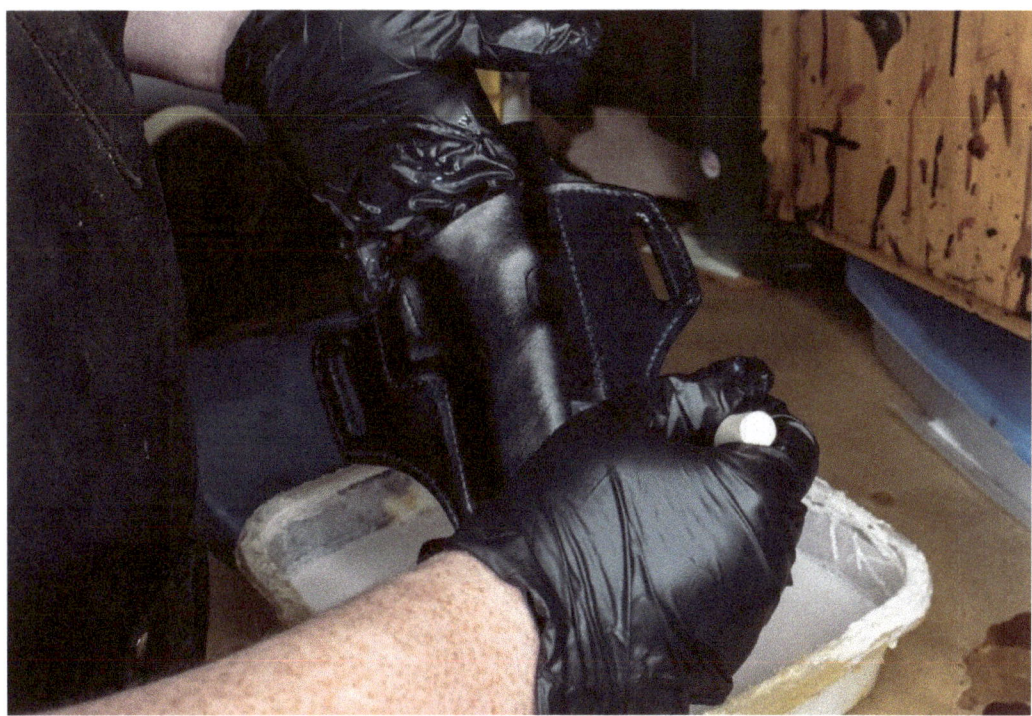
Figure 11-76

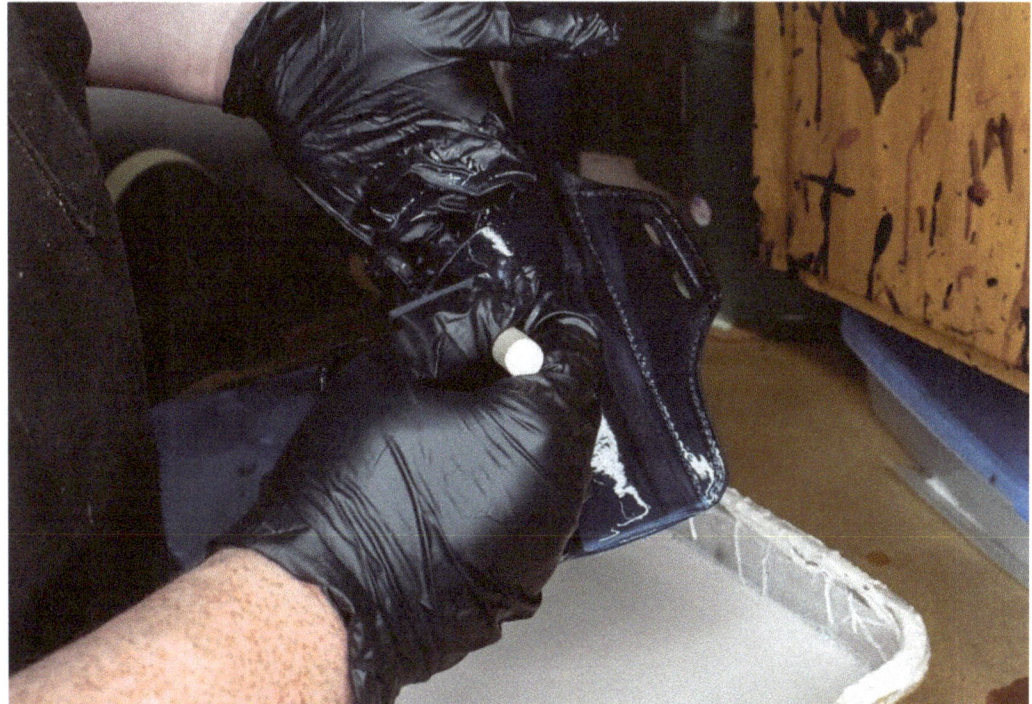
Figure 11-77

Once the front of the holster is covered, flip that thing over and let's get the back. Don't forget to coat the edges and the inside of the belt slots.

Figure 11-78

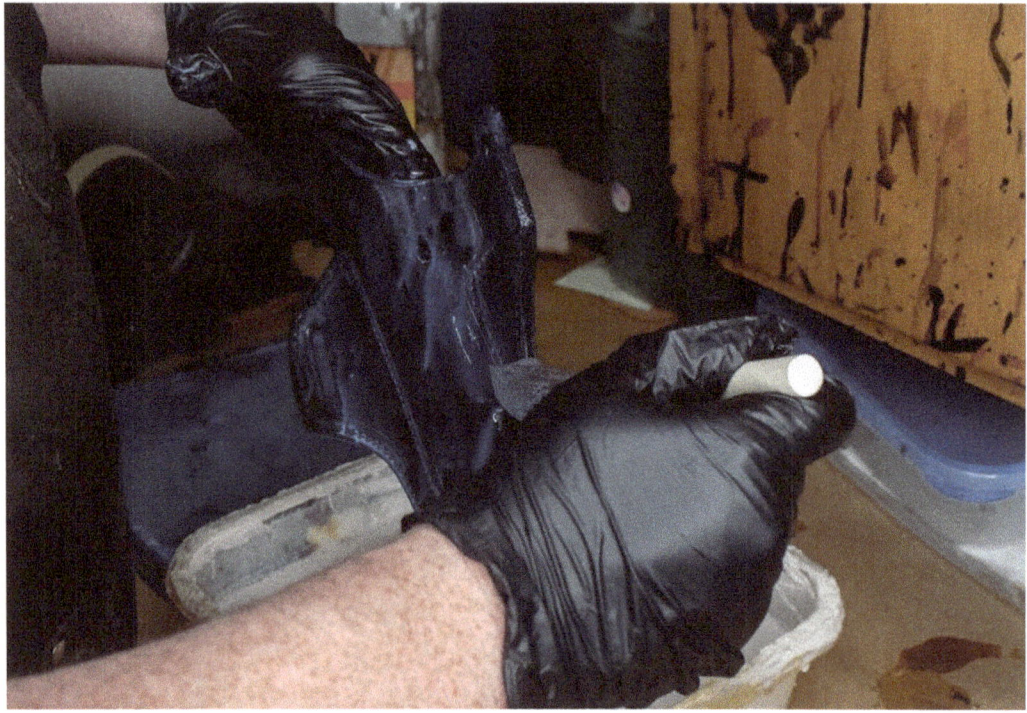
Figure 11-79

Don't forget the inside of the holster.

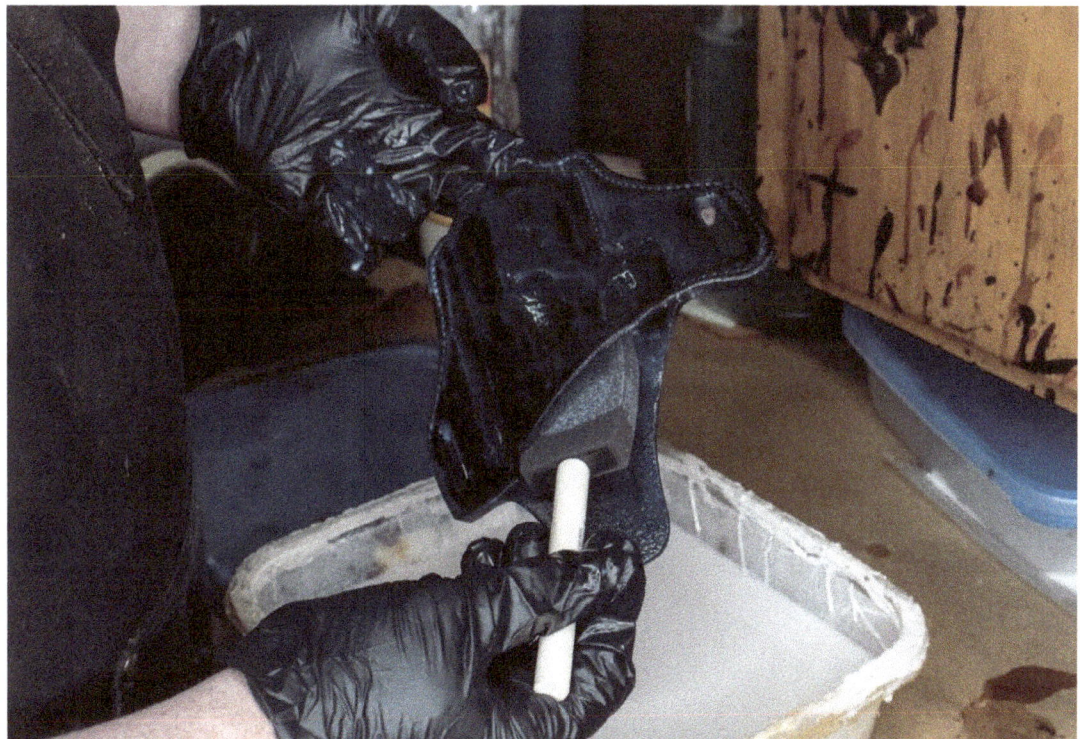
Figure 11-80

Figure 11-81

Grab a paper towel and wipe the excess finish from the outside of the holster.

You're going to have haze from the wet acrylic. Don't Panic! This'll go away as the Acrylic finish cures.

Hang this puppy up and let it cure.

Figure 11-82

We're closing in on our final goal!

After this thing is completely cured, we'll perform a final stretch to the holster. Then you'll get to put it on!!!

Chapter 12: Holster Building – Thumb Break Holster

Let's build our Thumb Break Holster Design.

Just like the last chapter, grab that pattern and make some photocopies! We always want to work from a copy and save our original!

Hold the pattern up to your belt and make sure the trigger guard and grip are pointing to the rear.

Let's mark the pattern with grain (hair) side or flesh side. We'll build our holster grain side out, making all marks on the flesh side of the leather.

Hopefully, your pattern will resemble this.

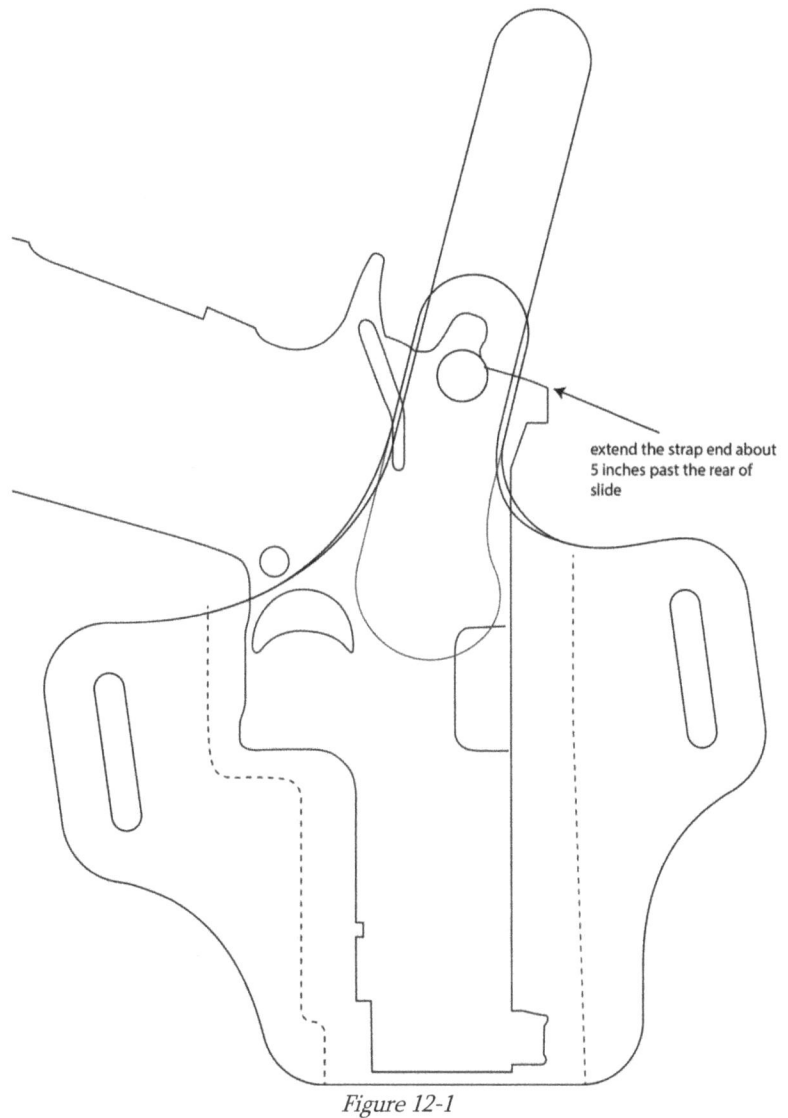

extend the strap end about 5 inches past the rear of slide

Figure 12-1

We have three pieces to cut from this pattern. You may want to start with three copies.

Here are the pieces;

Thumb Break Reinforcement (mark as flesh side).

Figure 12-2

Back panel (mark as flesh side)

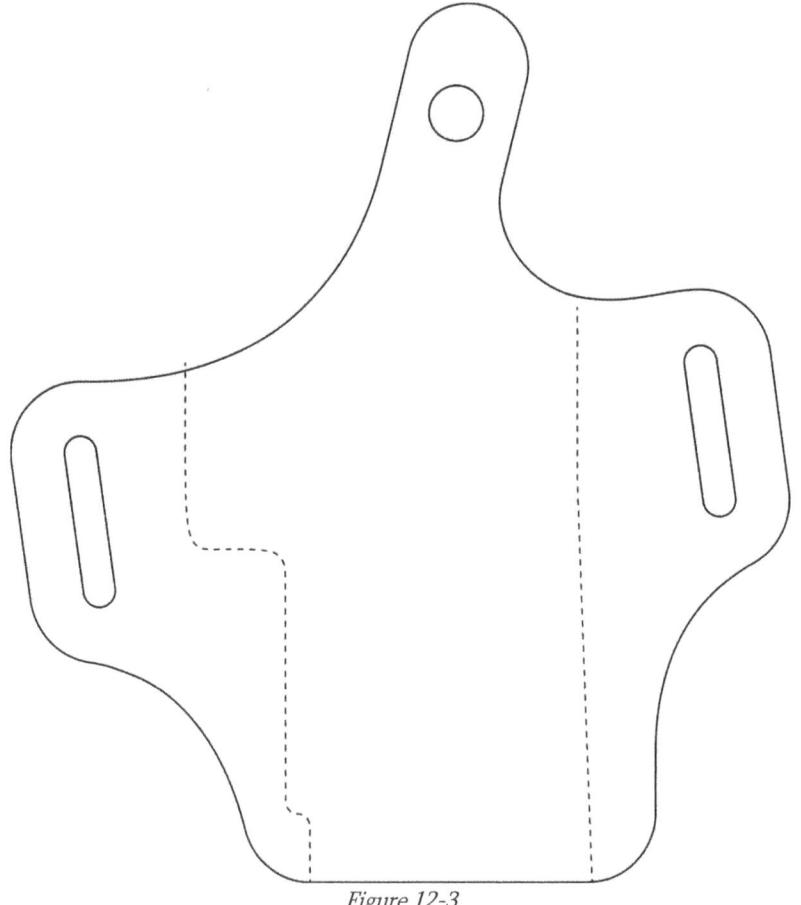

Figure 12-3

And the front panel. (mark as grain or hair side).

The thumb break strap will be longer than represented in the picture. We will trim the length only after we've set the snap.

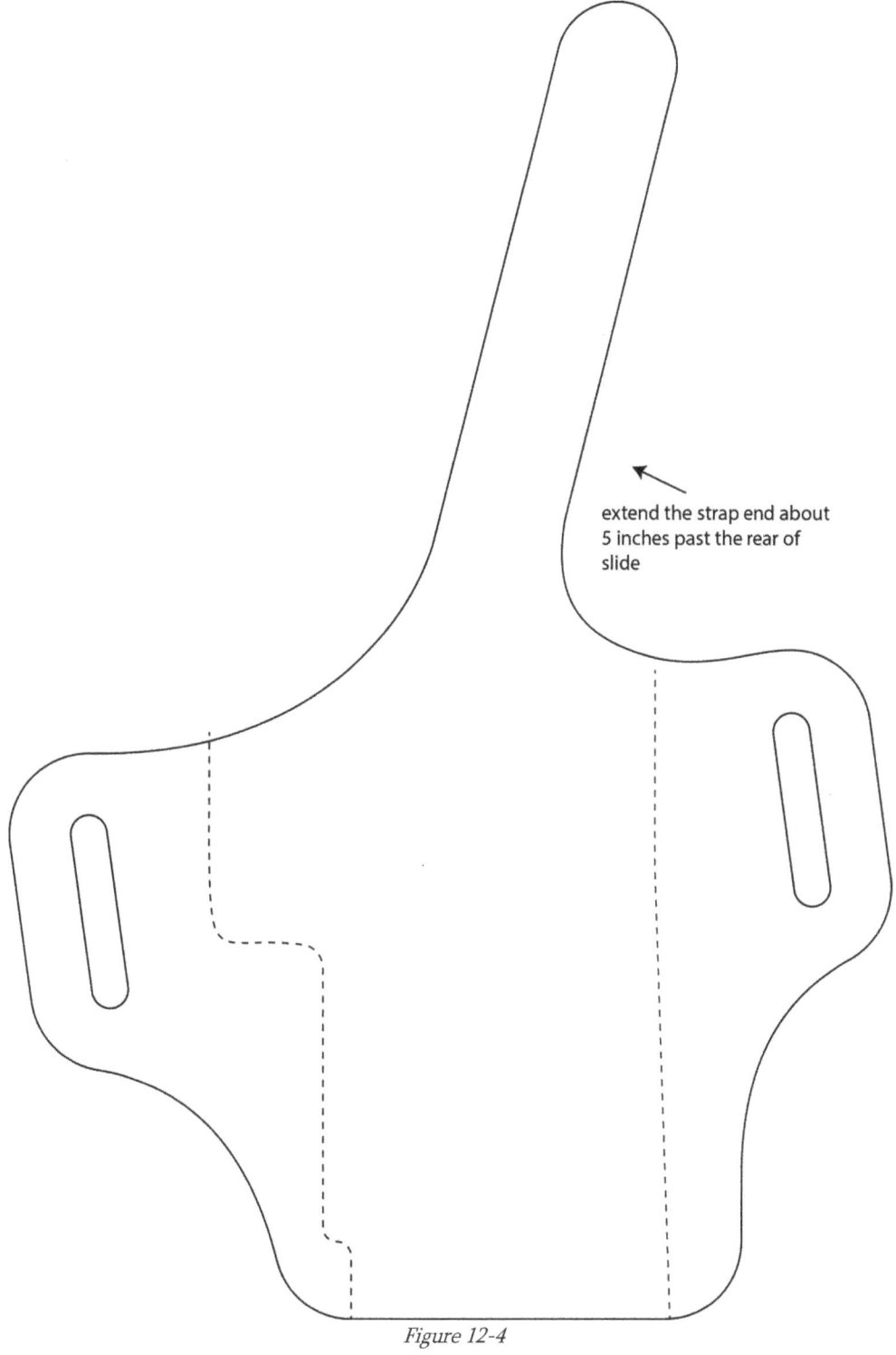

extend the strap end about 5 inches past the rear of slide

Figure 12-4

Chapter 12: Holster Building – Thumb Break Holster

Let's get to cutting out paper!
First we'll cut our front panel.

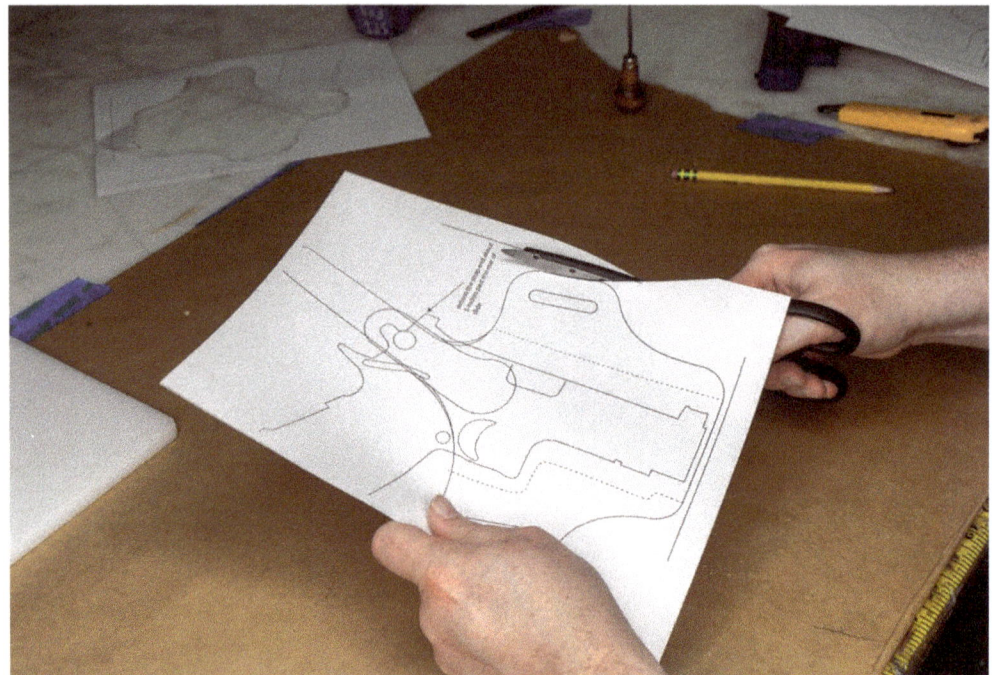
Figure 12-5

Looks like this!

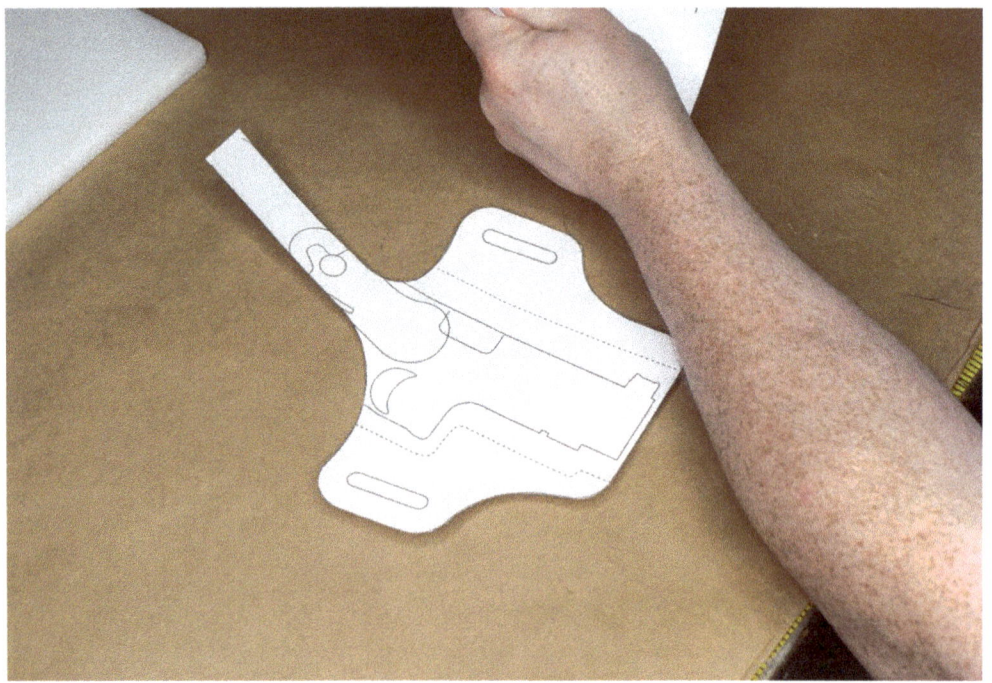
Figure 12-6

173

Now let's cut out the reinforcement.

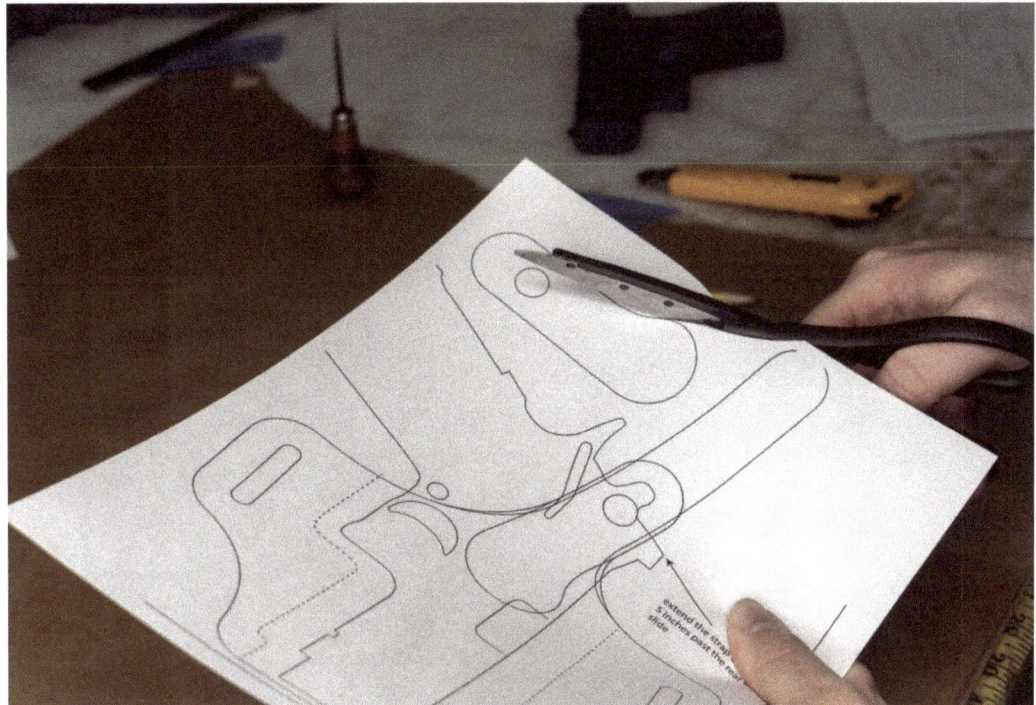

Figure 12-7

And the back panel.

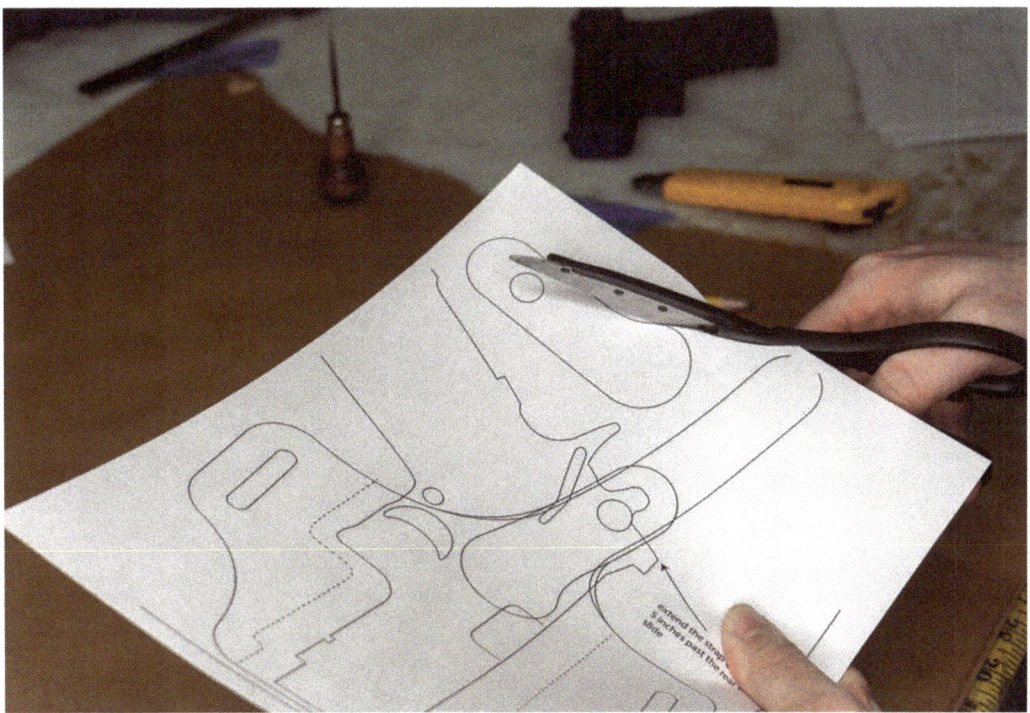

Figure 12-8

Now we have three pieces of paper.

Get your tight grained eight-ounce veg-tan leather and place it grain (hair) side up. We're laying this out on the grain, (hair side) of the leather.

The front panel will be pattern up and both, the back panel and reinforcement, are flipped.

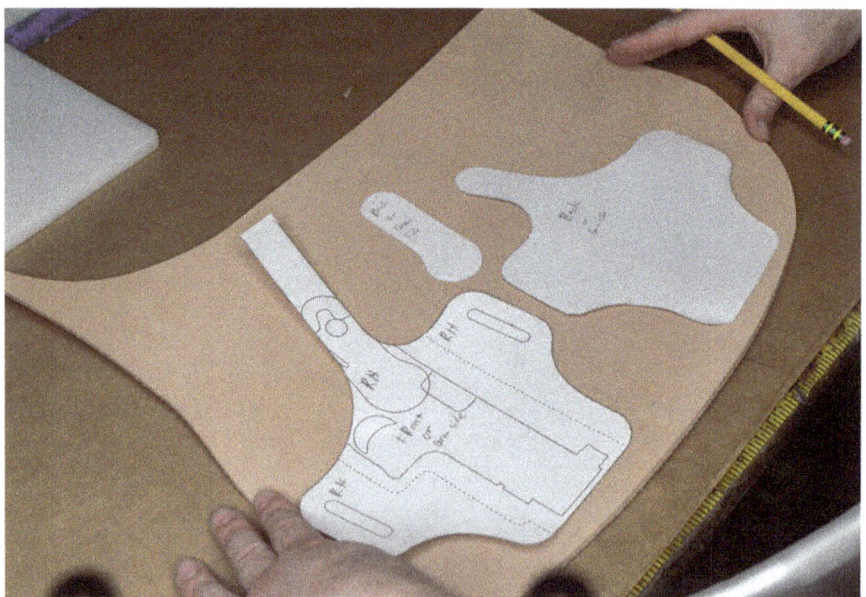
Figure 12-9

When marking patterns on the grain (hair) side of leather, use a pencil and mark lightly. You can always erase any errant marks.

Figure 12-10

Cheat whenever you can!

When cutting the long straight strap on the front panel, use a metal ruler to guide your knife!

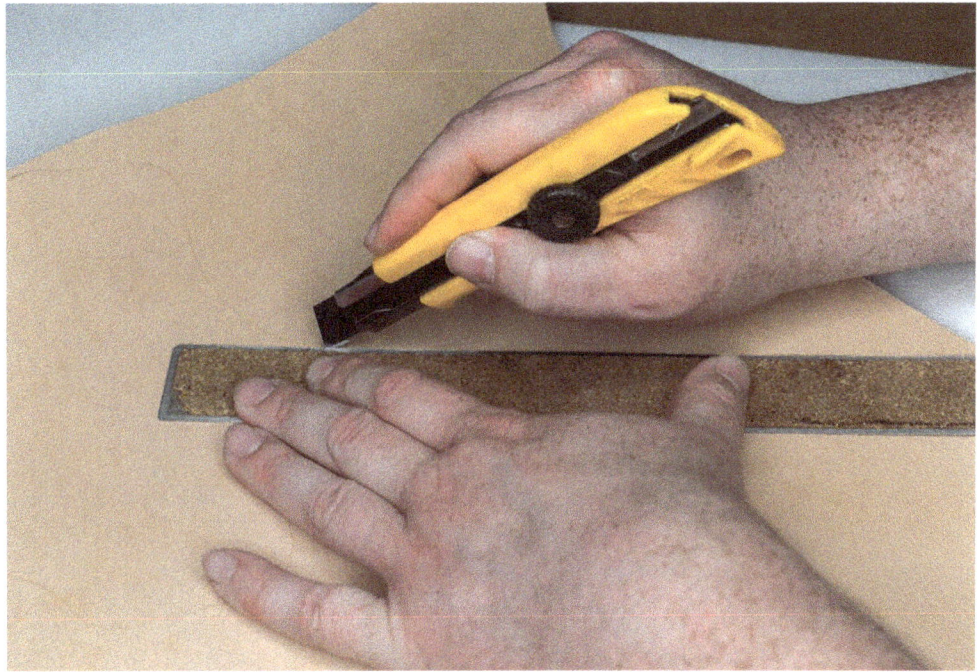

Figure 12-11

Everything is cut out. No blood on the table is a good thing!

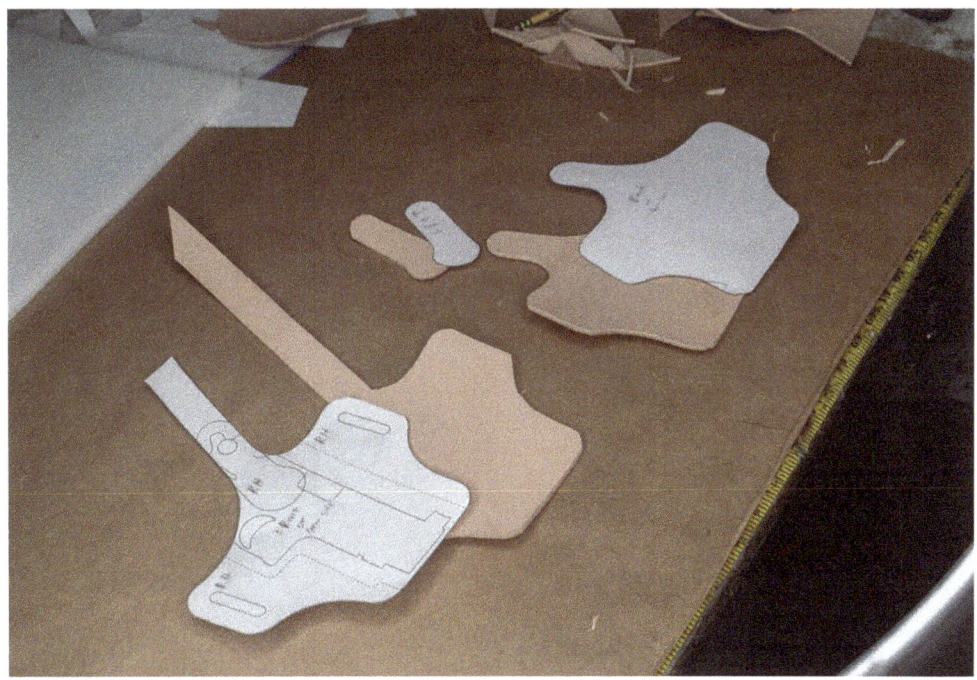

Figure 12-12

Here, we're going to deviate from the last build. We need to prepare the thumb break and thumb break reinforcement before putting this puppy together.

We're going to edge bevel and edge polish the thumb break reinforcement panel. Only edge bevel the grain (hair side).

Figure 12-13

Now let's grab our slicking solution

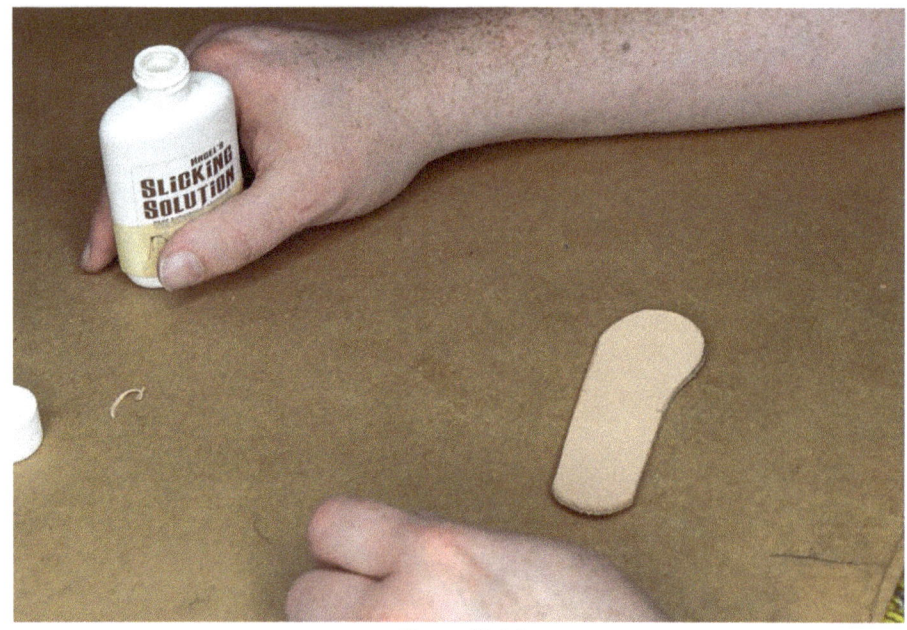

Figure 12-14

We only need to burnish the area that's going to be on top of the back panel, (the lower half).

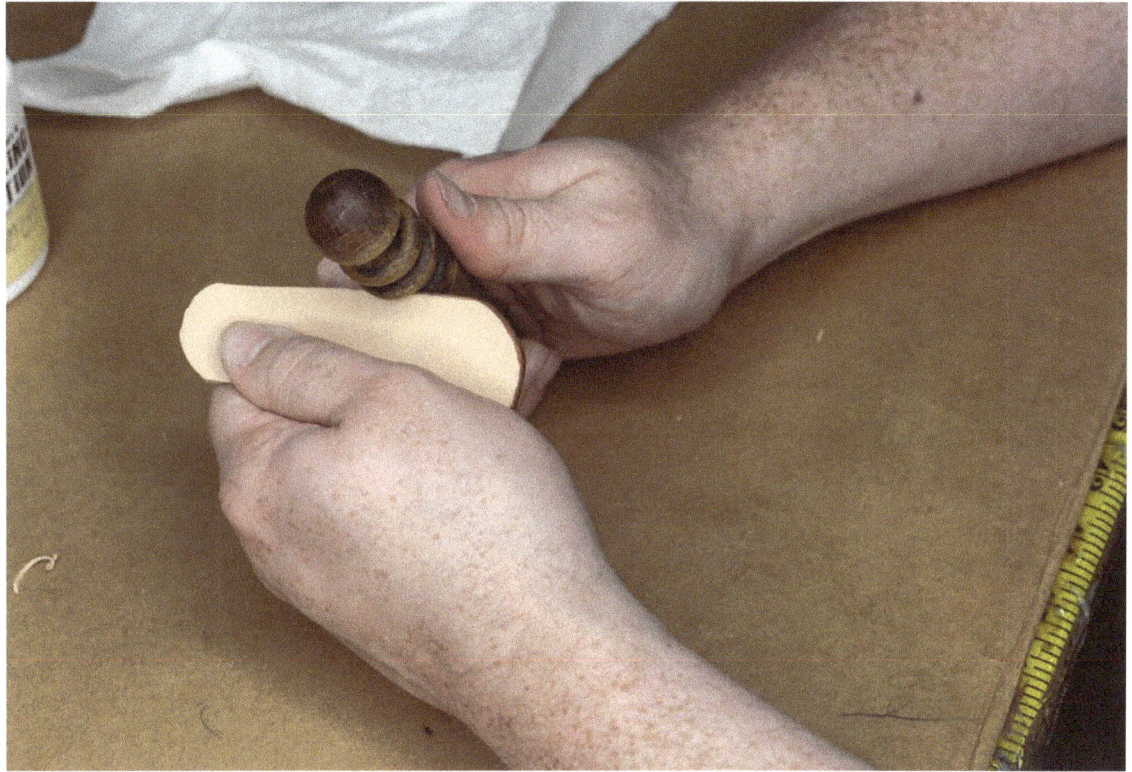
Figure 12-15

The red area will be on the back panel of the holster. The black areas will be on the edge of the break. You can burnish the two layers together.

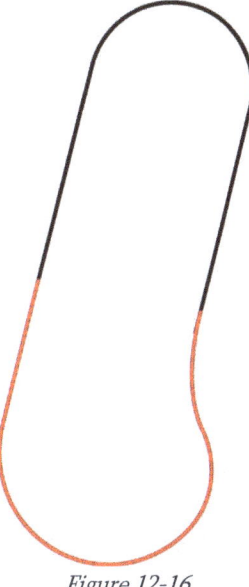
Figure 12-16

Chapter 12: Holster Building – Thumb Break Holster

Lay the Thumb Break reinforcement panel on the back panel of the holster and lightly mark its location in pencil. This will tell you where to glue later.

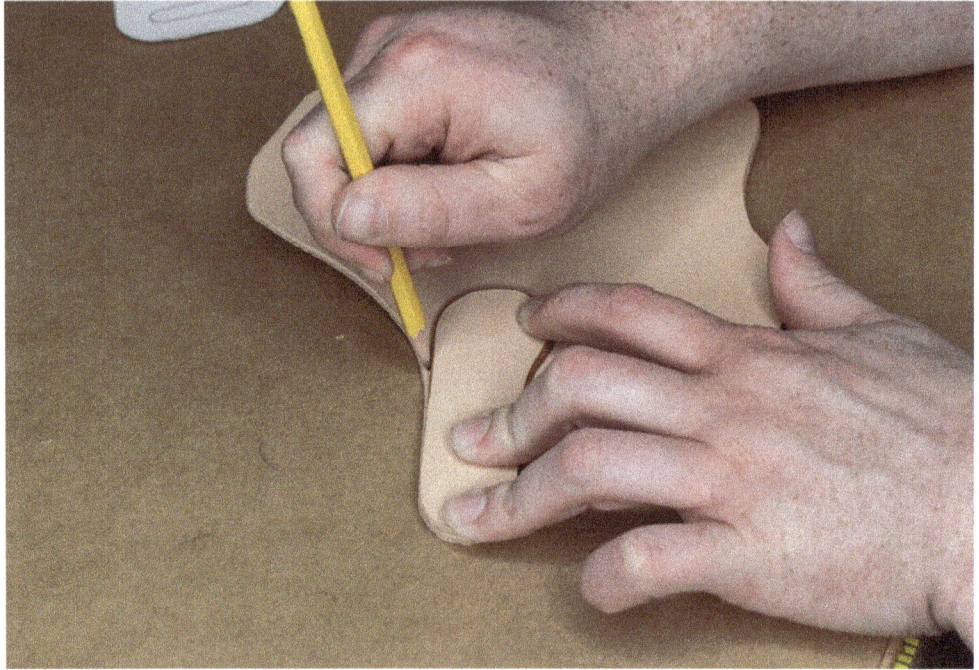

Figure 12-17

Gonna need some hardware and tools for this portion. We're going to be setting the hardware for the thumb break.

Figure 12-18

179

We're going to need our hardware, which consists of the female side of the snap, the cap for the snap, and the thumb break steel.

For our punches, we have a half-inch (1/2") punch and a one-eighth-inch (1/8") punch.

We also need our setter. In this case we're using the Barry King snap setter, and a hammer.

Take out your glue and have it ready. We'll need it to stick the rear reinforcement on with the thumb break steel and sandwich it between the rear panel and the reinforcement leather.

Also make sure you have a hard surface to set the snaps on. We use a small Harbor Freight anvil covered in masking tape to reduce the chance of any scratches on the leather.

Chapter 12: Holster Building – Thumb Break Holster

First up, let's use the half-inch (1/2") punch to punch the hole in our pattern.

Figure 12-19

Figure 12-20

Now that we have the hole in the pattern, let's line it up on the back panel.

Figure 12-21

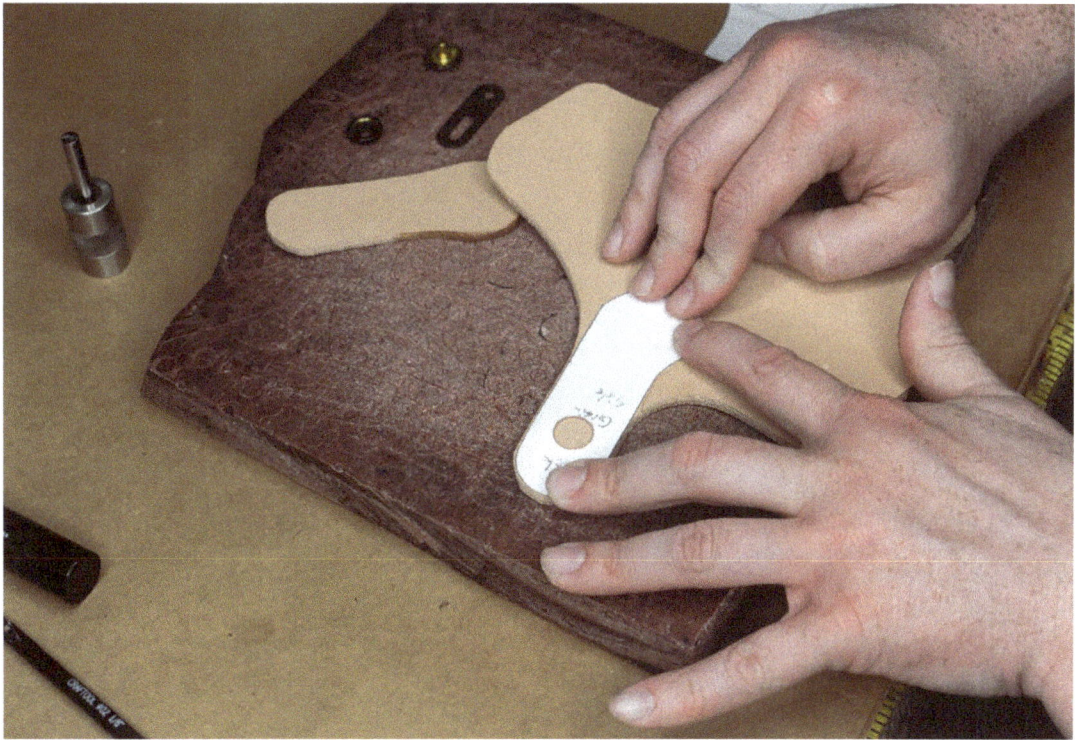

Figure 12-22

Next, we're going to take the punch and grip it hard to push a mark into the back panel itself.

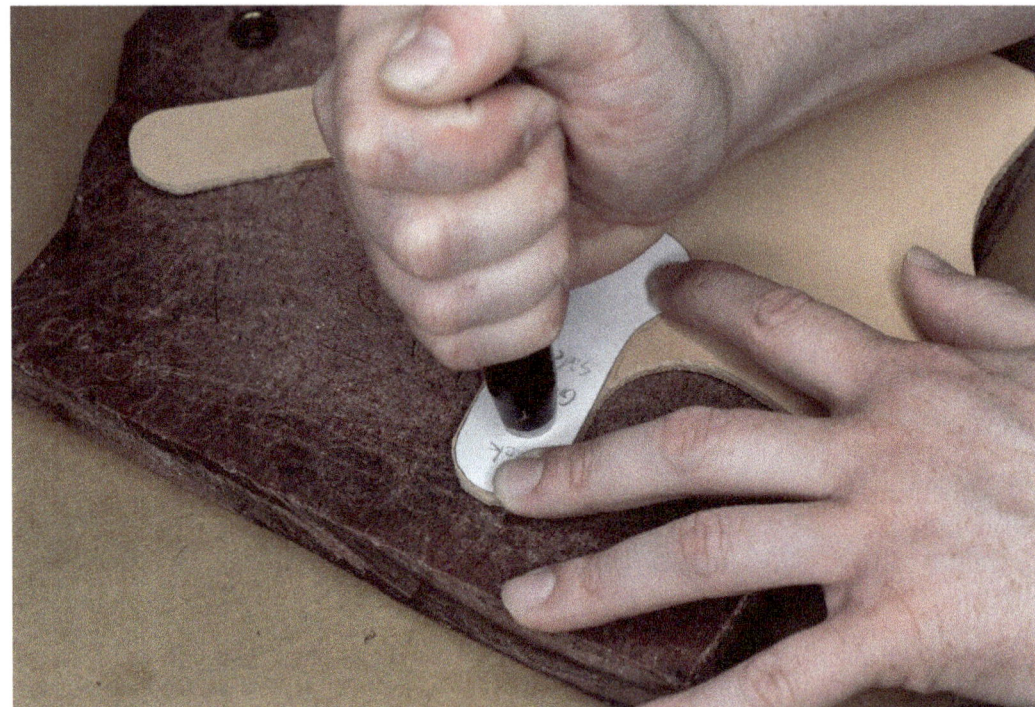

Figure 12-23

Figure 12-24

Now that we have that mark, we can remove the pattern from the rear panel and punch the hole.

Figure 12-25

Figure 12-26

This hole is where the female side of the snap will recede, minimizing the metal-on-metal contact when the firearm is in the holster.

It also reduces the chance of draw stroke interference when the firearm is removed from the holster.

Now we just need to make our hole for the post on the reinforcement.

First, take the reinforcement and either use your pattern or just line it up with the hole you just made in the rear panel. Now use a scratch awl to mark where you want to punch.

We want to do this just hard enough for the tip of the scratch awl to pierce the grain side, but not so hard that the entire awl goes through.

Figure 12-27

We can see where it came through. Now we can mark it again to make sure we see it.

Figure 12-28

Figure 12-29

Chapter 12: Holster Building – Thumb Break Holster

Get your favorite (not metal) hammer. We need to take our one-eighth-inch (1/8") punch and make our hole.

Figure 12-30

Figure 12-31

187

Now that our holes are punched, we can start the steps to get this reinforcement glued to the rear panel.

First, take the thumb break steel and lay it in place.

Now, trace around the steel with your pencil so you know where NOT to glue.

Figure 12-32

Figure 12-33

Do this on the back panel and reinforcement.

The reason we're doing this is, if we lay glue in this area, it'll squeeze out around the reinforcement and end up in the hole meant for the snap. We don't want that happening.

We're now ready for glue. Take out your preferred glue and get it ready.

Figure 12-34

Put the glue inside of the lines we made for the outer footprint of the reinforcement, but stay outside the mark made for the thumb break steel.

Do this on the grain side of the back panel and the flesh side of the reinforcement panel.

Figure 12-35

Figure 12-36

Now place the thumb break steel in-place and stick the two pieces together.

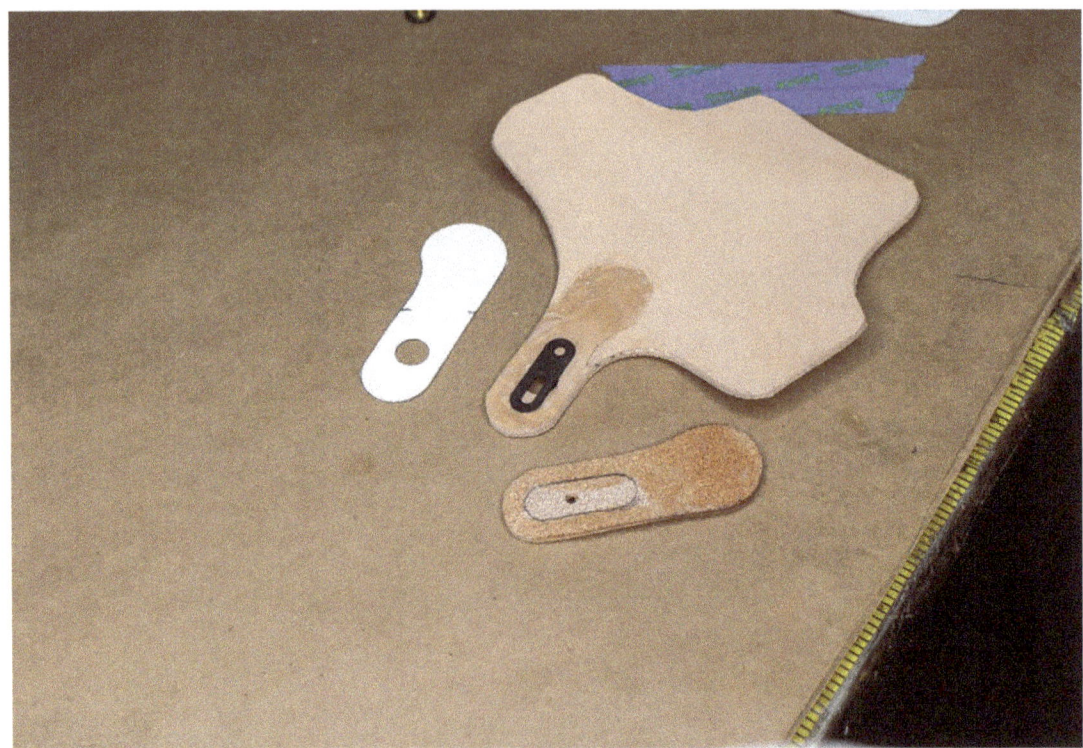

Figure 12-37

Figure 12-38

Grab your Cobbler's hammer and start tapping around the panel to make sure it's locked into place.

Figure 12-39

Now it's time for us to set our snaps.

Take out your anvil or other hard surface, the snap, the snap setter, and your hammer.

First, put the cap of the snap through the hole on the grain side of the leather. Then place your snap anvil on a hard surface.

Figure 12-40

Figure 12-41

Place the female side of your snap inside the half-inch (1/2") hole we made earlier, and atop the snap post.

Using your snap setter, get that snap set in there.

Figure 12-42

Figure 12-43

The snap is now in place and hopefully in the middle of your half-inch (1/2") hole.

Figure 12-44

Let's head on over to the sander and true up the edges between the reinforcement and the rear panel.

Figure 12-45

Good to go!

Now let's take our beveler and bevel the reinforcement edges.

Figure 12-46

Figure 12-47

Chapter 12: Holster Building – Thumb Break Holster

Don't forget the flesh side as well.

Figure 12-48

Once we've beveled the edges around the reinforcement, let's go back to our pattern and cut the wings out so we can mark the throat and toe of the holster, and get those beveled as well.

Figure 12-49

Just like with our 8-degree pancake holster, we need to edge bevel and slick the areas we can't reach once the holster is stitched together.
Front panel.

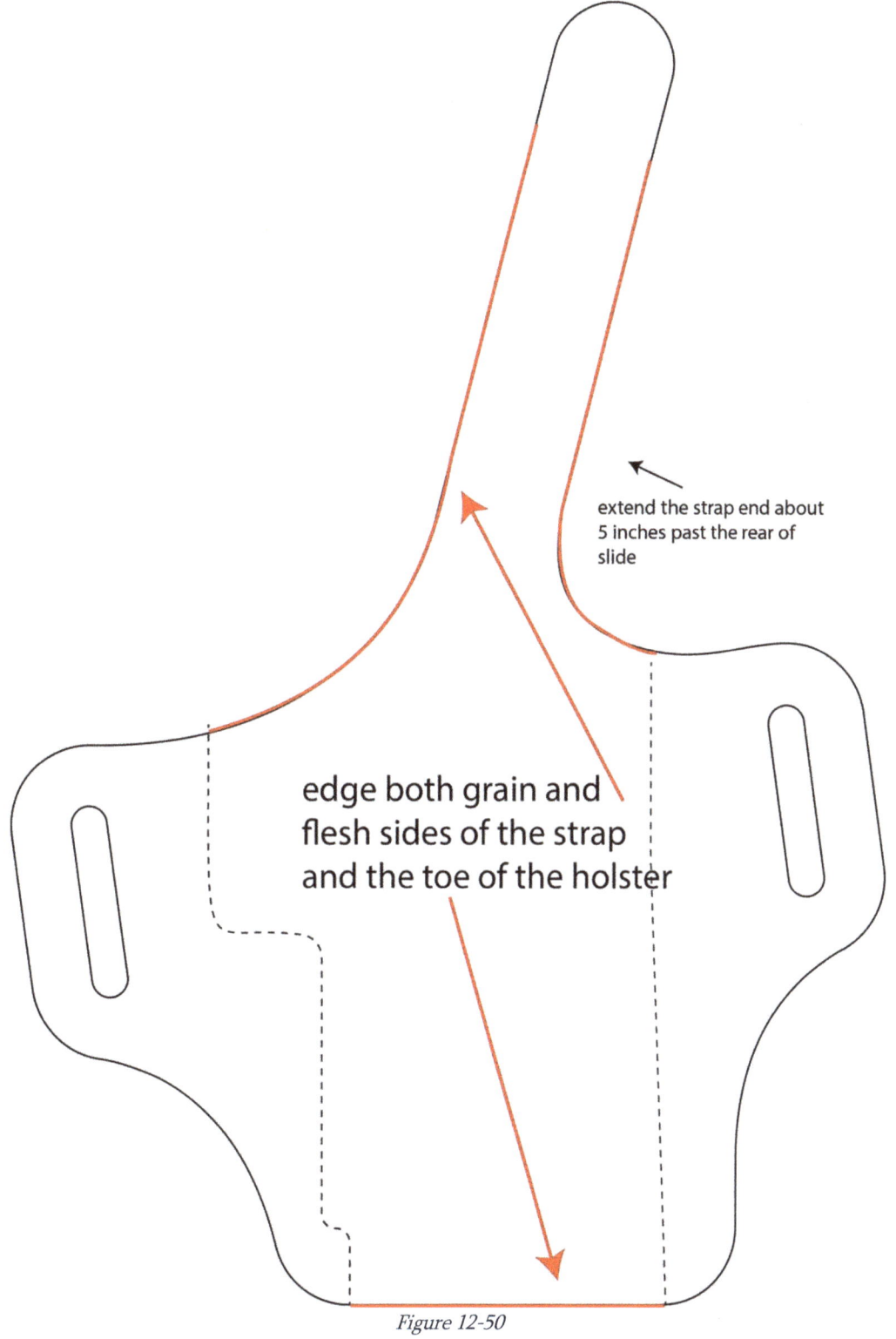

Figure 12-50

And the back panel

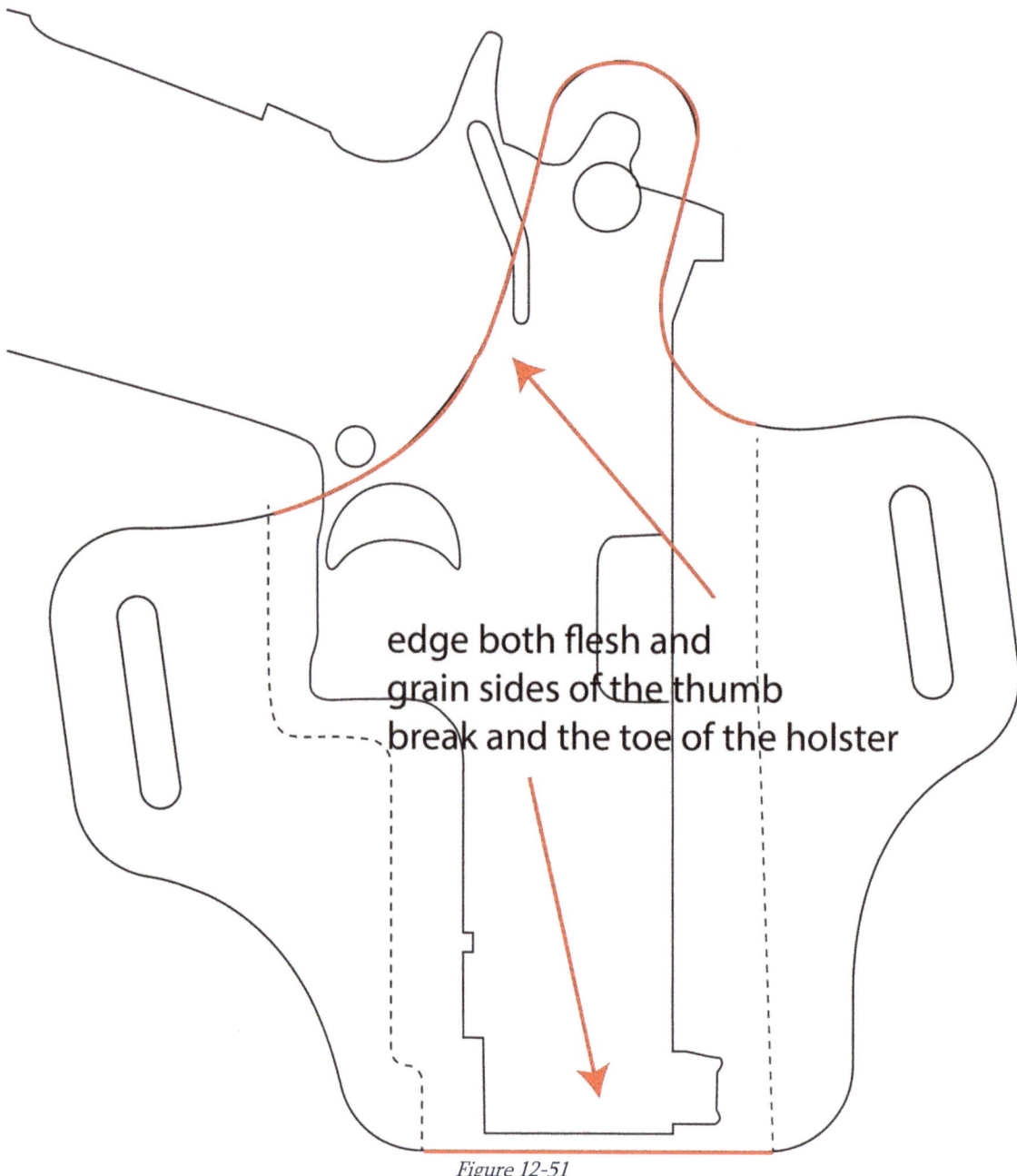

Figure 12-51

Let's cut off the wings and make top and bottom tic marks for the stitch lines.

Figure 12-52

Figure 12-53

Do this on both the slide side and the trigger guard side.

Now let's grab our edger and edge the red marked areas in figures 12-50 and 12-51.

Figure 12-54

Figure 12-55

Set your wing dividers to either one-eighth-inch (1/8") or three-sixteenth-inch (3/16"). Either size is acceptable.

Let's mark our stitch line for the reinforcement panel.

Figure 12-56

After stitching we can go ahead and polish the thumb break edges.

Figure 12-57

Now that we've got the thumb break assembled, we can start on the holster itself.

This'll go together just like the 8-degree pancake you completed earlier.

First, we need to place our wings back on the front panel of the holster. Then, using our punch, firmly press through the pattern to mark out the punch holes.

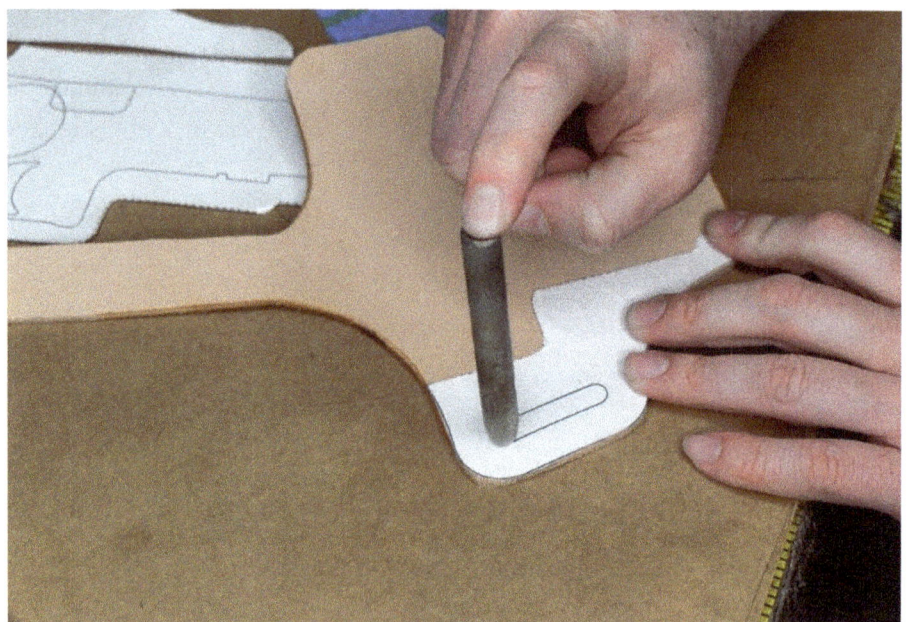

Figure 12-58

And the bottom hole.

Figure 12-59

Using your scratch awl, scribe the stitch line into the front of the holster. You'll be using this as your sewing guide later.

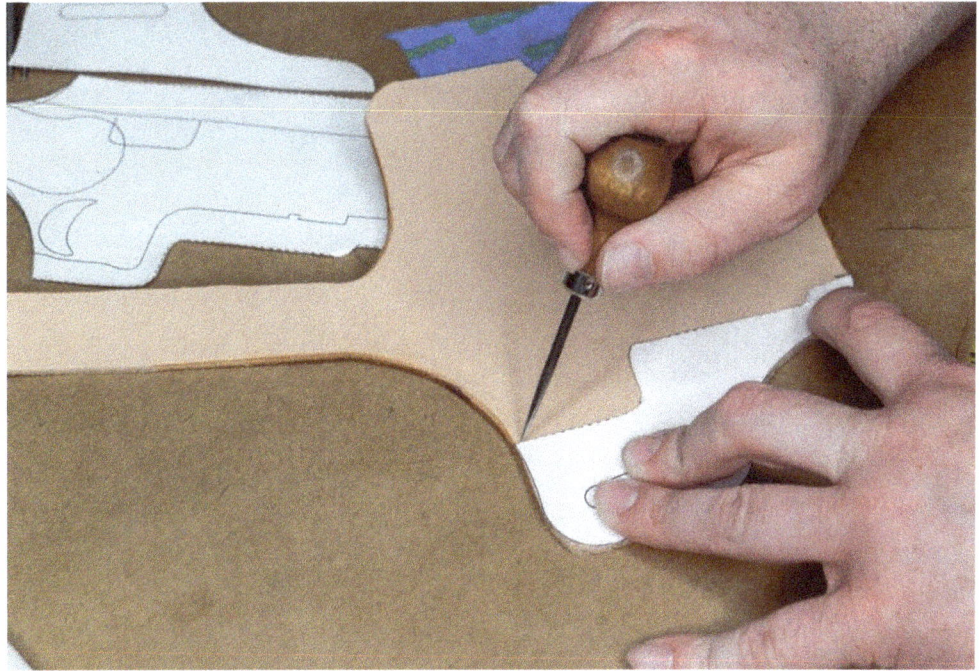

Figure 12-60

Now flip the panels over and, using a pencil, mark the stitch lines on the inside. This will be your glue guide.

Figure 12-61

Figure 12-62

Apply glue to both sides of the leather. Remember, always brush to the edge from the inside.

Figure 12-63

Glue both panels. Remember, contact cement sticks to itE.

Figure 12-64

Let it tack up for ten to fifteen minutes.
This is a good time to grab a drink and smell the volatile organic compounds.

Let's stick these puppies together!

Do your best to get the edges even. More care taken at this time means less sanding later.

Figure 12-65

Figure 12-66

Grab either a Cobbler's hammer, or place a piece of leather on top of your project and use the hammer you have.

We don't want to mar the grain of the leather with hammer marks.

Figure 12-67

Remember what I said about carefully lining up edges when gluing? Accurate glueing means less of this stuff.

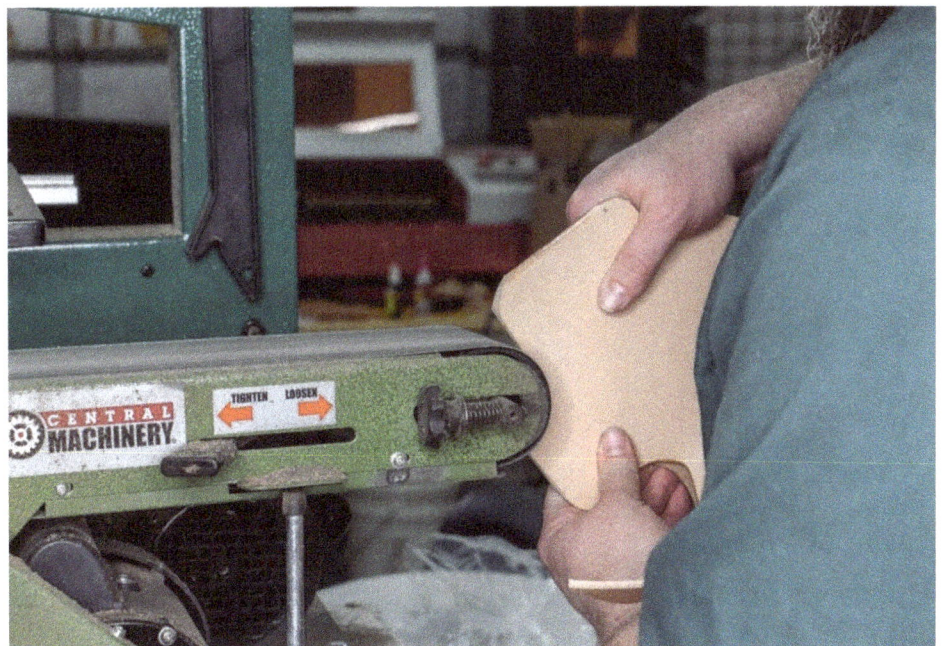

Figure 12-68

Let's grab your #2 or #3 edger and go around the outside of the holster on both the front and back panels.

Figure 12-69

Figure 12-70

Time to mark your stitch lines on the front of the holster.

Cut the ears off of your pattern, just like we did on the 8-degree.

Remember, the primary form of retention here is the thumb break, so you may want to cut your pattern on the outside edge of the stitch line instead of in the middle. This will reduce the stitch line tension slightly.

Both methods are correct, but you may want to experiment and see which one feels best for you.

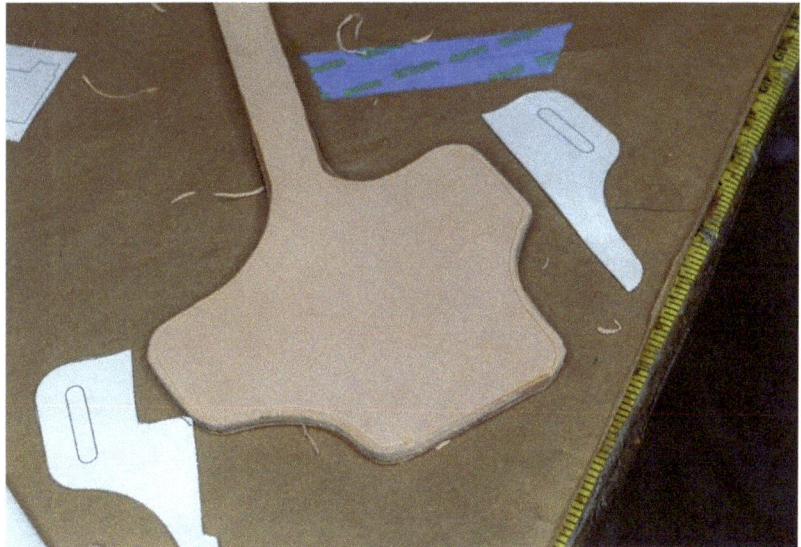

Figure 12-71

We'll start and end our stitch line on the ear of the holster where the belt will cover the overlap.

Figure 12-72

Run your stitch line in a racetrack, going entirely around the ear and along slide side stitch line. When finished, overlap by about three stitches.

Figure 12-73

And repeat the process for the trigger guard side.

Figure 12-74

On our last build we used a punch on the top and bottom of the belt slots, then connected them by cutting the leather between holes with a chisel.

On this rig we'll be using a Holster Slot Punch from Texas Custom Dies.

The dimensions of this punch are five-sixteenth-inch by one and nine-sixteenth-inch. (5/16" x 1-9/16"). This gives us one-sixteenth-inch (1/16") leeway on the belt.

Once you start building quantities of holsters you'll appreciate what this tool can do for you.

Figure 12-75

Figure 12-76

Let's get this rig wet and do our initial molding with a press. In our shop we use a twelve-ton H press with two-inches of Durometer: 40-Shore "A" Natural Gum Rubber above and below the holster.

Other options would be various foam rubbers. Holster Smith has Kydex presses and Kydex forming foams available as well.

Let's start with our mold gun.

Notice: We have a quarter-inch (1/4") wood dowel rod taped to the mold from the rear of the front sight, and extended to the muzzle side of the ejection port.

Figure 12-77

Now let's get that holster wet!

Figure 12-78

Don't forget to open the holster up and let water saturate the inside.

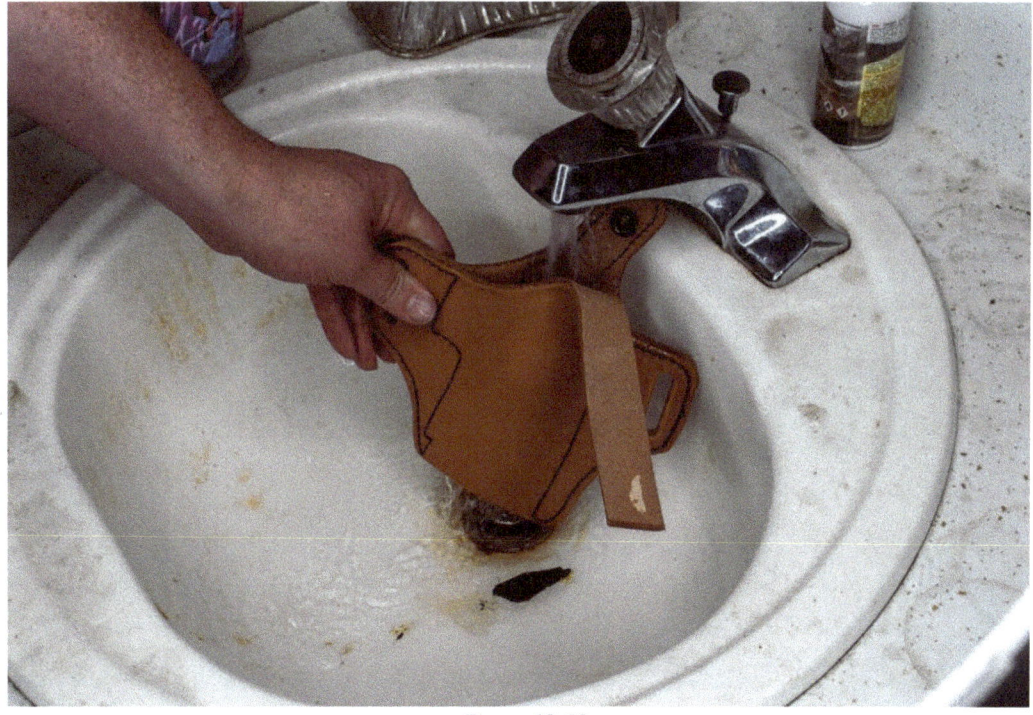

Figure 12-79

Now, let's get the mold into the holster.

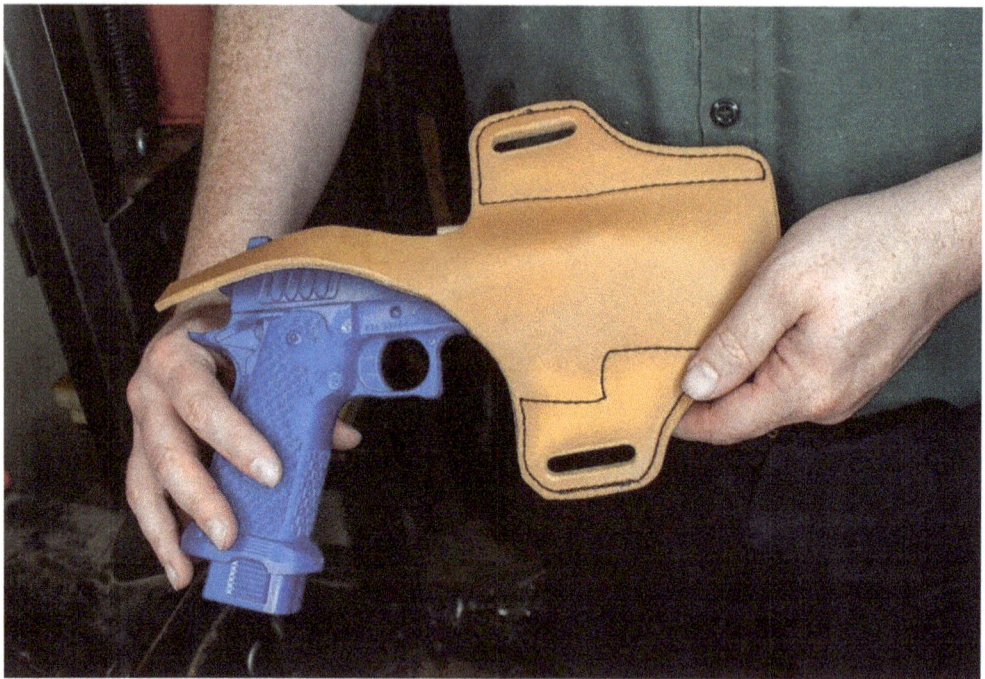

Figure 12-80

After you've firmly seated the gun mold into the holster, take a quick look at the muzzle end to ensure the mold isn't rotated.

Figure 12-81

Place the holster and mold into a plastic bag. This will help keep the rubber from burning the holster.

Remember falling on a hardwood floor during gym and burning your knee? The same can happen to leather.

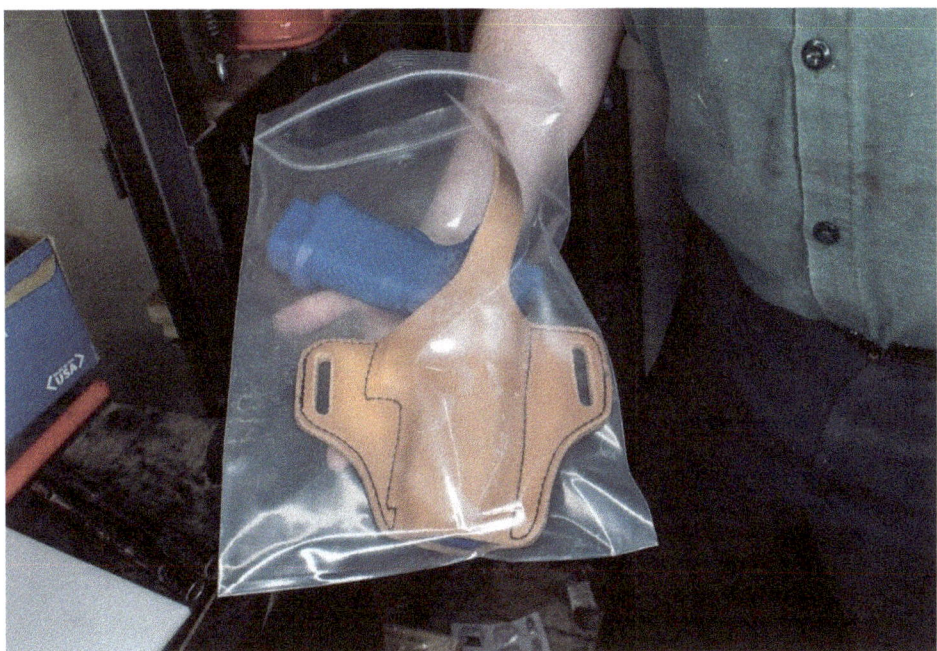
Figure 12-82

Make sure the holster is centered in the press.

Figure 12-83

Place the top layers of rubber above the holster and insert a plate and any spacers you may need.

Figure 12-84

Now smash the snot out of this critter!

Figure 12-85

Give it about five-minutes or so.

Note: If you leave and grab an adult beverage, or seven at this point, nothing in this press will hurt your holster. If you get tired and forget about it till tomorrow, all will be well!

Let's remove the holster from the press.

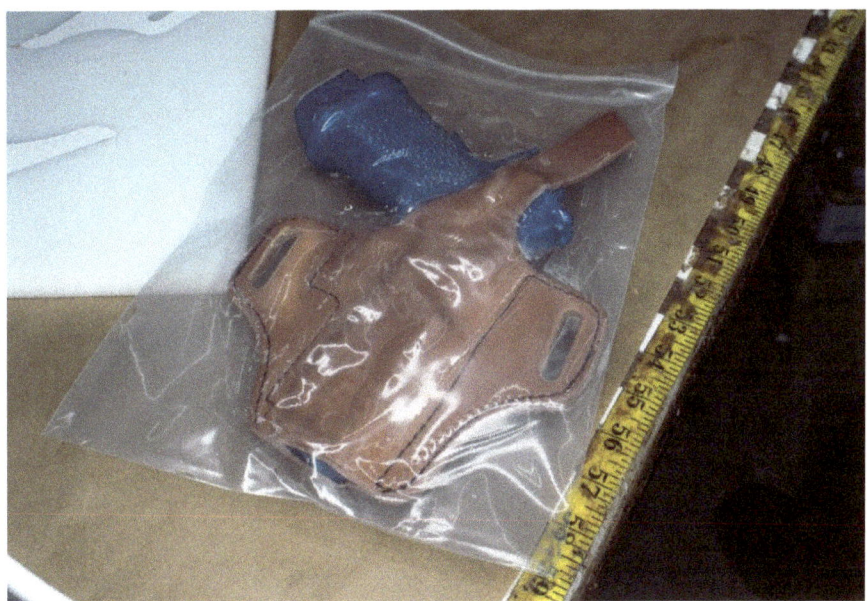

Figure 12-86

Remove from the bag and look at the definition we get from the initial block molding.

Figure 12-87

Because this is a thumb break holster, all we want to achieve with our molding is to make the holster attractive.

We won't be working retention areas into either the trigger guard or the ejection port.

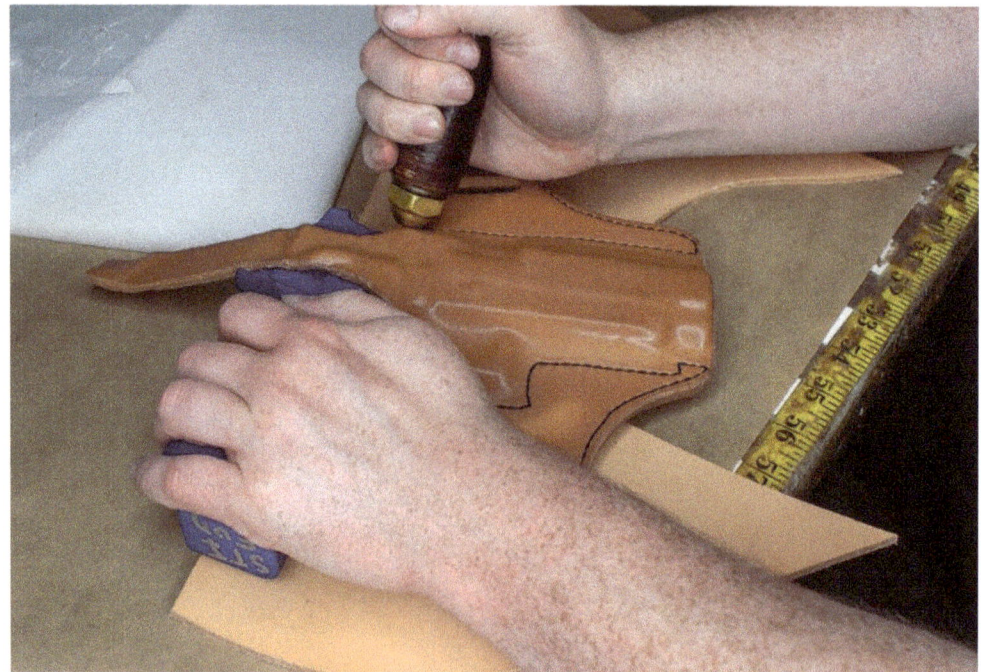

Figure 12-88

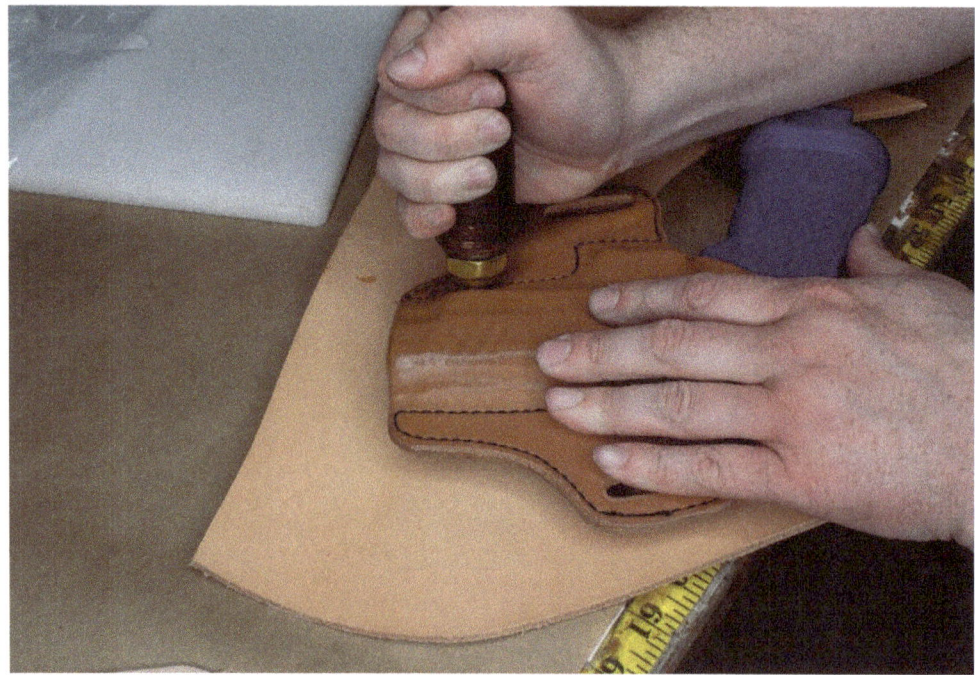

Figure 12-89

Remove the mold from the holster and let it dry completely.

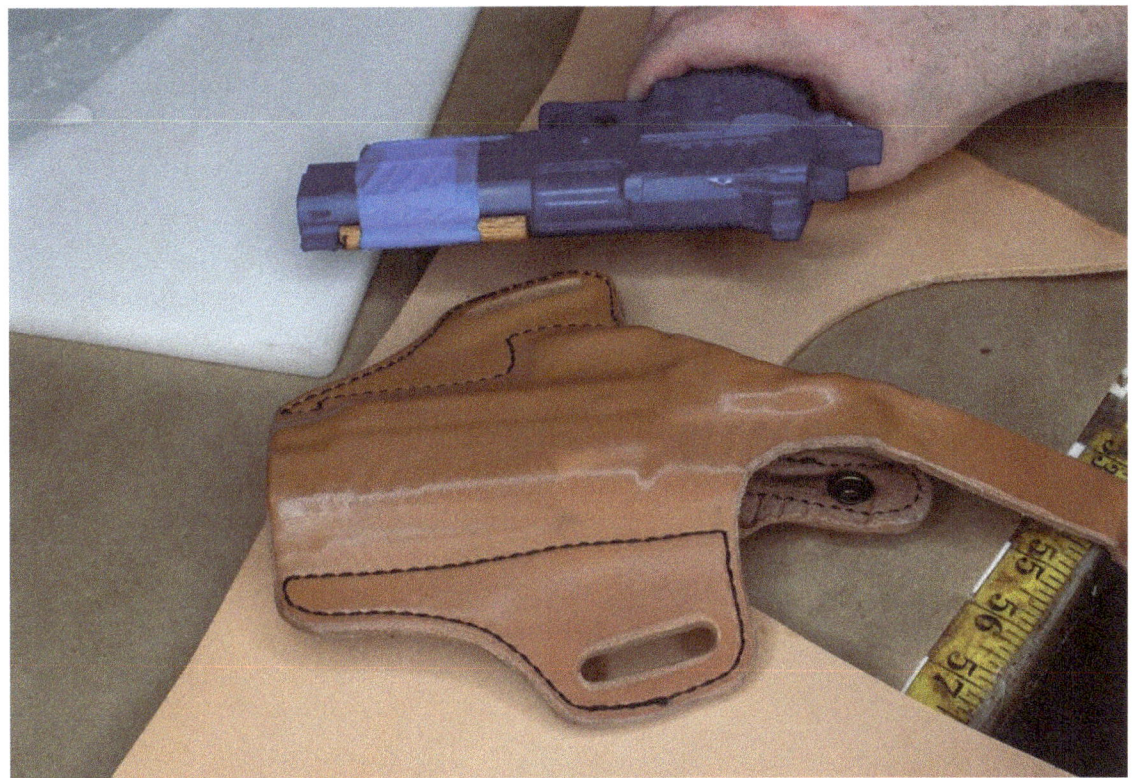

Figure 12-90

Chapter 12: Holster Building – Thumb Break Holster

In the last chapter we pre-dyed our leather and brushed on an acrylic after the molding was complete and the holster was dry.

On this holster we're gonna do things a little different.

We're gonna lightly oil the holster and put it in the sun so it can get a suntan. That's right, a suntan!

Start with your dry holster.

Figure 12-91

Put some neatsfoot oil in your hand. We're just rubbing a little oil on the surface. We do NOT want to saturate the leather.

Figure 12-92

221

We puts the lotion on the skin…
Whoops! Bad movie reference!
Rub that neatsfoot oil onto the holster.

Figure 12-93

Doesn't it look happy? Think of this as a 2nd Amendment spa treatment.

Figure 12-94

Now place the holster in full sunlight, and give it three or four hours. Don't forget to turn it. No one likes tan lines!

Figure 12-95

We left the holster in the sun for an afternoon. This is the beautiful mellow color we got.

Figure 12-96

We're going to dip the whole thing into acrylic sealer.

Here, we're using Angelus brand satin acrylic. You can also use Fiebings Resolene Acrylic Sealer as well.

The key to chemicals is to not cross the streams! If using Fiebings dyes, stick to Fiebings acrylics. The same can be said of Angelus products. If using Angelus dye, stick to Angelus Acrylics.

As you can see, we have a plastic bin full of acrylic sealer here.

Figure 12-97

Let's give it a dunk!

Treat this rig the way you always wanted to treat your Ex! Keep it under till it stops bubbling!

I want you to hold the edge of the bin and gently rock the finish back and forth, while keeping the holster moving back and forth.

Pay special attention to the stitching and making sure you get acrylic inside of the holster.

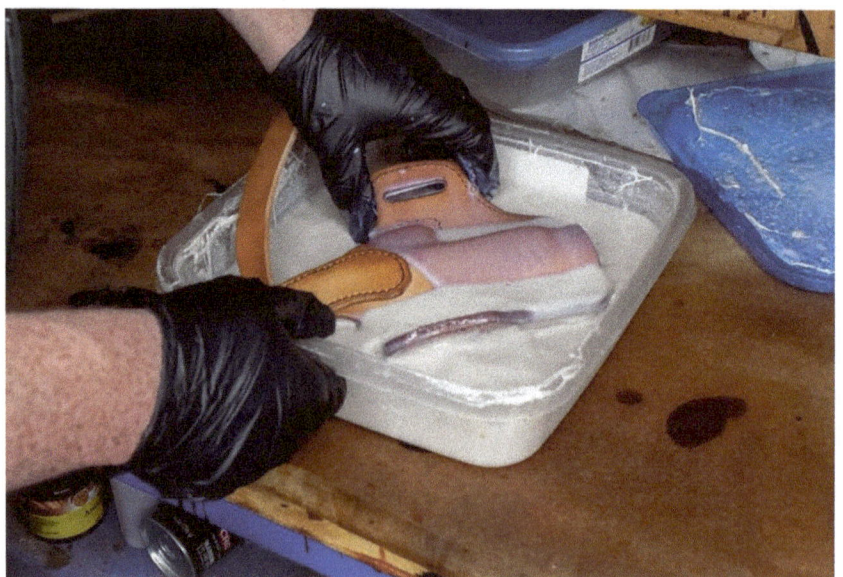
Figure 12-98

Thoroughly wipe the excess acrylic from the holster, both inside and out.

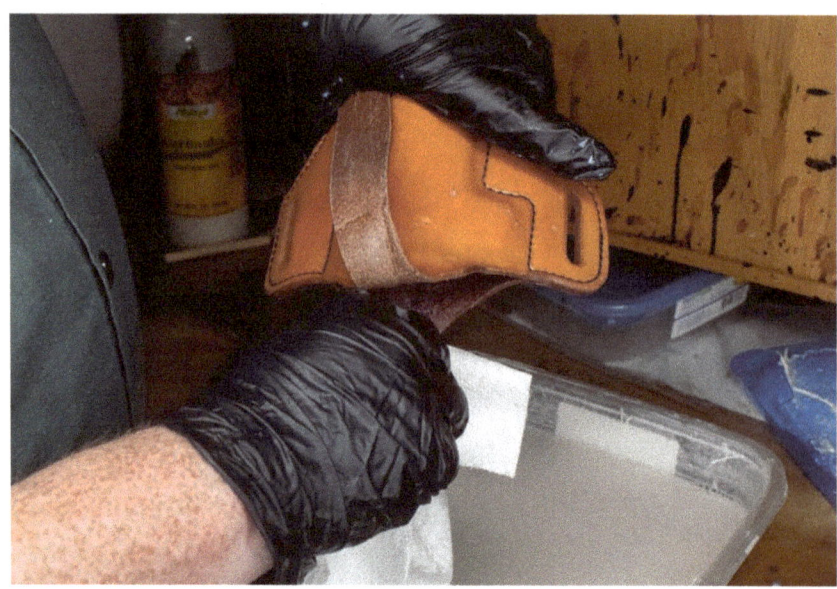
Figure 12-99

And outside…

Figure 12-100

Ensure you wipe any excess acrylic from the inside of the snap on your thumb break.

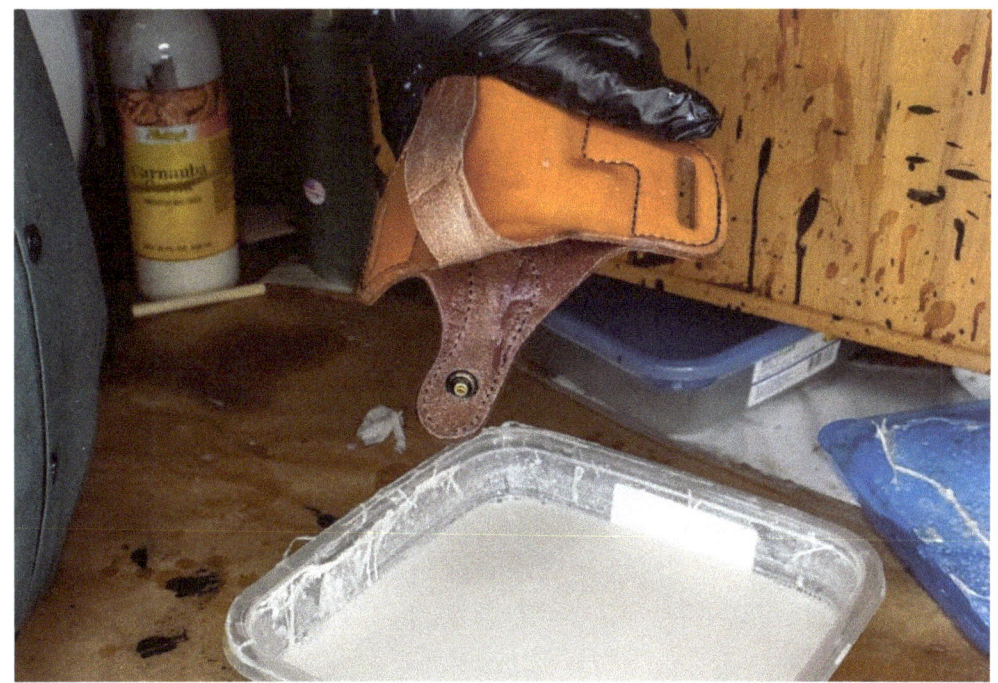

Figure 12-101

Let's give this holster a break and allow the acrylic time to thoroughly cure. Next up, we'll install the male post on the strap to complete the thumb break. You're going to need your snap setter, a one-inch (1") strap-end punch, a one-eighth-inch (1/8") punch, and your second favorite hammer.

Grab your BlueGun again and let's get it in the holster.

Figure 12-102

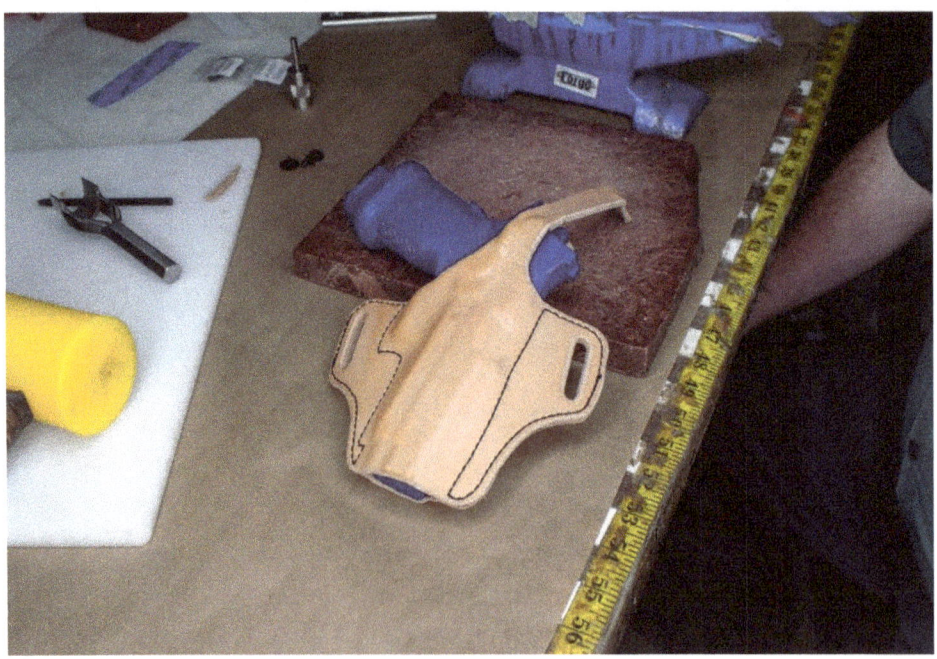
Figure 12-103

Dampen the strap of the thumb break and wrap it around the rear of the slide. Tuck the excess into the holster.

Now, back it out a little until you have about one-eighth-inch (1/8") gap between the strap and the hammer or rear of the slide.

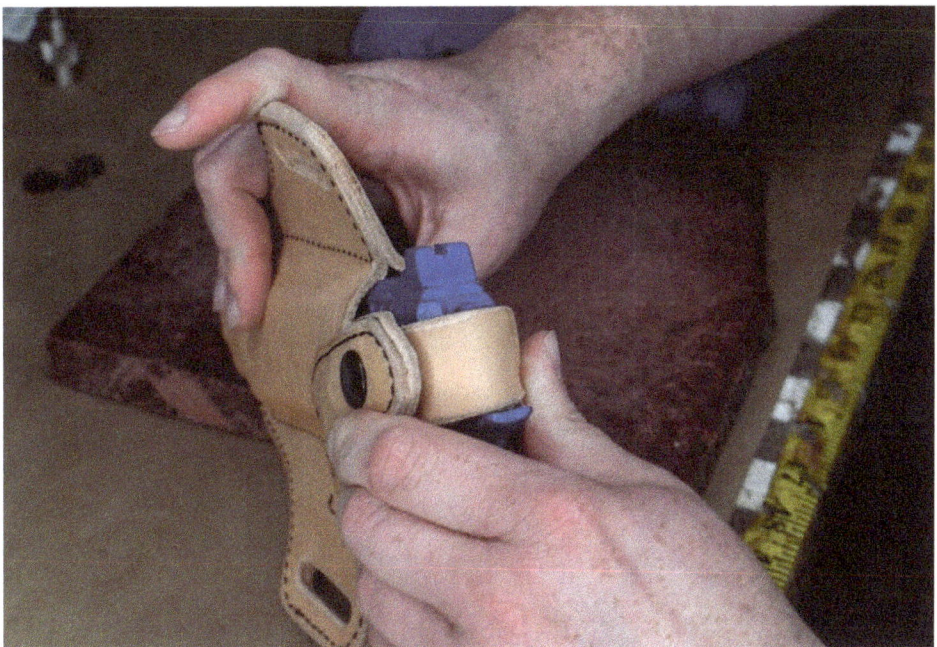
Figure 12-104

Check both sides and make sure the strap is centered on the rear break.

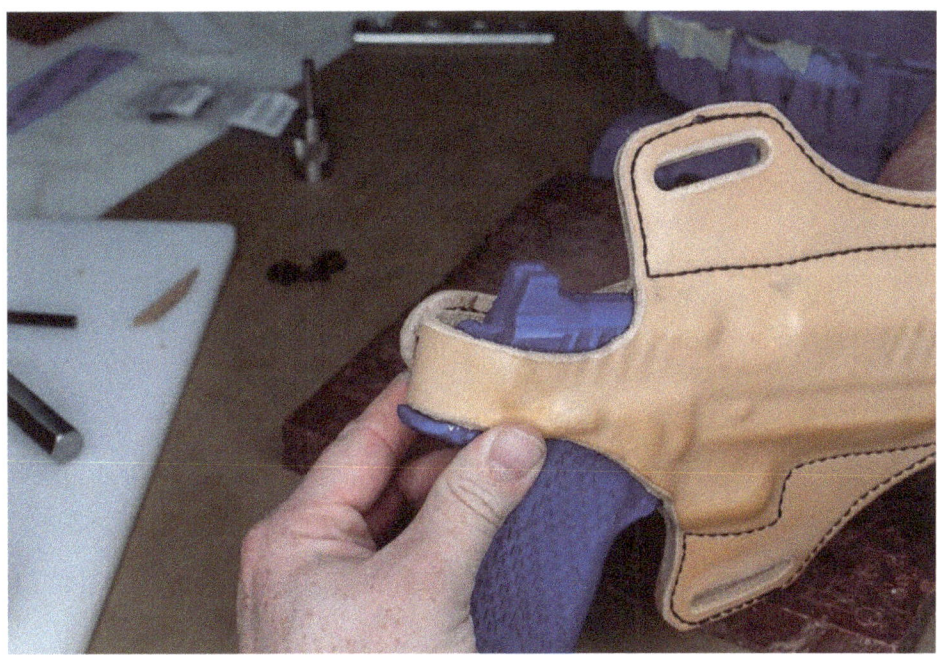
Figure 12-105

Press firmly, or give a gentle whack to the backside of the female snap. You want to make a little impression on the strap.

Figure 12-106

Mark the center of this impression with your pencil.

Then remove the mold gun and punch a one-eighth-inch (1/8") hole for your male snap.

Figure 12-107

Here are the three parts of our snap assembly.

From top to bottom: Hard-pull Line-24 Stud, Line-24 Post, and a nylon Snap Back Protector.

Let's set this puppy!

Figure 12-108

Grab your anvil and place the post of the snap through the hole, from the flesh side

Figure 12-109

Place the stud onto the post.

Figure 12-110

Here we're using a Barry King Line-24 Snap Setter. (It is the bomb!!!)

Figure 12-111

Give it a couple of whacks! You don't have to be gentle here.

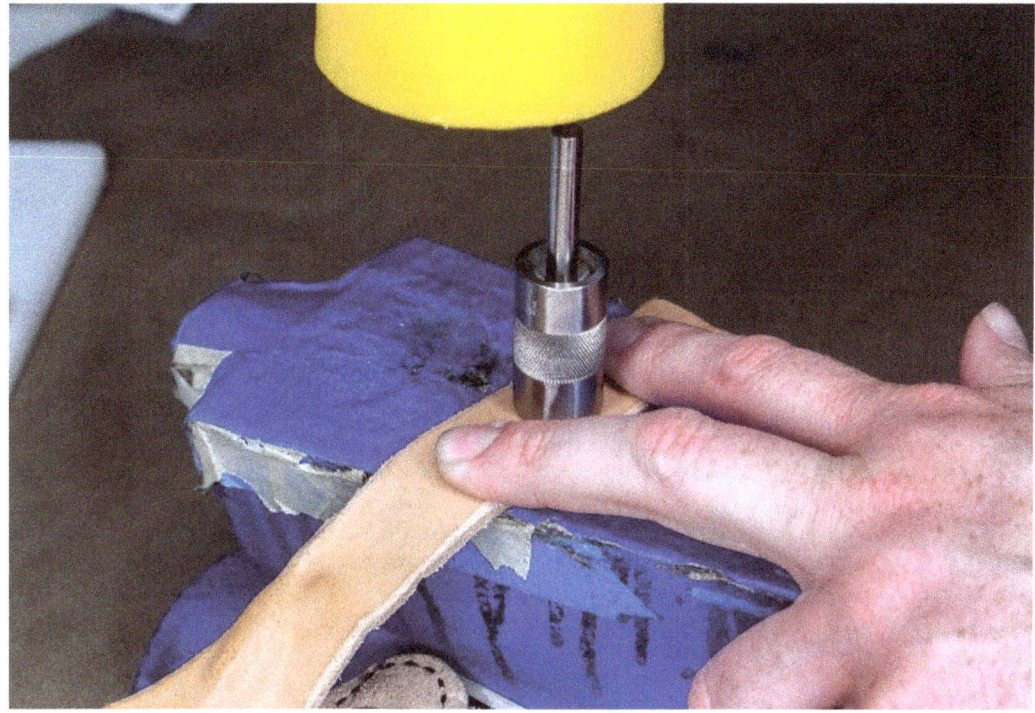

Figure 12-112

And we have a set snap!

Figure 12-113

What the heck is the nylon snap back protector for?

Ancient Holster Maker secret!

As you draw the firearm from the holster, the metal of the snap back will contact the gun.

Figure 12-114

Place the nylon protector on the back of the snap to keep this from happening.

Figure 12-115

Gently love tap it in and it will seat in the snap.

Okay, now it's time to trim the strap and see how your new rig works.

Here we use a one-inch (1") strap-end punch. You can also hand cut if you wish.

Figure 12-116

There's no science to where you cut the strap. We're about one-quarter-inch (1/4") or so from the flange of the snap stud.

Figure 12-117

Give it a whack and your strap is now trimmed!

Figure 12-118

Let's get the gun in the holster and see how we did!

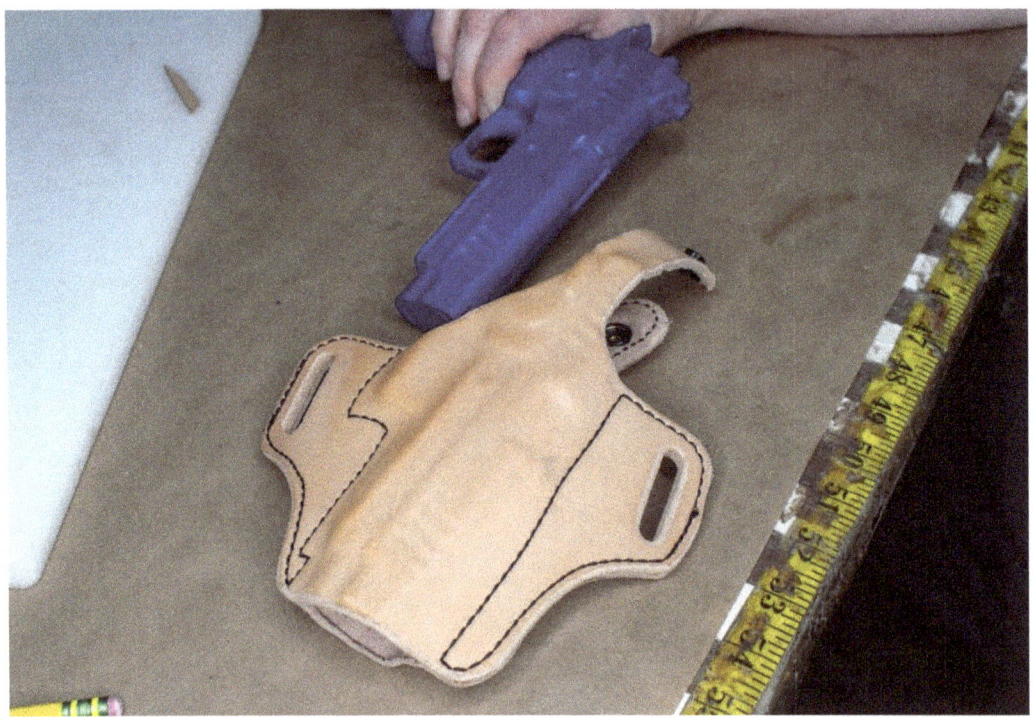

Figure 12-119

Slide the gun back into the holster.

Figure 12-120

And wrap the break over the rear of the slide and pinch the snap closed.

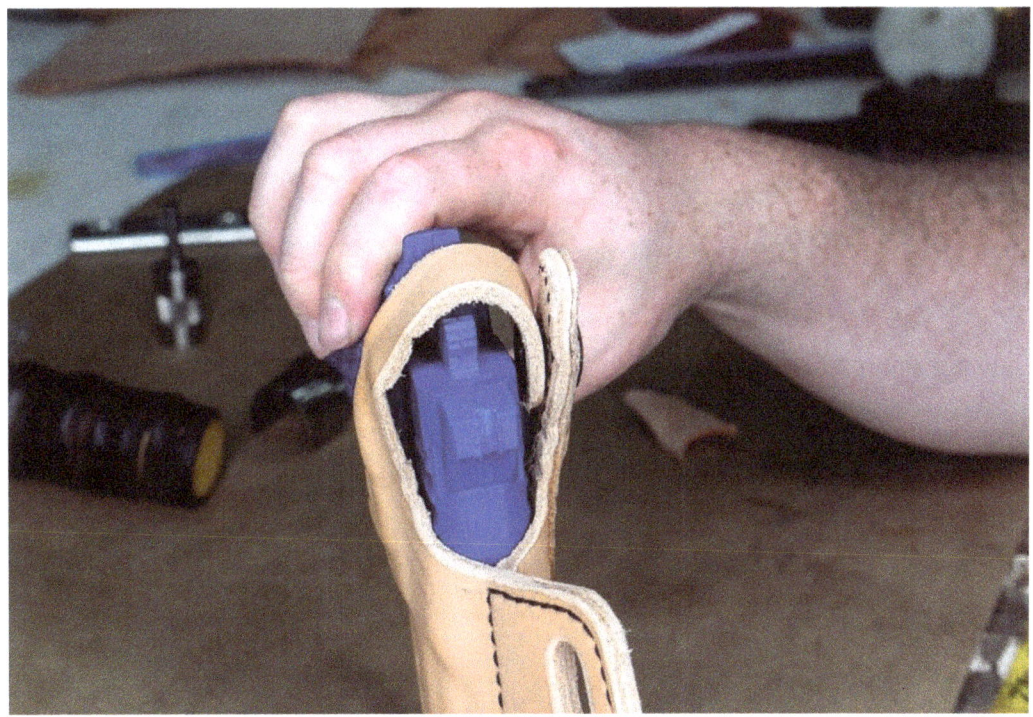
Figure 12-121

When you reach down to draw the firearm, keep the thumb straight.

Figure 12-122

As you tighten your grip, allow the thumb to tighten as well. The snap will *break*!

Figure 12-123

You've successfully designed and built an 8-degree thumb break pancake holster.

It may look different than the build in this book, but you now understand the goals of the design.

Congratulations! Grill up a big ol' steak and feel accomplished!

The advantage to having the steak is, now they have another hide to tan into holster leather!

Chapter 13: Holster Building – SnapCake Holster

Alrighty! Let's begin our SnapCake build.

On this one, we'll deal with setting T-Nuts, using a reinforcement panel, and setting snaps on the straps.

One thing to note: we use a special T-Nut setter that makes the process of setting T-Nuts much easier. However, if you don't have a setter, you can use a socket from a ratchet set that will fit over the T-Nut and cover the tabs that will be pushed into the leather and fold over.

With that out of the way, let's move into the build!

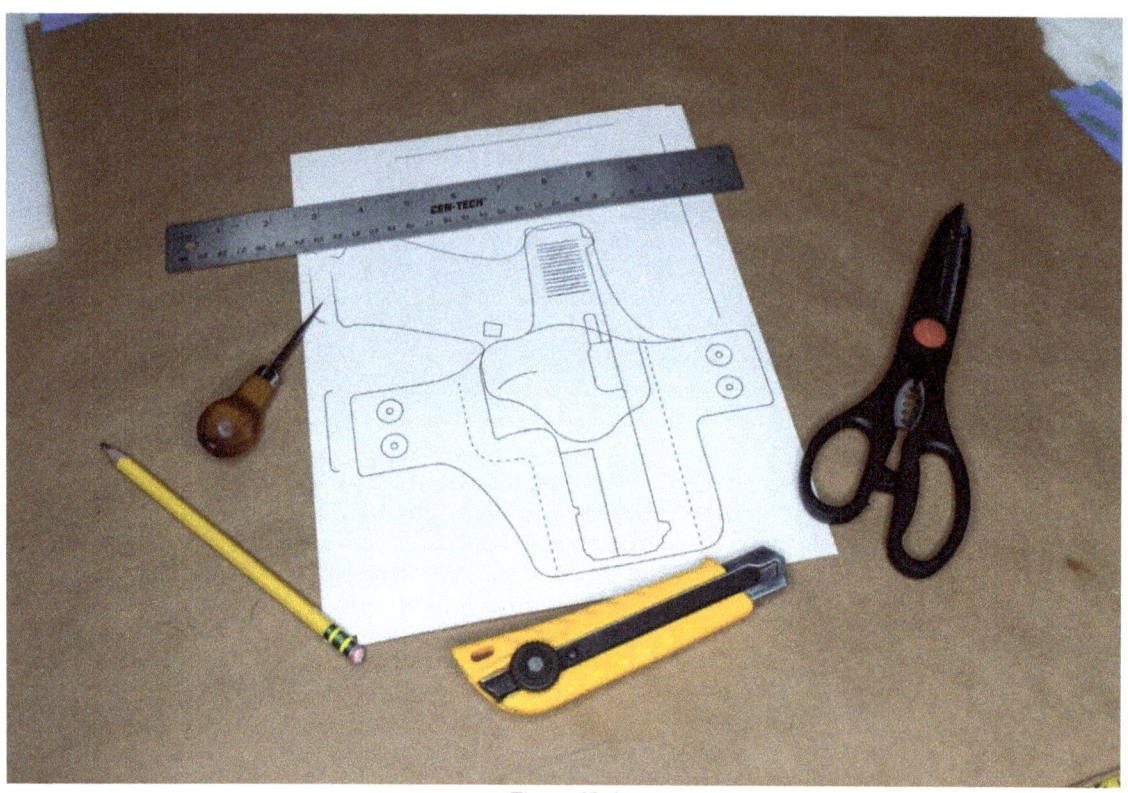

Figure 13-1

First up, cut out your pattern. When you're cutting make sure you don't cut down the dead center of your line. When you pick either the inside or the outside side of the line, it is easier to have a consistent cut.

Figure 13-2

Now that the pattern is cut out, it's time to take out our leather.

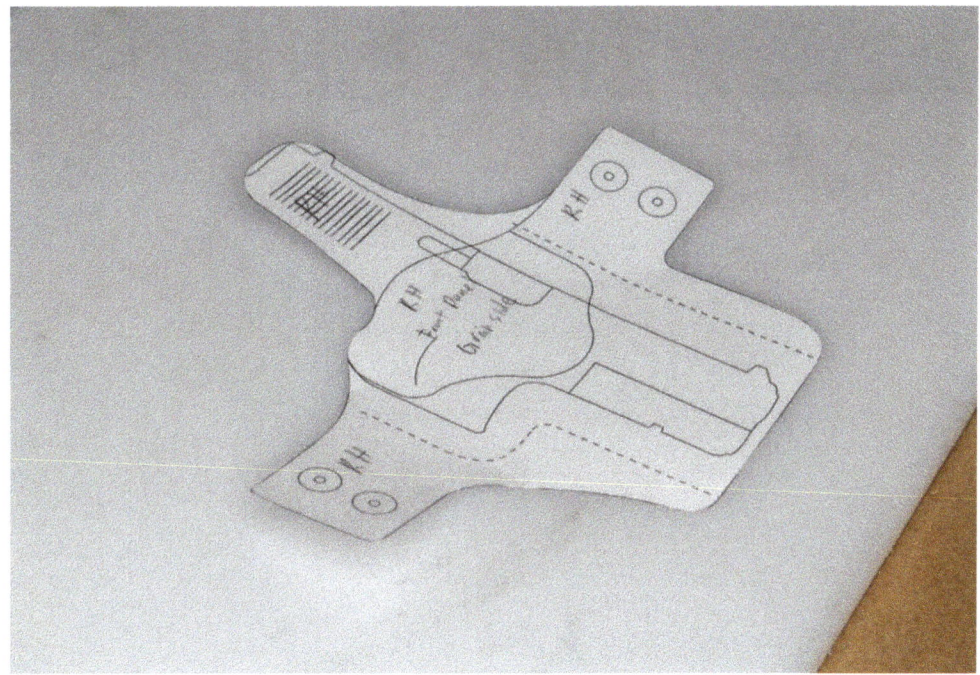

Figure 13-3

Chapter 13: Holster Building – SnapCake Holster

Place it on your leather and mark it up.

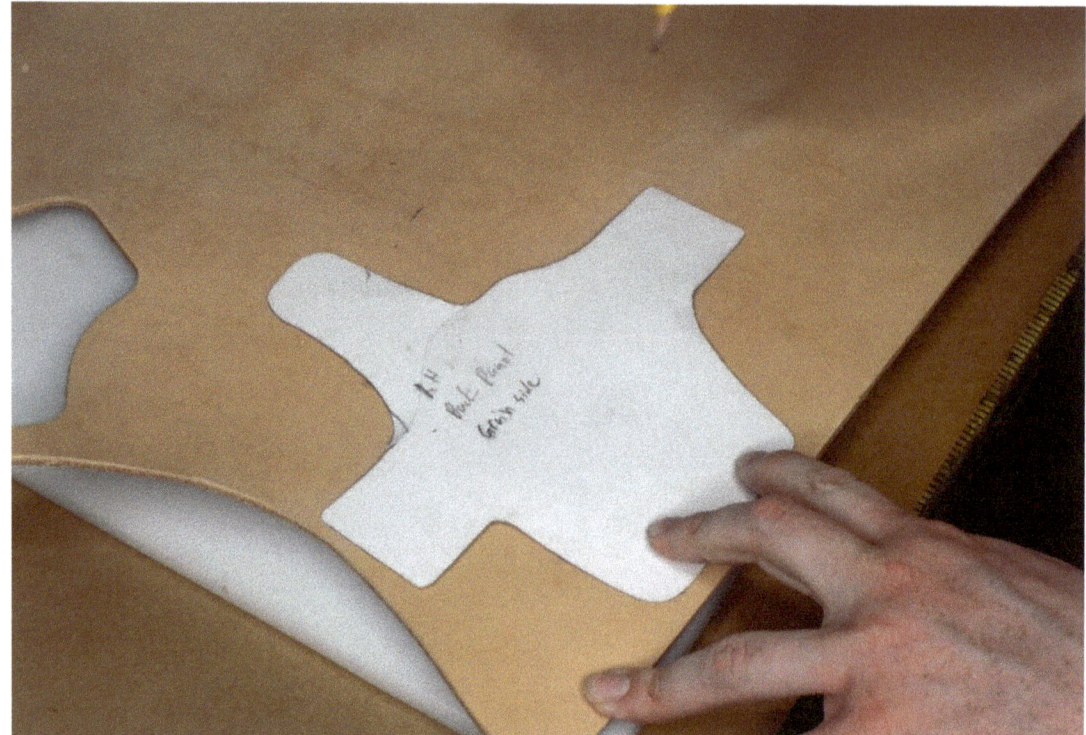

Figure 13-4

Figure 13-5

Now that the back panel is marked up, we can cut it out.

Figure 13-6

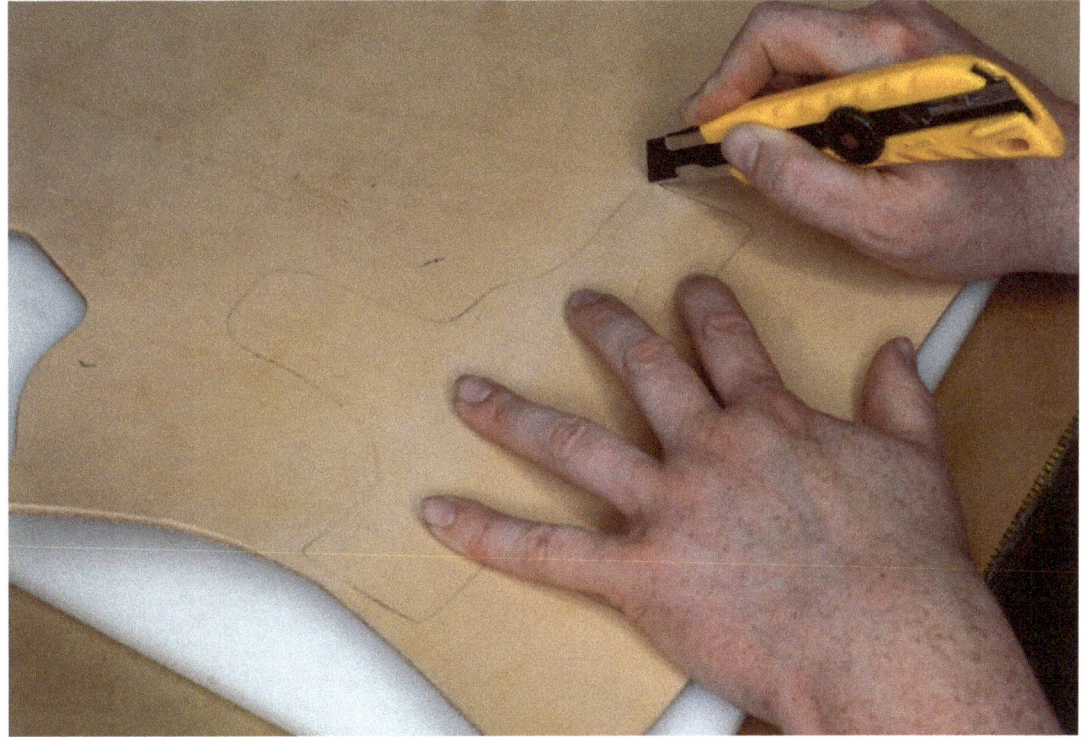
Figure 13-7

We're going to cut the sweat shield off and get ready to trace the front panel.

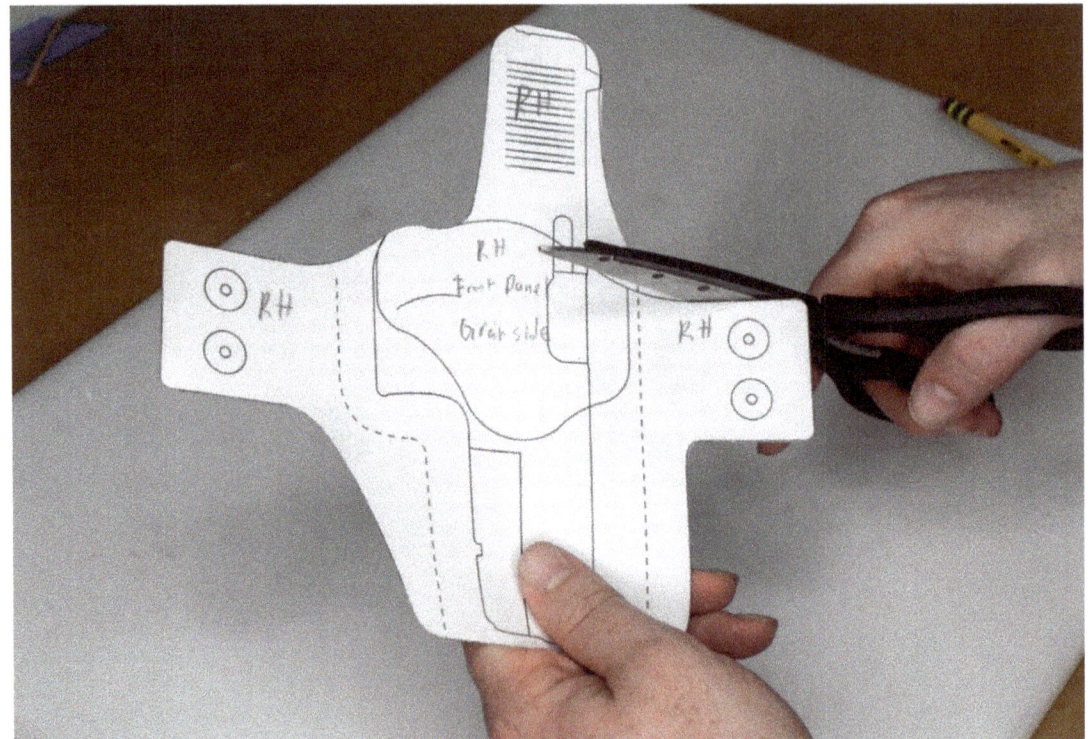

Figure 13-8

Figure 13-9

Let's trace the front panel!

Figure 13-10

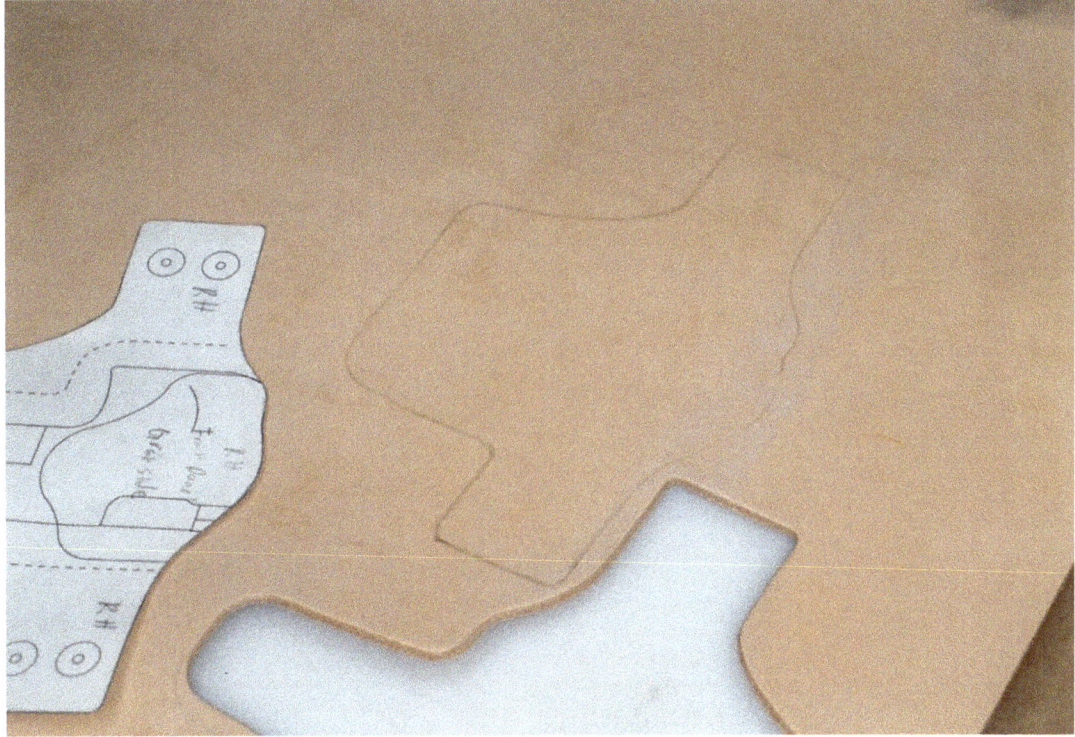

Figure 13-11

Once again, cut out your front panel.

Figure 13-12

Alrighty! Now that we have the front and back panels cut out, let's get our reinforcement panel cut from the pattern.

Figure 13-13

And once again, let's lay this out on our leather and trace it out.

Figure 13-14

Figure 13-15

And now to cut the reinforcement out.

Figure 13-16

The last thing we need to cut is the straps.

Take a piece of leather with a straight edge on one side and set your strap cutter to one and one-eighth-inch. (1-1/8").

We need two straps at about eight-inches long.

In this example we're going to cut one sixteen-inch strap and cut it in half.

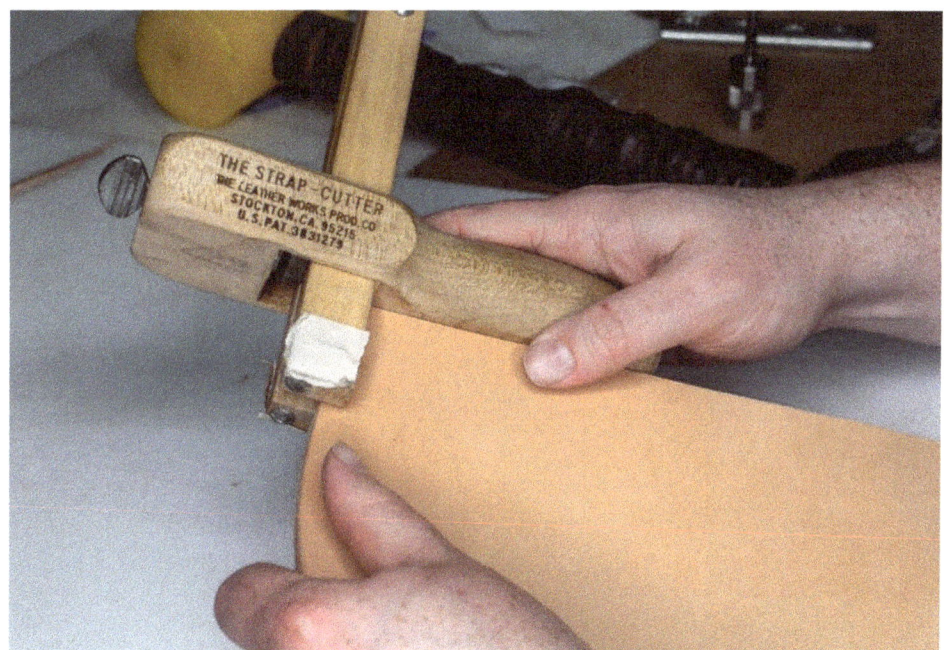

Figure 13-17

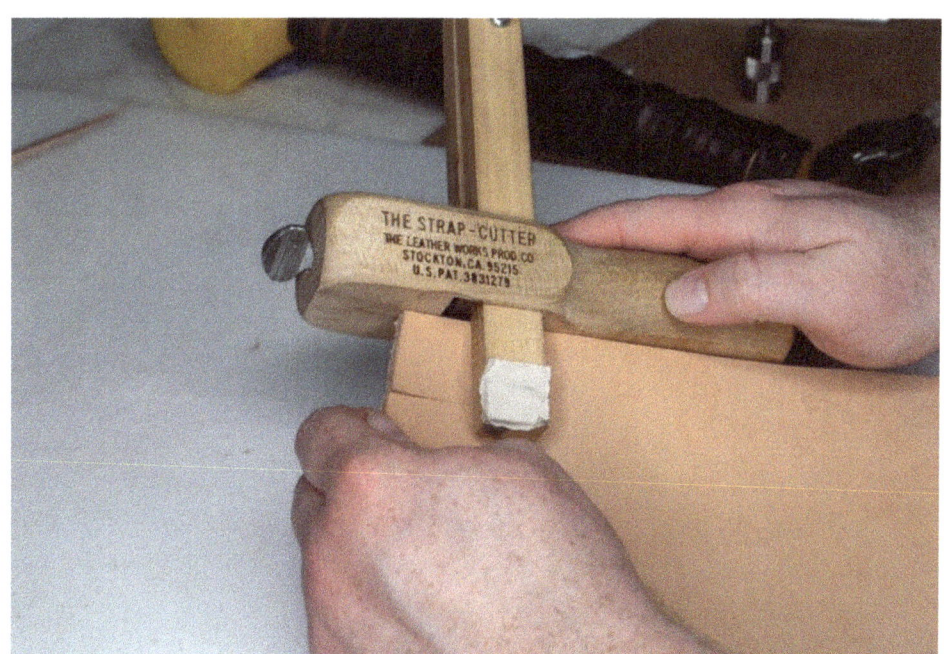

Figure 13-18

Chapter 13: Holster Building – SnapCake Holster

Now that our straps are cut, let's get them prepped so we don't have to worry about it later.

Take a round strap-end punch or just use a circle of the same size as the strap and round off the edge of the first strap.

Figure 13-19

Figure 13-20

249

If you're using one long strap like we did, measure out eight-inches (8"), and cut the long strap in half. Then round off the second end as well.

Figure 13-21

Now we need to punch the holes that will go over our T-Nuts.

Take a wing of your holster and lay it over the strap.

With the top edge of the strap about one-eighth-inch (1/8") from the top of the wing, mark (in pencil) where you need to punch your holes.

Make sure to do this on both straps.

Figure 13-22

Figure 13-23

Let's take our punch and get these holes knocked out.
Make sure you're centered on your strap and grab your hammer.

Figure 13-24

Figure 13-25

Don't forget the second hole.

Knock this one out, then make sure to do this step on the second strap as well.

Figure 13-26

Figure 13-27

The straps are now prepped. Let's move on from cutting and get into assembly!

Figure 13-28

This first big part we need to do is to get the reinforcement panel laid in on the front panel. We'll begin by laying our pattern over the front panel.

Figure 13-29

Next up, take your pencil and mark the front panel around cutout from the reinforcement panel.

One thing to note when marking this line: DO NOT mark it directly along the cutout.

Inset your line a little bit, around one-eighth-inch (1/8") give or take. This will help when you go to glue, making it less likely to squeeze out around the edge of the reinforcement panel.

Figure 13-30

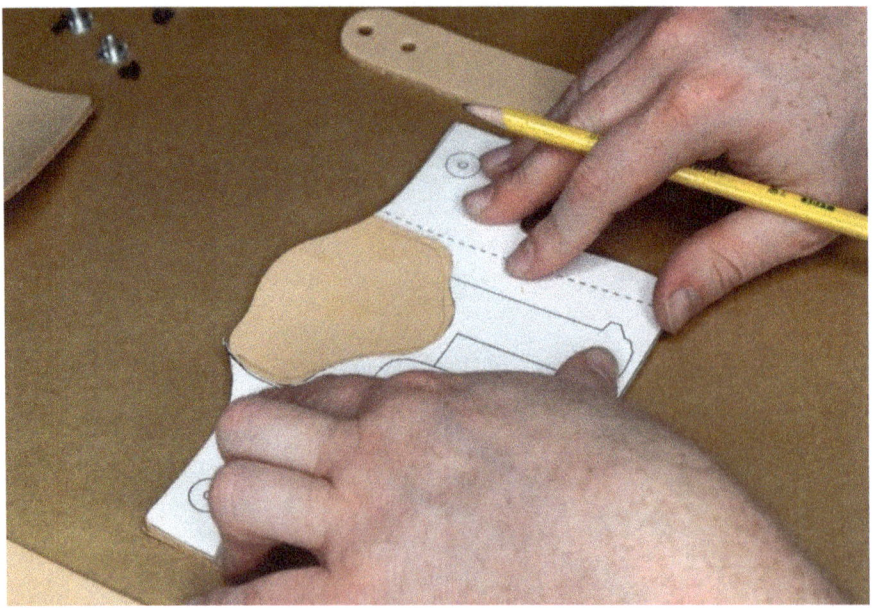

Figure 13-31

Since our reinforcement panel is going to be glued down, some edges will be unable to be reached later.

We must do all edging steps along the sides and bottom of the throat reinforcement before we can continue.

We'll only be edging the hair (grain) side of the reinforcement panel. Don't edge the flesh side or you'll have a gap between the throat reinforcement and the front panel of the holster.

Also, we won't be edging the top edge of the throat reinforcement panel at this time. That will be done after sewing.

Figure 13-32

Time to slick some edges! We use Hagel's Slicking Solution for this.

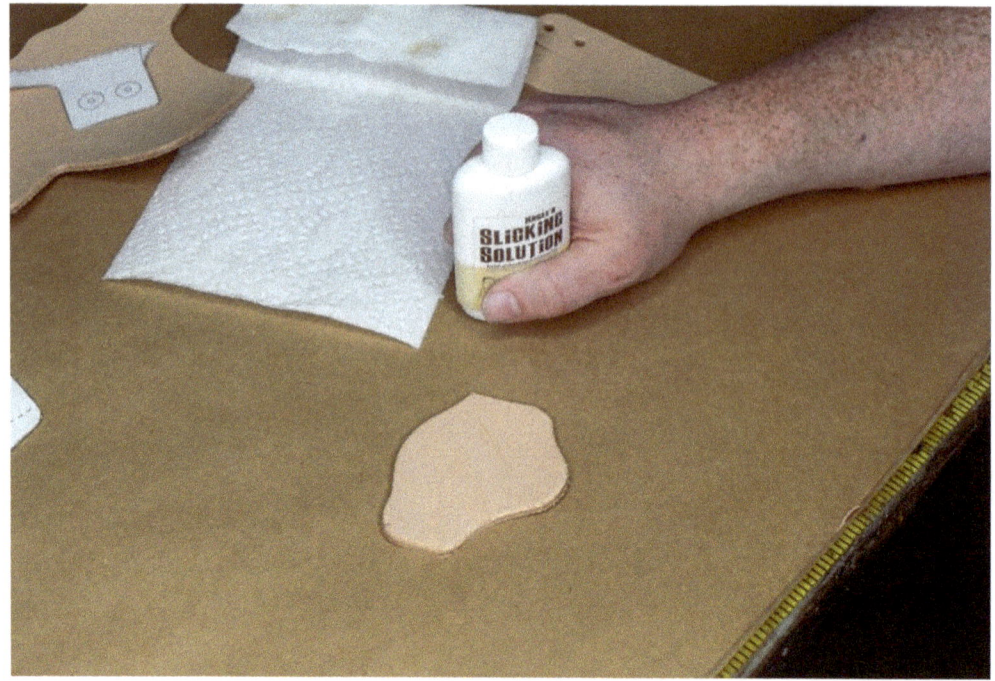

Figure 13-33

You can apply slicking solution many ways. We just use a little on a paper towel.

Figure 13-34

Grab your favorite slicking tool, and let's give this puppy a shine!

Figure 13-35

The Throat reinforcement panel has a nice slick edge on three sides. Remember, we didn't touch the top edge. We'll do that later.

Figure 13-36

Time for glue! Remember, the more accurate you are with where you stick the reinforcement, the less sanding you'll have in the next step.

To start this process, we use a roughing tool to rough up the surface of the grain side of the leather. If you don't have one of these, grab your scratch awl and use it. Keep the scratching on the inside of the line since this won't be recoverable if you go outside the lines.

Figure 13-37

We've roughed the grain side of the front panel. We don't need to rough up the flesh side of the throat reinforcement.

Figure 13-38

Time to pull out the glue pot, making sure to not sniff too much of it.

Once again, when gluing an area within a panel, work from your marked edges inward.

Figure 13-39

When glueing the entire piece, work from the center to the edge, being careful not to drag glue over the the edge of your project.

Figure 13-40

Let the glue sit for around ten minutes, then we will come back and stick them together.

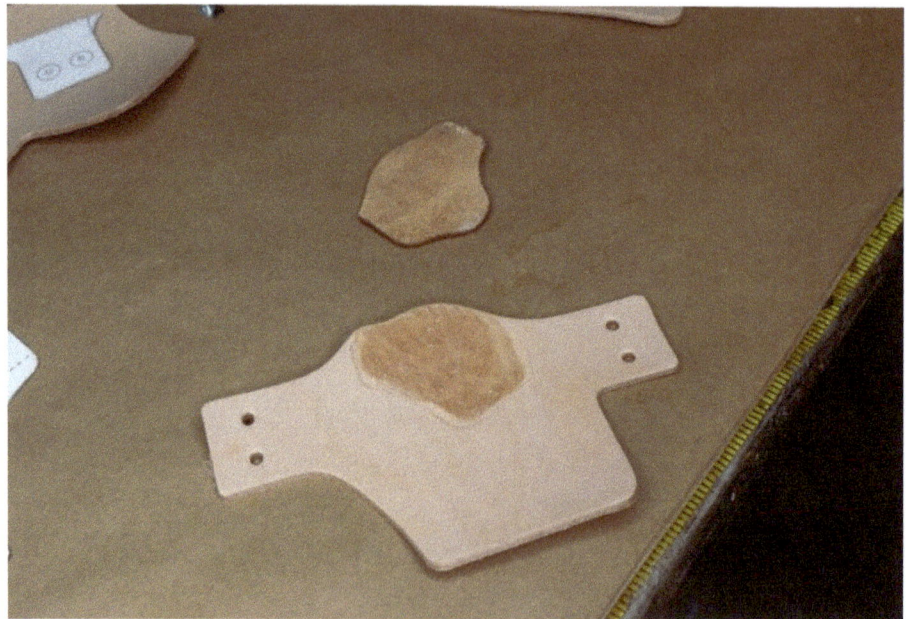
Figure 13-41

We're now ready to stick our reinforcement onto the front panel of our holster.

Carefully align the reinforcement before you place it on the front panel. Once you're satisfied with the alignment, stick it down.

Figure 13-42

Next take your Cobbler's hammer and beat the dog slobber out that thing!

Figure 13-43

Next up on the docket, we're going to set our T-Nuts in the front panel.

Once again, if you have a T-Nut Setter, you're good to go. If you don't have one, you can always use a socket from a ratchet set that fits over the T-Nut and covers the spikes.

Our goal is to drive these spikes into the leather and bend them flat so they pinch the leather and hold the T-Nut in place.

The reason we're choosing to use a T-Nut here is because, if, in the future, there's ever a problem with the strap or snaps, we can easily remove the strap and the snap and make a new one without needing to replace the whole holster.

Enough talking! Let's get these T-Nuts set.

First things first, punch two three-sixteenth-inch (3/16") holes for the T-Nuts.

Now we need to wet both sides of the front panel.

Figure 13-44

Next, bring out a hard surface such as a small anvil.

Notice: We've taped the top of the anvil. This keeps the steel from reacting with the tannins and making black marks on our leather.

Place your T-Nut on the anvil.

Figure 13-45

Now place the hole in your holster over the T-Nut.

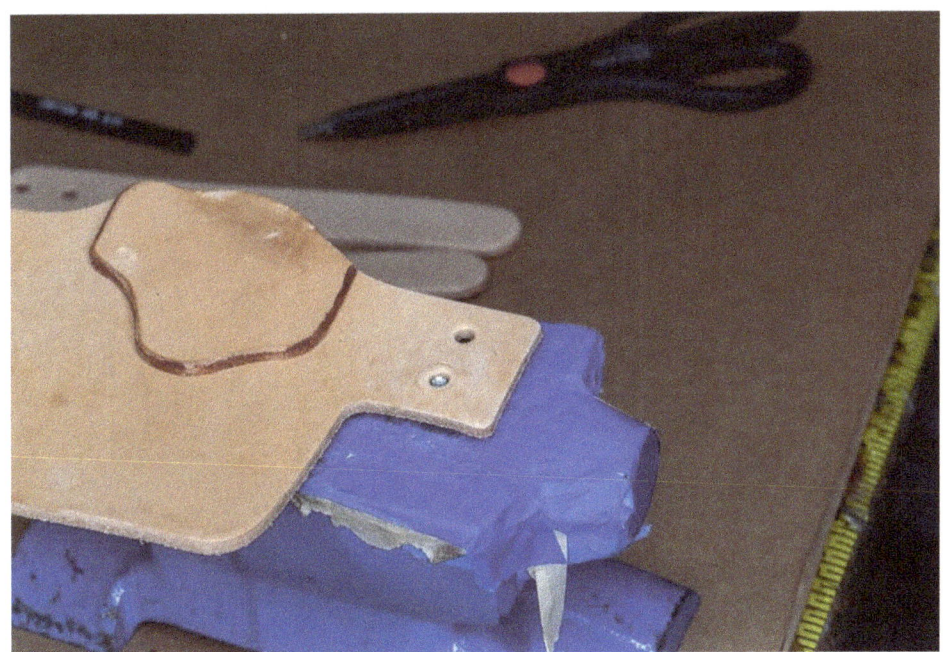

Figure 13-46

Place the setter over the T-Nut and give it a few whacks. Don't be gentle here. We want the points to bend over and *clinch* the leather.

Figure 13-47

Do this for all four holes in the front panel.

Figure 13-48

Install your screws into the T-Nuts now. This serves to protect the threads of the T-Nuts from damage, dye, and acrylic.

Figure 13-49

Next, we need to prep our holster for sewing the reinforcement to the front panel.

We're going to edge the throat area of the front panel and lay in stitch lines.

Before we do this step, if needed, sand the reinforcement panel throat area to make sure there isn't any ledges between the front panel and the reinforcement.

Figure 13-50

Once that's done, we're ready to mark our stitch line.

Figure 13-51

Once our stitch line is laid in place, we'll run an edger around the throat of the front panel, front and back.

If you need, you can cut out the wings of the holster on the stitch lines and use them as a reference for how far to run the edger.

Figure 13-52

Figure 13-53

Now we're going to sew the reinforcement with whatever method you prefer.

Figure 13-54

Afterward, we'll put on some slicking solution and slick the throat area.

Figure 13-55

Figure 13-56

Use your slicking rod and get the throat area nice and slick.

Figure 13-57

Now we're going to do the edges on the toe of the holster and put stitch lines on the front panel.

Take the punch you used for your T-Nuts and punch holes in the paper pattern.

Now, cut out the wings at the stitch lines if you haven't already.

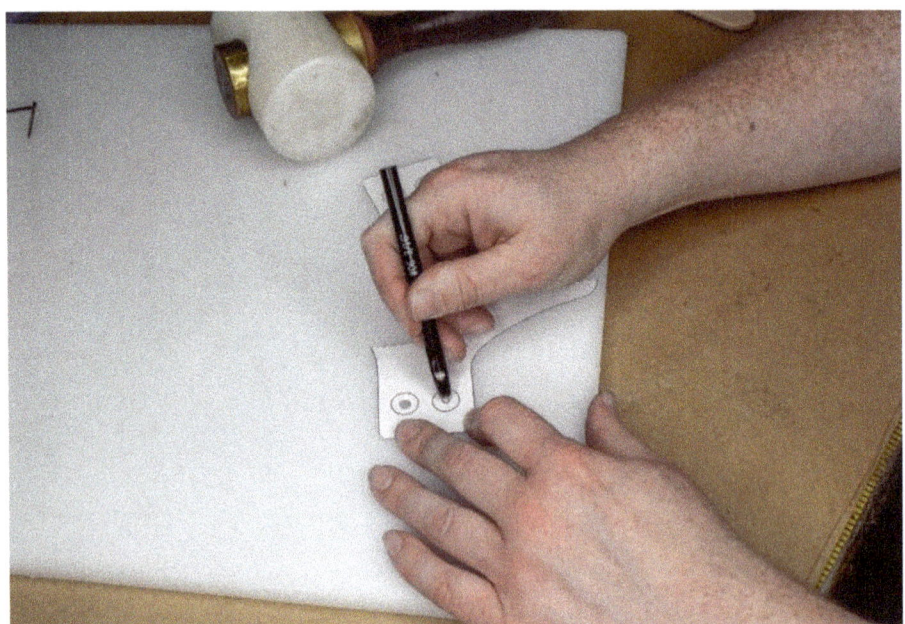
Figure 13-58

Slip the wings over the T-Nuts, and mark where you need to edge.

Figure 13-59

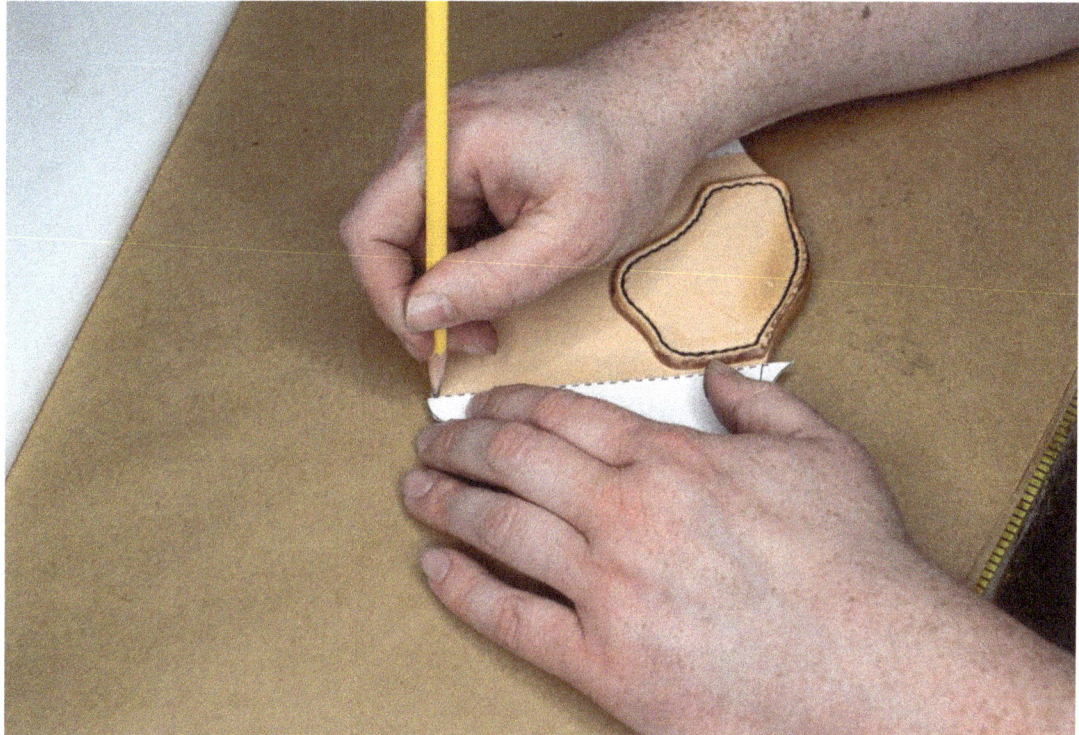

Figure 13-60

Do this on the back panel as well.

Figure 13-61

Figure 13-62

Now, run the edger between the lines on both sides of both panels.

Figure 13-63

Figure 13-64

And now the front panel.

Figure 13-65

Chapter 13: Holster Building – SnapCake Holster

Figure 13-66

Next, place the wings back over the T-Nuts and trace your stitch lines for the slide and trigger guard side.

Figure 13-67

275

Once complete, mark your glue lines on the flesh side of the holster with a pencil, using the wings as your guide on both the front and back panels.

Figure 13-68

Figure 13-69

Chapter 13: Holster Building – SnapCake Holster

Here's what we have so far.

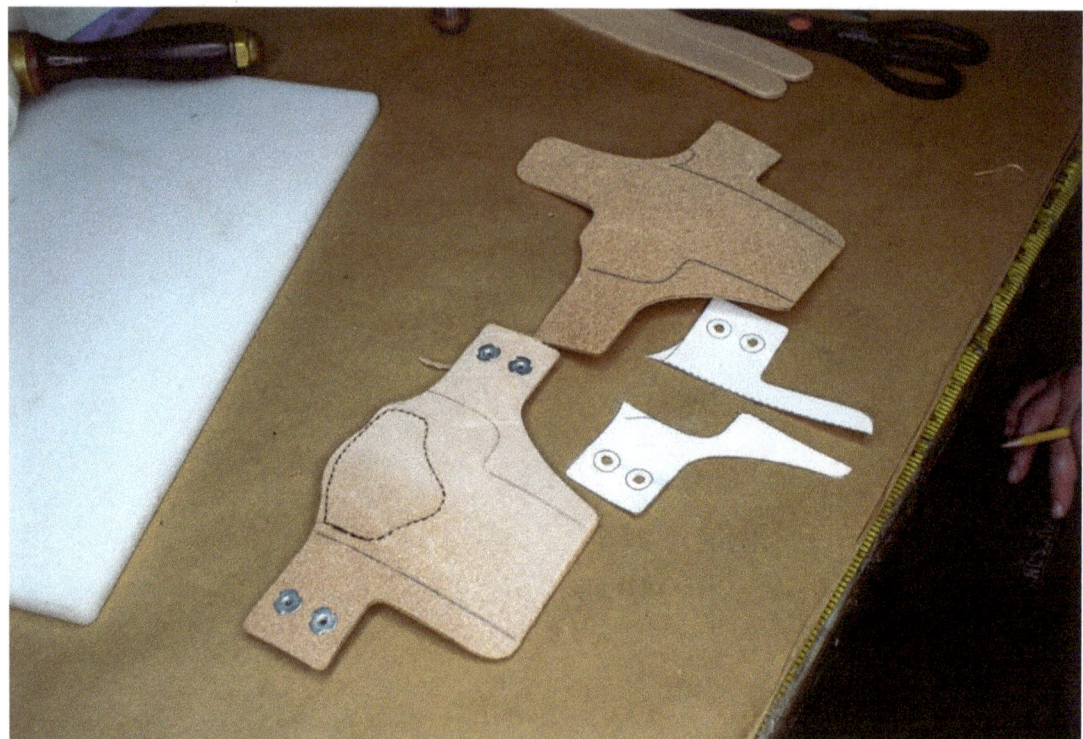

Figure 13-70

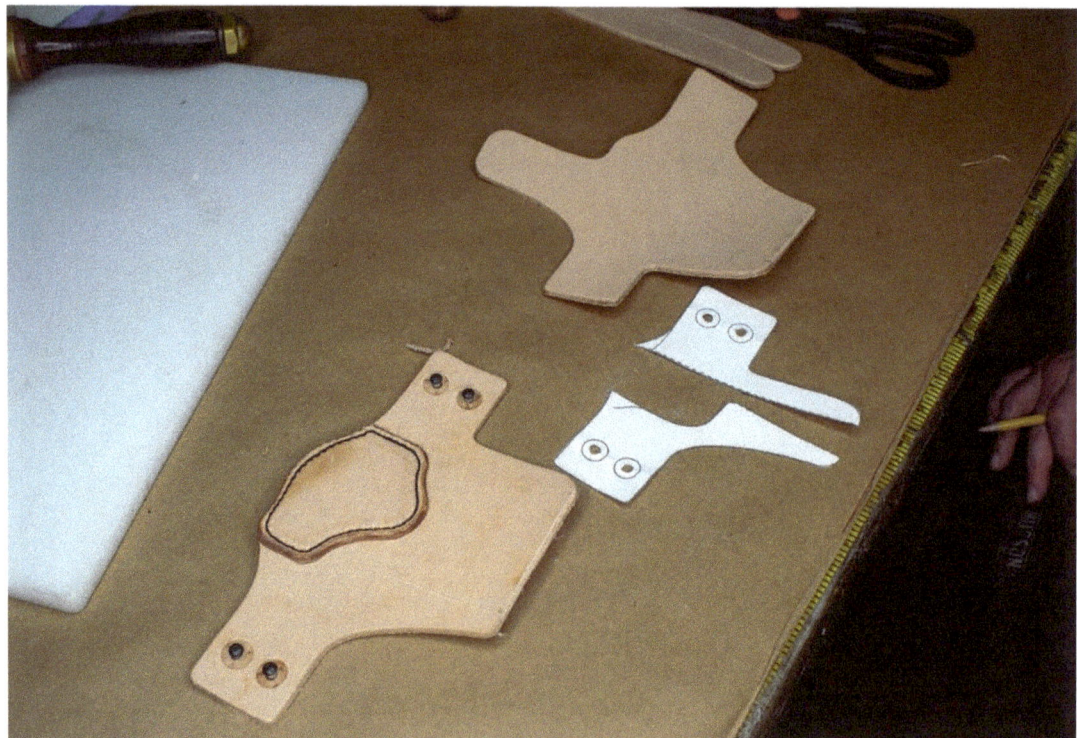

Figure 13-71

Now we want to edge finish the toe, where we ran the beveler earlier. Remember, we want to slick the toe of the front and the back panels this time.

Figure 13-72

Figure 13-73

The next step is our favorite. It's glue time!

Get out the glue and start applying it inside the glue lines on both halves of the holster.

Remember to always brush out to the edge when doing this to avoid getting glue all over the outside edge of the holster.

Figure 13-74

Once you've glued both panels, take your two halves and align them to the best of your ability.

Now, carefully stick the pieces together while keeping them aligned.

We like to generally work on getting one half stuck down and aligned before we press over to the other side.

Figure 13-75

Figure 13-76

Take your Cobbler's hammer and tap the two panels together. Leave it be and let the glue set before coming back and sewing.

Figure 13-77

Now all we need to do before we go on to molding is to sand, bevel the edges, lay the outside stitch lines on, and finally stitch it together.

While this may sound like a long list, don't worry, these steps go by extremely fast.

Let's either take out the sandpaper, or head over to the belt sander, and get these edges flush.

Figure 13-78

Now let's lay the outside stitch lines down with our calipers on both sides.

Figure 13-79

We want to run our edger around the whole holster, doing the grain (hair) side all the way around, and the flesh side of the sweat shield.

Figure 13-80

We're now ready to stitch!

Once everything is sewed together, we can start molding.

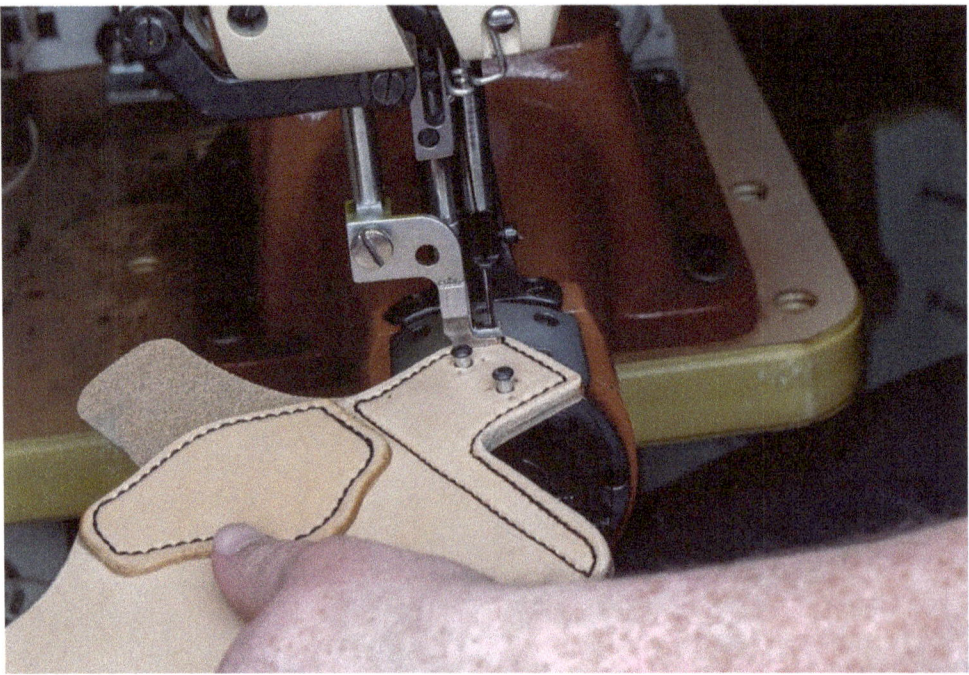
Figure 13-81

We need to prep our BlueGun before we mold.

We're going to use a cut-down dowel rod as our sight channel, which is going to be a molded area that is bigger than our front sight post. This is so the front sight does not catch on the leather and get obstructed when the firearm is drawn from the holster.

Take your dowel rod and cut it where it begins right behind the front sight, and ends right before the ejection port.

Figure 13-82

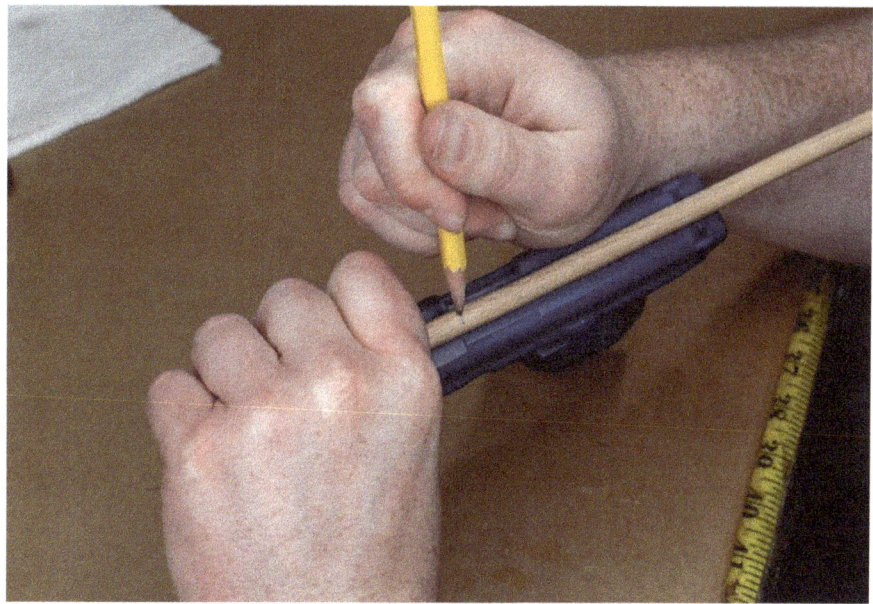

Figure 13-83

Now tape it to your mold.

If you're using a real firearm, you might want to consider cutting a channel into the dowel that you can simply slip over the front sight and into the holster once the firearm is seated and ready for molding. By doing this, you can avoid using tape.

You can also substitute dowel for anything that is circular and about the same size as the front sight.

Figure 13-84

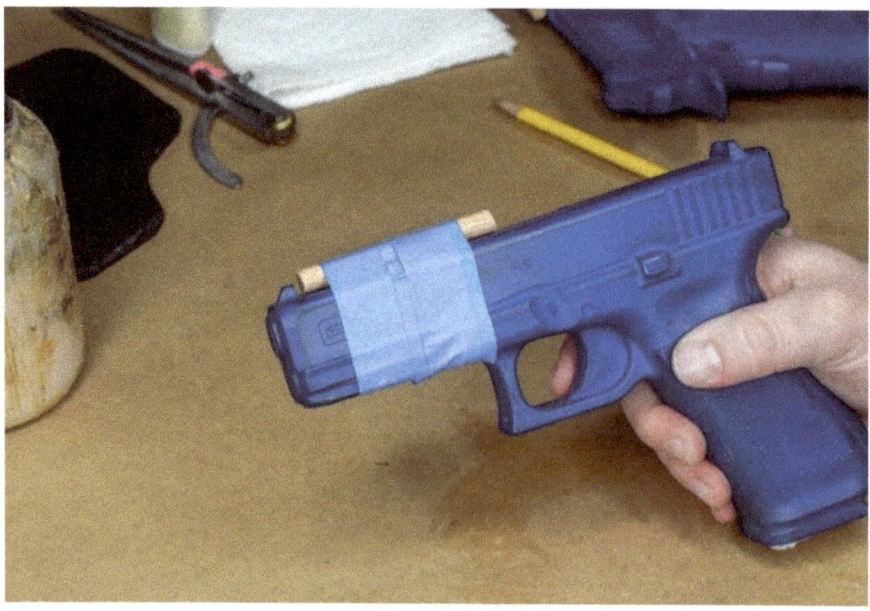
Figure 13-85

To begin molding, we need to get the holster wet.

Dunk it in some water or hold it under a running sink and make sure to get both halves and the inside.

Figure 13-86

Figure 13-87

Once again, if you're using a live firearm, make sure that it's clear and there are no live rounds in either the chamber or the magazine.

Also, stick it in a Ziplock bag so it doesn't get wet and try to rust.

If you're using a BlueGun you can skip that step as the mold will not absorb any water or rust.

Now stick the mold or firearm into the holster and make sure that you get it centered between the two panels of leather. We're looking for a 50/50 split, with the seam being right above the front sight, and not canted to one side or the other.

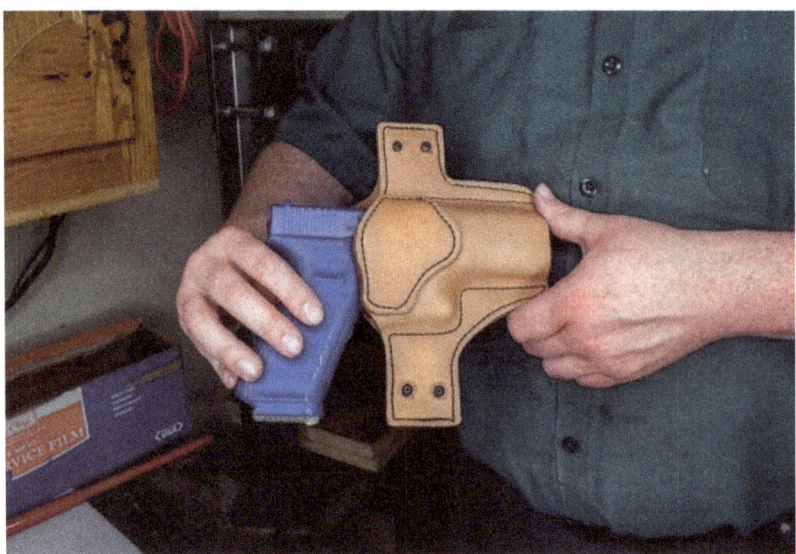

Figure 13-88

Figure 13-89

On this molding job, we're going to be using a combination of the press and hand molding.

Stick your holster in a plastic bag to avoid the rubber leaving marks on the leather.

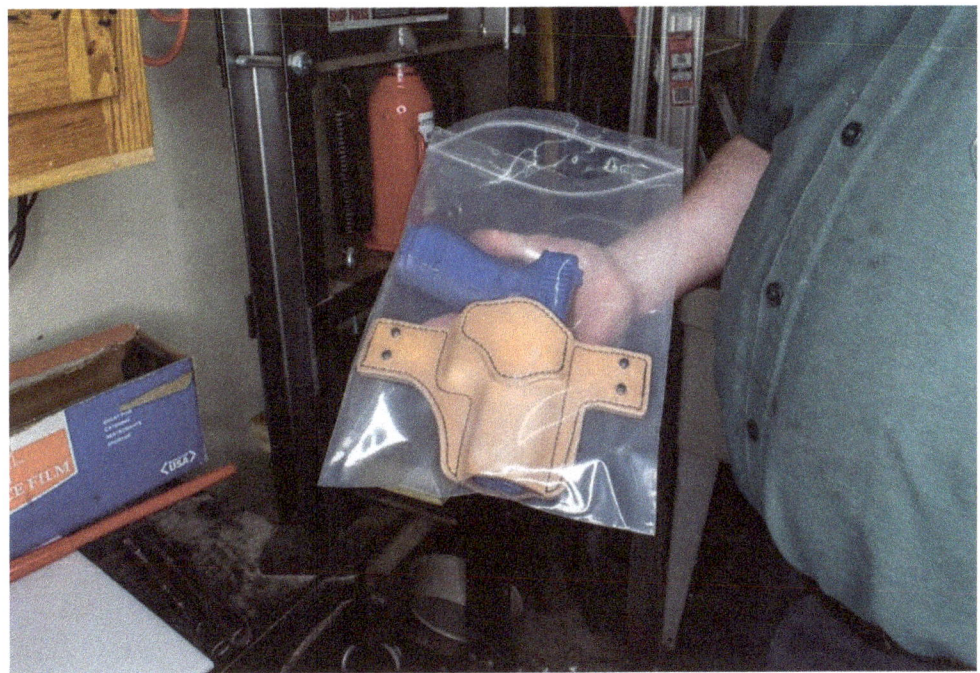
Figure 13-90

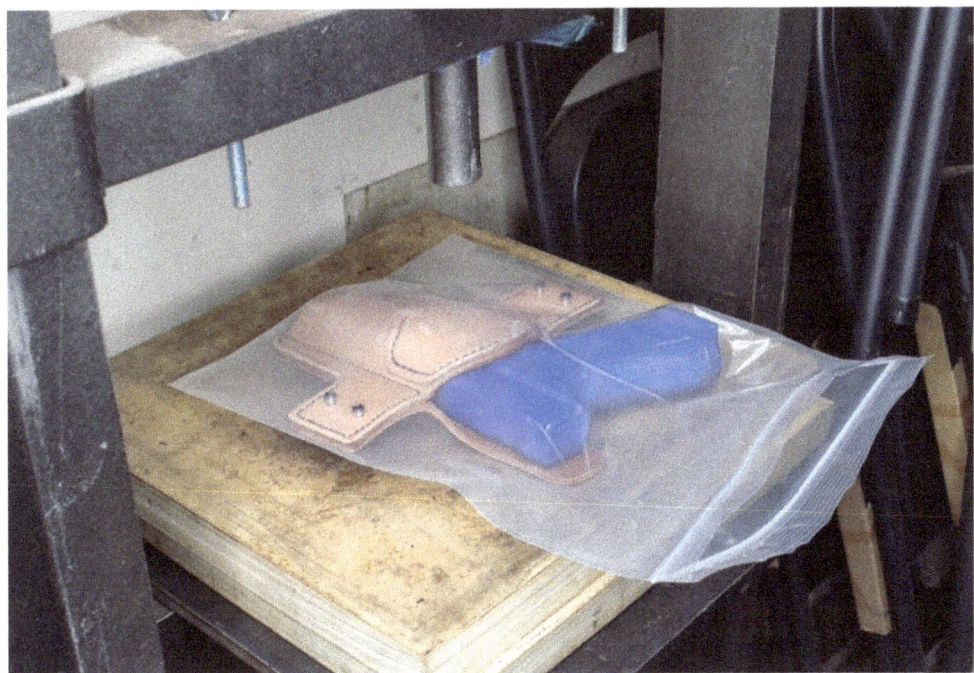
Figure 13-91

Align the holster under the middle of the press, and place your top layers of rubber and steel. Now start pressing!

Figure 13-92

Figure 13-93

If you stick your hand between the rubber while compressing, you can feel how much pressure you're putting on the holster. We don't want to break anything so we're just looking for a bit of squeeze on your fingers.

Figure 13-94

Now let that sit for ten to fifteen minutes.
We will come back and take it out of the press later.

Now that we have the holster out of the press, we can take a look at the tools we'll be using to mold this holster.

All the tools we have out are the tools we use day-to-day in molding holsters. These tools are expensive and there's no need to get them immediately.

However, when you're making a volume of holsters, they'll save your hands and wrists.

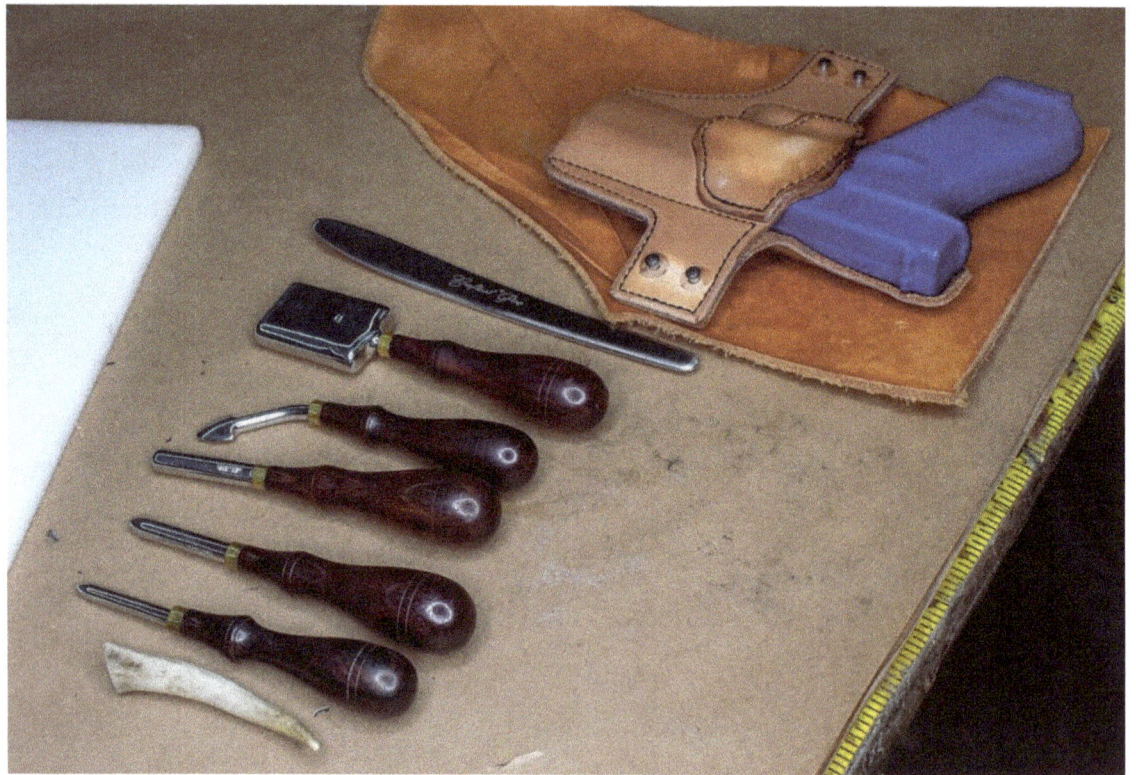

Figure 13-95

We're going to mold this holster how we normally do. However, these images will not show everything exactly as we do it. Much of this stage falls into personal preferences and what we think looks good.

You can build up your own style as a maker just by how you mold your holsters and the level of detail and precision you want to achieve.

Figure 13-96

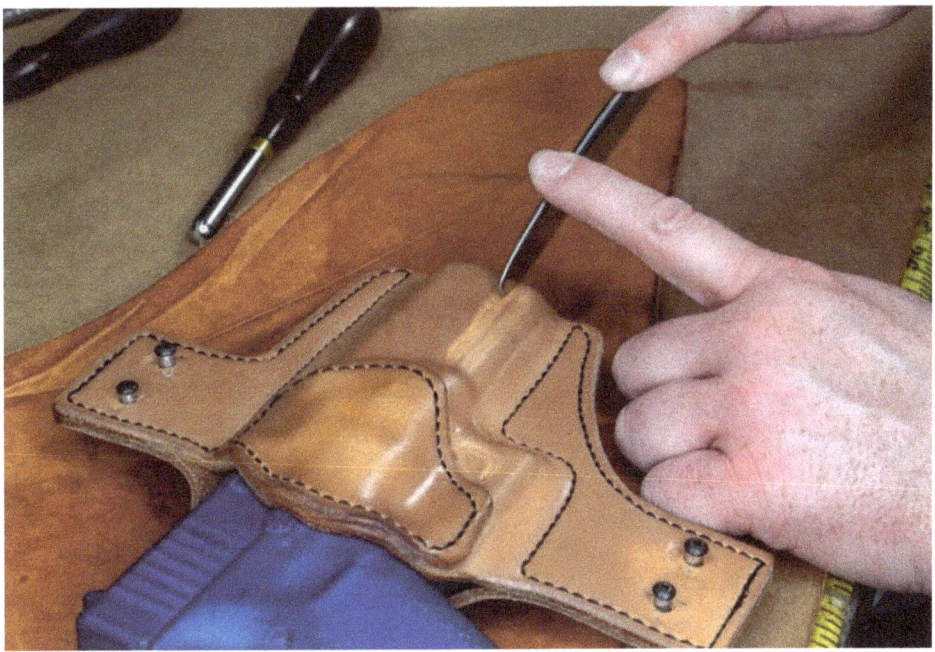
Figure 13-97

Chapter 13: Holster Building – SnapCake Holster

Here's the finished holster after we have molded it.

There are only a few steps left. We still need to dye and finish, and then we're done!

Figure 13-98

Figure 13-99

There are only two big parts left to do before this holster is finished.

The first being dye.

In this example, we're going to show you the way we dye holsters—dip dye.

First, pour dye into a container big enough for the holster. We use a shallow Tupperware container about twelve-inch-square.

Figure 13-100

Chapter 13: Holster Building – SnapCake Holster

Glove up, and prepare to dunk the whole holster in the dye.

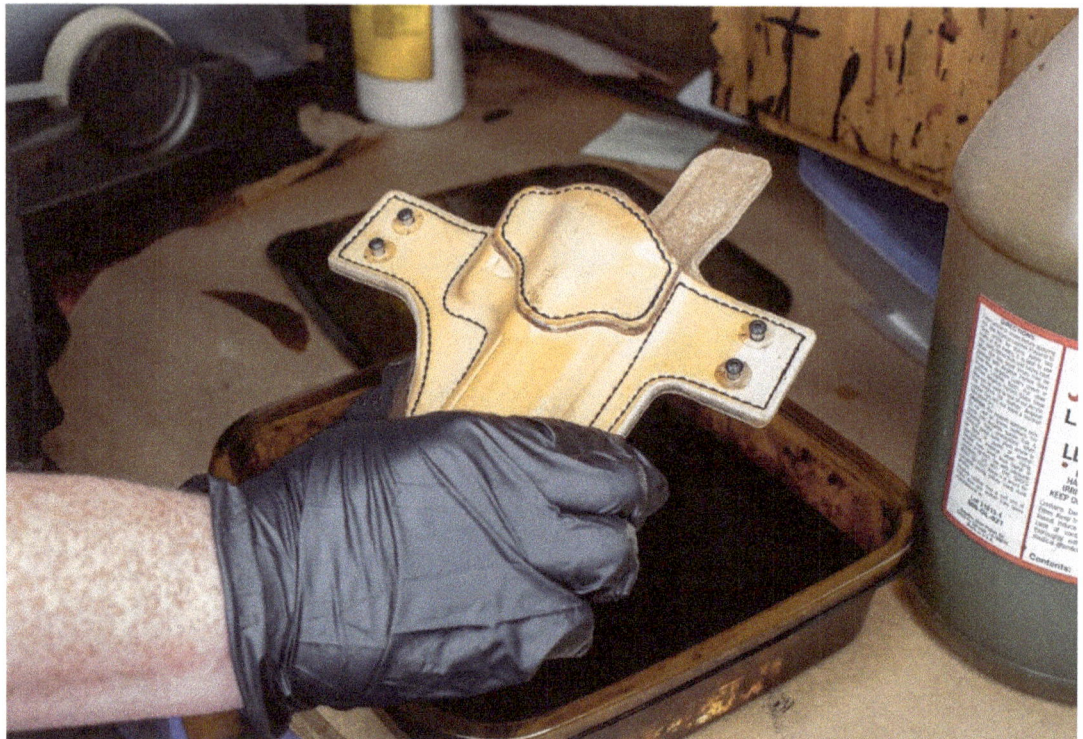

Figure 13-101

Figure 13-102

Dunk the holster into the dye and rock it back and forth, both horizontally and vertically, making sure to get some moving through the inside of the holster. Don't stop moving.

Flip the holster after a few seconds and do the same thing on the other side. Then lift the holster out of the dye.

Figure 13-103

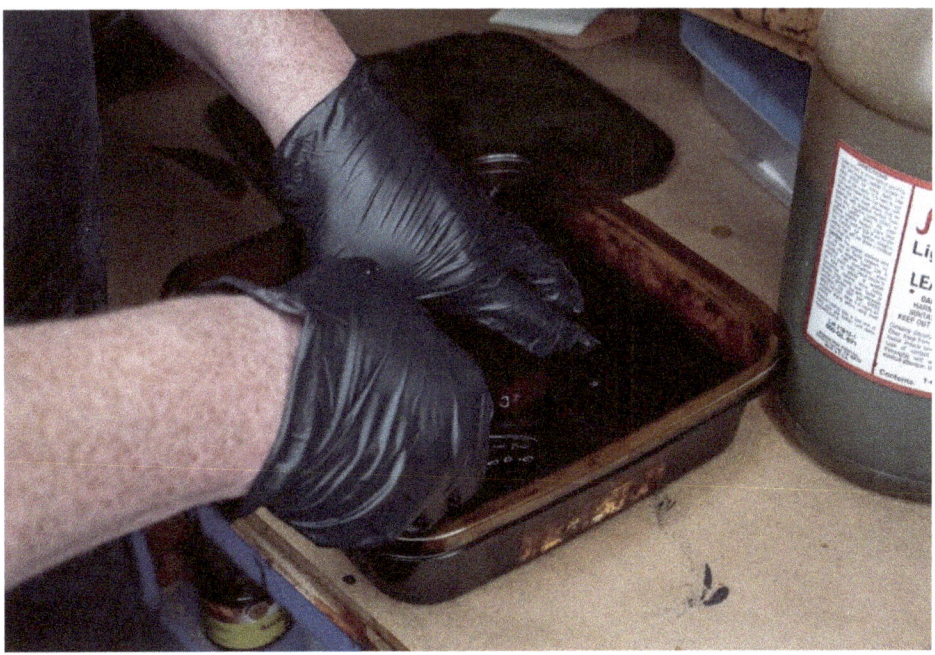
Figure 13-104

Chapter 13: Holster Building – SnapCake Holster

Hold the holster at an angle, letting the dye flow to the bottom edge.

Now, swipe it off the edges with a paper towel. If dye builds-up in a certain area, carefully swipe that up as well.

Keep doing this until the holster is no longer glossy on the surface. This is called *flash*, and it's when the spirits in the dye evaporate and leave a pigment.

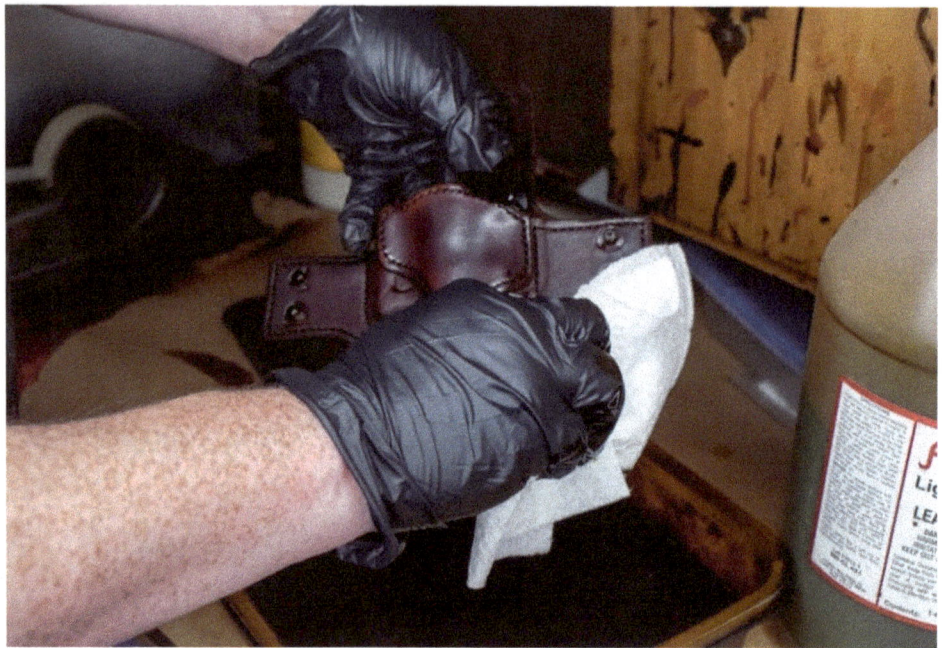
Figure 13-105

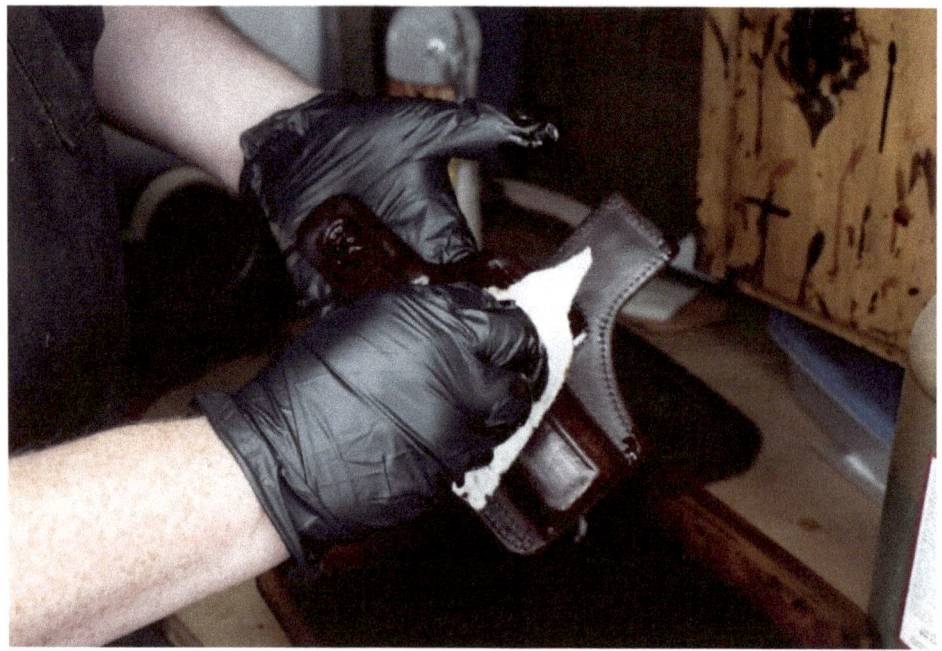
Figure 13-106

Once that's done you'll want to hang the holster.

We use a hotbox, but it's not entirely necessary. If you need, you can leave it on the table, but make sure it's on a cardboard box so any dye that may come off wont stain any tables.

Time for the straps as well.

Figure 13-107

Dunk them in and do the same thing you did with the holster, for about the same amount of time.

When you bring the strap out of the dye, hold it at an angle again and wipe the excess dye off the bottom edge as it accumulates.

Figure 13-108

Figure 13-109

You can see the flash we talked about earlier in these pictures. Repeat the process for the second strap.

Figure 13-110

Figure 13-111

We're finished with the dye!

We now have the holster dyed all the way through. The leather should be able to take any scratch and still show the color of the dye instead of natural leather.

All we need to do now is the tricky part.

Take a funnel and put it on your dye bottle.

Place a filter over it as well. We use paint filters commonly used for auto paint. It has fine metal meshes in it that block any particles or leather dust before they make their way back into your dye bottle.

This is extremely important, especially for brown dye which likes to dye uneven and splotchy. Given any extra opportunities such as particles in the dye, and it can make streaks and splotches an even bigger problem.

Do this next step in an area where it's all right if you spill the dye, preferably not on the kitchen table.

Very carefully, take your dye and pour it into the funnel. The best advice we have is to make sure your funnel is secure on the top of the dye bottle and commit to the pour. Once you start pouring, keep it going steady and stable. If you try to stop pouring, in our experience, it will only spill more dye everywhere.

Figure 13-112

We want this holster to be bone dry whenever we go to finish it.

If you live in a humid environment, it might take a day or more to fully dry. In an arid environment, it could dry faster.

Once the holster is fully dry, we need to get our finish ready.

We use Angelus Acrylic Finisher, but Fiebings Resolene is also a great product to use as well. One thing we can say is, if you're using an Angelus dye, use an Angelus finish. If you use a Fiebings dye, use Fiebings finish. Don't cross the streams.

For this holster, we showed dip dye, so we're going to show dip finishing as well.

Before we get our finish out, we need to buff the holster and take any dye particles that raised to the surface off. We showed this process with a rag earlier. Now we'll show it with our horsehair wheel.

The key when using one of these is to always keep moving. If we stay in one place too long, we can actually pull the dye out of the leather surface.

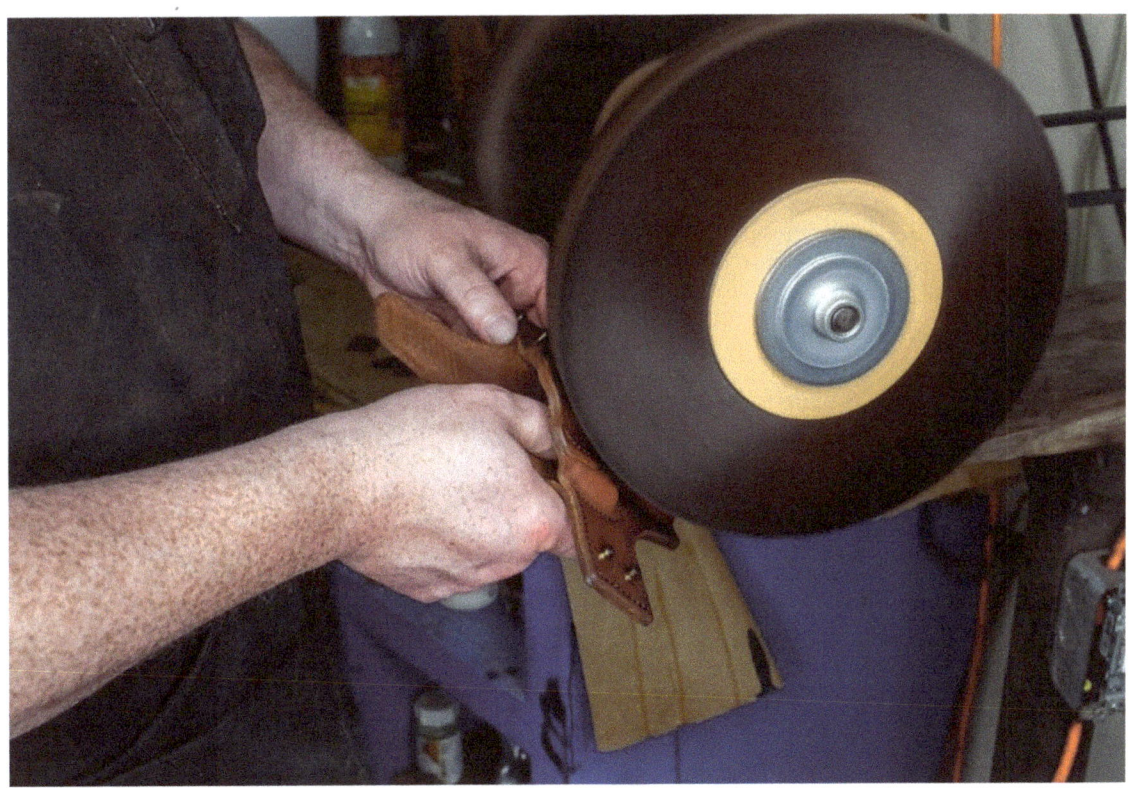

Figure 13-113

Chapter 13: Holster Building – SnapCake Holster

Once we have the holster and the straps buffed, we need to get the edges slicked before we put the finish on.

Let's get out our slicking rod and slicking solution, and start getting all the outer edges slicked down.

Figure 13-114

Figure 13-115

Don't forget the straps as well.
If you need to bevel them, do it now.

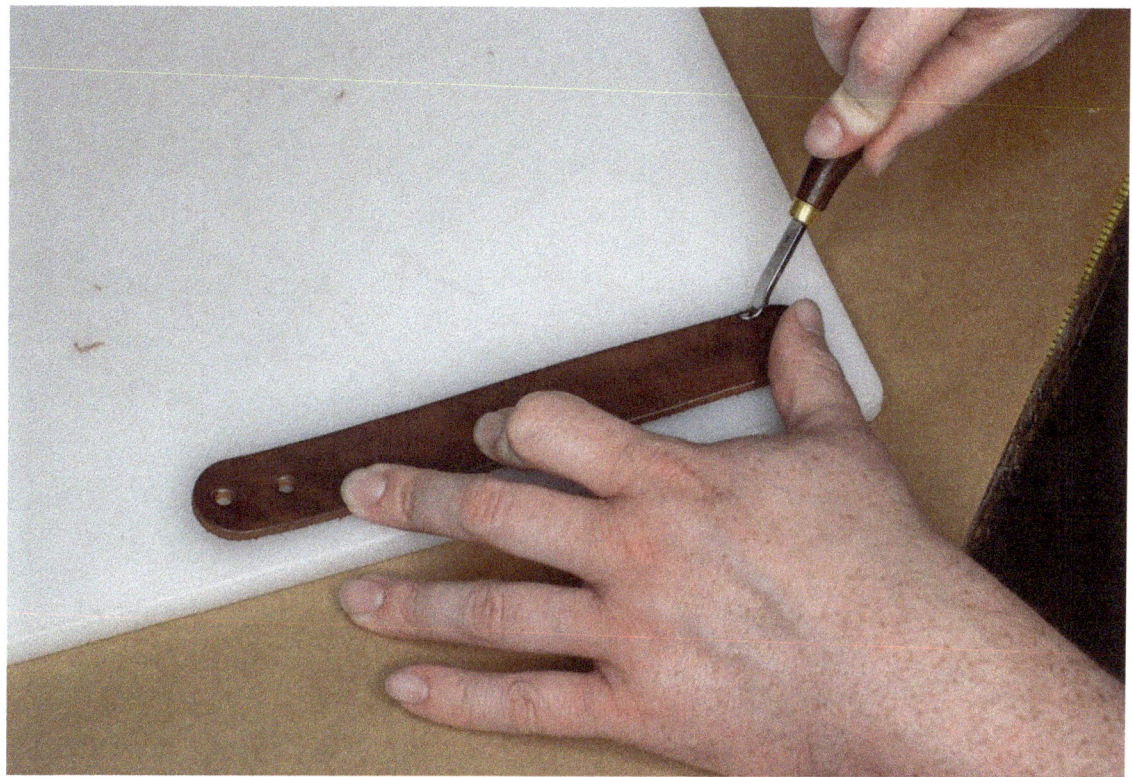
Figure 13-116

And now for the slicking solution and rod.

Figure 13-117

Figure 13-118

Okay, gang, let's finally get to finishing our holster.

Get out a container that's big enough for the holster to lay inside and pour your finish in.

If you don't already have the screws in, make sure your screws are in the T-Nuts, it is hard to get acrylic out of the threads. Trust us!

Hold your holster over the tub of finish, and have plenty of paper towels nearby.

Figure 13-119

Whenever you're ready, dunk the holster into the finish.

Just like we did with the dye. Keep it rocking and make sure to rock the finish inside the holster as well.

Once you have one side good and soaked, flip it over and get the other.

Figure 13-120

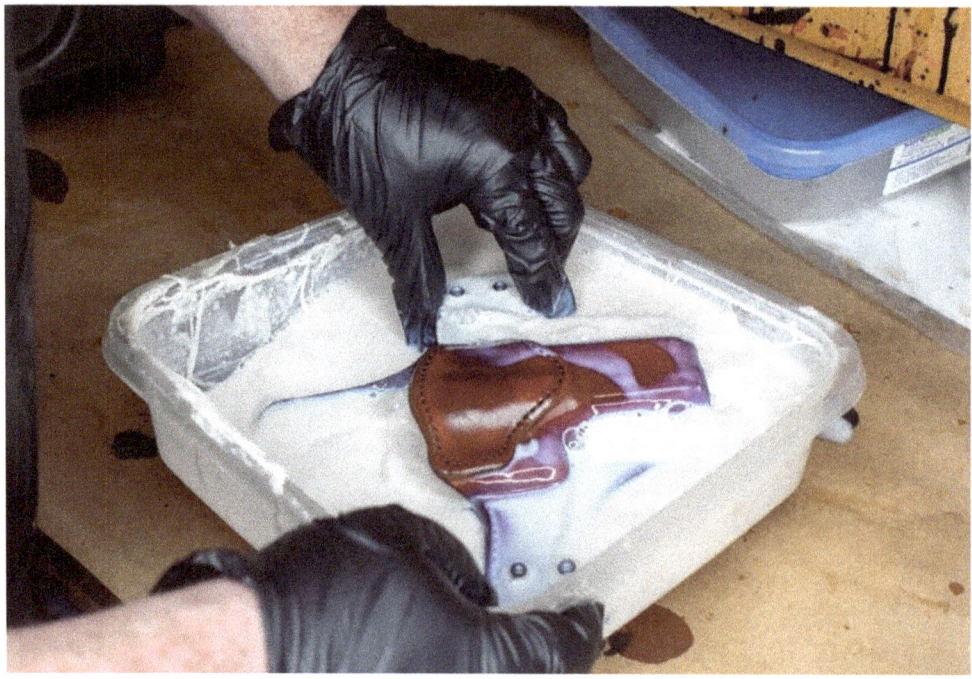

Figure 13-121

Lift the holster out of the finish and tilt it like we did with the dye. Then grab your paper towel and wipe the excess finish off the holster.

Do this quickly. We don't want to see any streaking of finish on your holster.

Figure 13-122

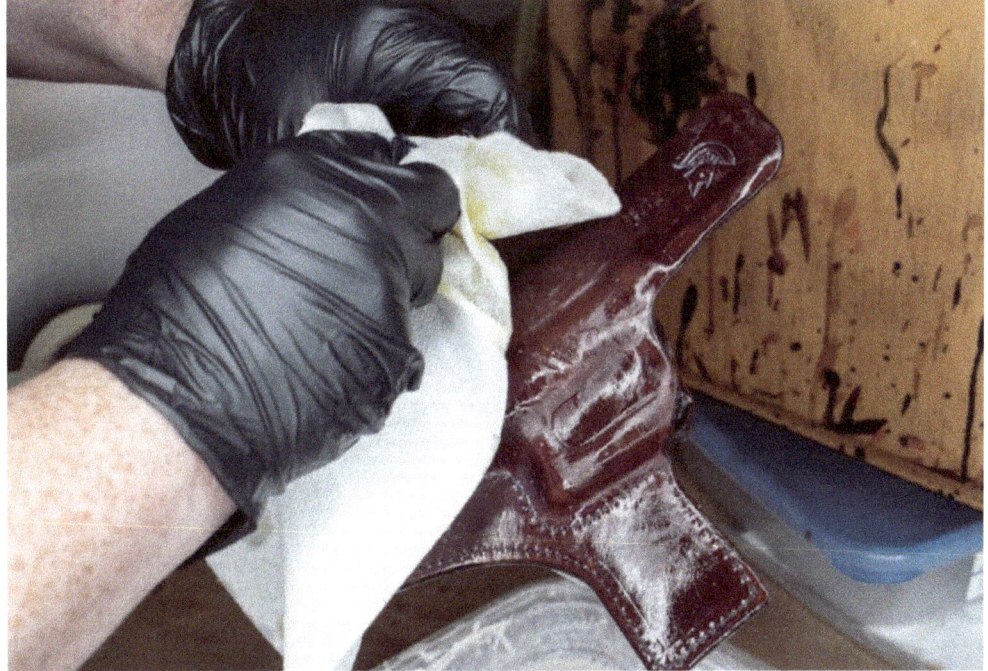

Figure 13-123

As quickly as you can without making streaks, wipe down both sides, and the inside as well.

Figure 13-124

Figure 13-125

Now on to the straps.

Since they have to bend and flex, the straps are not going to get the acrylic finish that our holster did.

For this we're going to use Angelus Leather Balm.

Figure 13-126

Put some on a cloth. We use old T-shirts because they're free and work better than a lot of rags sold in stores.

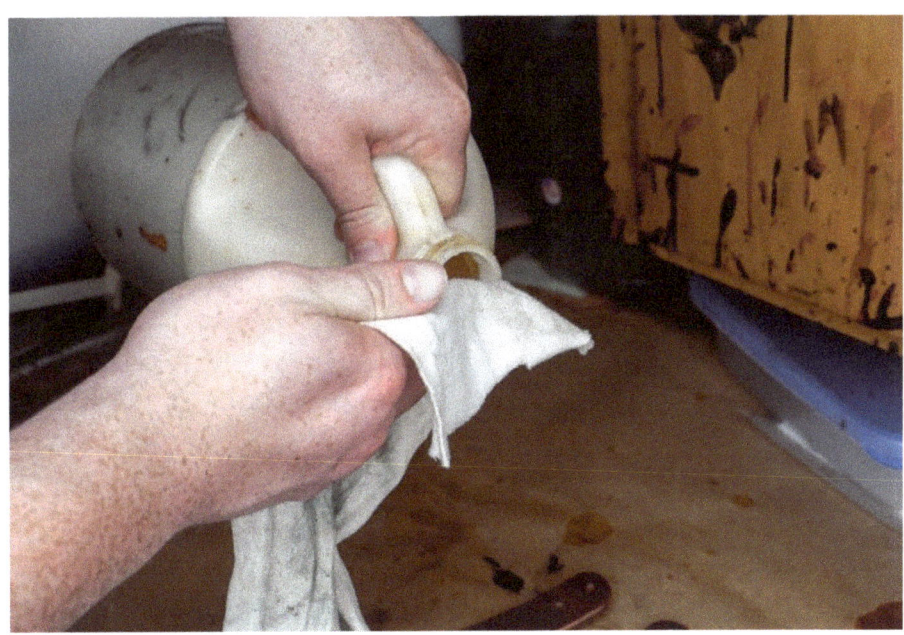
Figure 13-127

Rub down those straps! Put it over the front and back.

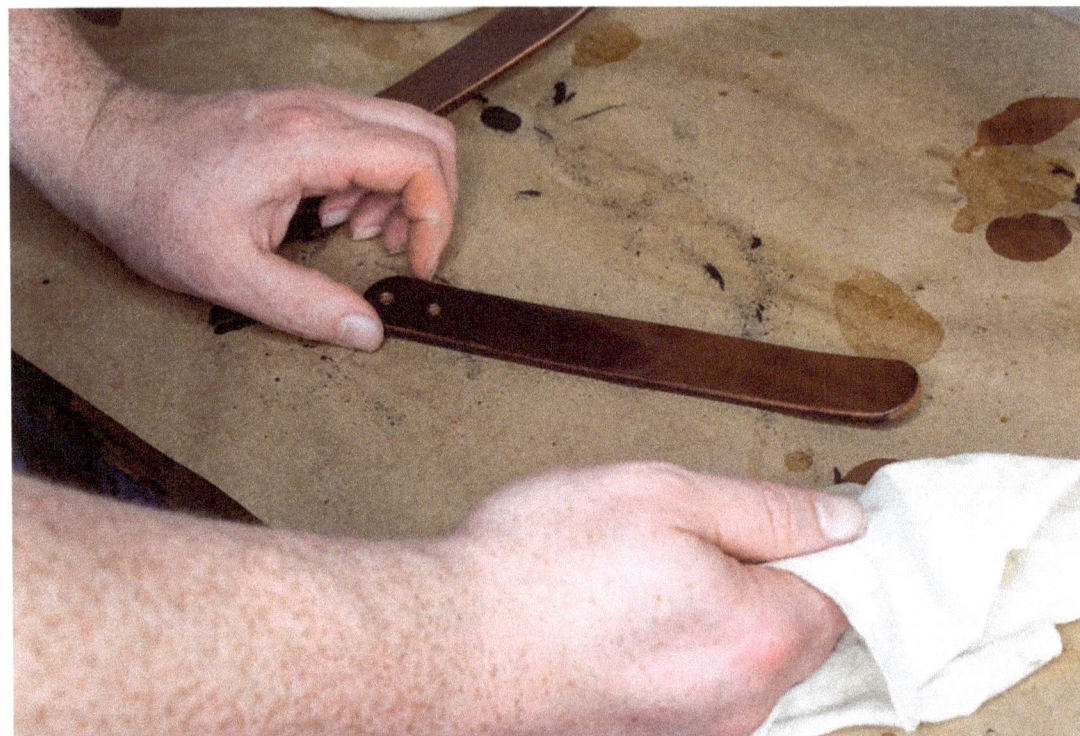
Figure 13-128

Figure 13-129

Now the finishing step is done!

Take your holster and straps and set them out to dry.

Once your holster and straps are completely dry and sealed. It is magic time!

This is where we will need our hardware and snap setter.

For the snaps in this build, we use one pull-the-dot (one-way) snap, and one hard-action snap.

The one-way snap goes on the top T-Nut, and the hard-action snap goes on the bottom T-Nut.

The reason we do this is to guarantee the holster will not unsnap and come loose from the belt unless the wearer intends for it to.

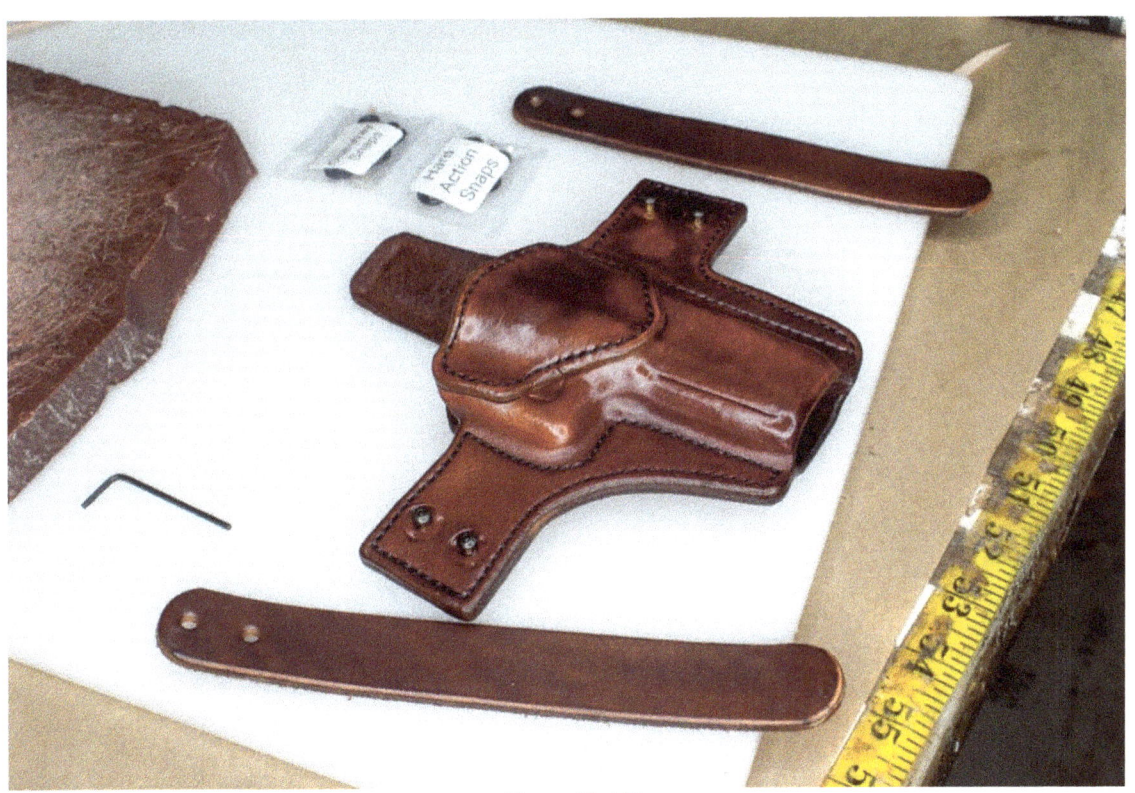

Figure 13-130

Take out a two-millimeter hex key/Allen wrench and undo the screws. One thing to note is the screws might be a touch stuck from the acrylic, but they shouldn't be too terribly bad to undo.

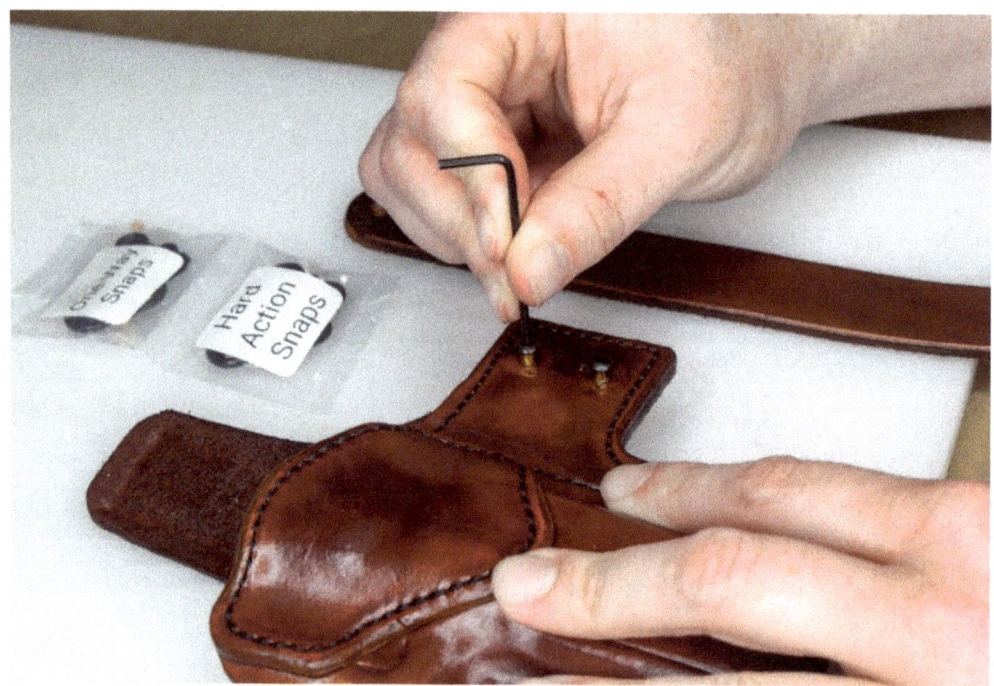
Figure 13-131

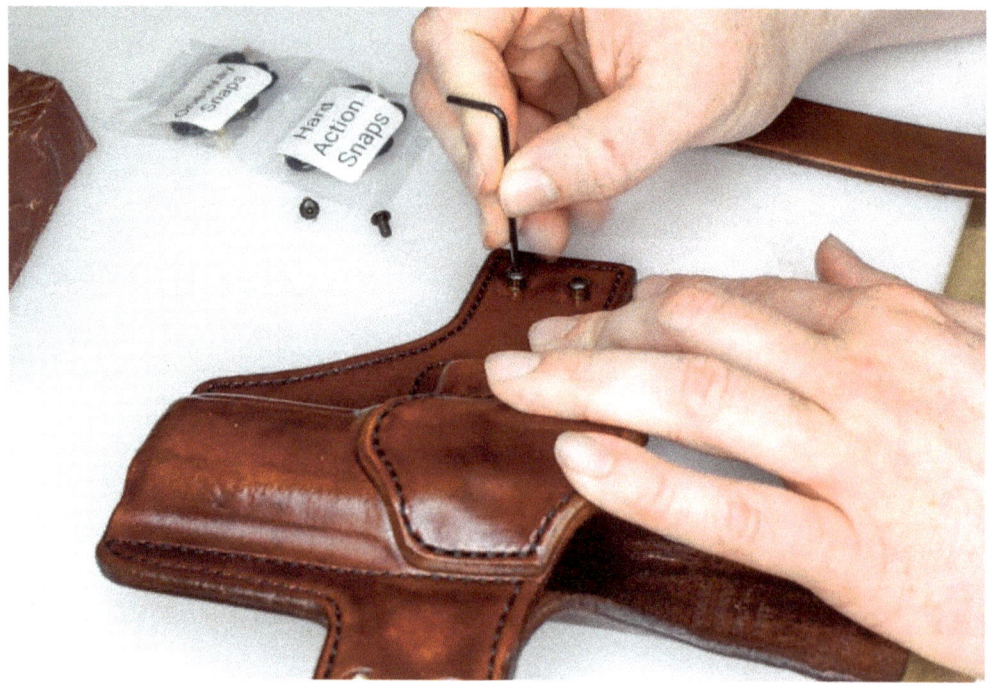
Figure 13-132

Lay your strap with the holes already punched over your T-Nuts.

Figure 13-133

Take the male piece of the one-way snap and lay it over the top T-Nut.

Figure 13-134

Use the screw to tighten the male one-way snap piece into place.

Figure 13-135

Now let's place our hard-action male piece so we can lock this strap into place.

Figure 13-136

Screw this guy down as well.

Figure 13-137

Now that we have this strap locked down, let's do it for the other strap as well.

Figure 13-138

Do the same steps again for the other strap. Place the strap over the T-Nuts.

Figure 13-139

Set the one-way snap male over the top T-Nut.

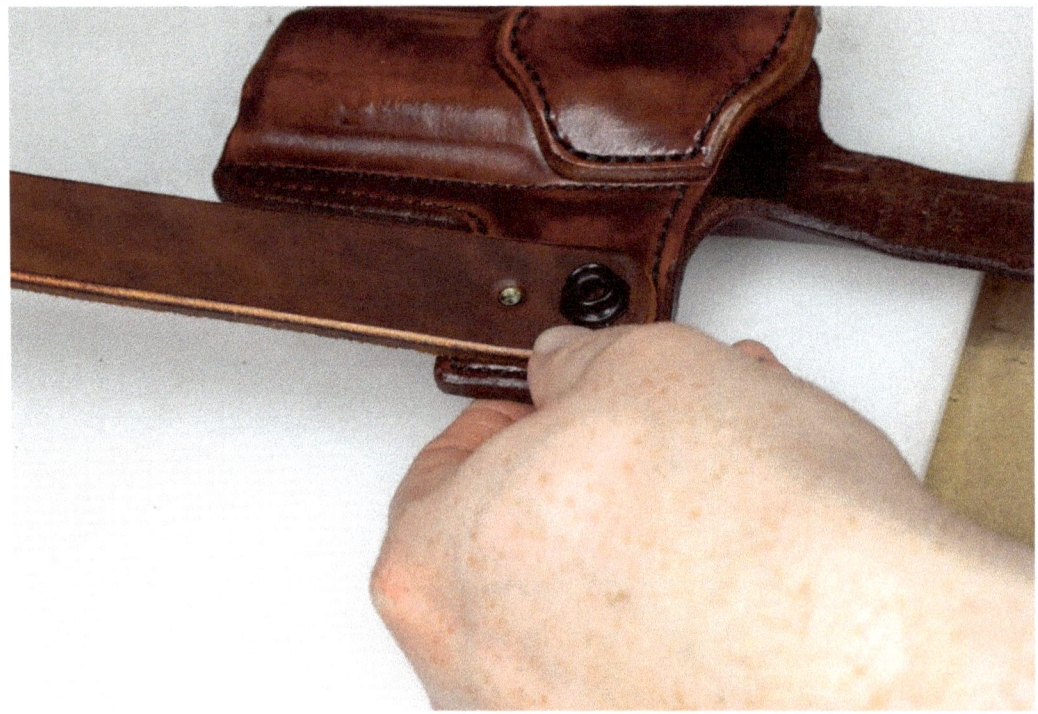

Figure 13-140

And screw it down.

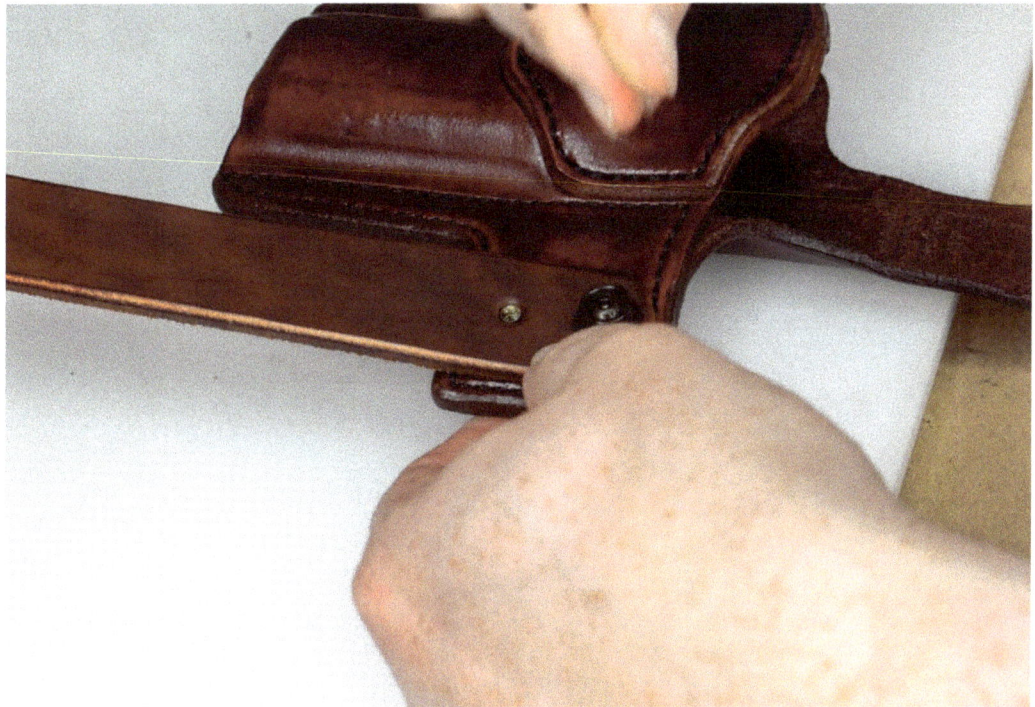
Figure 13-141

On the bottom T-Nut place in the hard-action male.

Figure 13-142

And screw it in.

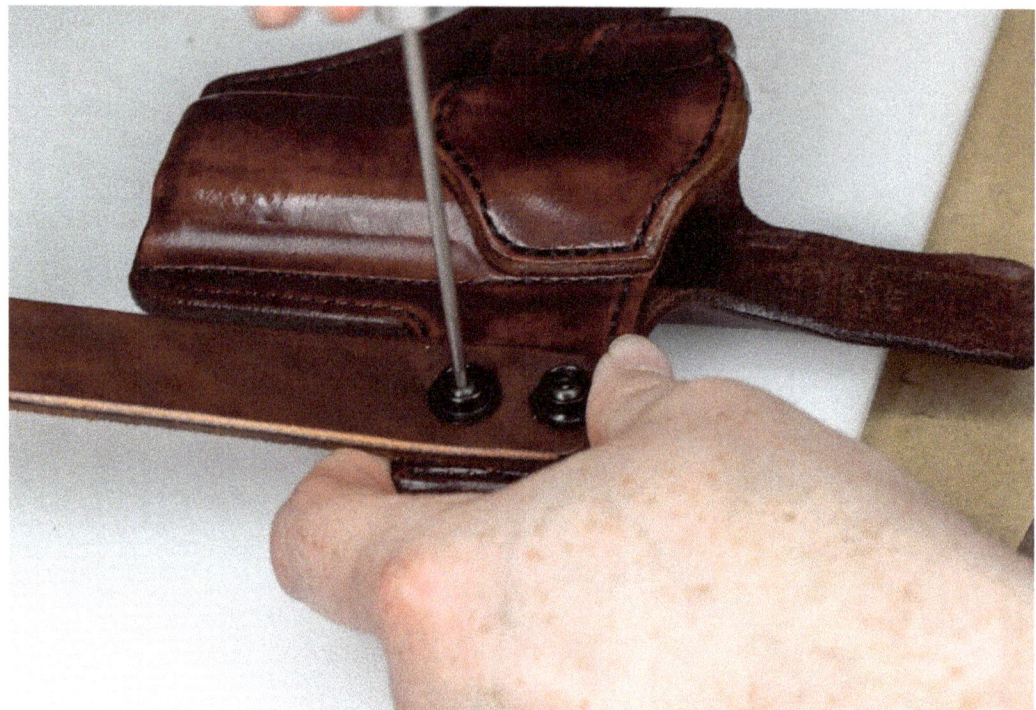

Figure 13-143

Now we have the straps secured to the holster body. It's time to find out where we need to put the female sections of the snaps.

For this step, we're going to use a belt blank.

We make all of our gun belts out of either two layers of eight and a half-ounce (8.5 oz.) Hermann Oak leather (combined max thickness of seventeen-ounces (17 oz.)) or out of two layers of six-ounce (6 oz.) with a reinforcement in the middle (combined max thickness of twelve to fourteen-ounce (12-14 oz.).

Not everybody makes a belt like we do. We understand that. So we want you to make your own belt blank that is built to the standard of your belts.

For us, the thickest belt we make is two layers of eight-ounce (8 oz.), so that's what we made our belt blank out of.

Figure 13-144

You might notice our belt blank is not stitched like a normal belt would be, and that is perfectly fine.

Trust us. A sufficient application of Masters Cement will never come apart whether it's stitched or not.

To find out where we need to set these snaps at, we need to fold our leather around the belt blank.

We don't want this strap wrapped around extremely tight. If you set the snaps at the point where it's very tight around the belt, then the user will never be able to get those snaps snapped when it's on their belt.

The method we use for straps is to wrap it around your belt blank, get it tight, then back it off about one-quarter-inch (1/4") to three-eighth-inch (3/8") give or take.

Here's an image of how our strap wraps around our belt blank for reference.

Figure 13-145

When you have the desired slack in your strap, take your thumb and press it hard over both snaps.

You want a slight impression on the flesh side of leather, so press hard.

Figure 13-146

Figure 13-147

Once you've done that, take the strap and flip it up to where you can see the impressions. Mark the center of the impression with a pencil. This will help you see it later.

Figure 13-148

Figure 13-149

And now your strap should look like this.

As you can see in the image, we have a slight impression where the snaps will be. In the middle of those impressions, we made a mark with our pencil.

Figure 13-150

Punch the holes for your snaps on those pencil marks and get out your snap anvil ready.

First up, let's set the one-way snap.
Place the cap for the one-way in the snap anvil.

Figure 13-151

This cap is going to go in the hole that is closest to the holster.
Place the strap over it.

Figure 13-152

Now let's place the female section of the snap over the post and get it set!

One thing to note: If you're using a one-way snap like us, place the snap so the tab on the back of the female part is facing the end of the strap, and the piece of metal that goes over the ring is facing up the strap and toward the holster.

Figure 13-153

Figure 13-154

Now that the snap is set, let's test it to make sure it'll work before moving on.

Figure 13-155

Figure 13-156

Let's repeat this process, but this time using our hard-action hardware. Place the cap in the anvil.

Figure 13-157

Place the strap with the hole farthest from the holster over the cap.

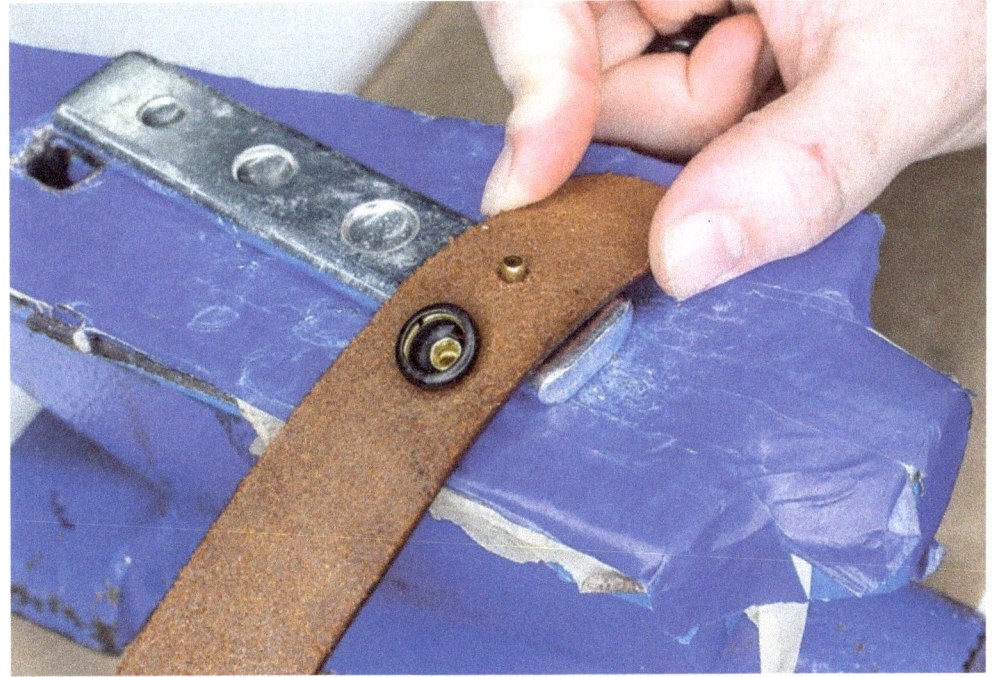
Figure 13-158

Place the hard-action socket over the cap.

This time you don't need to worry about any alignment like we had to do with the one-way snap.

Figure 13-159

And now set that snap!

Figure 13-160

Now let's check our snaps once again and make sure they do their jobs, and snap around the belt blank.

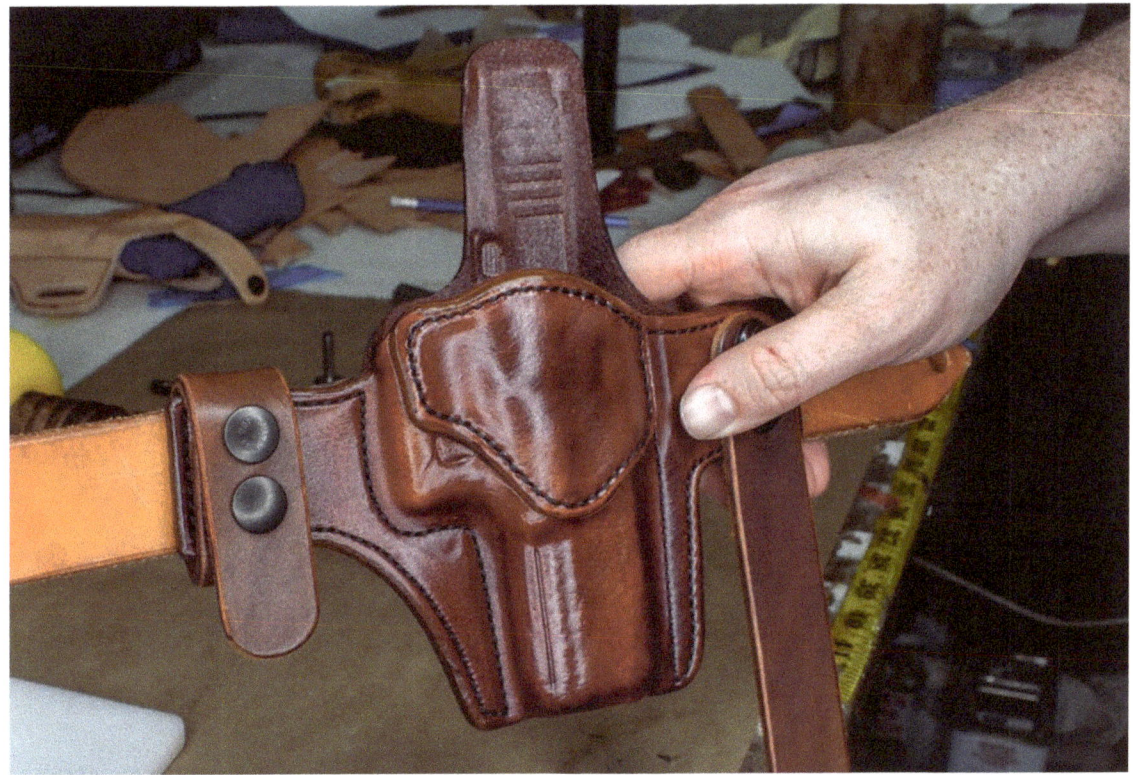

Figure 13-161

Looking good!

All to do now is repeat the steps on the other strap.

Once you're done with both straps, we're going to come back and use a strap punch to shorten up these straps.

This step isn't required, and everyone does it differently, but we'll show you how long we like our straps to be.

When trimming our straps, we flip the holster over and make a mark about one-eighth-inch (1/8") below where the strap wraps around the belt.

Figure 13-162

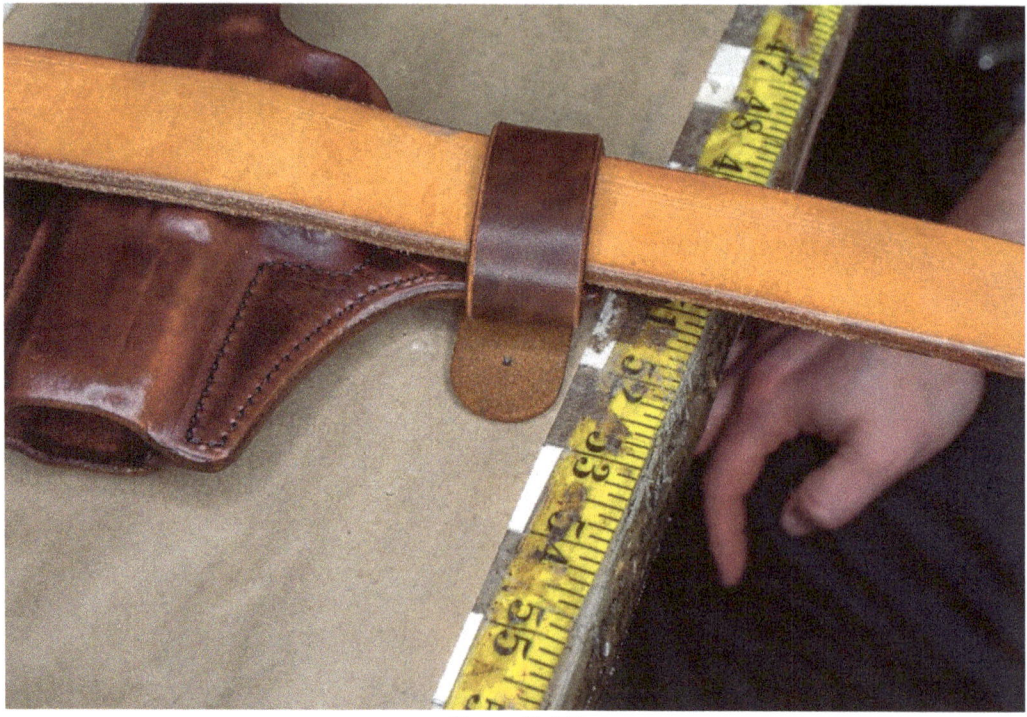
Figure 13-163

Now take the strap-end punch that you used earlier, and use it to cut the strap to the mark you made.

Real quick, once you're done with that, we can't forget that we need to finish that edge that we just cut on that strap.

Take out your edger and let's knock this out.

Figure 13-164

Then apply your slicking solution.

Figure 13-165

Use your slicking rod to lay all those fibers into a nice edge.

Figure 13-166

We can now take a look at our product in its finished state!

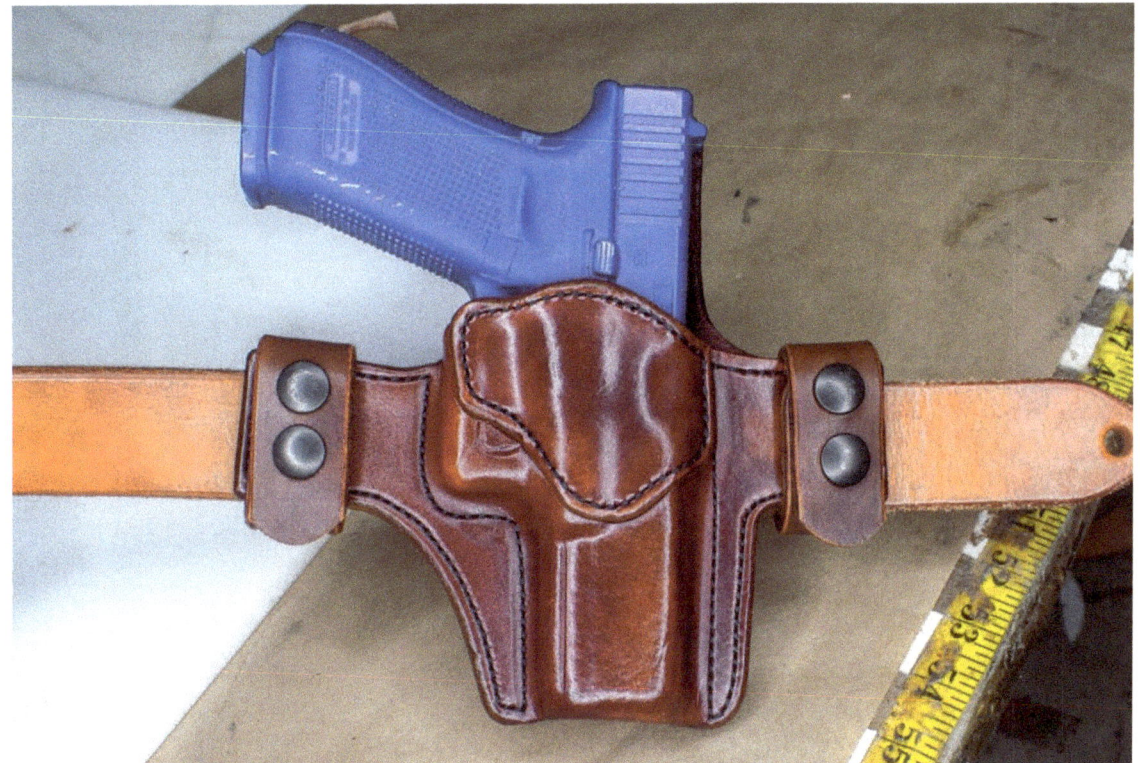

Figure 13-167

There's one more step that you must do before it can be sent out the door—Stretching!

Whenever you make a holster, even if you're using the real firearm that's going to live in that holster, the leather is going to shrink when you get it wet and then let it dry.

If you don't do the stretching process, you'll find that if you force the real firearm into the holster you might not be able to get it back out again by yourself.

Luckily this step is fairly simple. We will show you how to make sure your holster fits the firearm just right.

First let's take our holster and lightly spray the inside with water.

Figure 13-168

Wrap either your BlueGun, or preferably the actual firearm that's going to be in this holster, in a heavy-duty freezer bag.

This freezer bag is going to add three to four millimeters of clearance per layer around the mold.

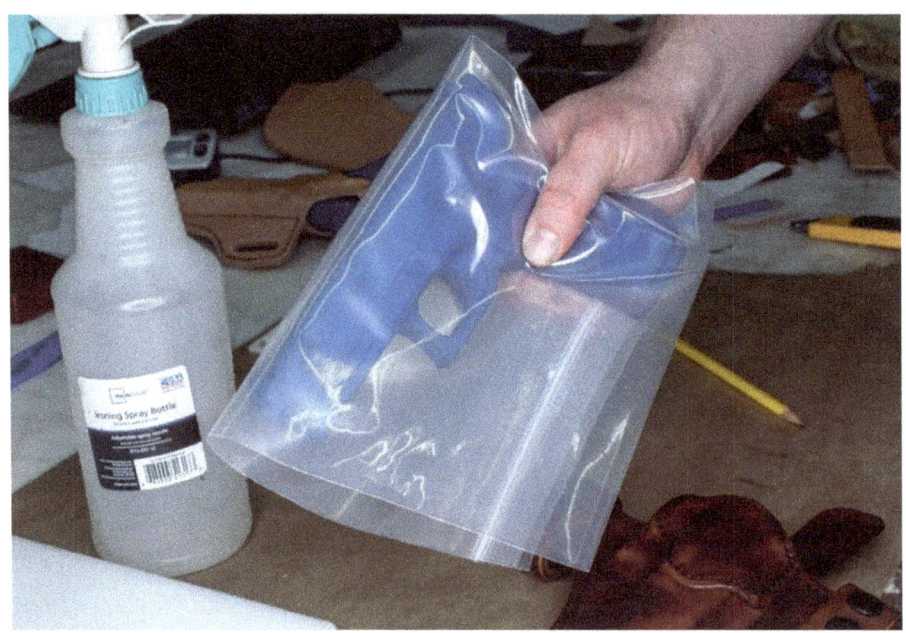

Figure 13-169

Shove your mold into the holster while trying to make sure the bag doesn't roll up the slide.

It can be tricky to do sometimes, but it is important.

Figure 13-170

Let the inside of the holster dry.

Once dry, you should be able to remove the mold with the bag.

Test the fit with the real firearm (make sure it's clear, with no rounds in the chamber or magazine), and decide if it needs to be stretched more or not.

Another quick tip: If it feels good when you test draw it in your hands, make sure to put it on a belt and give it a test draw.

Whenever you pull the ears of the holster back, like what happens when it's on a belt, the front of the holster will pull closer toward the back panel and increase retention.

You've now completed your build of the Zero-Degree SnapCake Holster!

You may very well decide that this is simply the most comfortable holster you've ever worn. And the sweetest part is, YOU BUILT IT!!!!

From all the guys at EDC Leather, Congratulations! We hope you've found this book helpful.

We have a ton of tools, patterns, and products designed to help the holster designer and maker with every step of the process.

Don't forget to visit our Facebook page at /EDCGunLeather or our website at EDCLeather.com. And if you like the book, tell everybody!

Enjoy,
Geo

Tools & Templates

The following pages include tools and templates mentioned throughout this book.

You may photocopy them for your own personal use.

If you prefer physical variants of these tools, we offer them in acrylic on our website, EDCLeather.com

Radius Tool

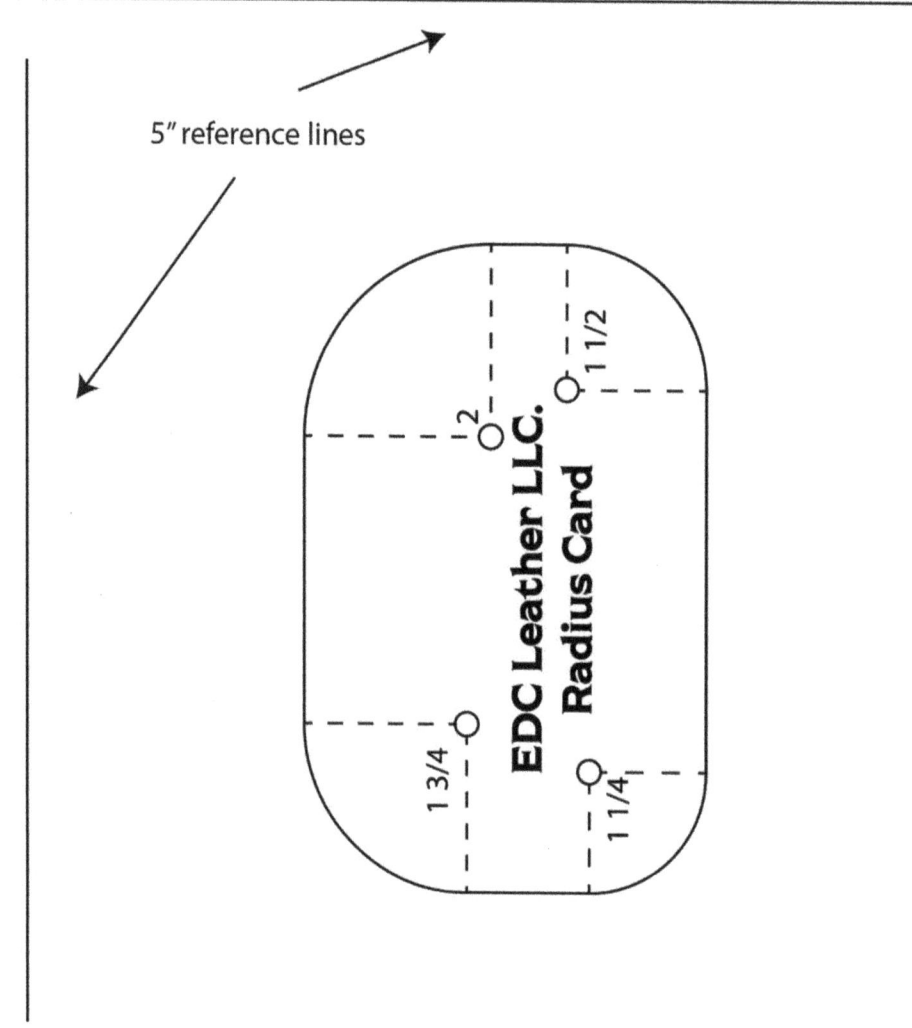

Thumb Break Template

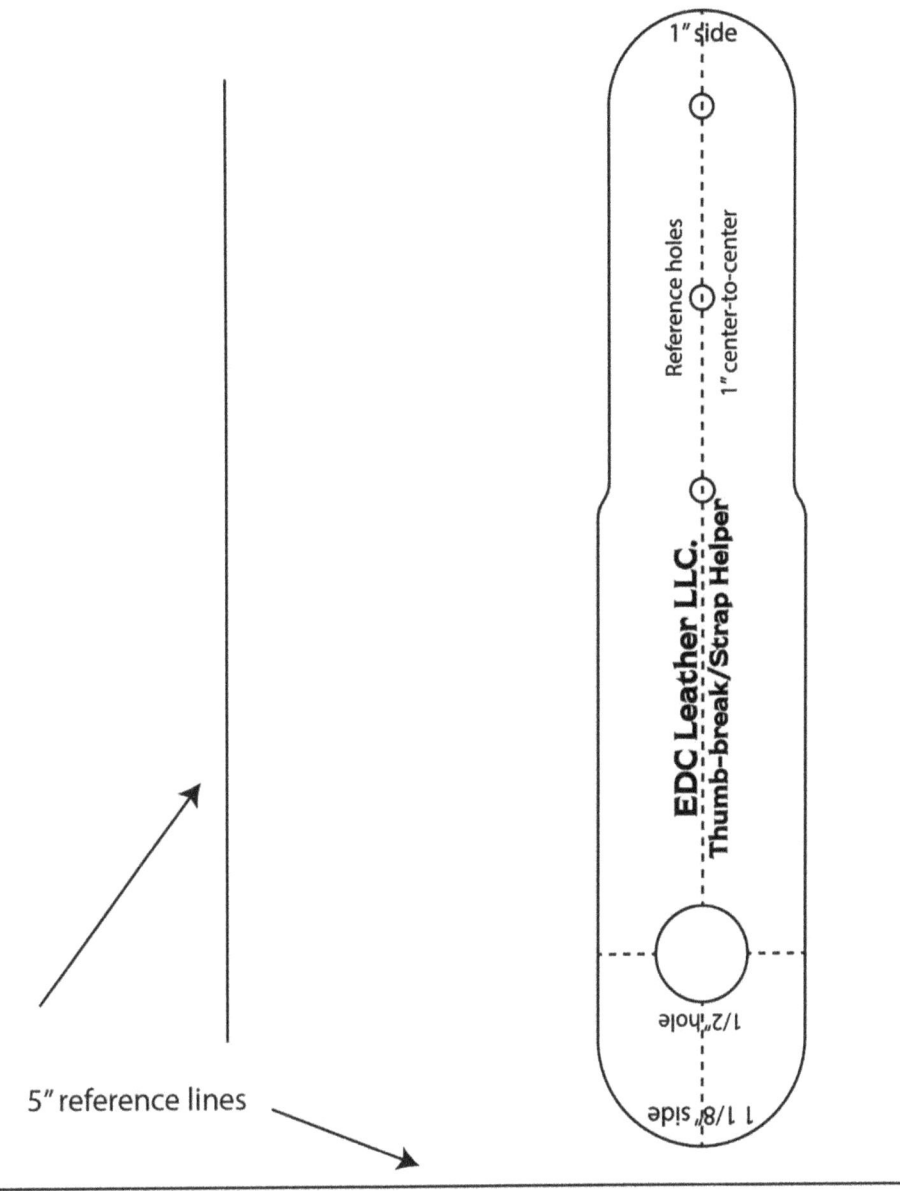

Chapter 13: Holster Building – SnapCake Holster

Belt Slot Template

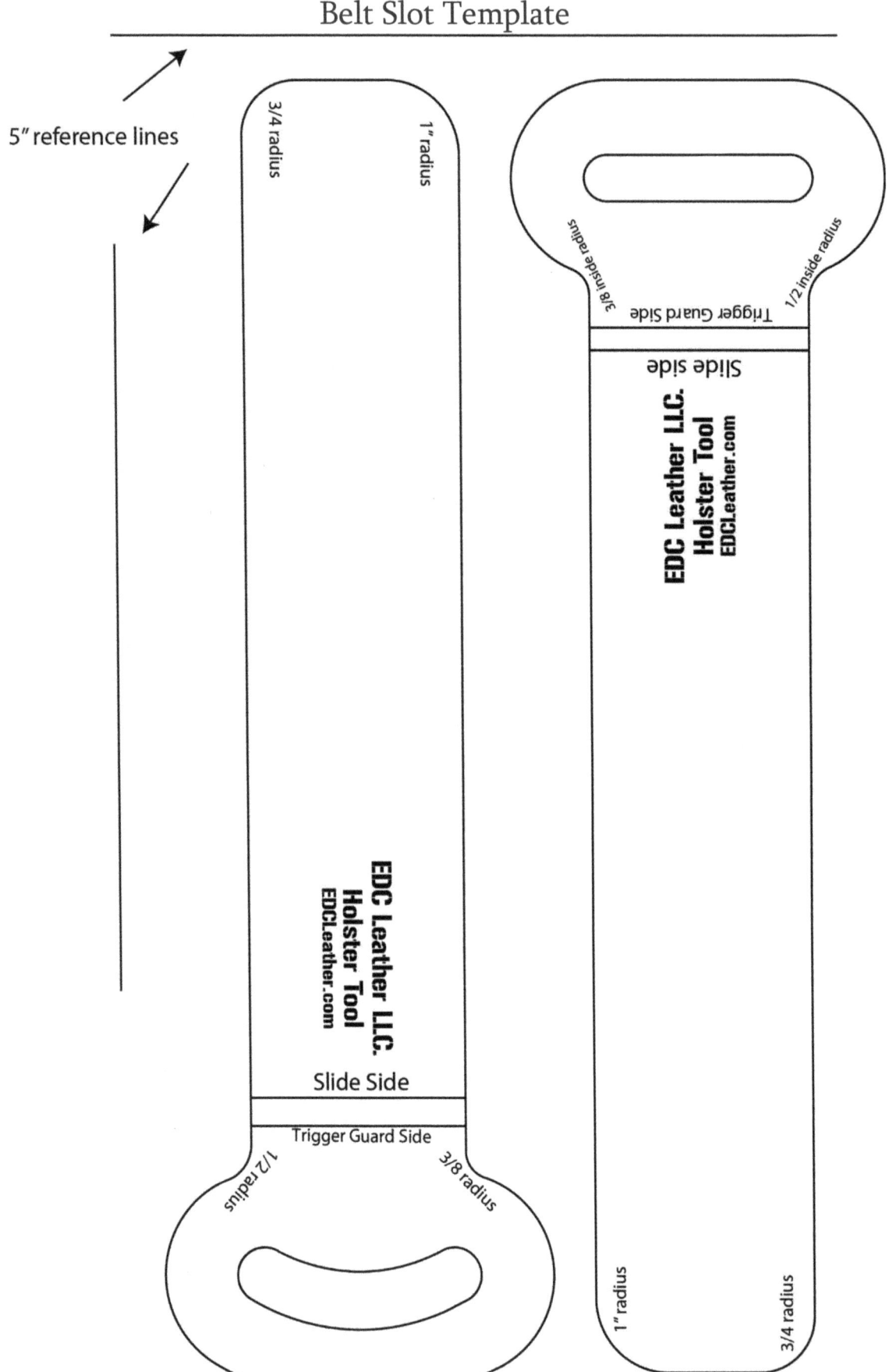

Cant Sheet

0 - degree

2 - degree

4 - degree

6 - degree

8 - degree

10 - degree

12 - degree

14 - degree

16 - degree

18 - degree

20 - degree

22 - degree

24 - degree

www.ingramcontent.com/pod-product-compliance
Lightning Source LLC
Chambersburg PA
CBHW041233240426
43673CB00010B/324